A Prosperous Past

Sam Segal

A Prosperous Past

The Sumptuous Still Life In The Netherlands
1600-1700

Edited by
William B. Jordan

SDU publishers, The Hague, 1989

SDU

© Sam Segal, Amsterdam 1989

Copyright reserved.
Subject to the exceptions provided for by law, no part of this publication may be reproduced and/or published in print, by photocopying, on microfilm, or in any other way without the written consent of the copyright-holder(s); the same applies to whole or partial adaptations. The publisher retains the sole right to collect from third parties fees payable in respect of copying and/or to take legal or other action for this purpose.

Revised edition

ISBN 90 12 06238 1

Translation: Mrs. P.M. van Tongeren, Amsterdam
Design: Herman Govers (SDU design), The Hague
Composing: IGS, Rotterdam
Photolithography: Nefli, Haarlem
Printing: Boom - Ruygrok Offset bv, Haarlem
Binding: Binderij Callenbach BV, Nijkerk

The first edition was published in conjunction with the exhibition *De Rijkdom Verbeeld / A Prosperous Past* held at the Stedelijk Museum Het Prinsenhof, Delft, Fogg Art Museum, Cambridge, Massachusetts and the Kimbell Art Museum, Fort Worth, Texas.

Foreword

Among the terms that have been used to refer to the variety of still lifes painted in Holland in the 17th century, *pronkstilleven* (roughly translatable into English as 'ostentatious' or 'sumptuous' still life) has been applied to works by artists like Jan Davidsz. de Heem, Abraham van Beyeren and Willem Kalf, among others. The term *pronkstilleven*, therefore, usually calls to mind rather elaborate compositions depicting luxurious, handmade objects and collectors' items, and denotes something quite distinct from 'flower piece,' 'breakfast piece,' 'fruit still life,' 'vanitas still life,' etc. There has never been a detailed study of the 'pronk' still life; therefore, this book and the exhibition it accompanies break new ground. In *A Prosperous Past* Dr. Sam Segal has endeavored to look beneath traditional typological classifications, which often tend to obscure rather than reveal the true nature of things, and to seek the thread of 'pronken' (to show off) which is woven through the development of many types of still lifes. From the earliest years of the 17th century until its end this major theme, little appreciated before now, was embedded at the core of many still lifes. It will come as no surprise to those who know Dutch culture of the 17th century that the theme of 'pronken' is present in these pictures not for purposes of anecdote or mere virtuosity, but rather for moral reasons. Indeed, the most affluent European society of its day, famous for its prosperity and conspicuous consumption, was preoccupied with its soul and revealed in its art a considerable ambivalence about its wealth. In probing the significance of these often spectacular pictures, Dr. Segal brings to bear a wide-ranging erudition which illuminates aspects of their meaning long forgotten. Some works reproduced here are published for the first time, many attributions are revised and inscriptions read accurately for the first time. It is hoped that this exhibition and its catalogue will open new doors of understanding and indicate new paths of inquiry that may one day clarify further the patterns being observed here.

This exhibition was conceived as a follow-up to two previous, highly successful ones, both of them also organized by Dr. Segal in conjunction with Charles Roelofsz. *A Flowery Past*, presented in 1982 at the P. de Boer Gallery, Amsterdam, and the Noordbrabants Museum, 's-Hertogenbosch, was a survey of Dutch and Flemish flower painting from 1600 to the present. *A Fruitful Past*, presented in 1983 at the P. de Boer Gallery, Amsterdam, and the Herzog

Anton Ulrich-Museum, Braunschweig, was a survey of the fruit still lifes of the Northern and Southern Netherlands from Brueghel to Van Gogh.

The inauguration of *A Prosperous Past* in Delft celebrates the 40th anniversary of the opening in June 1948 of the newly restored buildings of the former Convent of St. Agatha as the Municipal Museum Het Prinsenhof. The collection of Het Prinsenhof is focused on the art of Delft and includes 17th-century paintings and fine examples of Delft silver and Delftware, the latter made under the influence of the Ming and Transitional porcelain from China that was so avidly collected in 17th-century Holland. Against this backdrop it is especially meaningful to present an anniversary exhibition that so beautifully complements the collection of the museum and that has such a special historical relevance to the people of Delft. In the United States the exhibition represents perhaps the most extensive survey of Dutch still-life painting yet seen.

There are many individuals who deserve our thanks for helping to make this exhibition a reality. Foremost among them is Sam Segal, whose scholarship and connoisseurship form its basis. We are also grateful to Charles Roelofsz, of Amsterdam, who helped in the selection of works for the exhibition and lent his support throughout. Several dealers kindly assisted us in obtaining important loans from private collections. In that regard we are grateful to John Hoogsteder, The Hague, and Anthony Speelman, London. For bringing the Fogg Art Museum and the Kimbell Art Museum into the project as partners in its organization, we would like to express our appreciation to Bob Haboldt, of New York, and M. Kirby Talley Jr., Curator of Old Master Paintings at the Rijksdient Beeldende Kunst, The Hague.

We would like to offer a special word of thanks to William B. Jordan, Deputy Director of the Kimbell Art Museum, for his considerable assistance throughout the implementation of the project. We especially wish to thank Dr. Jordan, however, for his work in editing the English translation of Dr. Segal's manuscript.

A number of institutions also gave us support and assistance. In The Netherlands we wish to thank the Ministry of Culture (wvc), the Foundation for Cultural Exchange The Netherlands-usa, the Rijksdienst Beeldende Kunst, and the Municipality of Delft. Most especially, we must thank Ger Meesters, Evelyn de Regt and sdu Publishers, of The Hague, for their excellent cooperation as publishers of the catalogue. The international tour of *A Prosperous Past* is made possible by a generous grant from American Express Company. We wish to express our deep appreciation of this vital support.

Finally, we must thank the lenders to the exhibition, both institutional and private, who have shared our enthusiasm for its aims and who have been willing to make so many rare and beautiful works of art available to the public in Delft, Cambridge and Fort Worth.

Ineke Spaander, *Stedelijk Museum Het Prinsenhof, Delft*

Edgar Peters Bowron, *Fogg Art Museum, Cambridge, Massachusetts*

Edmund P. Pillsbury, *Kimbell Art Museum, Fort Worth, Texas*

Author's Preface

Writing about the *pronkstilleven*, or sumptuous still life, is a precarious business. The translation of the word itself is not easy, but the term tells us less than the pictures which it has traditionally been used to describe, mid- to late-17th-century still lifes by such painters as Jan Davidsz. de Heem, Abraham van Beyeren and Willem Kalf. Many of the earliest still lifes known to have been painted, however, works dating from around 1600, contain exactly the same elements, though they are painted in a more archaic style. To my knowledge no study has ever been made of this valid connection or of the consistent development of this still-life type. Such a study, I believe, can add valuable insight into the origins and development of the genre of the still life as a whole, especially as it was cultivated in The Netherlands.

This study, of necessity, is only a preliminary one, and we do not pretend it to be definitive in any regard. Thorough, critical oeuvre catalogues of the important artists represented in this exhibition remain, for the most part, to be written. Nevertheless, connoisseurship is a matter of importance to the advancement of knowledge in this field, and I have, in the text and notes, made suggestions for revised attributions. Research on the iconography of still lifes is in full swing, but it may take many decades before all the major questions have been answered. In fact, we are not now much farther along than the stage of asking questions: some of them may never be satisfactorily answered but are matters on which we can only speculate. The interpretation of symbols in art is a risky matter, because it involves speculation on the intentions of the artist, something about which we can know little. But there are patterns in Dutch intellectual life that indicate the validity of this approach to the still life, and there is already a large body of literature devoted to this subject.

The interpretation of symbols is difficult, moreover, because certain objects were highly charged with meaning in the minds of educated people in the 17th century. Often this meaning was not a unique possibility but a set of alternate, and sometimes opposing, possibilities. Only the context can indicate the direction for us, and even then we cannot always be certain. For this reason, I prefer to give the reader access to the range of alternatives, rather than to foreclose for him with seeming certainty the potentialities of a work of art that has aesthetic validity on various levels, including the completely nonsymbolic.

I would like to extend my thanks to the specialists in various fields who have helped me. Special thanks go to Dr. H. Coomans and R. Molenbeek for the identification or verification of all the seashells; to Dr. J. R. ter Molen and Mr. K. Citroen, who provided information on the objects of the goldsmith's craft; and to Mr. F. Lameris, authority on glass. Use was also made of a study undertaken together with Dr. H. Miedema on Chinese porcelain in still lifes.

It was a pleasure to cooperate once more with Mr. Charles Roelofsz., Drs. I. V. T. Spaander, Dr. E. P. Bowron and Dr. W. B. Jordan, who all made valuable contributions in selecting the works for the exhibition and to many aspects of realizing it. My thanks go also to Mr. P. van den Brink, who assisted me in preparing the bibliography and the technical data for the catalogue entries. I am indebted to Mrs. P. M. van Tongeren, who translated my manuscript under the severe pressure of a deadline, and I am especially grateful to Dr. Jordan, who edited that translation and invariably refined the expression of my thoughts. Mr. Herman Govers designed the catalogue, and I am pleased to have my work presented in such a beautiful format. Mr. G. Meesters and Drs. E. de Regt, of SDU Publishers, deserve my thanks for their patience, understanding and considerable skill in printing this book on a very tight schedule.

Although they were not directly involved in this work, I would like to pay my respects to my friends Professor I. Bergström and Professor E. de Jongh, who by their own work I consider to be my teachers and guides on the slippery path of still-life studies. Their pioneering contributions in this field have opened it for all the rest to follow. The Rijksbureau voor Kunsthistorische Documentatie has been for me an invaluable art-historical resource. I want to thank its staff members for their assistance throughout the many years of my studies.

Finally I wish to thank my wife Clara, not only for helping me with research into sources and with the translation of the Latin texts, but also for removing many stumbling blocks in the path of writing. Her part in the process of research and writing was essential for the completion of this study. My feelings and gratitude to her cannot be adequately expressed in words.

Sam Segal

Amsterdam, February 1988

Author's Preface (*second edition*)

The exhibitions gave ample opportunity for new observations and for comparisons, which led to new ideas. Some of these observations, if they correct the former text, have been incorporated in this second edition. I owe one to Mr. F.G. Meijer (p. 109, top).

Sam Segal

Amsterdam, April 1989

Lenders to the Exhibition

Denmark

Copenhagen
Den Kgl. Maleri - og Skulptursamling, Statens Museum for Kunst 58

France

Private collection 59

German Democratic Republic

Dessau
Staatliche Galerie Dessau, Schloß Georgium 21

Dresden
Gemäldegalerie Alte Meister der Staatlichen Kunstsammlungen Dresden 14, 25, 29

German Federal Republic

Münster
Westfälisches Landesmuseum für Kunst und Kulturgeschichte 30

Schlangenbad-Georgenborn
Hohenbuchau Sammlung 46

Stuttgart
Staatsgalerie Stuttgart 37

Private collections 1, 2, 13, 18, 19, 22, 24

Great Britain

London
National Gallery 36, 54
Thomas Brod Gallery 40
Richard Green Galleries 61

Oxford
Ashmolean Museum, Ward Collection 50

Westerham
Collection Mr. John Warde of Squerryes Court, Kent 43

Private collections 6, 7, 15, 31

Hungary

Budapest
Szépművészeti Múzeum 26, 41

The Netherlands

Amsterdam
Stichting Museum Amstelkring 60
Dutch Renaissance Art Collection 17
Charles Roelofsz Gallery 34, 35, 53
Rijksmuseum 28, 32, 44

The Hague
Rijksdienst Beeldende Kunst 3, 38, 48, 49

Heino
Stichting Hannema-de Stuers Fundatie, Kasteel Het Nijenhuis 16

Rotterdam
Museum Boymans-van Beuningen 23, 39, 62

Private collections 4, 10, 27

Switzerland

Lugano-Castagnola
Thijssen-Bornemisza Foundation 55

United States of America

Bloomington
Indiana University Art Museum 42

Cleveland
Cleveland Museum of Art 51, 56

Indianapolis
Indianapolis Museum of Art 57

Litchfield
Peter Tillou Gallery 47

Los Angeles
Los Angeles County Museum of Art 52

Private collections 5, 8, 9, 12, 20, 45

Otherwise

Private collections 11, 33

Contents

1 Introduction *15*

2 On Meaning and Interpretation:
The Abundance of Life and Moderation in All Things *29*

3 The Young Hieronymus and Frans Francken *39*

4 Laid Tables: Food for Thought *56*

5 Shell Still Lifes *77*

6 Flower and Fruit Still Lifes *93*

7 Sumptuousness in Sober Tones *121*

8 De Heem and his Circle *141*

9 Painters of the Broad Brush: Abraham van Beyeren *165*

10 The Sparkling Light of Willem Kalf *180*

11 Sparkle and Smoke *197*

Notes *207*

Catalogue *226*

Addendum *255*

Literature *259*

Photo Credits *276*

Chapter 1

Introduction

The Greek Aesop, who is said to have invented moralizing animal stories in the 6th century B.C., must have been the source of many fables which have come down to us through oral tradition. They were recorded and rewritten by Phaedrus, de La Fontaine and many others. One of these fables is the story of the magpie who tried to gain the friendship of some peacocks by putting peacock feathers in its tail. The peacocks, however, saw through this trick and pecked at the feathers. The magpie had, alas, to hop away. In another version it was a crow who used the feathers of other birds so that he might take part in the election of the king of the birds. He was also put in his place. In the commentaries on these stories, it is always pointed out that one should not 'show off' ('pronken' in Dutch) with borrowed plumes.[1] The Dutch verb 'pronken' often implies the meaning of showing off on purpose with something that does not belong to oneself or with something that one has obtained by improper means or that only seemingly has a shine of beauty, value, knowledge or wisdom. It therefore often has a slightly negative ring. The word 'pronken' is used to express a lack of humility, but, of course, it can also be used in a mocking sense by people who are jealous, by the have-nots. The word does not always have to have this negative ring, though; it can also mean the display of something that is beautiful and valuable or out of the ordinary, especially in combinations like a 'pronk' room, which is beautiful but in which the owner does not normally live, a 'pronk' bed in which he does not sleep, or a 'pronk' piece of jewelry which is worn only very rarely and then only on very special occasions. A *pronkstuk*, a show piece, is then something which is exceptional and brings the owner honor, or figuratively it denotes someone who excels by his exceptional qualities.

It is thus difficult to give an exact translation of the word 'pronken'. It expresses aspects of display and showing off, of ostentation, but also of gaudiness, of splendor or glitter, of lavishness and sumptuousness. The pronk still life, which is the subject of this study, is a still life in which an overtone of luxury is lent by precious handmade objects. After ample consideration we suggest translating it as 'sumptuous still life,' although this rendering lacks exactness. It is an advantage, however, that the word sumptuous is relatively neutral, as it comprises such connotations as opulent, luxurious and beautiful.

The objects depicted in a pronk still life include the products of gold- and silversmiths, fine porcelain, and beautiful glassware. Certain collectors' items, such as rare shells, exotic animals and other valuable things (e.g. wine, fruits or flowers from faraway countries) all appear in these still lifes and strengthen the aspect of luxury and preciousness, but they do not dominate. If they do, we speak of banquet pieces (*banketjes*), fruit or flower still lifes. Still lifes in which seashells predominate can be called shell pieces or shell still lifes. Of course, in reality there are many variations among these categories. Artists often had no intention of producing a 'pure' still life of one type or another but simply a beautiful painting. Such classification as this is only useful as an aid in creating a schematic survey, but it should not lead to a rigid systematization.

The art of the goldsmith is represented by silver and gilt objects, such as tazzas, pronk goblets, a *bekerschroef* (a gilt glass holder, i.e. an ornamented foot to which a glass is fastened), bowls, jugs and vases. Pronk goblets or beakers, with or without covers, are objects from which one might drink, but they were not produced primarily for that purpose as they are too valuable and sometimes too fragile. The cup can be made of silver or gold, sometimes crystal, but also a coconut can be used, or an ostrich egg, an exotic shell or other exotic objects. In the course of time one can discern a distinct change in taste and fashion in these objects. This also applies to glassware. The precious porcelain is for the most part Chinese from the Ming Dynasty (Wan-li) and, in the third decade of the 17th century, also so-called Transitional porcelain. A beautifully decorated cup of Chinese porcelain was called in Holland a pronk cup.

Dead animals are only rarely depicted in pronk still lifes, except for shells, lobsters, crabs, and sometimes game in transitions to game still lifes. Occasionally we see them as objects belonging in a curio collection, such as pelts or plumage of birds of paradise. But sometimes live animals are used to enliven the scene — for example, parrots, parakeets, or monkeys. Rather rarely in still lifes are religious objects depicted.

Inasmuch as the objects in pronk still lifes could inspire meditations on the material and spiritual values of life, they were regarded as vanitas objects. The concept of Vanitas relates to the transiency of earthly possessions and of man's life on earth. But, while the pronk still life in general is not a 'preachy' type of picture, there are borderline examples between the typical vanitas still life — with such attributes as a skull, an hourglass, a watch, or a candlestick with a smouldering candle — and the typical pronk still life. Since flowers are in bloom for only a short while, flower still lifes have often been interpreted, sometimes too insistently, as symbolizing transiency. The same applies to book and music still lifes. Musical instruments, though, appear from time to time in pronk still lifes.

Although we define the pronk still life as one in which precious objects play an important role in the composition, they need not necessarily be large in size. One can think of the large works by Jan Davidsz. de Heem and his followers or by Abraham van Beyeren, but I would call smaller paintings with only a few objects pronk still lifes as well, as long as they conform to the above definition. An extreme example is the 'portrait' of a single object, such as the beautiful work shown in fig. 1.1. Painted by Pieter Claesz in 1641, it shows a gilt pronk goblet with only a few additional objects.[2] The goblet still exists and is now in the Frans Hals Museum in Haarlem. It once belonged to the St. Martin's or Brewers Guild of Haarlem and is dated 1604. The decorations were executed by the silversmiths Jacob Pietersz. van Alkemade and Ernst Jansz. van Vianen after designs of Hendrick de Keyser, for the cover, and

INTRODUCTION

Pieter Claesz
Pronk Goblet of the St. Martin's Brewers Guild at Haarlem, 1641
Private Collection, U.S.A.

Hendrik Goltzius, for the medallions. The decoration depicts scenes from the life of St. Martin. The sculptural group on the lid shows the saint as he cuts his cloak in half to share it with the poor beggar, a sign of charity.

Several other works by Pieter Claesz can also be regarded as pronk still lifes, though in these the exclusive role of a single object is less obvious. Examples are cat. nos. 29 and 30, and also a work with a tazza.[3] Other pronk 'portraits' of this type were made by Willem Claesz. Heda,[4] Maerten Boelema, Jan Jansz. den Uyl, Paulus van den Bosch, Simon Luttichuys, Pieter Gerritsz. van Roestraeten, Willem Kalf, and others.

Pieter Claesz and Willem Claesz. Heda are known as the great masters of the monochrome banquet pieces. Some of their works can be called pronk still lifes, but the presence of less luxurious food, such as ham, mackerel, salmon (a common food in those days), cake and pastries, of less expensive pewter utensils and Dutch or German glassware makes the distinction between the pronk still life and the banquet piece rather vague. The true masters of the pronk still life are Jan Davidsz. de Heem, Abraham van Beyeren and Willem Kalf.

INTRODUCTION

There are many cases in which the boundaries between pronk still life and history painting overlap. Borderline cases with kitchen and market pieces, for instance, can be found among the works of Pieter Aertsen and his followers, as was clearly demonstrated by Sterling (1952) and later elaborated by Bergström (1956) and others.[5] Several subjects from history have lent themselves particularly well to depicting pronk, e.g. the proverbial wealth of Croesus, the magnanimity of Scipio, or King Solomon receiving presents from the Queen of Sheba, all subjects which were very popular in the 17th century. The Lydian king Croesus, who reigned in the 6th century B.C., made precious votive offerings to temples — among others, to that in Delphi. Pointing to his treasures, he asked the philosopher Solon who could be the most fortunate of mortals. Solon answered that nobody could be considered to be the most fortunate person before his death.[6] This subject was depicted by Frans Floris and several times by Frans Francken the Younger.[7] The story is closely linked to the view, widely held in the 17th century, that true life, eternal life, only begins after death. Earthly wealth, like man, is perishable.

The Roman general Scipio Africanus Major, after he had conquered Carthage, returned a beautiful virgin who was part of his booty to her bridegroom, Allucius, to whom he also donated the presents which he had received from Allucius's grateful parents.[8] This story was depicted hundreds of times by Italian, Dutch and other artists, among whom were Karel van Mander (in 1600), Jan Brueghel the Elder, Peter Paul Rubens, Frans Francken the Younger (at least seven times),[9] Gerbrandt van den Eeckhout, and Jan Steen.[10] The subject underscored the virtues of charity, sobriety and moderation.

The story of King Solomon and the Queen of Sheba is recorded in the Old Testament.[11] The theme was especially favored in Italian art, but there are also examples by Peter Paul Rubens and Frans Francken the Younger.[12]

PETER PAUL RUBENS
Sleeping Silenus
Akademie der Bildenden Künste, Vienna

ADRIAEN VAN UTRECHT
Pronk Still Life with an Alchemist, 1636
Musées Royaux des Beaux-Arts, Brussels

A remarkable painting with pronk objects is a work by Peter Paul Rubens in the Akademie der Bildenden Künste in Vienna (fig. 1.2.)[13] The principal figure is the sleeping Silenus, the tutor of the young Bacchus, god of wine, who is depicted behind him. The nymph who is pressing grapes probably alludes to the saying that the theater of the world changes with inebriety: Silenus is drunk most of the time and can no longer distinguish between reality and illusion.[14] He is shown dreaming here: in his intemperance he dreams of immoderate treasures and lust. Our attention is caught by the objects depicted at the right which were available in Antwerp around 1610: gilt bowls, jugs, chalices, a shell beaker, a pronk goblet, a Wanli cup and glassware, some of it *façon de Venise*. A number of these objects are similar to ones in still lifes of the period, for instance in the work of Osias Beert, who worked in Antwerp. Some of them, however, we seldom encounter, such as the glass drinking bowl with a 'bat' border from which the young Bacchus drinks. We find a similar bowl, clasped in a *bekerschroef*, in the pronk still life dated 1642 by Jan Davidsz. de Heem (fig. 8.3).

In 1636 Adriaen van Utrecht painted the large pronk still life in the Musées Royaux des Beaux-Arts in Brussels (fig. 1.3).[15] Here also there are a number of precious objects, such as glasses, Chinese porcelain and goldsmith's work, which would make the modern connoisseur envious. The large parrot, a macaw, became a familiar figure in the still lifes of this period. The alchemist in the background is, according to Sambucus, a fool who searches for the essence of life in worldly gain and thus misses his goal. The motto above the emblem reads: *Alchimae Vanitas*.[16] The biblical response to the alchemist's false quest can be found in the scene on the tazza lying in the left foreground. We see Melchisedek, the priest-king of Salem or Jerusalem, who brings bread and wine to the patriarch Abraham, who has been victorious in several battles, and blesses him.[17] This is the first time that Jerusalem is mentioned in the Bible. King David considered himself the legal successor of this priest-king.[18] Melchisedek, which means 'King of Justice,' is also generally seen as the precursor of Christ, and the offering of bread and wine to Abraham is a metaphor of the Holy Communion.[19] The story of Melchisedek and Abraham was painted often from the 15th through the 17th centuries. Notable examples are by Dieric Bouts and Peter Paul Rubens.

Nearly all profane art of the 16th and 17th centuries was a development, directly or indirectly, from religious art. Artists who made the first departures from traditional sacred formats, such as Leonardo da Vinci and Pieter Brueghel the Elder, were great innovators. But portrait painters forged the first link in the chain of transition. Jan van Eyck brought this branch of art to new heights. Yet in Renaissance portraiture religious overtones are stressed. Attributes of the sitters often express their faith, trust or hope — for instance in the form of a flower, often a carnation — and the realistic focus on those attributes represented in itself a new orientation of artistic vision.

Another link between portraiture and religion can be seen in the vanitas attributes and texts which from the 15th century were often placed on the verso of the panels, and later also on the back of the side panels with which a triptych can be closed. These images can be considered the precursors of vanitas still lifes. The oldest isolated vanitas still life in Dutch art, however, is a work by Jacques de Gheyn of 1603 which is now in the Metropolitan Museum in New York.[20] Together with a work by Johannes van der Beek, also known as Torrentius, by whom until now only one still life is known,[21] and a later vanitas piece of De Gheyn of 1621,[22] it forms the basis of a great tradition which blossomed, at first especially in Haarlem and Leiden, and of which Jan Davidsz. de Heem became the great representative. Presumably De Heem had great admiration for Torrentius: at least this would explain the name of his daughter Torentiana, who was born in Leiden in 1635.

De Heem was the originator of a special type of vanitas still life, the book still life.[23] Music still lifes are a later development of this theme.[24] The relationship of the vanitas theme to the development of the pronk still life, however, is only an indirect one. While vanitas attributes may appear in pronk still lifes, retaining the same symbolism, they may also signify something quite different. This applies especially to timepieces and, to a lesser degree, to musical instruments. However, as far as the clock or watch is concerned, the interpretation can shift from a warning of the approaching end — often with the hand pointing to 11 or nearly 12 — to a sign of regularity and an admonition of moderation. Musical instruments as an indication of harmony may have been derived from allegorical and genre paintings.

While the still life as we know it today evolved to an important degree out of developments in 15th- and 16th-century religious painting,[25] even more fundamental forces were at work which led to the emphasis and eventual isolation of objects from their original contexts. Not the least of these was the profound social change in Northern Europe away from a society dominated by the clergy and nobility toward one controlled by a class of commoners in which the profits from trade created a new aristocracy based upon wealth. Reflecting the influence of Renaissance thought in this society, we note the increasing importance of profane subject matter (mythological and allegorical scenes), for instance in the prints of the late 15th century in Germany, and somewhat later in Flanders and Holland. We see such profane themes in the work of Petrus Christus and Quinten Matsys, and on a much larger scale in Pieter Brueghel the Elder's genre paintings with peasant scenes.

Propelled by the force of Humanistic thought, which reached its peak in 16th-century Holland, a merging of sacred and profane themes occurred in the kitchen and market pieces of Pieter Aertsen and his followers (and in series of allegorical prints of the elements, the seasons and the senses).[26] We note in these works that the sacred themes have been pushed to the background while the still-life elements, often rich with concealed symbolic content, are emphasized in the foreground. This startling shift of emphasis encouraged the interpretation of the paintings on various levels — profane, religious, moralizing — and represented an intellectual game of sorts, understandable only to insiders.

In other types of paintings, too, objects themselves, both animate and inanimate, were scrutinized more sharply and stood out from their environment. This surely reflects in part the emerging scientific mentality, according to which plants and animals were studied not only as to their economic usefulness but also in the quest for a truer understanding of nature. The art of working in gold and silver, and that of glassblowing, reached new heights, the former at first in Nürnberg, the latter in Venice, stimulating the production of highly-prized articles and the embellishment of exotic natural objects. The importation of ornamental objects and naturalia from distant lands newly discovered in the age of exploration and economic empire-building aroused admiration for the richness of forms in Creation and inspired the formation of collections of curios and valuable objects on the part of the new class of wealthy elite. In this light, too, one should understand the excitement over collecting bulbs and other exotic plants. In general, the increasing secularization of art ran parallel to a development in which objects of luxury and natural curiosity assumed importance in the lives of the newly affluent. The importance of these objects in many cases was no longer tied to any symbolic meaning they may once have held. Nevertheless, a tradition of symbolic reference had grown during the late 15th and 16th centuries which inevitably contributed to the pronk still life.

One of the earliest scenes with prominent pronk objects is a painting by Van Eyck's pupil Petrus Christus. Depicting St. Eligius in his study (fig. 1.4) and painted in 1449, it is now in the Metropolitan Museum in New York.[27] In the background we recognize pronk goblets, among which is a coconut beaker in which the coconut is mounted on a golden foot. The coconut, like coral also shown in the painting, was a product from a distant and exotic land. The painting shows another pronk goblet with gold work around a cylinder of polished crystal. On the top shelf is a pewter predecessor of a *Buckelpokal* with gold ornamentation.[28] In addition, rings and other jewelry and also gold coins attract our attention. A rich young couple stands behind the saint, the woman dressed in gold brocade, the man in velvet

1.4

PETRUS CHRISTUS
St. Eligius in His Study, 1449
Metropolitan Museum, New York, Robert Lehmann Collection

Quinten Matsys
The Banker and His Wife, 1514
Musée du Louvre, Paris

and adorned with jewelry. In several regards there are similarities with a work by Quinten Matsys in the Musée du Louvre, dating from 1514, entitled *The Banker and His Wife* (fig. 1.5).[29] The weighing of valuables, which both paintings represent, not only serves the purpose of determining the value of the objects but also expresses symbolically 'the weighing of other values.' Above the head of the banker an orange lies on a shelf, symbolically understood as the fruit of the Tree of Knowledge of Good and Evil. The woman is choosing between spiritual values, represented by the manuscript with a miniature of the Virgin and Child, and material values, which seem momentarily to have a stronger attraction for her. The split-wood boxes are for the storage of valuables; we encounter them right into the 17th century as little cases in which collectors' items were kept.[30]
Unfortunately, the texts which once elucidated Matsys's work are no longer clearly legible. An inscription on the original frame reads: 'Statera iusta & aequa sint pondera.' This is from the philosophical tract *De Ludo Globi*, of 1463, by Nicolaes von Kues.[31] Von Kues wrote that in life there must be a balance between material and spiritual values. The text also refers to

Unknown Master
Objects in a Cupboard, 1538
Kröller-Müller Museum, Otterlo (the Netherlands)

Leviticus 19:15: 'Ye shall do no unrighteousness in judgment: thou shalt not respect the person of the poor, nor honor the person of the mighty: but in righteousness shalt thou judge thy neighbor.' The scales, of course, are a well-known symbol of justice. Perhaps more germane than the works of Von Kues, however, is the fact which one must keep in mind that Quinten Matsys was in close contact with the great humanists of his time, such as Desiderius Erasmus and Thomas More.[32]

One can imagine that paintings like *The Banker and His Wife* may eventually have led to attempts to bring the objects together without figures. Fig. 1.6, an anonymous work,[33] shows the archetype of this development. Several details remind us of the work of Matsys, but there are also considerable differences. In this painting, which is dated 1538, we are looking into a cupboard, an illusionistic effect and an excellent example of *trompe l'oeil*. An amusing detail is the mouse that is nibbling the bread. The cheese will return in the Dutch still lifes of the early 17th century.

From the last decades of the 15th century, especially in Flanders, we see in the marginal illu-

NICOLAES SPIERINC
Book of Hours of Mary of Burgundy, c. 1477
Österreichische Nationalbibliothek, Vienna

minations of manuscripts great attention paid to precious objects. The most beautifully illuminated manuscripts were commissioned by kings and princes. Fig. 1.7 shows a miniature from the book of hours of Mary of Burgundy.[34] Through an open window one sees Christ nailed to the cross. On the windowsill lies a brocade-covered cushion, used as a support during prayer, with a string of pearls as a rosary to which a pomander and a purse are attached. A pomander is a perfume ball which was filled with sweet-smelling herbs (see cat. no. 31). In the foreground on the left is a box of jewels, an earthy snail and a bottle with perfumed water, a sign of vanity that can be regarded as the antithesis of the book of prayers to the right in the foreground. On the canopy at the left St. Peter hands the key of heaven to an angel to open the gate for the praying faithful. In another miniature in the same book of hours, Mary of Burgundy is shown reading a book of prayers with jewels and flowers next to her. She sits in front of a window that looks out on Mary with the Child Jesus in a church.[35]
In the flourishing period of Flemish book illumination, the miniatures also contained profane scenes whose sources were from Antiquity. A scene in a French manuscript by Willem

Vrelant of Bruges shows the young and beautiful Juno surrounded by precious goblets, jugs and jewelry. A young knight on horseback is not seduced by this show of wealth, power and luxury, and rides on.[36] The young man reminds us of the *Miles Christianus*, the fighter for Christ whom we shall discuss later in connection with pronk goblets.

In the second half of the 16th century certain biblical themes lent themselves particularly well to the growing humanistic tendency to use objects to convey symbolic content. Because of its central religious significance, the Last Supper was chief among them. In the words of Matthew 26:26-28: 'And as they were eating, Jesus took bread and blessed it, and broke it, and gave it to the disciples, and said, Take, eat; this is my body. And he took the cup, and gave thanks, and gave it to them, saying Drink ye all of it: For this is my blood of the new testament, which is shed for many for the remission of sins.'

Bread and wine, or a beaker (with wine), are the eucharistic symbols of the body and blood of Christ, and wine or blood are each symbols of the Teaching of Christ, the New Testament. Christ called himself elsewhere 'the bread that came down from heaven.'[37] This implies spiritual food, as in Erasmus's *Convivium Religiosum* (the Spiritual Meal). This is one of the first dialogues in his *Colloquia Familiaria*, a book that had a profound influence on other humanists. In the course of the book's dialogue it becomes clear that the imitation of Christ is the proper way of life. The daily meal itself is associated in this text with the Last Supper: 'For truly if a meal was something holy to pagans, much more should it be to the Christians, for whom it is an allegory of the sacred Last Supper which the Lord Jesus took with his disciples.'[38] In 16th-century practice the walls of the room where the meal was served were often hung with paintings, among which the Last Supper and The Rich Man's Table and the Poor Lazarus were common examples.[39] The Last Supper as a pictorial subject, of course, has a long and old tradition. We find examples in the Roman catacombs from the first century A.D. and also in the mosaics at Ravenna which date from the Middle Ages. The Worcester Art Museum has a beautiful example of a fresco from Spoleto, of around 1300, with jugs, bowls, dishes, beakers and knives, as well as bread, fish and fruit.[40]

From details in certain 16th-century allegorical scenes, such as paintings by Hieronymus Bosch and prints by Pieter Brueghel the Elder, we gain insights, confirmed by textual sources, into the symbolic meaning of attributes. These insights are useful in understanding the meaning of early still lifes, even if the paintings themselves cannot be seen as direct precursors of still lifes. A different matter, however, are the paintings of Pieter Aertsen. Some of his kitchen pieces are without any doubt still lifes. That behind these still lifes lies hidden a deeper meaning is not only evident from the religious scenes in the background and inscribed references to biblical texts, but also from the comments of contemporaries such as the humanist Hadrianus Junius. In 1588 he wrote in laudatory terms about Aertsen's work, and again in 1610 about Aertsen's pupil Joachim Beuckelaer. He wrote that it was no wonder that his kitchen pieces were appreciated since 'many find pleasure in a kitchen with a deeper meaning.'[41]

Something similar was written by the humanist-geographer Abraham Ortelius about Pieter Brueghel. He wrote that by his masterly rendering of emotions Brueghel always suggests more than one can see directly.[42] There are diverging opinions as to how the kitchen and market paintings of Aertsen should be interpreted. The most extreme ones are the views of

INTRODUCTION

Grosjean, Emmens and Moxey. Grosjean (1974) assumed on the basis of Bax's research on Hieronymus Bosch that every object was an allusion to a well-known expression or proverb, and he interpreted the objects mostly in an erotic sense. Emmens (1973), referring especially to humanistic and related sources, came to suppose that there are fundamental contrasts embodied in the works, in terms of which he identified paired conceptions: for example *Fides* and *Diffidentia Dei* (trust and distrust in God), *Amor Dei* and *Amor sui* (love of God and love of self), *Castitas* and *Voluptas carnis* (chastity and lust), *Vita contemplativa* and *Vita activa* (a contemplative life or a career on earth) or, in general, an adherence to Christian virtues as opposed to a concern for material things. Moxey (1976) considered the scenes as naturalistic 'slices of life' and denied any moralizing character.[43] This view is unconvincing.

Most researchers before and after Emmens indeed perceived contrasts and were of the opinion that one had to seek such interpretations assuming the presence of disguised symbolism. Genaille's view was that Aertsen tried to combine two different styles and atmospheres in one work with the aim of confronting each with the other: '...un lien entre un univers de la fiction et un univers naturaliste.'[44] Irmscher (1986) based himself on Cicero and the Stoa and thought that one should distinguish three levels of meaning: erotic, religious, and ethical or political. I am of the opinion that a profane as well as a religious interpretation was intended, at least in a number of works, and that not different but the same figures and objects can be interpreted both *in bono* and *in malo*. In this view a painting as a whole can be interpreted either as earthly-materialistic or religious-spiritual or even entirely spiritual.[45] Such an interpretation of the still life of 1552 in the Kunsthistorisches Museum in Vienna (fig. 1.8) was

1.8

PIETER AERTSEN
Still Life with Christ in the House of Martha and Mary, 1552
Kunsthistorisches Museum, Vienna

INTRODUCTION

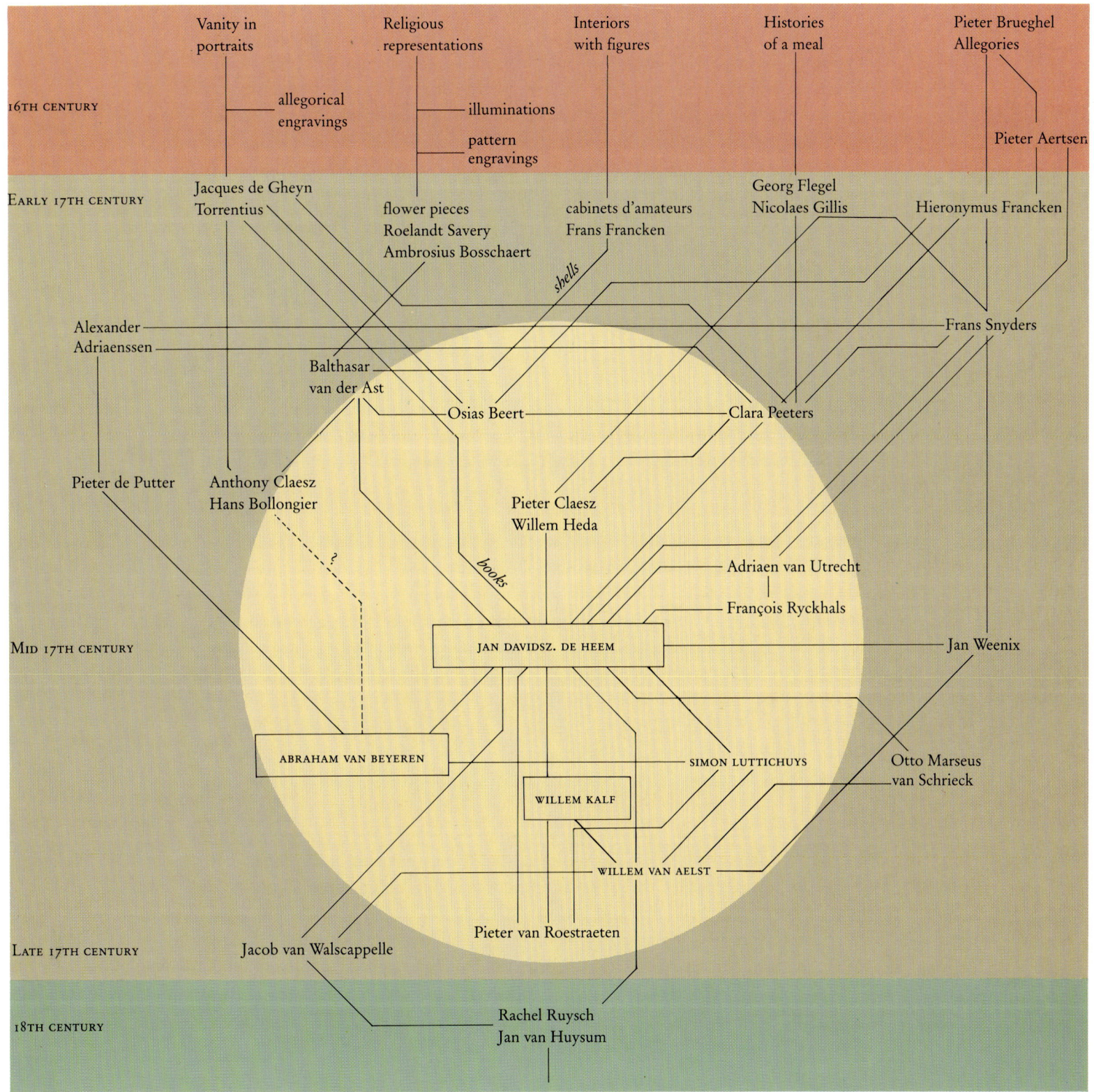

1.9 *Simplified chart of the development which contributed to the creation of pronk still lifes. The connection lines differ in significance.*

given by Anne Lowenthal in a lecture (1986) which is awaiting publication.[46] One of the reasons that Aertsen invented this approach must surely be that he witnessed the iconoclasm and wanted to safeguard his deeply-held religious beliefs, addressing a clientele who shared those beliefs during a dangerous time of religious strife. In the Escorial is a painting of the Judgment of Solomon, there attributed without foundation to Luca Giordano but certainly by Aertsen.[47] I believe that Aertsen would agree with me that we should leave the judgment of the meaning of the painting to the spectator, though admittedly a spectator of our day will differ in his understanding from one of the 16th or 17th century.

By the end of the 16th century sophisticated connoisseurs of art in Northern Europe were well accustomed to interpreting the concealed symbolism of objects in paintings (still more will be said about this in Chapter 2). Despite the familiarity of this intellectual activity, however, the pronk still life was not directly derived from scenes with objects in interiors or from the miniature marginalia of illuminated manuscripts or from the proto-still lifes of Pieter Aertsen. It was an outgrowth of early 17th-century still lifes with tables set for a meal — *banketjes* (banquet pieces) and *ontbijtjes* (breakfast pieces). The *banketje* is simply a richer form of the breakfast piece, but it was already being painted before the simpler *ontbijtjes* began to be produced in the third decade of the century. It is difficult, however, to draw a sharp distinction between the two, and in art-historical practice the term breakfast piece is applied so loosely that some authors use it to denote any painting in which a meal is depicted.

Others consider pictures of laid tables with many different objects painted in the first decades of the 17th century as a separate group. In this study (as developed in Chapter 4) I shall use the terms 'meal still life' and 'banquet piece' as an overall concept when pronk objects are present, and the term 'breakfast piece' only when pronk objects play a minor role or no role at all. Overlap between banquet pieces, breakfast pieces, and pronk still lifes will always exist, but each collective term covers a group of paintings which will be clearly recognizable as a group for anyone who is willing to make some effort to study this subject.

The central figure in the development of the pronk still life was Jan Davidsz. de Heem, the originator of the most eloquent and elaborate works in this genre (fig. 1.9). He was able to assimilate the different methods, concepts and ideas of his forerunners and contemporaries, which led him to new and lofty creative heights. The influence of Balthasar van der Ast is only clearly discernable in his earliest work, but from around 1640 on De Heem was the undisputed grand master of the still life in the northern and southern Netherlands and remained so for several decades. In 1635 he moved to Antwerp but often returned to the north and even stayed for several years in the town where he was born, Utrecht.

Jan Davidsz. de Heem had many direct and indirect followers. Hardly any still-life painter of the second half of the 17th century could escape his influence. Even Abraham van Beyeren and Willem Kalf, who each developed an individual style, were strongly influenced by De Heem. In fact, this influence penetrated far into the 18th century with painters like Rachel Ruysch and Jan van Huysum, and it was still noticeable even in painters of the 19th century.

Chapter 2

On Meaning and Interpretation: The Abundance of Life and Moderation in All Things

Dutch old master paintings have long been appreciated for their beauty, evocative atmosphere, great craftsmanship and appeal to the heart and intellect. It has become increasingly clear in recent decades, however, that seemingly secular paintings from the 17th century often express much more than the mere imitation of reality and that their function was not purely decorative. If we have the feeling that the artist's intention was more than to decorate or to delight the eye through imitation of the world around him, then a deeper study of the painting and its context can add an extra dimension to our visual pleasure. The search for meaning, however, can become a goal in itself, in which case the pleasure of looking turns into a mere intellectual fixation. It is like listening to music. One can enjoy great music without knowing anything about the theory of harmony. Knowledge can either increase or diminish our enjoyment.

After it was discovered that genre paintings often contain a message,[1] it was found that attributes in portraits also often had meaning,[2] and that even landscapes were not always devoid of symbolism.[3] Although symbolic meanings have been attributed to still lifes for a long time,[4] we have in recent decades gained new insights which have added to or corrected our former ideas.[5] This does not mean that there are not considerable differences of opinion among scholars about the degree and importance of symbolism in the paintings, about specific interpretations, or about the limitations of interpretation in general.

Dutch society in the 17th century was in some ways like our own but in other ways profoundly different. As we seek an understanding of the new art forms of that day, it will be helpful to examine, if only sketchily, the character of society and the ethical values that were held up to its members. The pronk still life, as it happens, is a vivid reflection of both.

In the Middle Ages the Netherlands had been ruled by the clergy and the nobility. Power was strongly decentralized in the 17th century, however, and was transferred to the cities and local authorities. The Republic of the United Netherlands, a federation of states without much coherence, developed with astonishing rapidity. The southern part of the Dutch-speaking provinces remained for a long time in the hands of the Spaniards, who also made occasional attempts to extend their control into the northern provinces. Towards the end of the 16th century the situation had become more or less stabilized, although the state of war with Spain was to continue for another half century.

The policies of local government were mainly decided by the merchants. They, together with the regents (governors), who were partly recruited from the powerful merchant class and partly from the nobility, began to form a new aristocracy based largely on wealth. The standard of living was high in comparison to that of other countries; in a short time the province of Holland, and subsequently the whole Republic, had developed into one of the most powerful countries in the world. Concomitant with this civic progress and prosperity, there was an exceptional blossoming of culture. In contrast to other countries, where the arts were cultivated mainly in the courts of kings and princes, in the Netherlands they were patronized in the cities and were influenced by the demands of the new aristocracy.

Prosperity for a substantial segment of the population was a new experience. Anyone who showed ingenuity and initiative was able to better himself. This prosperity was in particular a result of trade with neighboring countries and distant lands. Some of the profits were spent on estates, houses and other possessions. Possessions that could be seen increased one's prestige, and prestige was a coveted thing. It was reflected by the location and size of one's house, the number of servants, the garden, the furnishing of the interior with precious objects, and the quality of the table one kept. In addition, one could be admired for giving gifts to charitable institutions such as orphanages and almshouses.

The beginning of the 17th century was an exciting time with many new things and ideas. The new things were the products of trade; the new ideas were the fruits of the Renaissance, of humanism and the consciousness of certain religious values (which continually caused religious quarrels), of a scholarly curiosity, and of a scientific interest in the rich variety of nature. Immigrants from the southern Netherlands who had fled from Spanish oppression played an important, innovating role in the country through the development of the textile and other industries.

Nowhere else in Europe was there such a wide choice of food, and nowhere else was so much eaten, even among the lower classes. According to Simon Schama (1987), who has made an extensive study of 17th-century Holland, the Dutch were widely reputed to be gluttons. The supply of food included not only domestic products from the farms and fisheries of Holland but also exotic fruits, wines, spices, and later coffee and tea. Other amenities of life were also abundant. From Nürnberg and other centers of manufacturing and trade came gold and silver objects. Costly glass came from Venice; spices, exotic animals and seashells from the Indian archipelago; porcelain from China; and tobacco from America — all items which contributed to the unprecedented sense of luxury of the affluent.

Religion played an important role in the daily life of the people, both for the catholics and the protestants of various persuasions. The protestants had drastically reduced the central position that the Virgin Mary had held in medieval theology and had decimated that of the saints. Christ and his teaching were now at the center of theological thought. To follow Christ was the right path in life. It was generally considered that a righteous life on earth was the preparation for the real, eternal life after death. This belief gave special dimensions to the polar concepts of life and death and must have led many to pause and reflect. Curiously, it seems there was the potential for a sense of guilt in the midst of such plenty. For the poor and sick this may sometimes have meant hope and expectation, since it was generally understood that it was easier to gain Redemption by having led a sober life, even one with much suffering, than by a life of ease. The plague and other epidemics still flared up but had become less frequent as a result of better hygiene. Hunger was not so prevalent, although occasional unsuccessful harvests caused deprivation.

The church remained the principal moral arbiter of society, but people of the higher social classes who could read and write also turned for guidance to books in which new humanistic ideas integrated concepts from both Christianity and Antiquity. For a small group of humanist-oriented artists in Haarlem the ideas of Justus Lipsius and others were of great importance as they tried to give new life to classical stoicism.[6] Dirck Volckertsz. Coornhert had written in Dutch for the average man his *Zedekunst, dat is, Wellevenskunste...*, a sort of manual of daily behavior and thought. His point of departure, derived from classical philosophy, was the concept of self-knowledge, which meant that by becoming conscious of one's self one can achieve a virtuous life of his own free will. Everyone understood that this was, simply put, the way of Christ. In his third book Coornhert discoursed upon the virtues and vices, treating the kinds of choices with which men and women are continually confronted. One of the expedients was avoiding extremes and keeping to the golden mean in all activities and emotions.[7] The work of Coornhert was influential, but it did not attract a large readership. Later the books of Jacob Cats, some of which were emblem books, became the educational manuals for the general public. The books of Coornhert, Cats and kindred spirits were intended to help people to become aware of the struggle required to maintain a balance between material prosperity and moral sobriety and charity, to choose between virtue and vice.

Of course, the most important literary source, to which people were continually referred and which everybody regularly read or listened to, was the Bible. The influence of sermons was no doubt considerable, but just as nowadays this depended on the quality of the clergyman and the local circumstances. In cities where entertainment was more readily available and where social control was less rigid, the practicing of religion could easily become a mere duty, or even a matter of habit. The urge for reflection could be satisfied by owning moralizing prints and books, or even paintings.

There can be little doubt that still lifes were among the paintings which served this purpose. Contrary to what is often thought today, the new art form of the still life was probably the most 'philosophical' of its day. Still lifes were not mere technical *tours de force* and were in no way the result of a direct imitation of a real arrangement of objects. The combinations of things depicted were often significant. In a flower piece, for instance, we see flowers that in reality bloom at different times of the year and could not reflect a real arrangement; in a fruit piece we see fruit which is not available in the same season. The painter invented his own composition, often in a rapidly executed composition sketch. The composition sketch was often transferred in chalk to the white gesso ground of the panel or canvas on which the painting was to be executed.[8] He painted the objects either directly from nature, *alla prima*, or from studies in watercolor, bodycolor, or oil paint which he could use more than once, and also from his own finished paintings. It is clear from this that post-Cézanne painters have a completely different approach to the still life than painters of the 17th century.

To what extent early still-life painters intended to include a moral lesson in their works is difficult to say. There is reason to believe that originally the intention was there in many cases but that later purely pictorial concerns came to dominate, although even then there may have been from time to time a need for serious reflection. In a number of works, however, we can be certain about the message — when the scene is accompanied by a legend. In the catalogue *A Fruitful Past*, I have extensively discussed the possibilities of symbolism, conscious or not, and the perception of the viewer. Searching for an interpretation in the labyrinth of possibilities is not always easy — for some attributes there are scores of meanings — but context and logic can often show the way. Nevertheless, one must beware the pitfalls of over-interpretation and fantasy. There may be no *one* interpretation, no matter how seemingly watertight the arguments. And there may be no hidden meaning at all. The viewer will see in a given work what he will, and I believe that was understood by most artists. With this in mind I simply offer a few guidelines to assist in understanding the rich symbolic vocabulary of forms that was common currency among educated people of the 17th century, a vocabulary that has been all but forgotten in modern times.

A common language of metaphor and symbol, which was still very much alive at the beginning of the 17th century, had been nurtured throughout the Middle Ages in the encyclopedic compilations of such authors as Pliny the Elder, Isidore of Seville and Vincent of Beauvais, or in such specialized manuscripts as herbaria, bestiaria and lapidaria. With the advent of printing in the Renaissance many of these texts were published, followed by anthologies, summaries and adaptations, and efforts were made to integrate ancient knowledge with Christian belief. In the 16th century educated persons were familiar with such compendia of symbolic knowledge as Erasmus's *Adagia* and Valerianus's *Hieroglyphica*. We cannot believe that all artists knew such esoteric literature, but certain ones of a humanistic bent, such as Joris Hoefnagel, did make use of classical texts, and many were familiar with Ovid's *Metamorphoses*.

Prior to the explosion of 'new knowledge' in the 17th century — the result of exploration and scientific investigation — the fairly stable body of knowledge which had existed up to then had been poured over, collated, elaborated and paraphrased until a cohesive and elegant epistemological 'system' emerged. This system, which reached perfection in the works of 16th-century humanism, was of such utility and appeal that its use long overlapped 17th-century initiatives to study nature and organize knowledge along more empirical and objective lines. Inevitably in the works of painters of this period, we find visual expression of this overlap in the heightened focus on the true appearance of things as well as reminiscences of their symbolic meanings according to a system of knowledge that was destined to become irrelevant. As inheritors of the new system it is sometimes hard for us to believe that those who lived through its early years could credit both the new and the old. But that is surely the way it was, just as belief in the relevance of astrology far outlasted the realization that the true organization and influence of the heavens in fact bears little relation to medieval concepts.

In view of the strong evidence for the importance of symbolic thought in 17th-century life, it is well to take a closer look at how it worked. The difficulty of symbolic interpretation is due not only to the various meanings a single object might have but also to the several ways in which a specific symbol might be used and to the different levels on which its meaning might be interpreted. The different meanings of an object may simply reflect a general significance and a specific one, depending upon the context in which it is used as a symbol. Thus any fruit can be a sign of fertility in general, while a pomegranate can express certain forms of fertility, for example the Church with its faithful (the seeds) or the blood of the Martyrs (red seeds). Quite often the same object can have totally contrasting meanings, depending on the context. For example, Jacob Cats uses the lion in his preface to *Zinne- en Minne-beelden* as a symbol of Christ as well as the devil.[9] Meanings of the same object *in bono* and *in malo*, positive and negative, had been listed by Petrus Berchorius (1290-1362) in his influential *Reductorium Morale*.[10] The symbol of a negative action or a negative quality, such as drunkenness, can also have opposing meanings, according to how it is used — as an illustration or as a warning. In the latter case the effect of the meaning is the opposite, sobriety. A title like Pieter Baardt's *Deugden-spoor in de on-deugdhen des werelts affgebeeldt* (1645) — (A Depiction of the Path of Virtue in an Unvirtuous World) — illustrates the point. The book was intended as 'a mocking of the wicked and for the faithful a path of hereditary virtue.' In many authors one finds texts that can be interpreted on different levels — sometimes on two, three or even four levels. In the case of two levels, one finds usually a literal and a metaphorical meaning.[11] In the case of three levels, meaning is expressed in various ways,[12] though not always clearly. They usually are the three levels of knowledge as distinguished in the Middle Ages: *Cogitatio* (knowledge through the senses), *Meditatio* (knowledge through intellect or *ratio*), and *Contemplatio* (knowledge through the understanding of the soul and heart, in which extreme happiness and admiration are experienced). Contemplatio is regarded as the highest level, which brings one nearest to the Creator. A fourth level is sometimes applied to the interpretation of the Bible. Besides the well-known, four-part classification of Augustine,[13] the Jewish author of the mystical *Zohar* distinguished four levels which he compared to a nut: 'Just as a nut has an outer shell and a kernel, each word of the Torah contains outward facts, midrash, haggadah, and mystery, each of which is deeper in meaning than the preceding.'[14]

In still lifes it is sometimes possible to distinguish a literal, a moral and a religious level of meaning. The lesson to be drawn from these works, even when they are vanitas still lifes, is that one has to make a *choice* in life. This can be a choice between earthly and heavenly, material and spiritual, or transient and eternal values, between lack of freedom and redemption, between vice and virtue. At the root of choice is the biblical story (Genesis 3) in which Eve tempts Adam in Paradise to eat the forbidden fruit of the Tree of Knowledge of Good and Evil.

We come across the choice between good and evil in many texts and in legends on paintings and illustrations in books. We read about it in the introductions of emblem books,[15] some of which contain listed pairs of contrasts.[16] In the later Middle Ages Valerius Maximus's *Facta ac dicta memorabilia* (Noteworthy deeds and sayings), from the first half of the first century, became a popular work. It consists of stories and anecdotes about good and bad behavior. In the illuminated Flemish manuscripts of this work produced in the second half of the 15th century, we see scenes representing 'the tables of the sober and immoderate persons.'[17] This subject is linked to the *Rich and Poor Kitchens* of Pieter Brueghel the Elder and to *The Poor Man's Meal* and *The Rich Man's Meal* of Hieronymus Francken the Younger (Chapter 3). In the paintings by Brueghel we see attributes that are important for the interpretation of 17th-century meal and pronk still lifes. In *The Poor Kitchen* are: salted herring, a cooking pot with a ladle (see also later: the virtue Prudence), mussels and brown bread; in *The Rich Kitchen*: roasted game, ham, sausage and white bread (only later apparently was sausage seen as food for the poor).

Series of illustrations of virtues and vices were also popular. This tradition was already in existence by the Middle Ages[18] and was continued in engravings into the 17th century. In these illustrations we see a number of attributes which later were to play a part in pronk still lifes. In a psalter from around 1525 a number of virtues and vices were painted by the Fleming Gerard Horenbout.[19] Hieronyumus Bosch's *Seven Deadly Sins* in the Museo del Prado in Madrid is a famous example.[20] Pieter Brueghel the Elder made a series of engravings of both vices and virtues. Within this tradition the vices are represented by: jewels (Pride, Vanity); a pronk goblet (Pride, Avarice); a mirror (Pride, Vanity); a bottle with perfumed water (Vanity); money and a money box (Avarice); ham and roasted game (Gluttony, Dipsomania); a mussel (Lust); a snail (Laziness, Apathy).

The virtues are represented in Brueghel, among others, by: a mirror, a pot of porridge with a ladle (Prudentia, or Caution, and Providence); a pair of scales, a candle, a sword, a gallows and a legend on 'the straight path' (Justice); a dead peacock, a turkey, a cockerel, a sword and a snail (Fortitude or Strength). These attributes can be supplemented by later examples from Cesare Ripa's *Iconologia*. We must take more time, however, to look at Brueghel's print

PIETER BRUEGHEL THE ELDER
Temperantia, 1560
Museum Boymans - van Beuningen, Rotterdam

Temperantia (Temperance), of which fig. 2.1 shows the original drawing.[21] The central allegorical figure is holding a rein in his mouth (the verb 'to rein' means in this sense 'to restrain').[22] He has a clock on his head, in his hand is a pair of spectacles, and he is standing on the sail of a windmill. Behind him people are using measuring instruments. To the right a bookkeeper is busy, and at the back on the right a play is being enacted by an actor on a stage. These and other scenes around the central figure depict the seven Free Arts. The inscription under the engraving reads: 'Videndum, ut nec voluptati dediti prodigi et lvxvriosi appareameus, nec avara tenacitati sordidi avt obscuri existamus' (We must see to it that we do not give ourselves over to a life of lust, extravagance and waste, and that we not, because of miserly greed, behave despicably or meanly). Here Lust, Pride, Gluttony and Greed are arrayed against Temperance. We shall see later that these same virtues and vices are protagonists of the pronk still lifes of the 17th century. The central theme of these still lifes is Moderation, but at the same time the choice between good and evil is often represented, as are the contrast between eternity and transiency and that between spiritual and material values. We have already seen that the Dutch had a reputation for gluttony and that they knew very well how to drink the wine of the rich and the beer of the poor. From the time of Pieter Brueghel the Elder onwards they are shown eating in large groups in paintings of peasant weddings. We see them dining at Civic Guard dinners by Frans Hals, or feasting outdoors in works by Willem Buytewech, or indoors in paintings by Dirck Hals. We see them drinking and smoking in tavern scenes by Adriaen Brouwer or in brothel scenes by Jan Steen. A number of these scenes are linked to the tradition of depicting the Prodigal Son. Scenes of drunken revelry comparable to the works mentioned above can be found in engravings such as *The Prodigal Son* by Jacques de Gheyn after Carel van Mander, of 1596,[23] or that by Cornelis Jansz. Visscher after David Vinckboons, of around 1608.[24] An early example is an engraving of an elegant outdoor party by Johannes Sadeler after Maarten de Vos, entitled *Crapula et Lascivia* (Revelry and Dissoluteness).[25] In some outdoor parties by Lucas van Valckenborch, David Vinckboons, Willem Buytewech and Jan Miense Molenaer we notice details which could indicate that 'on the side' a hint is given that one should behave moderately. One of the most frequently occurring hints is the diluting of wine with water. The allegory of Temperantia pouring liquid from a jug, a ewer or a bottle into a drinking cup or bowl, or mixing the contents of two barrels, is a theme in engravings by Lucas van Leyden, Jacques de Gheyn, Crispyn de Passe, Hieronymus Wierix, and in emblemata by Gabriel Rollenhagen and Roemer Visscher.[26] Temperantia's opposite is often Gula (Gluttony), and the same attributes are used, but then *in malo*. An example of this is Wierix's pendant series of the Cardinal Virtues and Vices. In an oval medallion is an allegorical female figure drinking, and in the four corners are other figures eating, drinking and vomiting, and one who is pouring wine from a jug into a tazza.[27] However, Temperantia can also have other vices as opposites, as we have already seen in the Brueghel print. The text of an allegorical Temperantia engraving by Crispyn de Passe the Elder, of 1600, is as follows: 'Nec mihi deliciae gratae/ nec foeda voluptas./ Contemno luxum,/ vili contenta paratu: (Sweets are not agreeable to me, neither is shameful lust. I scorn wealth, I am content with simple apparel).[28]

Mixing wine with water goes back to a very old tradition. Molsdorf and Timmers give examples from the Middle Ages.[29] Such scenes are probably based on a play of words, since the latin word 'temperare' means not only to moderate or to control but also to mix in the right proportion. In Erasmus we find under the motto 'Dionysium aequore mergentum' (Dionysus must be plunged into the sea) the justification that, according to various classical authors, Dionysus (Bacchus) is always full of wine.[30] A 'pronk portrait' of a pronk goblet by Pieter Claesz, which is related to fig. 1.1, shows the figure of Temperantia pouring water into a drinking bowl in one of the oval medaillions on the goblet.[31]

Another motto of Erasmus that we come across in literature and in art is 'Ne quid nimis' (Not too much).[32] It reminds us of the Temple of Apollo in Delphi with the Greek inscriptions 'Not too much' and 'Know Thyself.' It is the motto of an emblem by Rollenhagen showing a woman who pours too much liquid from a ewer into a bowl so that it spills. The following explanation is added: 'Angustum quicquid superest, vas respuit, ergo / In fundas ne quid forte caveto nimis: (All that is too much the little bowl spits out. Take care that you do not pour too much into it).[33] Jan Davidsz. de Heem uses a related proverb 'Niet hoe veel, maar hoe êel' (Not how much but how noble) in a pronk still life which we shall discuss in Chapter 8. We also find this proverb in works by Roemer Visscher and Jacob Cats.[34]

The theme of moderation in eating, drinking, talking, love making, even in giving and in behavior[35] — staying on the middle course — crops up everywhere in literature, and we should not be surprised to find it in art as well. The variant 'Al te veel is ongesont' (Too much is unhealthy) is seen in emblem books and in an emblematic painting by Adriaen van de Venne.[36]

A third motto of Erasmus should also be mentioned: 'Musicus apparatus' (Harmonious equipment).[37] Harmony and moderation are linked here and also include music, as *temperare* also means 'to keep time.' The link between music and moderation is evident from the texts on engravings and sometimes in still lifes, as, for instance, in the painting of 1614 by Torrentius,[38] mentioned earlier, in which a sheet of music is depicted with the text 'Wat buiten maat bestaat, int onmaats qaat verghaat' (Whoever exceeds the measure is lost), fig. 2.2. De Jongh linked this painting to an emblem by Roemer Visscher about the mixing of wine with water and suggested a relationship between pronk still lifes and the theme of moderation.[39] The connection between music and harmony in life is further confirmed by many texts in engravings and emblems.[40] Roemer Visscher treats the theme under the motto 'Not how much but how noble.'[41] In Ripa, Harmonia is a beautiful noblewoman with a viola da gamba.[42] It is not surprising that pronk is easy to link with Vanitas (vanity) and, in view of the earthly, material aspect of precious objects, with transiency. In fig. 2.3, a work by Cornelis de Vos, the female figure is interpreted by Klessmann as an allegory of transiency.[43] The bubble-blowing boy is the symbol of 'Homo bulla' (Man is like a soap bubble). This symbolic image is very often used in paintings.[44] In vanitas still lifes the boy has disappeared, but the soap bubbles still float in the air. Earthly riches, beauty and power (the beauty of the woman, her apparel, her jewels, and the power symbolized by the crown and scepter) are transient. Here the musical instruments are not symbols of harmony but of transiency: the sound of music is of short duration.

In a similar way this relation is expressed in a work by Pieter Boel and Jacob Jordaens (fig. 2.4).[45] Not only is the bubble-blowing putto present here, but Death itself blows out the flickering candle, the last vestige of life. Two winged putti, two redeemed souls, are gamboling about behind him.

TORRENTIUS (JOHANNES VAN DER BEECK)
Temperance, 1614
Rijksmuseum, Amsterdam

CORNELIS DE VOS
Allegory of Transcience
Herzog Anton Ulrich-Museum, Braunschweig

PIETER BOEL AND JACOB JORDAENS
Life, Transcience and Death
Musées Royaux des Beaux-Arts, Brussels

SEBASTIAN STOSKOPFF
Transcience of Wealth and Power
Musée de l'Oeuvre Notre Dame, Strasbourg

Fig. 2.5 is a vanitas still life with pronk goblets and silver beakers painted in 1641 by Sebastian Stoskopff. Silver *Setzbechers* or *Häufebechers* were a specialty of Stoskopff paintings. They were made in sets of six or eight, each fitting into the top of the other. The engraving depicts Zani, a clown from the opera buffa, after Jacques Callot. The text inscribed in the still life reads as follows:

> «Kunst, Reichthum, Macht und Kühnheit stirbet
> Die Welt und all ihr thun verdirbet
> Ein ewiges komt nach dieser Zeit
> Ihr thoren, flieht die Eitelkeit.»[46]

(Art, riches, power and courage die. The world with its activities decays. After this time comes eternity. You fools, escape from vanity.)

Chapter 3

The Young Hieronymus and Frans Francken

If we regard the still lifes of Pieter Aertsen and Joachim Beuckelaer and also some watercolor flower paintings by Joris Hoefnagel[1] dated from 1581 as merely the forerunners of a tradition of Dutch still-life painting, then we should date the beginning of this tradition around 1600. Until now no oil paintings have been found of an earlier date than one by Nicolaes Gillis of 1601.[2] The dated still lifes of Jacques de Gheyn the Younger and Roelandt Savery date from 1603, and flower pieces by Ambrosius Bosschaert the Elder and Jan Brueghel the Elder from 1605. A painting once attributed to Hieronymus Francken the Elder in the Koninklijk Museum voor Schone Kunsten in Antwerp, whose date had always been read as '1607', is now known to be by Hieronymus Francken the Younger, and the date is 1604 (fig. 3.1).[3] It is a painting of a simple meal of bread and butter, pancakes, herrings and beer. At first glance it does not seem to have much to do with a pronk still life, but it is worthwhile looking at it more carefully. The drawing or print at the top of the scene is remarkable. It shows an owl on its perch and to its left a pair of spectacles; to its right is a candlestick with a lighted candle. Underneath is a text: 'AL HEEFT HY KAERS EN BRIL/...UYL NIET ZIEN WIL' (Although it has a candle and spectacles/....the owl does not want to see).

This painting can in many ways be compared with cat. no. 1. We recognize a number of comparable objects, such as bread, pancakes, sausage, a wooden plate with a fresh herring, a ladle, a knife, a drawing of an owl with candle and spectacles. In the Antwerp painting a stoneware bowl is just visible at the back to the left and also a tall stoneware jug. On further examination we notice more similarities in the details, such as the little hand as a mark on the jug and on the blade of the knife. The similarities in composition, style, use of color, objects, handwriting on the wooden plates, and the black chalk underdrawing which is in some places visible to the naked eye leave us in no doubt that we are dealing with the same artist. The *HF* monogram on the knife is legible, but the date has lost much of its clarity. Probably it has to be read as '1599'. This composition was apparently very popular as there are at least four other versions, of which three are in museums in Antwerp, Brussels and Rotterdam. Until recently they were attributed to Pieter Brueghel the Elder, Pieter Aertsen or Joachim Beuckelaer. All are marked on the blade of the knife, and in none of them is the date clearly legible. In the Brussels version the little plate seems to bear a date that could be 1599, but it has been strengthened by a later hand. In the Rotterdam version a date of 1549 has been, no

HIERONYMUS FRANCKEN THE YOUNGER
Banquet Piece with an Owl Engraving, 1604
Koninklijk Museum voor Schone Kunsten, Antwerp

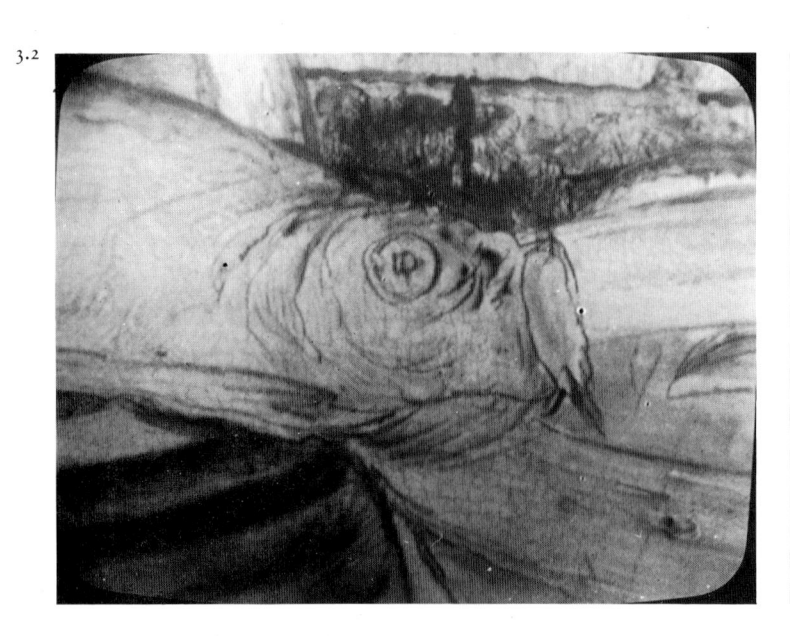

*Infra-red photograph of a detail of a Poor Man's Meal
by Hieronymus Francken the Younger*
Musées Royaux des Beaux-Arts, Brussels

HIERONYMUS FRANCKEN THE YOUNGER attributed
Herrings, 1597
British Museum, London

HIERONYMUS FRANCKEN THE YOUNGER
Rich Man's Meal, 1600 or 1601
Private Collection

doubt erroneously, read at the same place.[4] In another version the date looks more like 1601.[5] The Brussels version has a strong underdrawing which was examined with infra-red reflectography. This brought to light that many alterations had been made in the original sketch in black chalk on the white gesso ground.[6] Fig. 3.2 shows the infra-red photo of a detail of the head of the bloater on the stoneware pot with a handle.

A drawing in the British Museum, catalogued as 'Anonymous Flemish, circa 1600' (fig. 3.3),[7] should be seen in relationship to this painting. It is a study of two herrings lying crosswise on a wooden plate with a text. I have only been able to decipher the text in part. The handwriting seems the same as that on the wooden plates of the above-mentioned paintings. The text, in Dutch, starts with the date '1597' and refers to March 16 in London.

The painting with the bloaters, sausage, pancakes with batter and fresh herrings is, like the Antwerp painting of 1604, not exactly a pronk still life, only indirectly. It must be seen, however, in connection with another work of about the same size, of which there are also several versions (fig. 3.4).[8] Five versions known to me are in private collections; they are certainly pendants of the versions of cat. no. 1. Their similarities in technique, coloring, underdrawing and composition are striking, and together they depict — antiphonally as it were — the 'poor man's meal' and the 'rich man's meal.' A view of a landscape is painted on the right in *The Poor Man's Meal* and to the left in *The Rich Man's Meal*. The most precious object is a gilt goblet.⁹ The versions of fig. 3.4 have been described in catalogues of exhibitions and auctions under the names of Pieter Brueghel the Elder, Pieter Aertsen, Georg Flegel, Clara Peeters, Hans Antoni Françoi and Hieronymus Francken the Elder. They show the remains of a signature and text with a date on the *façon de Venise* flute glass that is ornamented with gold. In a version that formerly belonged to Willem Russell in Amsterdam, Bob Haak deciphered the inscription as *Hans Toni Françoi......1589*.¹⁰ In my opinion it reads *Hieronimo Francken F....1599*.

Fig. 3.4 is signed HIERONIMO/ FRANCKEN F/160(?), which could be read either as 1601 or 1600. The monogram HF can also be seen in the heart-shaped mark on the pewter plate, and the initials possibly also can be seen in the way in which the sweetmeats have been arranged on the plate. In comparing cat. no. 1 with fig. 3.4, a number of similarities as well as some differences make it clear that both paintings are related. We shall not go into all the similarities in technique, composition and style, but shall confine ourselves to a few remarks which are of importance for a better understanding of the development of the still life in general.

The paintings by Hieronymus Francken are very broadly composed with little fussing over details. The smooth manner of painting reminds us of the works of fellow-townsman Peter Paul Rubens, and also those of other members of the Francken family, of whom the younger brother Frans Francken the Younger is the best known because of his large production. It is remarkable that already at the beginning of the still-life tradition certain painters with a relatively delicate technique gave much attention to detail (such as Ambrosius Bosschaert the Elder and Clara Peeters) while others used a rather broad brush (such as Andries Daniels and Frans Snyders). In their color Francken's still lifes have dominant tones of brown and terracotta with secondary gray ones, linked by intermediary tones. These are the first 'monochrome banquets'. In *The Rich Man's Meal* the vermilion of the red wine provides an element of refreshing tension, and in *The Poor Man's Meal* the same effect is achieved with the white of the pancake batter and the vermilion of the sealing wax with which the drawing is affixed to the wall. The lustrous highlights in whites and grays do not yet show the delicacy which later Clara Peeters, Willem Claesz. Heda, and Jan Davidsz. de Heem were to achieve with such mastery when they depicted glass, pewter, silver, gold or a herring.

The vistas belong to the tradition of 15th- and 16th-century Flemish religious painting, and this tradition is continued for a while in the still lifes of, among others, Osias Beert the Elder, Frans Snyders, and members of the Brueghel dynasty. But the deliberate symbolic connection between foreground and background begins to become less strong in the second quarter of the 17th century.

The most important differences between the two paintings by Francken can be seen in the objects themselves. *The Rich Man's Meal* includes expensive and exotic food, such as citrus fruit, grapes, olives, wine, sweetmeats made from sugar, precious glassware, a knife with a silver handle and a gilt goblet. White bread takes the place of the brown bread of the poor man's table, pewter instead of the wooden plate and the stoneware, fresh oysters instead of smoked or pickled herring, sweetmeats instead of pancakes. The view in *The Poor Man's Meal* shows a shabbily dressed peasant couple on a winding path between two hills on which are, to the left, a gallows and, to the right, a windmill. In the distance is a town. The view in *The Rich Man's Meal* shows a splendidly dressed couple, the man with sword, walking on a straight road lined with trees on both sides. The menu has been written on the border of the plate: 'een Vis-Pekel Harinck Loolespot Bouckweycoecken Een pintthen bier sonder gout: (a Fish Salted Herring Stew Buckwheat biscuits A Pint of Beer without gold). The text is difficult to read in each version, partly since it is written in old-fashioned italics, partly since the paint is worn. Moreover, in each version the text is a little different. This also applies to the text on the drawing of the owl. In contrast to the Antwerp painting of 1604, the owl in this one is seen in a mirror. Above the mirror is written 'goeden dach bruer,' and underneath are the words 'vuilen spieghel.' The first expression is a toast, such as 'Cheers, brother,' and the second is a play of words on the name of the notorious rascal Tyl Uilenspiegel, a well-known figure in literature (*uilenspiegel* means 'owl's mirror' while *vuilen spiegel* means 'dirty mirror'). The owl in the mirror is a reflection of the stupid or ignorant person, for example a person who drinks immoderately. In *Iconologia* by Cesare Ripa (1593) we read that a mirror can either reflect a false or deceptive image, or, metaphorically, can help to know oneself, as one can only achieve this by seeing one's own faults.[11] When one, however, does not want to see stupid or bad things in a true light, then it is as if one is looking into a dirty mirror. The owl is considered to be a dirty animal. This is apparent from the drawing in the painting of 1604: even with the help of a candle and spectacles to see more clearly, this nocturnal animal is not better off. It is like a human being who, living in darkness, is blind to the essentials of life, or rather, does not want to see the truth.

Physiologus, who lived in the early Middle Ages, ascribed to the owl, a lover of darkness, many malevolent characteristics. A nocturnal animal cannot tolerate the light; it avoids the day, just as people who are up to no good. The animal fables collected by Physiologus, to which he gave a Christian moralizing tenor, had a great influence until the 17th century and even later. According to good Christian belief, the owl was a symbol of the unfaithful or the Jewish people who did not want to be enlightened.[12] Later the owl was an attribute for all sorts of mortal sin, as we can see in the *Dialogus creaturum* of 1480, published in Gouda, Holland.

In Ripa we see that the owl is an attribute of *Scorno*, Shame, but also of *Consiglio*, Wise Counsel.[13] The owl, with mirror, candle and spectacles, appears in an engraving by Nicolaes de Clerck (active 1599-1621), with the text 'NOSCE TEIPSVM-KENT V SELVEN...' (Know Thyself, see Chapter 2). The owl appears in a number of emblems which can be associated with the drawing depicted in the Hieronymus Francken painting. In 1540 it is shown with the motto 'Was hilfft mich sunn, licht oder prill. Weyl ich doch selbs nicht sehen will' (What good are sun, light or spectacles to me, if I do not want to see), and the accompanying text says 'Wer arges thut/hasset das liecht/ und kumpt nit an das liecht/ auff das seyne werck nicht gestrafft werden' (Who commits evil hates the light and does not come into the light so that his deeds will not be punished). This is a biblical text from John 3:20: 'For everyone that doeth evil hateth the light, nor cometh to the light, lest his deeds should be proved.' An accompanying text by Hans Sachs explains further that everyone is blinded by jealousy, lust for power, deceit, hate and envy, lust, gluttony, etc.[14]

In an engraving by Cornelis Bloemaert we read the following text: 'What is the use of spectacles if the owl does not want to see.'[15] In a dictionary of proverbs by Johan de Brune, published in 1636: 'What is the use of a mirror or spectacles for those who do not see or want to see. A thief can be nowhere better than on the gallows or the rope.'[16] This text is of a later date than the painting so that a direct relationship between the owl and the gallows in the background is not clear. The gallows is probably an admonition. The windmill on the hill opposite resembles the one in an emblem book of Marcus Antonius Gillis, published in Antwerp in 1556, which is a translation of the emblems of the Hungarian Johannes Sambucus.[17] The motto is as follows: 'Ledicheyt verwacht de fortuyne' (Idleness waits for a fortune). The text tells us that our forefathers built windmills on a hilltop so that they were driven by the precariousness of the winds, just like an idle man lets himself be led by fate. But the windmill can also be a symbol of the virtue of Christ, of Moderation or Regularity, and if it is used in this sense, then the people in Francken's painting can be seen as moving along a path between good and evil. A mill is often present in the background of 16th-century paintings of Mary and in those of Christ carrying the cross. A mill is situated on a high rock in the sunlight in the *Procession to Calvary* (1564) by Pieter Brueghel the Elder, in the Kunsthistorisches Museum in Vienna, while a gallows has been depicted in the background on a hill.[18] In the *Temperantia* engraving by Brueghel, from the series of the Cardinal Virtues, the windmill appears as a symbol of Moderation. I presume that Pieter Brueghel had a great influence on Hieronymus Francken, because one can in a certain way compare the rich and the poor man's meals with the Rich and the Poor Kitchens of the two famous engravings by Brueghel. We see the gallows in a number of Brueghel's paintings and in the engraving *Iustitia* in the same series of Virtues. Whether we apply the meaning *in bono* or *in malo*, we see in both cases the couple walking along a crooked path leading to a city in the distance, possibly heavenly Jerusalem, a path from which they could stray. The richly dressed couple from *The Rich Man's Meal* is walking along a broad, straight path. We read in Matthew 7:3-14: 'Enter ye in at the strait gate: for wide is the gate, and broad is the way, that leadeth to destruction, and many there be which go in thereat: Because strait is the gate, and narrow is the way, which leadeth unto life, and few there be that find it.' By the word 'life' is meant eternal life. This theme is dealt with in many ways in the impresas and emblem literature. Dante alluded to it in his *Purgatory* (x:3): 'After we had entered the Gate through which man cannot pass when he is sinful, As sin makes us think that the crooked path is straight....' I suppose that allusions to the narrow and the broad paths appear frequently in Flemish religious paintings.[19] We can relate both paintings with other works by Pieter Brueghel, for example with the print *Elckerlyck* (Everyman), a print within a print in which we see a person looking at himself in a mirror with the text: 'NIEMANT EN KENT HEMSELVEN' (No one knows himself).

This does not give a complete and unequivocal explanation of the pendant pair of paintings. We prefer to indicate a direction, an atmosphere which embraces both the intentions of the artist and the meaning as it was understood by his contemporaries without the pretention of being either certain or complete. Curiously enough, one can give to all the elements in both paintings a positive and a negative meaning, *in bono* or *in malo*. The simple food can signify the food of the righteous who search for virtue during their life, or spiritual poverty to which, among other things, the owl alludes. The owl drawing contains a message or warning that we have to choose how we want to see things. To see also includes our moral outlook. The rich fare indicates senseless excess (intemperance) and ostentatiousness which leads to an easy way of life, but leads nowhere. *In bono* the scene may mean: spiritual wealth which has been earned by righteousness and keeping to the straight path. In this sense the bread, wine grapes, and olives can be interpreted as Christ symbols, and to follow the teachings of Christ leads to the right path. The fruit would then be the fruits of labor, or the fruits of righteousness, according to the well-known biblical passages[20] and popular expressions. In this sense one could relate the fish to fasting. Fish was an attribute of fasting in Pieter Brueghel's *Fight between Carnaval and Lent* (1559) in the Kunsthistorisches Museum in Vienna.

In the background of *The Rich Man's Meal* a curtain seems to obscure a view. Again the question arises, as with the mirror: what is semblance, what is real, or where is the play of life staged, the *Theatrum vitae humanae*? Or would this be too abstruse?

As we have already said, there are indications that the artist has made a link with the widely-known story of Tyl Uilenspiegel. The salted herring could refer to the joker with the same name (Pekelharing) in that tale. Many questions are still unanswered: for example, the meaning of the little hand on the knife and the jug in the poor man's meal. Is it the sign of a guild or the trademark of Antwerp where the members of the Francken family worked? It was probably also a sign of poverty which was worn on their clothes by people who depended on charity.[21] Is it a coincidence that we also come across small marks on knives in the works of Jeroen Bosch and Pieter Aertsen? Or, that the words 'goeden dach bruer' appear in a different form in a painting by Pieter Aertsen, written on a plate under two little hands?[22]

Another question is whether the artist deliberately intended a composition with such potential for double interpretation. Many elements can be interpreted both *in bono* and *in malo*: the owl as symbol of wisdom or stupidity, the mirror of self-knowledge or vanity, the spectacles of self-knowledge and deceit, the fish of Christ or voluptuousness, the apple of discernment or sin, the wine of truth or intemperance, and many more. Or are the potential meanings of the objects so various that one can simply choose whatever interpretation he pleases?

Whether Francken does or does not link up here with Aertsen, it is certain that there are other links, both in objects and composition and in style and technique. The landscape vistas have been a compositional element in Flemish art since the time of Van Eyck and are also present in Aertsen's work.

Another scene by Hieronymus Francken the Younger shows an even greater connection with pronk still lifes. A number of versions of the work are in existence, of which some are obviously copies. It is a composition with silver and gilt tazzas, luxurious beakers, a gold chain, documents, money, a purse, money bags, gold rings with jewels, and some calculations.[23] Examples can be seen in the Wadsworth Atheneum in Hartford (fig. 3.5), in the Szépművészeti Múzeum in Budapest, the Museum van Stad en Lande in Groningen, Holland, and in the Musée des Beaux-Arts in Valenciennes. I have studied these and some other versions, but the state of the paintings is generally such that the signatures are difficult to read. My examination has not yet been concluded, but a few preliminary conclusions are worth mentioning.

In some of these works, fragments of a signature or monogram are visible which point in the direction of Hieronymus Francken. They can be found most often on the pawn tickets. In the painting in Hartford the initials HF can be seen on the silver tazza; in that in Groningen the signature is on one of the coins dated 1602, a date *post quem*. This same date can be seen in some of the other versions, including that in Budapest, which, according to Agnes Czobor,[24] is the authentic painting, painted by Christaen van der Perre of Antwerp, whose name is signed below on the right on the sheet of paper: PERRE FT. The Valenciennes version has the date 1613 on one of the coins and, in the legend in the view, 1617. Haverkamp Begemann sees the dates on the coins of the Hartford version as either 1610, 1619 or 162(5?) and attributes it to the circle of Frans Francken the Younger.

The background view shows an episode in the life of a rich man and the poor Lazarus as it is written in St. Luke's gospel 16:19-31. This story was popular and was painted many times in the last quarter of the 16th century and the first quarter of the seventeenth. We shall return to it in the following chapter (cat. no. 6). The scene represented in the background vista, as Bergström has shown,[25] goes back to a woodcut in *Ars Moriendi* from around 1470 but can also be seen to be connected with *Death and the Miser* by Jeroen Bosch in the National Gallery of Art in Washington, D.C.[26] This scene is also, according to Gibson, related to *Ars Moriendi* but to another engraving from it.[27] *Ars Moriendi* (the art of dying) was comprised of popular devotional images that were often reprinted in Germany and the Netherlands. It describes how the dying mortal is exposed to a series of temptations in which devils try to deflect him from the straight path, but angels are at hand to guide him.

Other still lifes by Hieronymus Francken the Younger have also been attributed to other artists. One of these is the painting in the Musées Royaux des Beaux-Arts in Brussels that is

3.5

HIERONYMUS FRANCKEN THE YOUNGER
Allegory of Worldly Riches
Wadsworth Atheneum, Hartford (Connecticut), Ella Gallup Sumner and Mary Catlin Sumner Collection

HIERONYMUS FRANCKEN THE YOUNGER
Sweet Meal
Musées Royaux des Beaux-Arts, Brussels

listed as by the 'Monogrammist BDC?' (fig. 3.6).[28] The monogram on the napkin, however, can be read as HF if one ignores the damages. The style of painting fits in with the works which have already been discussed but also relates to the early works of Clara Peeters, Nicolaes Gillis and Georg Flegel.

In other ways the Franckens can also contribute to a better understanding of the early development of still lifes, namely by their paintings of *cabinets d'amateurs*, some of which can almost be regarded as true still lifes. They contain other still-life elements and give us a special perspective on the theme of prosperity. From 1612 onwards such works were especially painted by Frans Francken the Younger, and some were executed by or with the assistance of Hieronymus. Later, other painters such as Cornelis de Baeilleur, Willem van Haecht and David Teniers also painted works of this kind. In a derivated form, we come across paintings of *konstkamers* (literally the art rooms of private collectors) by Jan Brueghel the Elder, made around 1617 or 1618, sometimes in cooperation with Peter Paul Rubens. The former also collaborated with the Franckens.

The earliest dated work of this type that we know of is a piece by Frans Francken from 1612.[29] In a relatively small space we see a wall with paintings, small sculptures on a ledge and, through the doorway, three scholars, one of whom is taking measurements with his compasses. They personify the *Artes Liberales*, or the humanities, which include the visual arts.³⁰ A group of scholars, nearly always depicted in an inset, can often be seen in Francken's works (or his copyists' and followers'), as for instance in fig. 3.7. This small *cabinet*, which we could almost call a still life, is in the Historisches Museum in Frankfurt.³¹

Around a small, round portrait we read FRANSOIS · FRANCKENS · AET · 55, and underneath an · F, for *Fecit* (or a monogram). The work has always been regarded as a painting by Frans Francken the Younger, but it is also reminiscent in its details of Hieronymus Francken the Younger and is certainly in harmony with his early still lifes. The small portrait cannot be a self-portrait of Frans Francken the Younger, who was 55 years old in 1636, as that date seems improbably late. Frans the Elder was 55 in 1597, and according to Härting (1983), who made a study of Frans the Younger with an oeuvre-catalogue, it could be a portrait of the father, who died in 1616. Although a number of art historians have written articles on this painting, important details and relationships went unnoticed. A complete explanation cannot be given here either, but some observations and suggestions will be offered.

The painted wreath of flowers encircling the Madonna and Child is the central feature. On the carved banderole on the frame we can read with some difficulty: ANDRIES DANIELS...FRANS FR. Andries Daniels and Frans the Younger worked together on a number of flower wreaths around medallions, in which Daniels painted the flowers. The motif of the Madonna with Child is repeated in the sculpture at the left; above on the wall we see other religious scenes. Most of the other objects on the table are precious collectors' items: antique coins, one of which has the inscription CAESAR AUGUSTUS and his effigy, seashells, rings and jewels. At the upper left is a resplendent sculpted river god with a cornucopia, probably an allegory of the river Scheldt or Antwerp.

3.7

FRANS FRANCKEN THE YOUNGER
Cabinet d'Amateur with Scholars
Historisches Museum, Frankfurt am Main

The stoppered bottle to the right is very remarkable, with its flowering plants, enormous snail, and a number of animals whose proportions are completely wrong, even when we take into account that we see the two dogs — a greyhound and a bulldog — in reflection. To the left also are a frog and a goldfinch. Is this a depiction of a microcosm? Behind the bottle to the left is a globe, representing the earth, and to the right we see documents, probably meant as symbols of earthly transiency, as is the oval painting of a fire.

In this painting the scholars are sitting talking to each other at table in a small entresol room, surrounded by books. One of them is holding a round object in his hand, probably a globe.[32] While the presence of the scholars could represent Learning in general, the man with the globe may represent a specific individual: Abraham Ortelius, the famous cartographer. Speth-Holterhoff has identified one of the scholars from another gallery piece by Francken as the Flemish humanist Justus Lipsius (1547-1606).[33] Lipsius and Ortelius have already been identified in two other paintings by Frans Francken.[34] Ortelius is portrayed in a gallery piece by Frans Francken in the Kunsthistorisches Museum in Vienna, his name being written above the square little portrait. In this painting we see three scholars in an entresol room in debate, with books on the table and in their hands. Lying in the foreground are seashells, medals, jewelry and documents.[35]

Another large group of cabinet pictures by the same artist features scenes of a completely different sort than the one of the scholars. These background views represent figures, some with a donkey's head, others with that of an owl, who are destroying with sticks paintings, sculptures, musical instruments, globes and books or, as to the right in fig. 3.8, setting them

FRANS FRANCKEN THE YOUNGER
Cabinet d'Amateur with Iconoclasts, 1618
Rubenshuis, Antwerp

HIERONYMUS FRANCKEN THE YOUNGER
Private Collection

FRANS BADENS
Private Collection

JAN BRUEGHEL THE ELDER
Sight (from the Series of Senses), 1617/18
Museo del Prado, Madrid

on fire with torches. The painting hangs in the Rubens House in Antwerp.[36] It is clearly an allusion to the desecration of the churches during the Reformation, and the iconoclasts (those who do not appreciate Art and Learning) are intended to represent Ignorantia. Since Antiquity donkeys' ears have stood for stupidity in reference to the famous story of king Midas who was misled by his own ignorance.[37]

Both the flower wreath around the medallion and the bouquet are painted by or after works of Andries Daniels. The drawings in the sketchbook and some of the paintings can be identified.

I agree with Winner (1957) and Härting that the scholars, or in some paintings art connoisseurs, and the iconoclasts could be seen as antipodes, although we have no evidence that we could be dealing with pendants. In various works by Francken both scholars and iconoclasts are seen.[38]

We come across a chained monkey in some of the gallery pieces by the Franckens, for instance a painting attributed to Hieronymus the Younger and Jan Brueghel the Elder in the

Walters Art Gallery in Baltimore.[39] In this work the iconoclasts are depicted in a painting that the artist has placed probably on purpose on the ground against a chair. The chained monkey is a long-tailed one and stands for man, bound to lust, vanity and other sins,[40] or the 'Genius luxuriae.'[41] In a *konstkamer* by Jan Brueghel the Elder with figures by Peter Paul Rubens, we see a monkey with two pairs of spectacles (fig. 3.9), as if one pair were not already too much for the ignorant who are only interested in pleasure. It is one of the five works of the well-known series of the Five Senses in the Museo del Prado in Madrid, of which two are dated 1617 and 1618.[42] Brueghel has continued here the concept of the Franckens. The gallery picture represents the Sense of Sight and can well be related to Prosperity. We see paintings, drawings, prints, sculptures, rugs, gold- and silverwork, jewelry, Chinese porcelain, a purse with coins, seashells and exotic animals. On a cupboard is a vase of flowers. An opening in the rear wall gives a view of the palace in Brussels of the Archdukes Albert and Isabella, who are portrayed in a double-portrait in the room, with Albert appearing again on horseback. Symbols of the visual arts, architecture and science — many measuring and optical instruments — have been brought together here. In the *Temperantia* print by Pieter Brueghel the Elder, we also see measuring instruments.

According to Müller Hofstede (1984) Juno is the personification of Sight, as can be seen in Valerianus,[43] who himself refers to Roman sources. Juno explains to the winged Genius a picture in which Christ heals the blind.[44] In the New Testament the healing of the blind is related to accepting the Word of Christ, as in Luke 18:43: 'And immediately he received his sight, and followed him, glorifying God.'[45] Without going into the extensive and not always well-founded iconographical explanation of Ertz,[46] or Müller Hofstede's attack on this explanation and the latter's own cumbrous theory, one can summarize that various levels of experiencing and symbolizing the Senses, in particular Sight, have been depicted in this painting: looking without attention or understanding is equated to being like the monkey, and such instruments as spectacles will not help. The painting on the floor against the chair, a Bacchanal, represents earthly beauty and profane love, while the Madonna and Child in the wreath of flowers represents heavenly love. Here the artist has touched a theme of Pieter Aertsen, though with a completely different approach: the choice between the *vita activa* and the *vita contemplativa*. Or in other words, through visual clues we are made to think in a moral way about the different ways and degrees of looking: sight, insight, and seeing through things.

JEREMIAS VAN WINGHEN
Rijksdienst Beeldende Kunst, The Hague

GEORG FLEGEL
Private Collection

CHAPTER 4

LAID TABLES: FOOD FOR THOUGHT

The years in which the earliest still lifes were painted were complex ones characterized by deep social, political, religious and cultural changes and the moving about of people from one place to another. It is impossible, therefore, to consider the early history of the still life in Holland without also considering certain artists who worked in other parts of Northern Europe. Frankfurt on Main was the most important center outside the Netherlands for artists who created still lifes in the manner of the Dutch painters. By 1595 Georg Flegel of Olmütz (now in Czechoslovakia) was already assisting the painter Lucas van Valckenborch there by painting in some of his works extensive still-life details of high quality, for example in a series of Seasons of that year.[1] Dated independent still lifes by Flegel are known to us only from 1630 on, but no doubt he had produced such pictures much earlier. Jeremias van Winghen was working at the same time in Frankfurt. He was the son of the better-known Jodocus van Winghen, who in 1585 had moved from Brussels to Frankfurt for religious reasons. Jeremias was born in 1578 and was an apprentice of his father and, after the latter's death in 1603 or 1604, of Frans Badens in Amsterdam. Later Jeremias worked for some time in Rome and married the rich Johanna de Neufville in 1616. His production was small, possibly as it was not necessary for him to paint for a living during a considerable part of his life. Apart from still lifes he painted market pieces and portraits.

Frans Badens was born in Antwerp in 1571. In 1576 his father fled with his family to Amsterdam to escape the Spanish onslaught, and Frans remained there until his death in 1618. Between 1593 and 1597 he traveled together with the engraver Jacob Matham to Italy. His pupils, aside from Jeremias van Winghen, included Adriaen van Nieulandt and the Dutch poet Gerbrand Adriaensz. Bredero. Details about Badens' life can be found in Karel van Mander (1604).[2] Frans Badens painted and drew mainly historical works of a mythological or religious nature but also made portraits, masquerades and conversation pieces. Several of his scenes remind us somewhat of Caravaggio, for instance a *Judith and Holofernes* in the Victoria and Albert Museum in London, in which a candle illuminates the interior.[3] Some works were signed by him in full, and a few are dated. Sometimes he only signed with his initials, *F.B.*[4] According to Van Mander, Badens painted many banquets, but not a single one has been traced before now. In a private collection in Germany, however, I have seen a small painting by the artist which is signed *F.B.* (cat. no. 2). It reminds us of later works by Georg

56

Flegel and Gothardt de Wedig but also shows similarities with the work of Peter Binoit (the same Siegburg jug with a pewter lid can be seen in a painting by Binoit from the twenties which is hanging in the Nationalmuseet in Stockholm).[5]

Flegel, Van Winghen and Binoit worked in Germany in Frankfurt or in nearby Hanau, and De Wedig in Cologne. While a relationship with such Netherlandish contemporaries as Nicolaes Gillis, Floris van Dyck and Clara Peeters is not so evident, one can see a definite parallel with the candle-lit interiors of Osias Beert the Elder. The little still life by Frans Badens, for example, is full of atmosphere, especially due to the oil lamp which creates strong effects of light and shadow. Recently I have been able to attribute to Badens a second still life and a drawing of a lobster dated in 1608.[6]

White sweets similar to those we see in Frans Badens' painting are depicted in many still lifes of the early 17th century. Cane sugar, the primary ingredient of these sweets, was an expensive and exotic product. Originally from India, it was eventually introduced and cultivated in Asia Minor and some parts of the Mediterranean region. The best white sugar, though, came from Madeira and the Canary Islands.

Only a few works by Jeremias van Winghen are known. A beautiful still life, the date of which has been erroneously read as 1667, is in fact dated 1607. It belongs to the collection of the Rijksdienst Beeldende Kunst in The Hague, where until recently it was attributed to Jacob van Walscappelle. This is impossible in view of the date and the signature which reads *I.V.W. 1607*. It is a splendid piece (cat. no. 3), in fact a pronk still life that prefigures elements of later works by Osias Beert, Georg Flegel and Peter Binoit. One can see, for instance in a painting by Binoit, little lobsters, a *bekerschroef*, a split-wood box, an orange and sweetmeats which show a strong resemblance to those in this painting by Van Winghen.[7] Outstandingly beautiful is the depiction of the German *bekerschroef* with swans and cherubs on its base and with clamps in the form of chameleons which hold the foot of the *roemer*, or glass.[8] The *bekerschroef* was an important object at festive parties, as it was handed around to confirm ties of friendship.

Together with a kitchen piece in the Historisches Museum in Frankfurt this still life forms the key to the attribution of a number of paintings to Jeremias van Winghen. The kitchen piece is signed and dated IEREMIA.VAN.WINGE FECIT 1613.[9] (In this study we shall not discuss further the relationship of this work to Pieter Aertsen and Joachim Beuckelaer nor its remarkable resemblance to works by Sebastian Stoskopff.) Also by Jeremias van Winghen is a kitchen piece given to the 'Monogrammist IF,' which recently appeared at auction in Monaco. The date was read by the auction house as 1635 and by Greindl (1983) as 1655. In fact, it reads $\overline{IF} \cdot 1615$ (fig. 4.1).[10] $\overline{IF}$ stands here for IEREMIA....FECIT, and the horizontal line above IF indicates that it is an abbreviation. The latter work shows not only a relationship with Stoskopff but also one with the painter Hans van Essen, while both scenes also prefigure elements of much later works by Elias Vonck and Abraham van Beyeren.

Another signed still life by Jeremias van Winghen (with the monogram *IVW* and a hallmark on a knife) was recently sold at auction in Monaco, where it was offered as an Osias Beert.[11] These data allow us to attribute a few other works to Jeremias van Winghen. In the first place are two flower still lifes, one of which is in the Musée des Beaux-Arts in Lille, while the other was recently on sale in the art trade as a work by Georg Flegel (fig. 4.2).[12] By a detailed

JAQUES DE GHEYN THE YOUNGER
Private Collection

OSIAS BEERT THE ELDER
Private Collection

LAID TABLES: FOOD FOR THOUGHT

4.1

Jeremias van Winghen
Kitchen Piece, 1615
Sale Sotheby's, Monaco, 1987

4.2

Jeremias van Winghen
Flower Piece with Fruits
Private Collection, formerly Waterman Gallery, Amsterdam

4.3

Georg Flegel and Martin van Valckenborch
Storeroom
Sale Ader, Picard & Tajan, Paris, 1987

comparison of these two paintings to signed or well-documented flower pieces by Flegel it appears that they differ rather strongly from his works.[13] In the meantime I believe that I can attribute a few more works to Jeremias van Winghen, kitchen pieces as well as still lifes.[14] Since the important study on Flegel by Wolfgang Müller (1956), our views on this artist have undergone a change. Müller himself has been able to attribute a number of recently discovered works to Flegel, but for others the attribution had to be withdrawn.[15] As we mentioned above, Flegel had cooperated well before 1600 with Lucas van Valckenborch, and later with other members of the Valckenborch family. We can see an excellent example of this cooperation in a painting (fig. 4.3) which was recently auctioned in Paris.[16] The figure in the painting was attributed to Lucas van Valckenborch, who died in 1597, and the still life to Georg Flegel. There is no doubt about the latter's contribution. The painting contains a bouquet, and the composition, colors and technique are typical of Flegel. It also contains a large number of individual flowers which we recognize from other works by Flegel, including a narcissus variety with four instead of six petals.[17] Also other objects can be traced to certain works by Flegel, but a number of the objects in the painting cannot be connected with any known works of the artist, for instance the beautiful coconut beaker, the grape beaker, and the *façon de Venise* glasses. The little basket with glasses and other details show similarities to the work of Sebastian Stoskopff. Whether the figure should not be attributed to Martin van Valckenborch rather than to Lucas is worth further research.

The more one gets acquainted with paintings by Flegel's contemporaries who worked in Hanau the clearer it becomes that some shifts in traditional attributions are necessary. The influence of Van Winghen, Flegel and Binoit on each other was considerable, and they in

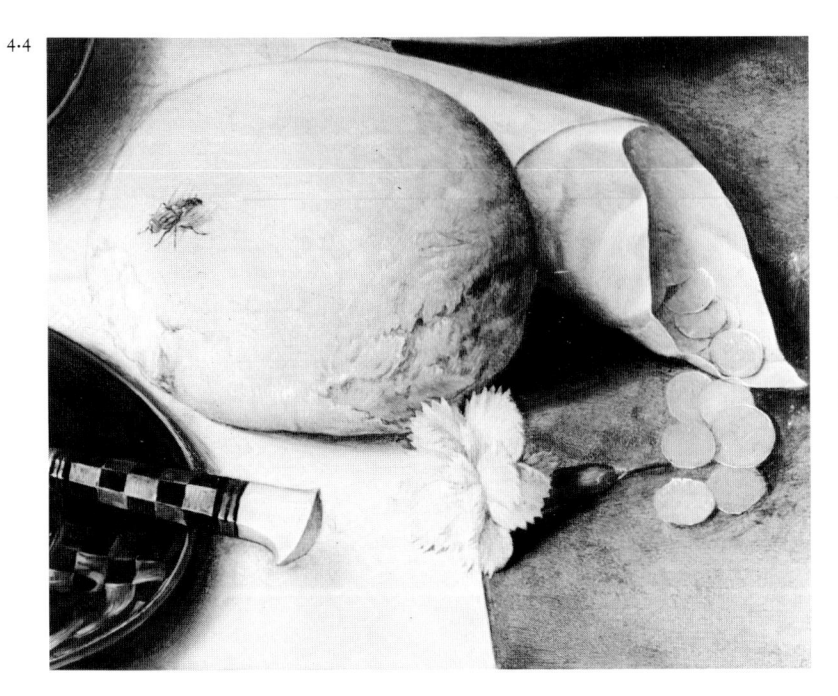

GEORG FLEGEL
Detail of cat.no.4

GEORG FLEGEL
Meal with a Mouse and a Parrot
Alte Pinakothek, Munich

8

Illustration cat. no. 7 see p. 82

CLARA PEETERS
Private Collection

CLARA PEETERS
Private Collection

their turn influenced other artists in Hanau, such as Isaac Soreau and Sebastian Stoskopff, or De Wedig in Cologne. To this must be added the undeniable interaction with painters in the Netherlands. Peter Binoit, for example, clearly borrowed certain elements from several of his contemporaries. Most of the time his works can be clearly distinguished from those of Georg Flegel, for instance, whose compositions, brushwork, use of color and description of detail are more subtle. Cat. no. 4 is a work which has long been attributed to Peter Binoit but which in reality shows all the characteristics of Flegel, including the manner in which the highlights, shadows and minor effects are realized.[18] The similarity of certain objects and details in works is completely convincing. Some objects are nearly identical, as is shown by the comparison of coins and carnations in a detail of cat. no. 4 (fig. 4.4) and similar forms in a still life by Flegel in the Alte Pinakothek in Munich (fig. 4.5). Two other versions of cat. no. 4 are known to me, one of which is in the Musée du Louvre in Paris[19] (in our catalogue *A Fruitful Past* the work is still attributed to Peter Binoit, and there possible symbolic meaning of the painting is discussed). Other paintings by Flegel are also known to exist in several versions.

The gilt *bekerschroef* with lion masks and little rings looks like Netherlandish rather than German goldsmith's work. The silver tazza might be from Antwerp. We can assume that the earthenware jug comes from Siegburg, as closely related jugs have been preserved. A black and white checkered knife like the one in Flegel's still life, with silver and ivory inlay in ebony, can be encountered again and again in works of the early 17th century, both in the Netherlands and in Germany, but similar knives have not been preserved. This strengthens the supposition that the painter may have used the knife to express a symbolic meaning: the knife as a symbol of separation or discernment, of black and white, of good and evil. Products of the silversmiths were mainly spread over Western Europe by means of the free year markets. The most famous was that of Frankfurt. These markets were also centers where ideas were exchanged. Many products thus obtained an 'international' character and were produced in similar form in places like Nürnberg, Augsburg, Hamburg and in the Netherlands.

We have already mentioned Antwerp as one of the centers of development of the still-life tradition. Over the years many artists moved from Antwerp to the northern Netherlands or elsewhere. One of them was Jacques de Gheyn the Younger, who came to Haarlem in 1581. One of his works (cat. no. 5) is a painting which until recently had been attributed to other artists: the names of Osias Beert and Gottfried de Wedig have been suggested. The attribution to De Wedig was based on an incorrect interpretation of the monogram on the knife, a monogram which can be found on many of the drawings and engravings of Jacques de Gheyn. The resemblance to works by Osias Beert is considerable, but the simple composition with little overlap of the objects, the lighter colors and the differences in technique show clearly that it cannot be a work by Beert, while the similarities in technique with other works by De Gheyn are obvious.[20] No other fruit still lifes by De Gheyn are known to us, but in 1738 a fruit piece by 'De Ghyn,' from the collection of Baron Schönborn, was sold for 23 guilders at an auction in Amsterdam.[21]

Here again we see a black and white checkered knife, now with a blade that is gilded at the base and the top. On the knife a little hand has been impressed, just as in the painting by

Hieronymus Francken (cat. no. 1). De Gheyn, who was a Roman Catholic and therefore had not come to the northern Netherlands for reasons of religion, probably maintained relations with Antwerp and also visited that town. In his vanitas still life of 1603, in the Metropolitan Museum in New York, we find coins with portraits of the Roman Catholic couple Charles and Johanna of Aragon, which seems to confirm this.

The fruit piece by De Gheyn (cat. no. 5) is probably an early work painted around 1600. All the objects can be found in later works by Osias Beert, and it is plausible that this or similar works of De Gheyn exerted a considerable influence on Beert, and also on other artists such as Clara Peeters. De Gheyn's vanitas and flower still lifes also had a great influence on his contemporaries.

Cat. no. 6 is a remarkable work by Osias Beert the Elder. We recognize immediately the wine glass from Jacques de Gheyn's fruit still life, and it is interesting to compare the small but characteristic differences in technique. The brush of De Gheyn is more restrained and works to a cooler effect; that of Beert is more nervous and painterly. High-quality works by Beert always have a somewhat mysterious atmosphere which is created by his rather strong chiaroscuro effects. It is evident that the work of Hieronymus Francken also influenced him. In this painting, for example, we see sweetmeats, bread and oysters, and also — rather unusual for Beert — a background view. Comparison with Francken's still life in fig. 3.5 is interesting, since depicted there, just as in the work of Beert, is an episode from the life of the rich man and the poor Lazarus. Rich and Poor have been contraposed in a special manner within the same scene. The view may be the work of Hieronymus Francken the Younger, who is known to have collaborated with others, among them his brother Frans Francken the Younger.

As we have mentioned already in our considerations of Hieronymus Francken, the story of the rich man and the poor Lazarus was very popular in the 16th and 17th centuries. Especially common was the scene in which the rich man sits at a well-provided table while Lazarus lies on the ground, the dogs licking his wounds — the scene in the background of Beert's painting. According to St. Luke, 'There was a certain rich man who was clothed in purple and fine linen and fared sumptuously every day; And there was a certain beggar named Lazarus who was laid at his gate, full of sores; And desiring to be fed with the crumbs which fell from the rich man's table; moreover the dogs came and licked his sores....'[22] Lazarus goes to heaven after his death, and the rich man sees from hell that Lazarus will receive eternal consolation. Virtue and vice are clearly opposed. The parable was depicted in many engravings, sometimes in series. Cornelis Cort, for instance, made a series of four engravings after Maerten van Heemskerck.[23] The text under fig. 4.6, one of this series, reads in translation: 'The rich man is dining sumptuously, while Lazarus, a beggar, is lying at the door.' Crispyn de Passe the Elder made a similar series after Maarten de Vos,[24] while Crispyn de Passe the Younger did the same after his own designs.[25]

The rich meal in the foreground of Beert's work contains a message which is clarified by the background scene, an incitement to Christian charity. This must also be the meaning of the sweetmeats in the form of a cross. This motif returns in several other works of Beert. The bread and the wine could be interpreted as eucharistic symbols, as an exhortation to follow the teachings of Christ.

CORNELIS CORT
after Maerten van Heemskerk
The Rich Man and the Poor Lazarus, Engraving

We know of no dated works by Osias Beert, but there exist some paintings on copper which carry on the back the mark of the panelmaker Peeter Stas with the dates 1607, 1608 or 1609 (the consecutive years indicate that the copper plates were used soon after they had been made). The 'trick-glass' on the left in cat. no. 6 can be found in a work of around 1608 in the Gemäldegalerie in Berlin-Dahlem.[26] The glass also appears in the fruit still life by De Gheyn (cat. no. 5). Drinking from such a glass is problematical unless one is experienced, since, when the glass is tipped, the wine stays in the four chambers until a bursting air bubble releases it in one flood. Remarkably enough, the goldsmith's work in Beert's paintings seems to originate from the northern Netherlands. The *bekerschroef* in the painting in Berlin has been attributed to the Amsterdam goldsmith Leendert Claesz and can be dated around 1605. The tazzas are also probably of northern origin. One should compare the tazza in our painting with that in fig. 4.7, which is marked 1609 on the back.[27] Whether these are different works by the same goldsmith, or made of different parts which could be screwed together, or whether the artist took certain liberties, we cannot say, since only a few of these objects have been preserved. We find an example of such artistic license in the painting of glasses, however, where Beert painted the same cup on different feet, or vice versa.[28] The Beert

OSIAS BEERT THE ELDER
Banquet in a Niche, c. 1609
Private Collection

painting of 1609 shows some relationship with cat. no. 3 by Jeremias van Winghen, of 1607, but the characteristics of Beert's technique are clearly recognizable. These include the abundant use of white lead in the highlights, the use of gold pigment on the pastry,[29] and the sinuous, pasty delineations of the oysters and the bread.[30] A replica of this painting is known but without the background view.[31]

A few early works by Clara Peeters have recently come to light, and our views on this artist have slightly changed. A signed and dated painting of 1607 (cat. no. 7) reveals a few primitive distortions of a beginning artist, but it already shows some of her characteristic traits, such as the fine stippled highlights and other features of her brush technique. The confusing picture which has recently been created by Vroom (1980), who added to her work paintings by Pieter Claesz, must, for this and other reasons, be ignored.[32] It is not difficult to find in this simple work a link with the oeuvres of Hieronymus Francken, Frans Badens and Osias Beert. It is even not impossible that Beert derived his sweetmeats in the form of a cross from Clara Peeters.

This elegant and restrained little painting does not dazzle us with wealth the way that Beert's did, but it represents, nevertheless, objects of a certain luxury. A gold and silver ring with a ruby and five thin golden pendants, nearly all attached to a branch of rosemary, are the most precious objects. Sweetmeats and wine were certainly not food for the poor, who would also not have had a glass goblet with a gold-ornamented stem. The gold objects, the sweets and the pastry give only short-lived pleasure; they, the candle and the fly represent the transient, material things in life. The artist included a reference to herself in this category in the form of the P-shaped pastry; in other works she sometimes did this by painting a reflection of her face in shiny metal objects. The positive elements are represented by the wine (the blood of Christ) and the rosemary. As the leaves of this plant keep their smell for a long time, rosemary became a symbol of eternity. The dead were given branches of rosemary in their graves.[33] One can read this in a poem which Joost van den Vondel, one of the most important Dutch poets of the 17th century, wrote on the death of his eight-year-old daughter Saartje in 1633, in which a friend weaves a garland of rosemary for her dead playmate.[34] Rosemary was also considered to be a medication for many diseases, and in the Middle Ages it was already believed to strengthen one's memory. This is a reason why it was considered a plant for the relatives of the departed in their grief. But it was a plant connected not only with death but also with life. It played a role in wedding ceremonies and was included in bridal garlands as a reminder of faithfulness.

4.8

CLARA PEETERS
Pronk Goblets, Flowers and Shells, 1612
Staatliche Kunsthalle, Karlsruhe

Cat. nos. 8 and 9 form a pair and were painted by Clara Peeters in 1612. One might consider the works as a rich man's meal and a poor man's meal, but the precious Wan-li dish with butter does not entirely tally with the idea of poverty. Of course, there are also links with the work of Hieronymus Francken and Frans Badens, and several details such as the cut artichoke remind us of paintings by Jacques de Gheyn and Osias Beert. But what a development the still life has gone through! With what attention to detail and refinement have the scratches on the wooden plate been painted, and the gritty surface of the Siegburg jugs, small dents in the pewter, or small chips on the foot of the porcelain! Not to overlook the subtle way in which the gilt pronk goblet has been rendered. The same goblet appears in a still life in the Staatliche Kunsthalle in Karlsruhe (fig. 4.8).[35] That work was also painted in 1612, and its vanity aspect is evident. The artist herself, with palette and brushes in hand, is reflected on several of the gleaming knobs of the pronk goblet on the right. Her face is also vaguely visible on the pewter lid of the beer jug in cat. no. 8.

Many of the objects in both paintings are characteristic of still lifes of the early 17th century, and we see them in the work of various artists from Antwerp, the northern Netherlands and south Germany, including Frankfurt and Hanau. These include the wooden plate with a herring, the cut artichoke, the Siegburg jug, sweets and pastry, and the combination of almonds, raisins and figs. Also certain types of knives, gold and silver objects, and bread are characteristic of this period.

If these two still lifes were indeed conceived as a pair, then perhaps we could apply to them the coupled interpretation of earth and heaven, of material and spiritual values. The course products like the earthenware and bread would then be seen in symbolic contrast to the gold articles and fine pastry. However, fish, cherries, artichoke, bread, butter, and the knife can also be interpreted as spiritual and religious, and the sweets and precious objects as material and earthly. Perhaps this view is defensible.[36] But perhaps we should not regard the two paintings as a pair but simply as works which were painted on panels of the same format ordered at the same time.

A painting which is similarly signed and dated 1612 is in the Kunstmuseum in Poltawa in the USSR. This still life with oysters, small lobsters, shrimps, pepper and a small paper bag with a text was shown at an exhibition held in 1983 in Dresden.[37] A signed flower piece of the same size was sold at auction in Berlin in 1932,[38] and a large number of works is known which have more or less the same dimensions. One may presume that a certain size indicated a certain price.[39] In the collection of the Museo del Prado in Madrid are three works of 1611, and also here the question arises whether they must be considered as a series or as individual works.[40] Gilt pronk goblets often appear in pronk still lifes. They are precious objects not only because of their expensive materials gold and silver but also because of the highly skilled work of the artist-goldsmith. Nürnberg was renowned for this goldsmith's work, but there were also other centers, both in Germany (Augsburg, Hamburg) and in Holland (Amsterdam, Haarlem and Utrecht). Being precious objects, pronk goblets can easily be related to the theme of material wealth, but probably we have to seek any symbolic meaning they may have in still lifes in another direction. We find some indications for this in Ripa's *Iconologia*, in which Iustitia, Justice, holds the cover of a chalice in her hand; the accompanying text reads: '...and the chalice means that Justice is a matter of God.'[41]

It is striking that many pronk goblets in paintings have a cover on which a warrior in armor is depicted with helmet, shield and spear. However, only a few goblets with such a cover have been preserved.[42] In view of the fact that so many goblets exist which have covers with floral or animal motifs, it seems improbable that there could have been many in existence with the warrior. One may therefore suppose that the warrior motif expressed some symbolism, and the other scenes on these pronk goblets confirm this. The soldier is probably a *Miles Christianus*, a knight of Christ who must protect and defend Truth. His way of life leads to Christ, which we can also see in Van Eyck's *Adoration of the Lamb* in the Ghent Altarpiece. This medieval concept was elaborated by Erasmus in his *Enchiridion Militis Christiani* (Handbook for the Christian Soldier), which was published in Antwerp in 1503. In this work Erasmus defends pure Christianity based directly on biblical sources, and he puts little value on ceremonial proceedings. He compares man to a knight who must fight to achieve eternal Salvation. The book was among the most influential of its century and was often reprinted and translated into many languages.

According to St. Paul the knight or soldier must put on the armor of God to resist the temptations of the Devil: 'Stand therefore, having your loins girt about with truth, and having on the breastplate of righteousness; And you feet shod with the preparation of the gospel of peace; Above all, taking the shield of faith, wherewith ye shall be able to quench all the fiery darts of the wicked. And take the helmet of salvation, and the sword of the Spirit, which is the word of God:...'[43]

A lance is substituted for the sword on these pronk goblets and on most others in still lifes. The warrior, in the apocryphal book of Wisdom, is armed with the armor of justice, the helmet of unerring judgment, the shield of right and the lance of divine wrath.[44] St. Paul admonishes the soldier to fight on the side of Christ, to defend Truth, and to accept the crown of the martyrs. Elsewhere he speaks of the breastplate of faith and love and the helmet of hope and salvation. These spiritual weapons were associated with the choice between Day and Night, wakefulness and sleep, sobriety and inebriety,[45] all metaphors of the choice between awareness and oblivion, between the spiritual and the material, virtue and vice. This is exactly the message that many of these still lifes contain. The symbolism of the warrior may also have been derived from Valerianus and from the description of Ripa's 'Fortezza', the strength of purpose and courage.[46]

The other decoration on pronk goblets is usually comprised of the traditional motifs: volutes, cornucopias, garlands, festoons, fantasy flowers, fruit and masks. On the goblet in Clara Peeters' work, however, we see a ram's head, a symbol of Christ or of Imitation, and cherubs which express the freed soul. Also represented are hunting scenes, and these especially deserve our attention. The deer hunt symbolizes the search for the pure soul, or the longing for Christ. The deer, or hart, as a symbol of Christ is derived from the Song of Solomon, on which St. Gerome elaborated in the Middle Ages, citing Psalms 22:16: 'For dogs have compassed me: the assembly of the wicked have inclosed me....'[47]

In the same year that Clara Peeters painted the two still lifes we have just considered, Nicolaes Gillis produced cat. no. 10. Until recently the date of this work was given in the literature as 1611, but the date actually reads 1612. We know another still life by Gillis dated 1601 (fig. 4.9),[48] but works from the period between 1601 and 1612 have not been identified with

NICOLAES GILLIS
Banquet Piece, 1601
Private Collection

certainty. As we have seen, Hieronymus Francken and Gillis had both painted the earliest dated meal still lifes by 1601. This was a hard year, due to bad harvests and naval wars with the English and Scandinavian powers which interrupted normal supplies.[49] In such a climate of deprivation pictures of such abundance must certainly have attracted notice.

Gillis's works of 1601 and 1612 depict a number of objects which, if not identical, are certainly comparable to each other, such as a *roemer*, oranges, Ming porcelain, and strawberries, whole and half walnuts, pastry, and a *bekerschroef*. The compositions are also comparable, with groupings of precious objects placed towards the left rear and right rear, respectively, on broad tables with a high horizon. New in the 1612 work are the white linen damask tablecloth trimmed with lace over a pink-red silk damask undercover, the more natural arrangement, stronger light effects, and much sharper detail. In terms of technique one can also see great advances by 1612, perhaps influenced by the example of Clara Peeters especially, for example, in the rendering of the reflections on the *roemer* glass, which is far more skilled. The combination of a damask tablecloth and a pink-red undercover can also be found in a work of 1614 by Gillis and in a number of paintings by his contemporary and fellow-townsman Floris van Dyck, a well-to-do man for whom painting was not a necessity of life and whose production was therefore small. Because of the closeness of their styles, it is necessary to review critically attributions to one and the other.

For a few years beginning around 1610 the works of Gillis and Van Dyck shared a number of other elements in common, among them depictions of a half apple and cut citrus fruits (they also shared porcelain bowls of apples, pears and quinces). Cut or partly peeled lemons remained an especially favored element in breakfast pieces for a long time, leading us to wonder if this motif may not have had some deeper significance. The melon as a possible symbol of temperance will be discussed in Chapter 8.

The fruit of the Tree of Knowledge of Good and Evil has often been depicted, both in literature and in paintings, as an apple. The use of the apple as a symbol *in malo* is derived from the latin word *malus*, which means both apple and bad. It is, as the object of temptation, also connected with Original Sin. *In bono* it is a symbol of discernment, the knowledge of good and evil. Citrus fruit can replace the apple in symbolic language as the fruit of the Tree of Knowledge. The Dutch word *oranjeappel* for a Seville orange is an indication of this. The fact that the apple is halved indicates even more clearly that two interpretations are possible. Moreover, the knife which cuts the fruit is also a symbol of discernment. The concept of Original Sin is emphasized in Gillis's painting by the fly on the piece of apple. That lemons

4.10

NICOLAES GILLIS
Storeroom, 1615
Private Collection

and citrons took over the symbolic meaning of the apple is perhaps connected with their sour taste. A sweet-tasting common orange did not become available until the 18th century.[50] The *oranjeappel* was already depicted by Jan van Eyck as the fruit of the Tree of Knowledge in his *Adoration of the Lamb* in Ghent. We also encounter a half apple with a fly in a triptych of Mary and the Child Jesus, attributed to the Master of Frankfurt. The apple lies on a stone bench to the left of Mary.[51]

A half apple was painted in 1610 by Floris van Dyck (cat. no. 11), two years before the painting by Gillis. Here we find parts of the concept of Gillis's painting of 1612 (the fly is missing), though with a change of objects. Floris van Dyck's painting has greater clarity and simplicity, and the composition is more balanced. Van Dyck's painting of 1613 in the Frans Halsmuseum in Haarlem (fig. 4.11) contains more detail,[52] for instance in the definition of the peel of the apple with little spots, and the perspective is better developed. The compositional scheme is nearly the same, but part of the damask pattern of 1610 can now be seen on the silk cloth. The vanishing point has also been shifted from upper left to upper right.

In both works part of the food can be interpreted both *in bono* and *in malo*. Presumably the bread and wine are meant as eucharistic symbols. The possible meaning of the cheese, which has such a central place in the work of Van Dyck, Gillis and their contemporaries, is rather puzzling. We find a discussion of the interpretation in De Jongh,[53] in which he rejects the one-sided (Roman-Catholic) interpretation of Lammers, who regards cheese as a Christ-symbol.[54] It is perhaps useful to look at other sources. In the encyclopedic works of the Middle Ages and the Renaissance cheese is often regarded as an indigestible food, in particular old cheese. On the other hand, an authority like Dioscurides is more positive. Compilations

4.11

FLORIS VAN DYCK
Banquet with Cheese, 1613
Frans Halsmuseum, Haarlem

and new editions of these encyclopedias were published until around 1600.[55] The physician Beverwyck relied for his wisdom on such sources, perhaps against his better judgment, since cheese in his time had already become a very common food, as has also been observed by De Jongh. Recipes for how to make cheese were common knowledge and could be read in many books which were frequently reprinted and translated, such as Etienne de Liebault's *Maison Rustique*.[56] Perhaps we should simply regard cheese as an abundant food which then serves as a counterpart to the precious, exotic foods such as grapes, citrus fruit and apricots. In Erasmus we find a proverb which already may point to this: 'Caseum habens non eget obsonio' (who has cheese does not need a dessert). Erasmus added to this proverb, which has a Greek origin, that one can feel satisfied with the least and the cheapest.[57] Simply for the sake of completeness, I should point to another possibile interpretation, which, nevertheless, seems improbable to me. When Job complains to God about his distress, we read: 'Remember, I beseech thee, that thou hast made me as the clay; and wilt thou bring me into dust again? Hast thou not poured me out as the milk and curdled me like cheese?'[58] If indeed this biblical text were connected with the representation of cheese in the paintings, then the cheese would represent Man, formed from God, who has to go his own way until he decays and has to suffer his fate but is free to choose — a choice that may enable him to inherit eternity.

Without doubt Frans Snyders was the most dynamic artist among the great early still-life painters. His earliest works, executed at Antwerp, come out of the tradition of Hieronymus Francken, and his rich compositions, especially his kitchen pieces, are clearly descended

4.12

FRANS SNYDERS
Storage with a Squirrel and a Cat
Wallraf-Richartz Museum, Cologne

FRANS SNYDERS
Fruits with a Squirrel, 1616
Private Collection, formerly Speelman Gallery, London

from the work of Pieter Aertsen and his followers. Soon, however, he went his own way. Gillis's still life of 1615 with dead hares and birds lying around a Wan-li *kendi* — a bottle with a wide, short spout (fig. 4.10)[59] — shows certain influences of Snyders. The latter soon developed a broad, direct and forceful brushwork that resembles that of Rubens, with whom he often collaborated. He made use of more striking color combinations than his

FRANS SNYDERS
Fruits, Carnation and Squirrel
Private Collection, formerly Müllenmeister Gallery, Solingen (Germany)

contemporaries. The white of a tablecloth, a goose, a swan or a heron, or the vermillion of a cloth or lobster, for example, strongly contrast with greens or other more subdued colors. These color combinations, together with dramatic light effects, twisting and waving lines and the manner in which game and objects are piled upon each other contribute to a sense of dynamism. He further enhanced this dynamic effect by the inclusion of live animals – dogs, cats, monkeys, squirrels and parrots. Sometimes these animals are so active that they create nearly slap-stick scenes in which we can almost hear them screech. His lobsters, placed on tilting Ming platters, appear later in the pronk still lifes of Jan Davidsz. de Heem and his followers. The smaller still lifes of Snyders are relatively more quiet.

One of the characteristics of Snyders' work is the cutting-off of objects along the borders of the painting. This creates the effect of seeing the scene through a window. These cut-offs have been incorrectly interpreted by several art historians who thought that the canvases were cut in later years.[60] How original Snyders' approach was becomes evident when we try to imagine the paintings with the objects completely depicted: the compositions lose much of their vigor. Three examples – figs. 4.12, 4.13, and 4.14 – may make this clear.[61] In these paintings other peculiarities are also noticeable. When we look at the squirrel we see that the animal and its surroundings have been depicted in each work from a progressively closer point of view. The third painting has a really close-up character when compared with the first work. This tells us something about Snyders' powers of observation which also contributed to the dynamic effects which he achieved. In each of the three paintings we see grapes of different colors. In the Ming bowl on the left in the first painting, and on a branch which sticks out of the basket in the second, we see mulberries, which in art-historical publications are nearly always mistaken for blackberries. We have already seen them earlier in the painting of Jacques de Gheyn (cat. no. 5). The leaves of this tree that originates from Persia are the food of the silkworm. The mulberry tree grows slowly but gives an abundance of fruit. Hence the motto 'Moram ubertate rependet' (He reimburses his slowness with abundance). This is a play of words, as *mora* and *morus* mean delay and mulberry respectively.[62] We notice further in the work of Snyders a rhytmical repetition of lines and forms. In itself this is a normal occurrence in still-life compositions, but it concerns here lines that project outward and ones that curl. In fig. 4.12 these nearly parallel lines are those suggested by the bouquet, the tail of the pheasant, the filbert-nut (which is related to the hazel-nut) in the top of the fruit basket, and the bundle of asparagus. In fig. 4.13 the curl in the tail of the squirrel is beautifully repeated in the cherry branch with curling leaves (fig. 4.13), the leaves and tendrils of the grapes, and the ears of the Wan-li bowl. The same bowl with plaited handles was depicted by Snyders three years earlier in a large 'storeroom' together with a beautiful nautilus cup, an excellent example of goldsmith's art.[63]

Abundance is a recurring motive in Snyders' oeuvre, especially in his 'storerooms' and kitchen pieces. In Dresden is a large kitchen piece with no less than eight Wan-li dishes and bowls, two baskets of fruit and piled-up game, enlivened by a dog, a monkey and a parrot.[64] Just as in fig. 4.12, a vase of roses, a seemingly nonessential element, has been put into the midst of all this. This work is clearly from a later date, probably from the thirties.

Chapter 5

Shell Still Lifes

Seashells have always fascinated people. Walking along the beach, one can hardly resist the temptation to pick them up and admire their shapes and colors. Many a child, and adult too, has brought them home to start a collection. From early times shells have inspired artists and craftsmen in their creation of ornaments and decorations. The shells themselves, or mother-of-pearl, were often incorporated into expensive jewelry and other objects of luxury. Shell beakers or shell cups were made of shells mounted on silver or gilt stands. For these cups large shells with a sheen of mother-of-pearl were used, either the *Nautilus pompilius* or the *Turbo marmoratus* from the Indian archipelago. Sometimes the outer layers of the shells were stripped away with the aid of acids in order to expose the nacreous lining; others were engraved. Although shell beakers could be used as drinking cups, they were not primarily made for that purpose: they served as rich display objects. The foot of a shell cup was often modeled in the shape of a dolphin, a turtle, a Triton (half human being, half fish), a mermaid or another fictive creature; on the top was often a figure of Neptune or another mythological or allegorical being.
Collections of exotic shells from the tropical seas were already being formed in the 16th century. Shells were so expensive and prestigious that they kept their value as an investment. Depending on fashion and rarity some sorts were very expensive, sometimes costing several thousand guilders for a single shell.[1] It is therefore not amazing that Roemer Visscher in his emblem book *Sinnepoppen*, published in 1614, flared up about the mania of collection shells (fig. 5.1). This emblem is often referred to in the art-historical literature as a comment on vanity or pride. The translation of the text which accompanies the emblem, entitled 'It's sickening how a fool spends his money,' is as follows:
'It is surprising that there are people who spend large sums of money on shells and mussels, whose only beauty is their rarity. They do it because they notice that great potentates, even Emperors and Kings, commission people to look for them and pay them well. Oh, you monkeys (= imitators), you do not understand the ins and outs of the game. King Louis XI of France ordered rare animals from neighboring kingdoms to make people believe that he still had a great appetite for life, though actually he was already physically very weak. I do not mean to condemn the people who earn their living from this: they are cunning enough to see a profit in this game.'[2]

> 5.1 Tis misselijck waer een geck zijn gelt aen leijt.

ROEMER VISSCHER
Sinnepoppen, 1614

This emblem, by the way, is immediately followed by one in which the buyers of tulip bulbs are ridiculed, more than twenty years before the 'tulpomania', or speculation in tulip bulbs, reached its height.

Philibert van Borsselen, however, had a different opinion, as we can see in his didactic poem 'Strand, oft Ghedichte van de Schelpen...' (Beaches, or Poem on Shells....in Praise of the Creator of All Things), written in 1611. It is about the silver-mounted *hulck*(shell), the *Turbo marmoratus*:

'Just as this shell receives its beautiful lustre from Heaven's greatest Light and reflects it back on man's face and cheers his spirit, thus must man whose heart has been gladdened further the honor of God and edify his fellow men. And man should not delve into his unfathomable heart, the treasure which God has given him, but lend it out everywhere as a pawn, and it will bring profit.'[3]

There is in this verse an admonition against greed and usury, and it is pointed out that what we acquire has only been lent to us temporarily and has to be handed on. The all-important message is that all beauty and lustre are reflections of the Creator, the Grace of God. The riches of nature have been given by Him, and we have only to wonder, to praise and to thank. This is probably the idea which several painters of shell and flower still lifes had in mind, as we can see from the legends on their works, for instance in Joris Hoefnagel's albums of watercolors of the Four Elements in the National Gallery of Art in Washington, D.C., and the engravings after him made by his son Jacob for *Archetypa Studiaque...* of 1592.[4]

The poem of Van Borsselen treats in nearly two thousand lines the great variety found in a collection of shells. He cites extensively the literature from the Renaissance and Antiquity on his subject. The praise in 'Praise of the Creator of All Things' is not only in the title but also pervades the poem throughout. The poet attributes to the polished Turbo shell mounted as a beaker an unparalleled beauty and purity which 'puts to shame the most beautiful lustre of pearls.'[5] He feels that an artist cannot do justice to Nature when he tries to express the beauty of shells: 'Oh sensuous Painter, although your hand be highly praised, here it falls short, neither your paint nor brush can do justice to this beautiful lustre.'[6]

Here in fact the author supports the argument of the superiority of Nature over Art. Such was also the case in paintings based on the pastoral scenes in Pieter Cornelisz. Hooft's then famous play *Granida*, of 1605, for instance in a painting by Dirck van Baburen, of 1623, in Brussels.[7] A conch with water is offered here to the hunting princess Granida by a shepherd, later her lover. But Van Borsselen's lines may have been meant more as a challenge to a painter. Hendrik Goltzius gave the allegorical Pictura a brush in one hand and a nautilus shell in the other.[8] In 1603 he painted a portrait of the art collector Jan Govertsen of Haarlem (fig. 5.2) with various shells on a table and a polished *Turbo marmoratus* in his hand.[9] We can also see the Turbo in a painting by Goltzius's pupil Jacques de Gheyn the Younger (fig. 5.3), lying in between Neptune, who is holding a nautilus, and his wife Amphitrite. Van Regteren Altena (1983) saw in the detail of Amor examining the contents of the nautilus a barely disguised erotic symbolism.[10]

HENDRICK GOLTZIUS
The Collector Jan Govertsen, 1603
Museum Boymans-van Beuningen, Rotterdam

JACQUES DE GHEYN THE YOUNGER
Neptune and Amphitrite
Wallraff-Richartz Museum, Cologne

It goes without saying that shells appear in paintings of sea-gods and sea-nymphs. Among the most frequently depicted scenes are the wedding of Peleus and Thetis and the triumph of Amphitrite, who, along with Thetis and Galatea, was one of the fifty Nereids, the daughters of Nereus, god of the sea. These subjects were often painted by a group of artists around Goltzius in Haarlem, such as Cornelis Cornelisz. van Haarlem, Karel van Mander, and Jacques de Gheyn, and in Utrecht by Abraham Bloemaert. In Antwerp we know these subjects from Rubens, Hendrik van Balen and Frans Francken the Younger. The latter painted the triumph of Amphitrite several times.[11]

Two paintings[12] should be mentioned separately, as the shells in the foreground take up so much room. One of them (fig. 5.4) is a true shell still life and has a mythological scene in the background. I believe that these are works of Frans Francken's brother Hieronymus Francken the Younger. We can recognize several nautilus shells and a *Turbo marmoratus*. Beautiful shells were also depicted in several paintings of Perseus freeing Andromeda, who was chained to a rock and left to be devoured by a sea-monster. Attractive examples are by Joachim Wttewael (1611)[13] and Gillis Claesz. de Hondecoeter (1627).[14] In these we also recognize the *Nautilus pompilius* and the *Turbo marmoratus*.

Another shell that was often depicted is the Triton shell, *Strombus gigas*, from the Caribbean area. This shell is used by Triton or the Tritons in the retinue of Neptune as a blowing horn. Van Borsselen uses the Strombus as a metaphor of the 'steadfast loyalty' of subjects for their king. The paper nautilus, *Argonauta argo*, from the Mediterranean floats like a ship on the waves, with its aperture pointing upwards. Van Borsselen therefore compares it to a wise admiral or a ship's pilot who is in control of the sea under all circumstances. For Van Borsselen it is like the pious man who has to save his 'badly battered ship' during the course of life to

5.4

HIERONYMUS FRANCKEN THE YOUNGER attributed
Shells with Neptune and Amphitrite
Private Collection, formerly Schweitzer Gallery, New York

'land at last at heaven's safe coast where he will gain forever the supreme reward.' This meaning conforms to an emblem published by Camerarius in 1604, where the paper nautilus is a symbol of steadfastness, with the motto: 'Tutus per summa, per ima': (Just as safe on the top as at the bottom [of the waves]).[15]

Reusner had already depicted this in 1581 in an emblem with Venus seated on a 'Pompilus ille sacer (dictus quoque Nautilus)' (that holy man Pompilus [also called Nautilus]).[16] These scenes can be traced back to Aristotle, Pliny and other classical authors[17] who knew the paper nautilus from the Mediterranean area. In later times this symbolism was transferred to the *Nautilus pompilius* from the East Indies.[18] The shells of the nautili (or 'pearl ships') are in fact shells of the cephalopod mollusks and belong to the order of octopoda. *Nautilus pompilius* does not float on the surface like the paper nautilus but swims at a much greater depth in the sea, down to 600 meters.

Among the works of Otho Vaenius from Antwerp we find an emblem with shells lying on the beach and a motto derived from Ovid: 'Litore quot conchae, tot sunt in amore dolores...' (There are as many sorrows in love as there are shells on the beach...).[19] This motto may be applicable to a number of mythological scenes, for instance in works of Frans Francken, but we cannot be sure of such a relationship.

Iconographically, shells can have several other meanings: for example, as a sign of the element Water, the Sea, the river Jordan (since Christ was baptized there), but also of the wind (in view of the fact that one can blow on the Triton shell). Some sorts, as we have already seen, can have their own individual meanings, but, of course, they can also be depicted simply as shells, without symbolism. The pilgrim scallop, *Pecten jacobeus*, is an attribute of St. James, the son of Zebedee, as we can see in the central panel (*The Adoration of the Lamb*) of the Ghent Altarpiece by Jan van Eyck. But it is also a symbol of nobility and virtue.[20] A well-known example is the *Birth of Venus* by Botticelli in the Uffizi in Florence, where we see the goddess on a scallop shell. We have mentioned already that she can avail herself also of another sort of shell. In the emblem literature we sometimes see a purpura (*Murex brandaris* and *Murex trunculus*), the snail which produces a precious purple pigment. Purple, of course, is the royal color.

The oyster and the mussel are much more important iconographically; although they play no role in the shell still lifes, they have a function in other types of still lifes and in genre paintings. The oyster and the mussel often have the same meaning. Both are food that can be eaten during Fast, and both are unclean foods according to the Old Testament. The mussel was a food of the poor, and the oyster of the rich ('the oyster, the dish for the great lords').[21] With regard to the oyster we read in some texts that it is an unhealthy food,[22] but in others that it quickens appetite and libido; in still others it is compared to the female genitals.[23] Valerianus, referring to Plato, compares the oyster to man and calls it a symbol of the soul which is locked up in the dark dungeon of the body, the shell.[24]

The oyster with a pearl inside has a number of special interpretations in the emblem literature: it is often used as a symbol of Mary's humility. Based on Physiologus,[25] the mussel is especially related to Christ, the shells representing the Old and the New Testaments. Physiologus, referring to texts in Isaiah, also makes a comparison between the conch and Mary's giving birth to Christ.

CLARA PEETERS
Private Collection

NICOLAES GILLIS
Private Collection

SHELL STILL LIFES

In the margin of one of the pages of the Book of Hours of Catherine of Cleves a miniature contains eleven oysters and a crab representing the eleven Apostles and Judas. The shell of a mussel, like that of a snail, can also signify the security of one's home. The shells of mussels were sometimes of practical use to artists, who used them as paint trays.

Most of the above interpretations are hardly, if at all, applicable to the iconography of seashell still lifes. In these still lifes we must see the shells primarily as precious collectors' items, luxurious showpieces, which, however, are related to the theme of Vanity in a double sense: vanity and transiency. They were kept in the curio cabinets and art rooms of collectors, in which one often sees them depicted.

Tropical shells were brought to Holland from the Far East in ships of the Dutch East India Company, after having been collected along the shores from Indonesia to Japan. Others came from Brazil, the West Indies and the Caribbean area. The ships from Indonesia also brought parrots from the Moluccas and the plumage of birds of paradise; from Mauritius came the Dodo, a large bird that was killed en masse and soon became extinct. From America came the turkey, and from the West Indies large tropical butterflies of beautiful colors.

GEORG HINZ
Collection of Curiosities, 1666
Castle Statni Zamek, Rychnov (Czechoslovakia)

BARTHOLOMEUS ASSTEYN attributed
Sheat from an Album
Fondation Custodia (Collection F. Lugt), Paris

SHELL STILL LIFES

In the third quarter of the 17th century the North German painter Georg Hinz specialized in the depiction of *Kunstschranken* (curio cabinets) containing rare and precious objects. In fig. 5.5 we see an example of this in a painting from the collection of Castle Statni Zamek in Rychnov (Reichenbach), Czechoslovakia. It is a typical trompe l'oeil painting: it creates the illusion of a real cabinet and its contents.[26] The two oval medallions near the center are little portraits of the Emperor Leopold I (1640-1705) and his consort Margarita Teresa of Spain (1651-1673). They married in 1666, and the painting dates from the same year.[27] Some of the objects in the cabinet have been preserved, for instance the ivory goblet with mythological scenes of putti, satyrs, Bacchus, Venus, and Hercules slaying the Nemean lion. The glass goblet has engraved inscriptions containing congratulatory greetings for the emperor extolling his virtues. The small gold skulls are explicit references to transiency; the watches — one pointing to one o'clock and the other to eleven — refer to the cycle of life and death. The reliefs and sculptures indicate struggle and victory in man's life. In the collection are also a number of precious naturalia and semi-artifacts, among which, on the left, is a *Nautilus pompilius* decorated in fretwork, a *Strombus gigas*, on the right, and a red coral.[28]

Several artists made drawings of individual shells, probably commissioned by collectors and scientists, but it was not until the end of the 17th century that illustrated books appeared with methodical lists of shells. One of the most important series is in the collection of the Fondation Custodia in Paris. It is part of a larger series of watercolors, mainly of flowers but some of marine animals, including shells. The sheets must have originally been part of a large album with numbered sheets which are now dispersed in many collections. On many of the sheets one finds the monogram *BA*, which has been interpreted by Bol as Bartholomeus Assteyn.[29] In fig. 5.6 we see an example.

In a painting by Jan Brueghel the Elder, dated 1593, we see people collecting shells. The main theme of the work is whale fishing with many ships and figures, as well as various other scenes which would not seem directly to fit into that context. On further consideration, however, they pose an intriguing iconographical connection — the rhinoceros hunt and St. John on Patmos who saw a vision of the Apocalypse with an enormous dragon in the sky.[30] Hunting on monstrous beasts stood for hunting the devil or slaying the bad.

Real shell still lifes always show only a small number of species, but they should be seen as only a part of a collection. We may assume this for certain if the painting also shows the familiar boxes or little cases in which the shells were kept. One of the oldest examples is by the French painter Jacques Linard (cat. no. 12), who was clearly influenced by Dutch artists. It is dated 1621, or 1624 (the last number is not clear). None of our familiar shells — *Nautilus pompilius*, *Turbo marmoratus*, or *Stombus gigas* — is present here, except for the paper nautilus, *Argonautus argo*, in the middle in front of the box. The latter is the only species from Europe: it is found in the Mediterranean region. Most of the others come from the Far East. They are, from left to right: on the box, *Conus episcopus* (Pacific), *Spondylus princeps* (Pacific), and *Hexaplex cichoreus* (Indian Ocean); and in front, the big *Hippopus hippopus* (Indo-Pacific), *Otala punctata* (Mediterranean), *Turbo petholatus* (Indo-Pacific), *Turris babylonia* (Indo-Pacific), *Turbo petholatus*, *Conus ammitalis* (Indian Ocean), *Archtectonia trochlearis*, (Indian Ocean), *Hepaplex saxicola* (Philippines), *Argonauta hians* (tropics), *Chlamys spec.*, *Mitra papalis* (Indo-Pacific), and *Muricanthus radix* (California-Peru).

12

FLORIS VAN DYCK
Private Collection

JACQUES LINARD
Private Collection

Jacques Linard painted several other shell still lifes. Most of them are known under the names of other artists, such as Clara Peeters and (in the Fondation Custodia) Balthasar van der Ast.[31] A charming small work (fig. 5.7), signed in gold *I^s Linard* and 1638 *a Paris*, shows shells in and around a small chest of drawers.[32] Several works by Sebastian Stoskopff are related to the shell still lifes of Linard. Cat. no. 13 is a beautiful example depicting a polished *Nautilus pompilius* and a panther shell, *Cypraea mauritiana* (Indo-Pacific), next to a chipwood box. We are familiar with these boxes from other works by Stoskopff, for instance one with shells in the Musée du Louvre in Paris.[33] Stoskopff started working in Hanau, near Frankfurt, and was influenced by Georg Flegel and Jeremias van Winghen but soon developed his own style. In 1640 he settled in Strasbourg after having worked for some time in Paris, where he must have seen the work of Linard.

The most famous of the Dutch shell painters is Balthasar van der Ast. His shell still lifes developed from the flower pieces with a few shells by his teacher and brother-in-law, Ambrosius Bosschaert the Elder, but also from his own earlier compositions of flowers, fruit and shells. A good example is the shell still life from the museum in Dresden (cat. no. 14) with peach branches in the background and red currants, lilies-of-the-valley and forget-me-nots in the foreground. The shells from left to right are: *Conus ermineus* (Caribbean); *Murex pomum* (Caribbean); *Conus marmoreus* (Indo-Pacific); *Murex spec.*; *Turbo marmoratus*, polished (Indo-Pacific); *Melongena morio* (Caribbean); *Cypraea tigris* (Indo-Pacific); *Cittarium pica* (Caribbean); *Murex brunnens* (IndoPacific); and *Harpa harpa* (Indo-Pacific).[34] The marbled conus (*Conus marmoreus*) is one of the best-known shells in art because of the famous etching by Rembrandt of 1650 (fig. 5.8), which the artist made more than ten years after the painting by Van der Ast. An often-depicted sort is the Pica-shell (*Cittarium pica*), which we shall encounter later in a work by Pieter Claesz.

The Dresden painting is closely related to a fruit still life with shells and a carnation in the Alte Pinakothek in Munich,[35] and even moreso to a fruit and shell still life with a carnation, lilies-of-the-valley and forget-me-nots which was shown in the exhibition *A Fruitful Past*.[36] In the Munich work all three shells are identical to ones in the Dresden painting, and in the other work seven find exact counterparts in the same picture. The well-known shell still life in the Boymans-Van Beuningen Museum in Rotterdam is richer in variety but different in atmosphere. It is probably later in date, but even here six of its 21 shells are identical to those in the Dresden work.[37]

In Van der Ast's work the shells are probably vanitas symbols. It is also possible, however, that the artist at the same time meant to express the glory of God's creation by the richness of their shapes. Ordinarily attributes of worldliness and transiency are depicted in contrast to symbols of heaven or eternity, such as the butterfly. This is true in Van der Ast's shell still life, but in this case the artist has elaborated his meaning with other symbols as well: the lizard and the spider and its web. Animals that lose their skin during metamorphosis or that wake from hibernation are often symbols of resurrection. This also applies to the lizard, but *in malo* it is a symbol of deceit, thus of sin.[38] In a number of still lifes, however, this symbolism is related to the idea of Physiologus that the lizard becomes blinded by the sun in old age and loses its eyesight. But guided by its instincts, it finds a crack in a wall facing east and by morning regains its sight. Taking into account that the lizard renews its skin, the commen-

JACQUES LINARD
Collection of Shells, 1638
Fischer Gallery, Lucerne

REMBRANDT VAN RIJN
Marbled Conus, 1650, Etching

tary is important: 'And you, O man, if you have the clothing of the old man, see to it that when the eyes of your heart are clouded, you seek out the intelligible eastern sun who is Jesus Christ and whose name is 'the east' in Jeremiah.[39] As the Apostle says, 'He is the sun of justice.' He will open for you the comprehending eyes of your heart, and for you the old clothing will become new.'[40] This quotation can be even better understood in the light of the relevant passages from the Bible,[41] cited in several commentaries on Physiologus. The details on the life of the wall lizard are derived from antique sources.[42]

The meaning of the spider in the web can perhaps also be traced back to Physiologus. The spider weaves its intricate web to catch flies: 'They [webs] are snares for you, fly, dainty and suitable morsel, to catch you as you flit.... Man follows the example of these small insects when he cheats his own friends and consumes them in their misery; and he is extremely pleased with himself when he can injure another. But whatever evil deeds he does, he falls when he dies like the web on which the aforesaid spider runs.'[43] Ultimately the web leads nowhere: 'the first breath of air pulls it and spreads it out; it is broken and falls into nothing.' Other shell still lifes by Balthasar van der Ast are known, most of them small in size. Also in his fruit pieces and those which combine flowers and fruit, shells are seldom missing. A very beautiful example of a flower-shell still life with a sea urchin is represented by cat. no. 15. The shells are, from left to right, *Murex pomum* (Caribbean), *Conus striatus* (Indo-Pacific), *Hexaplex cichoreum* (Indo-Pacific), *Tridacne maxima* (big clam, Indonesia, a relative of the giant clam *T. gigas* which was and is sometimes used as a font), the latter placed on a smaller pilgrim scallop (the edible *Pecten jacobeus* or *P. maximus* from the Atlantic). The big clam is filled with flowers. We see the lizard again. The caterpillar is the antithesis of the butterfly, here a Queen of Spain fritillary. A bumble bee is hovering over the flowers. To our eyes, this

13

Sebastian Stoskopff
Private Collection

BALTHASAR VAN DER AST
Gemäldegalerie Alte Meister, Dresden

is one of the most beautiful and poetic of all shell still lifes. Another example of a flower-shell piece with a bouquet in a shell is reproduced in the catalogue *Masters of Middelburg*.[44]

16 A sea urchin is also included in a still life by Willem Kalf (cat. no. 16) in which shells are arranged on an oriental rug in front of a Japanese lacquer box. The cup of the shell beaker is a polished *Turbo marmoratus* mounted on a figure of Neptune with his trident.[45] Among the shells, we recognize: the Indo-Pacific *Murex haustellum*, to the left of the sea urchin (in front of it another *Murex*); *Conus imperialis*; an *Astraea* in front; an unpolished *Turbo marmoratus*, in front of the branch of coral at the right; and *Conus aulicus*. A related picture without a shell beaker is in the collection of the Kunsthaus in Zürich.[46]

The shell beaker or shell cup is one of the typical show objects in pronk still lifes. An early example is Hermann tom Ring's painting in the Alte Pinakothek in Munich depicting the sibyl Samia,[47] painted around 1560. The sibyl is shown in front of the sea with ships, and at the back is a vista. At the bottom edge of the composition we see several attributes: a book, a string of pearls with a cross, a Pacific shell (*Haliotis*), and a shell beaker — in this case a nautilus cup. The sibyl's prophesy of the Incarnation of Christ can be read below in the stone, painted as if it had been chiselled. Kuechen believes that the pearls, the Haliotis-shell with its sheen of mother-of-pearl, and the polished nautilus are related to the symbolism of the oyster and the pearl as signs of Christ born of the Virgin Mary. The Nautilus cup could be compared to the chalice of the New testament.[48] That the Nautilus cup is meant as a Eucharistic wine chalice is obvious.

In 1611 Philibert van Borsselen described a mounted *Turbo marmoratus* shell beaker, such as the one in the work by Kalf, with the following words:

'Here follows a silver *Hulck*, the net of shell which holds the pearl, that is placed on the table on a golden foot, so that one can drink from the clean cup the joyful wine. This costly cup reflects the sun on man's face and miraculously shows the rainbow, painted so often, which crowns the earth.'[49]

Van Borsselen also mentions that in the East Indies mother-of-pearl is made from shells and is used as decoration on all sorts of objects. Mother-of-pearl is derived from the pearl oyster and from the *Turbo marmoratus*, *Nautilus pompilius*, and *Haliotis* species.

Among the most delicate shell still lifes are a few small works by Adriaen Coorte, exquisite
17 little jewels, painted in the last decade of the 17th century. A splendid example is cat. no. 17, dated 1697. Four shells glow against a dark background, brushed by rays of oblique light which fall across the thick slab of marble. The two horny ones are the spotted Indo-Pacific *Terebra subulata*, at the front, and the ribbed *Fusinus colus*, at the right. As usual, Coorte has combined big shells with a few small ones.[50] The number of shells in his works can vary from four to six, and they are always displayed on a stone slab with a crack and small joints, just as in his fruit still lifes.

CHAPTER 6

FLOWER AND FRUIT STILL LIFES

Although art-historical discussion of Dutch still-life painting has tended to perpetuate the categories into which such pictures are usually grouped, there are sometimes good reasons to ignore such strict classification. When flower and fruit still lifes, for example, are considered in the same light in which we have been examining the pronk still life, some significant affinities can be seen.

The flowers painted in most 17th-century still lifes — certainly those painted during the first half of the century — were items of considerable luxury and prestige. In value they were comparable to shells. The flowers themselves were in bloom for only a short while, but as perennials in the garden they retained their commercial value. Gardens could, in a way, be compared to shell cabinets. Each plant was given plenty of room, and the layout was like a 'collection', as we can still see in botanical gardens. A garden could contain an exquisite variety of rare and costly plants, a great array of species and colors. The flowers we see depicted in early flower pieces, however, did not all bloom in the same season, demonstrating without question that these painted bouquets were not mere painterly excursions in naturalism. They were instead compositions carefully and meaningfully composed from studies made when the flowers bloomed in their seasons.

Like the shells we have already discussed, the flowers depicted in early still lifes were mostly exotic ones. They were mainly imported as bulbs, or as rhizomes or seeds. Most of the plants came from Asia Minor and Southern Europe, some from Central Europe, and only a few from America and South Africa. But the distant origins of these flowers had little effect on artists and collectors, since horticulturists soon began to cultivate them, creating great variety and catering to fashion. The tremendous variety of species was partly the result of spontaneous cross-breeding. In nature hybrids have much less chance of survival, since they cannot compete with other plants and are, moreover, usually sterile. In gardens, however, this can be remedied by taking cuttings or by splitting and giving prized plants extra attention. In addition, species from different parts of the world can be used in cross-breeding. The most expensive plants were tulips, which were traded as bulbs. For certain shapes and color patterns extraordinarily high prices were paid, sometimes thousands of guilders for a single bulb. Tulips were the object of speculation, and the bulb trade was sometimes in the hands of merchants who knew nothing about the product. They sold them in the seasons in

BALTHASAR VAN DER AST
Private Collection

WILLEM KALF
Stichting Hannema-de Stuers, Castle
Het Nijenhuis, near Heino (the Netherlands)

which they did not bloom. Flowering was in any case limited to only a few weeks each year. The sale was sometimes accompanied by a certificate from the bulb grower and by a colored drawing. The result was not always reliable, however, partly because of the hybridogene nature of the flower and also because of a spotted pattern often caused by a virus, something not discovered until the end of the 19th century.

Breeding was highly sensitive to fashion, so that, on the basis of the flower, one can often date a 17th-century still life to within ten years. There was also a clear distinction between the taste and culture of the northern and southern Netherlands. Such distinctions and other variations in the types of flower pieces seen over the centuries have been treated in the catalogue *A Flowery Past*. For fruit pieces the same development has been treated in *A Fruitful Past*.[1]

Not only were the flowers depicted in still lifes items of great luxury, but so were the vases in which they were arranged. They could be simple glass vases with a smooth surface or with prunts, produced in the Netherlands, or costly Venetian vases into which lapis lazuli was sometimes incorporated. It is difficult to be certain whether the latter were produced in Italy, by Italian glass blowers who had emigrated to the north, or by their followers in the Netherlands and Germany, and it is preferable to refer to them as *à la façon de Venise*. From the beginning of the 17th century Chinese porcelain vases were used, mostly from the Wanli period (1573-1619). In fruit and pronk still lifes Chinese plates, basins, bowls and cups are also familiar objects. They appear so frequently in still lifes that we may lose sight of the fact that they were costly items which only the well-to-do could afford. This also applies to the exotic varieties of fruits, such as grapes, peaches and apricots, which were also included in many still lifes.

In rare early Netherlandish flower pieces we come across decorated glass or majolica vases, such as in the flower piece by Hans Memling from the end of the 15th century in the Thyssen-Bornemisza Collection in Castagnola.[2] Also in illuminated manuscripts, especially in Flemish books of hours of the late 15th and early 16th centuries, such vases are often seen. By the end of the 16th century baroque vases had become popular, either imported ones or copies of Italian designs. We know of them, however, almost entirely from the flower pieces seen in engravings, some dated before 1600.[3] Fig. 6.1. shows such an engraving by Hendrick Hondius after the artist Elias Lucasz. Verhulst (b. Malines, fl. and d. Delft, 1601), a painter of flowers, shells and animals.[4] An open niche shows a vista of a distant landscape with the sea, cities and mountains, such as we see later in paintings by Ambrosius Bosschaert. The vase shows symbolic elements of all-nourishing Nature,[5] the enormous assortment of flowers being intended to evoke our awe at the diversity of God's Creation.

The presence of insects and birds in early flower pieces serves a symbolic function. They introduce thematic notes of transiency and redemption, which we shall discuss further in specific works. The parrot probably represents the *vita activa*, and the goldfinch the *vita contemplativa*.[6]

Around the middle of the 17th century we begin to see the appearance of ornamented silver vases, especially in the work of Willem van Aelst. A little later we also see vases of ivory, for instance in the works of Maria van Oosterwijck and the German Georg Hinz. But such vases remain exceptions to the norm. Smooth glass vases are the most commonly used con-

Hendrik Hondius after **Elias Verhulst**
Flower Piece, 1599, Engraving

tainers for bouquets in that period. Later we see tooled bronze vases and decorated stone and terracotta garden urns, but by then we are already in the 18th century. Later still we see marble and alabaster urns and, especially in the 19th century, vases of cut crystal.

Flower still lifes derived in part from the symbolic role of flowers in religious paintings. Other antecedents can be found in decorative prints. The original religious sources, often symbols of Mary and — after the Reformation in the northern Netherlands — of Christ, can be clearly traced in several flower pieces. For instance, a conspicuously placed white lily at the top of a bouquet was commonly understood to signify the Annunciation or the Immaculate Conception, when serving as a symbol of the chastity of Mary or the purity of Christ. The arranging of flowers in triads seems also to have played a symbolic role in early still lifes. For example, three conspicuously placed roses, tulips or other flowers — or ternate leaves, such as the Columbine or the Strawberry — or flowers whose shape or color show triplicity, such as the Iris or the Pansy, were very often understood to symbolize the Holy Trinity.

ADRIAEN COORTE
Private Collection

JAN BRUEGHEL THE ELDER
Private Collection

The 17th-century flower piece is practically always associated with the theme of transiency, and innumerable sources, among them the legends on engraved flower pieces which cite relevant biblical texts, make this clear.[7] Furthermore, Redemption is frequently suggested as a positive note in this context by a butterfly or dragonfly, symbols of the redeemed soul which has earned eternal life. Just as the butterfly develops from a crawling caterpillar and the dragonfly from an imago without wings, so too can man be resurrected from the dead and enter into real life. That true life begins only after death was a commonly accepted belief.

Flowers were transiency symbols because they only bloom for a short time. The themes of Vanitas and Pride were often associated with the transiency of luxury articles, including flowers. Luxurious things, or vanitas symbols, consequently held a clear message: To gain eternal life one must perform good deeds on earth and lead a God-fearing life. This meant that a choice had to be made between Good and Evil.

The earliest dated flower still life by Jan Brueghel the Elder is from 1605.[8] It is a bouquet in an earthenware pot with 72 species and varieties of flowers and four butterflies. In the foreground lie some diamonds. In three other versions of the composition the diamonds have been added to or replaced by other precious articles: gold coins, a ring or another piece of jewelry, or shells. A still life representing a bouquet in a gilt tazza is dated 1612, but this painting was last documented in 1928.[9] There are other autograph versions of this painting, as well as imitations. Fig. 6.2, from a private collection in Spain, shows one of these versions.[10] Later Jan Brueghel painted a flower wreath around a more robust tazza in a typical vanitas painting with jewels and coins in a lacquer box. There are also several versions of this paint-

JAN BRUEGHEL THE ELDER
Flowers in a Tazza
Private Collection

JAN BRUEGHEL THE ELDER
Flowers and Jewels, 1618
Musées Royaux des Beaux-Arts, Brussels

ing; one of them, of 1618, is in the Musées Royaux des Beaux-Arts in Brussels (fig. 6.3). Examples of the Renaissance hairpin and pendant have been preserved.[11]

Cat. no. 18 shows us a bouquet in a Wan-li *kendi* (ewer) decorated with plants and animals. Again, there are more versions of this painting, but only this one is signed. The bouquet is less dense than in most of the other flower pieces by Jan Brueghel. This and other stylistic characteristics point to a relatively later dating, probably around 1620. One may wonder if the grasshopper on the body of the bottle, which has a rather devilish appearance, was meant to be an opponent of the placid bird on the bottle's neck. The symbolic meaning of a bird goes more or less hand-in-hand with that of the butterfly and the dragonfly, here represented by a blue and a damselfly. The bird is often a symbol of the Idea or of the Soul. The painting is also furnished with two ladybirds, two more beetles, a fly and a lively grasshopper. According to contemporary literature and to emblem books, the grasshopper is frequently a symbol of gluttony, calling to mind the plague of locusts in the Bible.[12] As a sign of gluttony and its bad effects the grasshopper was also a warning to be moderate (Temperantia).[13] The fable of the cricket and the ant, which was common knowledge in those days, probably contributed to this idea. The cricket represents someone who lives without a thought of tomorrow.[14] That the cricket and the grasshopper were often confused is apparent from illustrations accompanying the texts of various authors. One should be cautious, however, with an interpretation *in malo*. In Camerarius the grasshopper is also a symbol of Spring and thus a sign of Resurrection.[15] The fact that it sheds its skin from time to time supports this interpretation.

The earliest dated flower piece that we know of by Ambrosius Bosschaert the Elder is also of

AMBROSIUS BOSSCHAERT THE ELDER
Flowers in a Wan-li Vase
Thyssen-Bornemisza Collection, Castagnola (Switzerland)

PETER BINOIT
Private Collection

BALTHASAR VAN DER AST
Private Collection

1605 and represents flowers in a Wan-li vase mounted on a gilt foot.[16] The flower piece in fig. 6.4, from the Thyssen-Bornemisza Collection in Castagnola, was painted a few years later.[17] The same Wan-li vase mounted on a gilt foot can also be seen in a work of 1609 in the Kunsthistorisches Museum in Vienna.[18] Both the vases of 1605 and 1609 are decorated with floral motifs (and a cut pomegranate), and the feet are practically identical.

19 The Wan-li vase in a work by Peter Binoit (cat. no. 19) is also decorated with floral motifs but is contained in a more complicated, German gilded mount. By comparing this painting from the Hermitage in Leningrad with dated flower pieces, it would seem to have been painted in 1612, or possibly 1613. What is perhaps not so obvious at a first glance is that this work contains no fewer than 32 species and varieties of flowers and ten insects, including a butterfly, a blue, a caterpillar, a damselfly, ladybirds and ants. In Binoit's flower still lifes we see the marked repoussoir effect of objects overhanging the edge of the plinth. In his early paintings these are often carnations, stag-beetles or shells, sometimes in combination. In his later works, from 1620, they are wreaths of flowers with fruits and parakeets.

The carnation is often seen in both religious paintings and portraits of the 15th and 16th centuries, usually associated with the belief in Christ. This is, inter alia, expressed in such flower names as Oeillet de Dieu (Eye of God) and Clove. The old French name Giroflée, which is related to the clove (a Passion symbol), was also used for the Gilliflower, which was also often depicted as a symbol of Christ (but for different reasons too). Rosemary is seen in numerous early flower pieces, among them those by the German artist Ludger tom Ring of 1562. The plant is usually without flowers, but in the painting by Binoit, depicted at the lower left, it is in flower. We have discussed the meaning of Rosemary in Chapter 4. The hole in the rose petal and the fly on the rose evoke the theme of transiency. Perhaps the position of the caterpillar at the bottom, in contrast to the resting butterfly and dragonfly high at the top of the bouquet, is not a coincidence. It is possible that Binoit is playing with a trinitarian symbolism with this and with his three tulips at the top near the iris, which is also a triple flower. In a flower painting dated 1611 there are three irises at the top as well as three red anemones and three red tulips. Similar examples can also be found in other flower pieces, e.g. in a painting, dated 1620, with three sorts of Turban lilies.[19] It is interesting to note that the assortment of flowers in flower pieces by masters from neighboring Frankfurt, Germany, differs somewhat from those in Antwerp and Holland and that changes in the dates at which species were depicted are observable.

In Binoit's painting of 1611 the Peruvian Small Garden Nasturtium (*Tropaeolum minus*) is seen. The familiar, larger Garden Nasturtium (*Tropaeolum majus*) was not brought to Europe until more than a century later than its smaller brother.[20] In Binoit's painting, however, we can distinguish two varieties of the smaller Nasturtium, one of which is unknown today. The Small Nasturtium can also be seen in the lovely flower piece in the Philadelphia Museum of Art by Christoffel van den Berghe, dated 1617 (fig. 6.5), painted in Middelburg, on one of the islands of Zeeland between Flanders and Holland.[21] The diversity of nature represented in this small work is quite large: 21 variations of flowers, with five butterflies and eight other insects, including three caterpillars and a damselfly, as well as two Indo-Pacific shells (*Conus mustelinus* and *Conus generalis*) and, at the right, an Indonesian snail (*Amphidromus*). This richness of form, as well as the composition, the facture of the leaves, and

CHRISTOFFEL VAN DEN BERGHE
Flower Piece with Shells, 1617
Philadelphia Museum of Art, John G. Johnson Collection

other qualities (especially the sense of atmosphere) remind us more of Roelandt Savery than of Amborsius Bosschaert. It also resembles very little the style of Jan Brueghel. In many respects this work is unique and shows the individuality of a real master, for example in the miniaturistic details in even the most hidden corners of the painting, in the visual tension which is evoked by the many cracks in the side of the niche and the shelf, and the poise of the butterflies which one can almost see alight or fly away. The two Wan-li cups are practically identical to bowls which have been salvaged from sunken East Indiamen, such as the *Witte Lelie*, which sank in 1613 and from which the Rijksmuseum, Amsterdam, acquired a perfect example in 1977.[22]

With the work of Balthasar van der Ast we see again the influence of Bosschaert, although that of Roelandt Savery is also undeniable. The lizard and the large dragonfly in cat. no. 20 also show his influence. Van der Ast alloyed the static and fashionable forms of Bosschaert with the sensitive and suggestive tension of Roelandt Savery to create a controlled and harmonious style of his own. His compositions are at once clear, warm and subtle, but not all his artistic impulses were logical. For example, the long shadows cast in different directions often lend his works an air of mystery. Such subtle details are the first to disappear in inexpert restorations.

BALTHASAR VAN DER AST
Schlossmuseum Georgium, Dessau (German Democratic Republic)

JAN BAPTIST VAN FORNENBURGH
Private Collection

Whether Van der Ast's, like Brueghel's, Wan-li vases decorated with plants and birds — or, in the case of cat. no. 20, with an enormous grasshopper — actually existed, or were his own combination of existing shapes and motifs, is not certain. The landscape with the small gate looks very Dutch. The grasshopper could have a symbolic meaning: symbolism could still be at work here, but not so emphatically as in the still lifes of his predecessors. Gradually symbolism makes way for decoration *pur sang*, although Jan Davidsz. de Heem did bring about a considerable revival of symbolism, and other artists occasionally experimented with symbolic elements.

In still lifes combining flowers and fruits, such as Van der Ast's work of about 1623 (cat. no. 20), we can see a distinct vision of Creation and the cycles of Nature expressed in a single composition: spring flowers, such as the lily-of-the-valley and the tulip; the young, ripening buds of summer roses; the fruits of the autumn; and finally the return of the lizard awakening in spring from its winter hibernation. The butterfly and the dragonflies which renew themselves from the wingless state of their youth also fit into this cycle of nature. To do this successfully called for considerable descriptive skill. Van der Ast was one of the first artists who was able to paint currants so transparent that we can discern the seeds inside. He also rendered excellently the varying stages of ripeness — from pale to clear red — which suggest the on-going processes of life.

Balthasar van der Ast often sketched his compositions directly in black chalk on the white gesso ground of the canvas or panel. In the course of time such sketches often begin to show through the thin pigment on top. This has happened in this case. With some flowers, such as the rose in the middle, it is evident that the artist did not keep to his original sketch and made alterations in certain details.

In later works Van der Ast often included vases of flowers, bowls or baskets of fruit, as well as shells, in the same painting. This sometimes resulted in complicated compositions with objects at different levels step-wise behind each other, and Ming basins positioned obliquely on top of another container. One or more parrots might also enliven the scene. In the early compositions the insects are generally rather static, but in his later ones he frequently depicted them in flight, such as the butterfly in a work belonging to the Castle Georgium Museum in Dessau (cat. no. 21), in which we also see two lizards crawling along the window jam toward each other. The other insects — a caterpillar, a dragonfly, a fly, a beetle and, at the top, a grasshopper — are all depicted in true-to-life poise. The much nibbled fruit leaves add greatly to the painting's atmosphere and underscore the sense of transiency. Among the shells, we recognize: the Indo-Pacific *Conus marmoreus* and *Murex haustellum* and the Indonesian left-whorled snail, *Amphidromus*, on the window sill; the West Indian *Cittarium pica* and other mainly Indo-Pacific species, such as *Conus omaria* and *Conus textile*, on the table. This painting was made during the period when Van der Ast was living in Delft, from 1632 until his death in 1657, probably in the 1640s. Through the window on the left we look out on a building which resembles the town clerk's office, which is still standing today. The Wan-li vase is decorated with ducks and a duckling and is mounted on a gilt foot.

Jan Baptist Fornenburgh of The Hague worked more or less in the style of Van der Ast. When he used Ming vases in his flower pieces, whether in paintings or in drawings on vellum, they were vases with large birds, sometimes in flight, such as in cat. no. 22. In fig. 6.6, a detail, we see an insect on the surface of the vase near the bill of a flying bird of paradise, a nice trompe l'œil effect. A white butterfly, which flies during the day, can be interpreted as the counterpart of the earthly caterpillar, or of the moth, which flies only at night. The mouse is often the symbol of Gula, gluttony. The parrot, like the Ming vase, was an item of great luxury.[23] The theme of transiency is strongly suggested here by the cracks in the plinth and the background wall and by the fallen leaves.

Dirck van Delen is primarily known as an architectural painter who depicted both interiors and exteriors. The niches and paneling in the only still life that we know by him (cat. no. 23) reflect his architectural orientation.[24] In this work in the Boymans-Van Beuningen Museum in Rotterdam we see a single tulip in a *kendi* similar to the one we saw in Jan Brueghel's painting (cat. no. 18). The decoration on Dirck van Delen's *kendi*, however, almost certainly sprang from his own imagination. The tulip is the rare and precious *Generael der Generaelen van Gouda*. That Van Delen should have painted such a still life with a tulip in 1637 is not surprising. This was the year in which tulipomania reached its peak and the bulb market crashed. It was easy for contemporary moralists to associate this historical event with vanity, and the shells in the painting therefore have clear meaning as symbols of vanity. They are: the Indo-Pacific *Murex ramosus* (Thorny Horn), to the left at the back; the *Nerita polita*, on the left in the middle; the larger Argonautilus, *Argonauta argo*, at the front; and to its left, the *Strombus fasciatus* from the Red Sea.

Two still lifes by Johannes Goedaert, who like Dirck van Delen came from Middelburg in Zeeland, are known to us. Both represent flowers in a Chinese vase.[25] They reveal the same positive characteristics as his drawings and writings: considerable knowledge of natural science, a keen observation, and accuracy in depiction. Fig. 6.7, a detail of the blue-winged grasshopper (*Oedipoda coerulescens*), shows how Goedaert could achieve the clarity of a drawing with a fine painter's brush in oil. In his book *Metamorphosis Naturalis* he relates how caterpillars turn into butterflies and also how the metamorphosis of other insects takes place. His observations were partly based on his own breeding tests. The engraving in

JAN BAPTIST VAN FORNENBURGH
Detail of cat.no. 23
Private Collection

JOHANNES GOEDAERT
Detail of cat.no. 25
Private Collection

DIRCK VAN DELEN
Museum Boymans-van Beuningen, Rotterdam

JOHANNES GOEDAERT
Private Collection

24 fig. 6.8 shows the same butterfly, a red admiral, as in cat. no. 24. Counterbalancing the ethereal butterfly in the diagonal corner of the composition, a snail represents the earthly element. In Goedaert's other flower piece a bumblebee is examining a *Rosa Mundi*, and an ant is crawling across a striking tulip that forms the top of a bouquet. Although the same intimate and poetic atmosphere emanates form both works, the result is surprisingly different. What a world of difference we see when we look at the great flower still life by Jan Davidsz.
25 de Heem (cat. no. 25) from the Gemäldegalerie in Dresden. Goedaert appeals directly to the heart, and his somewhat static naïveté is very charming, but De Heem opens up an entire new world. This is due not only to his mimetic virtuosity but also to the atmosphere ripe with meaning which he conjures up with explicit symbolic references, the strong light effects, the teaming insects and the vibrant color composition. His rendering of texture seems perfect when we look at the nacreous sheen on the surface of the Turbo shell, the reflection of the studio window in the glass vase, or the folds and tears in the paper. The poise of the three butterflies and the 16 other insects (13 species) is true to nature, and the large variety is noteworthy. The 25 varieties of flowers, the wheat and the fruit have been painted with unparalleled skill. We see here new and different elements, such as apple and pear blossoms, ears of grain and wild plants like white deadnettle, which we came across more than a hundred years earlier in Flemish religious paintings.

De Heem's approach to the symbolism of transiency is also new. On the document underneath the shell and skull we can read the inscription 'Memento Mori' and the signature of the artist; thus the artist has implicated himself in this reminder of death. The fly on the skull, an image that is familiar from early vanitas paintings, strengthens the vanitas theme.[26] The majority of the symbolic meanings attributed to the fly are connected to sin or corruption, and these are based on Ecclesiastes 10:1: 'Dead flies cause the ointment of the apothecary to send forth a stinking savour....'[27] The skull is wreathed with ivy, traditionally a symbol of immortality because it does not shed its leaves in winter,[28] thus symbolizing the hope of eternal life or immortal fame.[29]

Ears of wheat are a recurring theme in De Heem's flower paintings. The meaning of this motif as a resurrection symbol stems from the influential emblem book of Claude Paradin of 1557 that ran to many editions and was also published in translation (fig. 6.9).[30] It is the last emblem in the book. In the Dutch edition of 1615, which contains many additions, we read under the motto 'Spes altera vitae:' 'Another stronger hope of life after death makes us less unprepared to be deprived of worldly goods.'

The explanation continues: 'The grain and also the seeds of other herbs, sown or thrown over the earth and withered there, become green again and achieve a fresh and new growth: and so also the bodies of men, decayed by death, will rise again to glory and eternal joy by the universal resurrection.' We find the original source in John 12:24: 'Verily, verily, I say unto you: Except a corn of wheat fall into the ground and die, it abideth alone: but if it die, it bringeth forth much fruit.' More specifically, the ear of corn is the symbol of the Resurrection of Christ.

We can point to several paintings by De Heem which are related to this theme. In the collection of the Alte Pinakothek in Munich is a flower piece with a white lily at the top, the same Turbo shell to the right and a skull with a wreath of ivy and ears of grain on the left. A cruci-

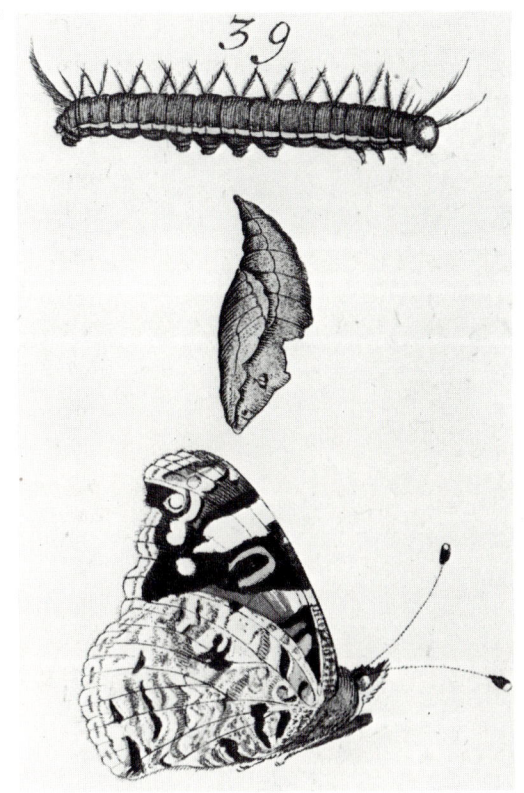

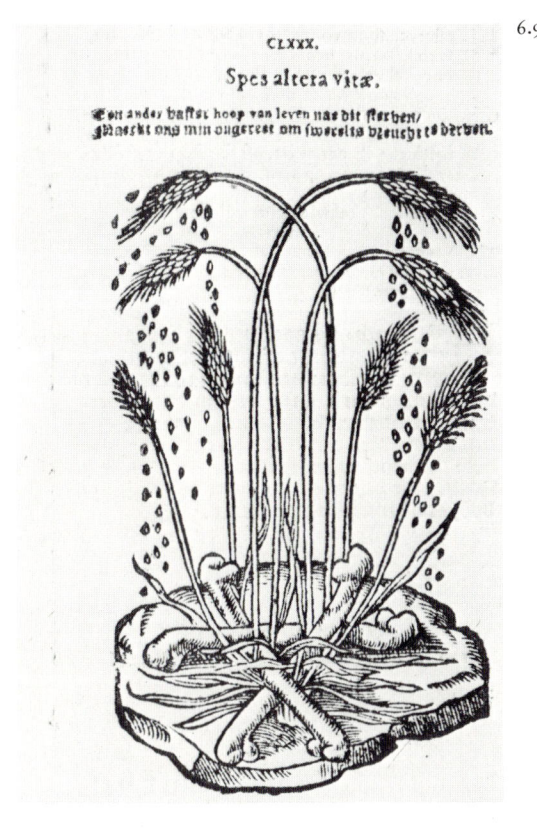

JOHANNES GOEDAERT
Red Admiral in 'Metamorphosis Naturalis,' 1662

CLAUDE PARADIN
Last Emblem of 'Devises Héroïques,' 1557

fix has been placed obliquely in front of the skull. The text of the letter refers to the 'Most Beautiful Flower.' Here the symbolism of Christ and the Virgin Mary has been combined with the symbolism of transiency. In the foreground a timepiece is lying on the table with the hands pointing to eleven o'clock: the last hour has struck.[31] A painting in the National Gallery in Dublin has a festoon of fruit with a skull on the right and the same crucifix seen from a different angle (fig. 6.10). The bread and the glass of wine on the left are Eucharist symbols. A snake, the symbol of Sin, is twisted round the foot of the cross. In a sculptured relief on the right we see cherubs playing, souls which have evidently already gained heaven.[32] The combination of a skull and a crucifix can also be found in depictions of St. Jerome and Mary Magdalene, where they allude to meditations on death and resurrection. In the festoon grapes, pomegranates and ears of corn play an important role. Grapes are explicitly symbols of Christ, and pomegranates are a symbol of the Church.[33] Without intimating that they are pendants, the paintings in Dresden and Dublin are certainly complementary to one another. Both are on canvas, and the measurements are nearly the same. Presumably all three works were created around 1653, a dating supported by dated works by De Heem. In all three paintings the symbolism transiency and resurrection is reinforced by caterpillars, butterflies and other insects.

25

JAN DAVIDSZ. DE HEEM
Galerie Alte Meister, Dresden

JAN DAVIDSZ. DE HEEM (former attribution)
Szépmüvészeti Múzeum, Budapest

JAN DAVIDSZ. DE HEEM
Festoon of Fruits, 1653
National Gallery of Ireland, Dublin

In the composition of the Dresden painting the repetition of lines and forms plays an important role, for example in the bent stems and stalks and the parallel curves of the shell and the skull. Is it only in the imagination that one can see a cross in the arrangement of the bouquet? The top flower in De Heem's bouquets is nearly always the most prominent. In about half of the approximately 20 flower pieces with genuine signatures by the artist an opium poppy is placed at the top, and in the others a clearly symbolic white lily, a sunflower or sometimes a tulip. The question arises whether the poppy occupies this place for purely decorative reasons. The poppy as an attribute can have contradictory meanings, as is so often the case with symbolism. The opium poppy can mean sleep and oblivion, or vigilance and memory. As the immature fruits provide the raw material for opium, the relationship with sleep is obvious; hence the interpretation of the opium poppy as an attribute of Venus.[34] Its association with vigilance is closely connected to the fact that attributes *in malo* are warnings, and as such the poppy appears in emblems, mottos and impresas with the words 'Per non dormire.'[35] As an attribute of Ceres (or Cybele) the opium poppy often has the connotation of fecundity, on account of its abundant seeds.[36] If De Heem introduced the poppy as a symbol on purpose, it is practically certain that he used it in the sense of vigilance. This was probably not based on the above-mentioned sources, as they were not generally known. He was perhaps inspired by a source as yet unknown to us or by popular association that had been handed down by tradition. However, it could also have been derived from the general belief that the opposite of what is meant *in malo* can be construed as a warning *in bono*.

Fruit pieces developed naturally from early 17th-century still lifes depicting meals, in which fruit always played an important role. Already in works of Osias Beert we come across still lifes with a Wan-li basin filled with fruit accompanied by only a few other relatively inconspicuous objects. It was only a small step for painters like Jacob van Hulsdonck, Jacob van Es, Frans Snyders and Alexander Adriaenssen to develop this further. Fig. 6.11 shows an extraordinarily fine fruit piece by Jacob van Hulsdonck which is in the J. Paul Getty Museum in Malibu, California.[37] It depicts lemons, oranges and pomegranate in a Chinese bowl, and orange blossoms help to evoke a sense of fragrance. It is not surprising that we detect a butterfly and a fly: a blue and a blue-bottle.

Adriaen van Utrecht and Joannes Fyt were later important fruit painters in Antwerp. In the northern Netherlands, after sporadic experiments by Ambrosius Bosschaert the Elder and Nicolaes Gillis, Balthasar van der Ast, Floris van Schooten and Roelof Koets became important painters of fruit still lifes.

Fruit pieces flourished after the debacle of the tulip trade around 1640. The impulses came partly from Antwerp, where Jan Davidsz. de Heem had settled in 1635. De Heem had developed a technique that was more painterly than the usual smooth glazing techniques of his predecessors, reflecting the influence of the freer brush strokes of Van Es and Snyders. An example by a follower is the still life with oysters in the National Museum of Budapest (cat. no. 26), in which the lemon peel was painted with the back of a thin brush and afterwards partly covered with a flowing layer of glazing. It is stylistically close to work by Christiaen Luyckx.

From the same museum is a fruit still life with a rummer by Abraham van Beyeren (fig. 6.12).

6.11

JACOB VAN HULSDONCK
Fruit Piece
J. Paul Getty Museum, Malibu (California)

117

PIETER CLAESZ
Private Collection

PIETER CLAESZ
Rijksmuseum, Amsterdam

6.12

ABRAHAM VAN BEYEREN
Fruits, Bread and Wine
Szépmüvészeti Múzeum, Budapest

Here again we see relatively broad brush strokes, but the differences from De Heem are considerable. De Heem combined in his paintings varying gradations of detail, using both quick, broad brush strokes and minutely elaborated ones. His techniques were astonishingly manifold, just like Rembrandt's, and at the same time he succeeded in building up a harmonious composition of colors, lines and planes. Van Beyeren painted fluidly and deftly, and one can appreciate his effects especially when viewing them from a distance. His is a different vision, and one of great artistry, but it did not find many followers. The later fruit pieces by Willem van Aelst and Jacob van Walscappelle, and even those of Jan van Huysum in the 18th century, are always, either directly or indirectly, connected to De Heem. This applies as well to their flower still lifes and is a further testimony to the greatness of this artist.

CHAPTER 7

SUMPTUOUSNESS IN SOBER TONES

The course of the 1620s witnessed profound changes in Dutch art, and the still life was not exempt from these. Among the changes was a coloristic restraint that pervaded many genres of painting and resulted in what has been have called the monochrome banquet piece. The artists most often identified with this style are Pieter Claesz and Willem Claesz. Heda, but others, such as Jan Jansz. den Uyl, Jan Jansz. Treck and others produced remarkable works. The new style appeared rather quickly, but we can see it evolving in certain works by artists of both the older and the younger generations.

As we saw in Chapter 3 above, the paintings of Nicolaes Gillis and Floris van Dijck are colorful displays of objects arrayed on broad tabletops seen from a high point of view. These and other characteristics of early banquet still lifes[1] can be seen in a work dated 1617 by Floris van Schooten (fig. 7.1),[2] who also lived in Haarlem. The arrangement of the objects, with a row of taller ones at the back, is the same as in the early work by Gillis of 1601. The table has been set with a white tablecloth on top of a red silk damask cloth. In fact, red tones accent this composition everywhere: in the red currants, the strawberries, the mulberries, the cherries and the foliage and flowers of the pronk goblet on the left. We can count as many as eleven Wan-li basins and bowls.[3]

Cut branches with berries, such as those in Van Schooten's still life of 1617, can also be seen in the works of Nicolaes Gillis. Gillis and Clara Peeters were very influential in the development of the banquet piece. Branches of red and white currants, black currants and gooseberries are also seen in the later works of Gillis[4] and in the early works of Pieter Claesz.[5] These paintings can hardly be described as colorful: pink and red are the only colors that catch the eye against a harmony of green, gray and white. It has been unknown until now that Gillis also began to paint banquet pieces in the monochrome style as Pieter Claesz and Willem Claesz. Heda did in the 1620s. Most of these works had been attributed to Pieter Claesz and sometimes had false signatures. An example of this is fig. 7.2, in which vestiges of the monogram NG are legible on the rim of the front pewter plate, with a date that can be read as 1625.[6] It is likely that in the beginning Gillis had influenced his young fellow-townsman Claesz but that the latter soon outstripped him and that Gillis later adopted some of the ideas of Claesz.[7]

Cat. no. 27 is undoubtedly an early work by Pieter Claesz painted around 1623. This paint- 27

29

PIETER CLAESZ
Galerie Alte Meister, Dresden

PIETER CLAESZ
Westfälisches Landesmuseum für Kunst und Kulturgeschichte
Münster (Federal Republic of Germany)

FLORIS VAN SCHOOTEN
Laidtable, 1617
Private Collection, formerly Lorenzelli Gallery, Bergamo (Italy)

NICOLAES GILLIS
Banquet Piece, 1625
Hoogsteder Gallery, The Hague

ing shows clearly the traces of Gillis's influence, for example in the overturned glass, the different sorts of berries and the basket with cheese. The top of a knife case is hanging over the edge of the table, the knife blade is resting on a slice of bread with strawberries, and the pewter plate protruding over the edge of the table provides a feeling of immediacy and strengthens the illusion of space. The point of view is lower than in the earlier Haarlem paintings, and we can see one side of the table, by means of which — together with the folds of the tablecloth — we can extend the lines of perspective to a vanishing point that lies at the upper left, outside the painting's space.

This early work by Pieter Claesz is not the first time that we come across a tazza. In the still lifes of Van Winghen, Beert, Flegel, Snyders, Brueghel and others, tazzas are often filled with sweetmeats, pastry, fruit or flowers. That was not their real function, however, as they were originally meant as drinking bowls for wine and, like pronk goblets, were handed round as a sign of friendship. We can see this illustrated in the Pers edition of Ripa's *Iconologia* (1644) under the motto 'Confermatione dell'Amicitia.'[8]

It is a small step from this painting to the monochrome *banketjes*, with their mainly gray, white and brown tones and a green that is attuned to them — a step that was taken in but two years. In most cases pronk objects are still present, such as the gilt tazza and the Ming plate, which in our painting is filled with butter and placed on top of the cheese. Soberness in coloring became a fashionable trend in the art of the still life, and remained so until around 1640, and even until after 1650 in the work of some artists. It could have been a reaction against the previous high-keyed palette with its many sharp and contrasting hues spread over the painting without a clear harmony. It could also express a tendency to moderation which developed as a consequence of the growing influence of Calvinism. The new narrower range of colors was also accompanied by an attunement in their clarity and pitch. The new sober tonality is seen in vanitas and fish still lifes and is even noticeable in the flower pieces of Roelandt Savery and Balthasar van der Ast. Later to an even greater degree, it can be found in works by Anthony Claesz and Hans Bollongier. Around 1640 still lifes — at any rate flower pieces and pronk still lifes — again became more colorful, now, however, with a deliberately harmonious orchestration of values and hues. This broad line of development in the use of color was not confined to the still life. The history of the Dutch landscape shows, more or less simultaneously, a similar trend in which the more colorful style (e.g. that of Gillis van Coninxloo) is followed by the monochrome manner of Jan van Goyen. This in turn made way for the fuller yet balanced chromatic scale of Jacob van Ruysdael. The monochrome tendency can also be observed in marine paintings and in historical and allegorical works of the 1620s and thirties.[9]

While Pieter Claesz continually introduced new objects into his paintings, there was at the same time a tendency to simplification and clarity in composition. We see that he starts making small panels with only a few objects, but those works are full of atmosphere and even occasionally achieve monumentality.[10] In the 1650s Claesz was still painting monochrome *banketjes*. Cat. no. 28, from the Rijksmuseum in Amsterdam, is an example which dates from 1647. The small Ming dish on the saltcellar is filled with capers, the pickled flower buds of the Capparis shrub from the Mediterranean area. Capers can also be seen sprinkled

WILLEM CLAESZ. HEDA
Rijksmuseum, Amsterdam

WILLEM CLAESZ. HEDA
Private Collection

on the fried mackerel. Hexagonal 'diabolo' saltcellars were made in both silver and pewter; the one in the painting is probably pewter.

In a number of still lifes by Claesz a fish occupies the central position. The banquet still life with a herring or a mackerel has a long tradition which began with Hieronymus Francken and was still flourishing in the 1670s in the work of Willem van Aelst. If such still lifes with fish — or fish still lifes in general — do indeed convey any symbolic message, one could think of the cryptic legend beneath an engraving of a kitchen by Jacob Matham (after Pieter Aertsen?), fig. 7.3: 'IESUS IN FRACTIONE PANIS AGNOSCITUR' (Jesus is recognized by the breaking of the bread).[11] This could be a *double entendre* in which the fish, because of its shape, can also be interpreted as a symbol of sensuality. The fish as a symbol of Christ was already in use in Roman times. In this engraving with fish in the foreground we see that someone has drawn back the curtain in the background to show us Christ at the Supper at Emmaus, where he was recognized by his disciples when he broke bread. The double meaning may also be inferred by the central position of the lobster, an animal that can crawl both backwards and forwards. We shall refer to the lobster again later in this study. Fish could, perhaps, have still another meaning: it was, generally speaking, food for the poor. In this sense fish could contrast with precious comestibles or objects. Salmon, which occurs in many banquet pieces, is known to have been a very cheap food.

7.3

JACOB MATHAM
Kitchen Piece with Fishes, Engraving

Apart from *banketjes*, we know that Claesz later made some fish still lifes and tobacco pieces, as well as a number of vanitas still lifes and pronk still lifes with vanitas elements. An early example (1624) is cat. no. 29, from the Gemäldegalerie in Dresden. The skull on the right, almost hidden behind a book, had been invisible for a long time, as a previous owner must have found it a lugubrious detail. When the work was cleaned recently the skull was brought to light again. A technical examination revealed that the curtain was also original and had not been added later, as had previously been thought. It makes a 'stage set' of the display on the table. The objects can be seen as vanitas symbols. We recognize among the shells the large Nautilus; the spotted Pica, to the left of the timepiece; and the Marbled Conus, to the right. The costly gold watch can be seen as an admonition of the inexorable passage of time. The red and white carnations are symbols of the Passion and purity of Christ. We see the familiar *Miles Christianus* on the pronk goblet, high above the symbols of temporality and redemption. In the background to the left we can see a couple making love in the doorway of a country house: the life of the young, now blossoming with the possibility of fertility and riches, will be short-lived. It is not easy to trace the date and maker of the pronk goblet in this painting. Most of these goblets belong to an 'international' style, made in several places in Germany and the Netherlands. The cup in cat. no. 29 can be compared to the earliest surviving object by the Utrecht silversmith Adam van Vianen, made in 1594.[12] A remarkable still life by Pieter Claesz in the Westfälisches Landesmuseum in Münster (cat. no. 30), a work painted in 1636 despite the fact that its date has always been misread as 1634, is close to what we call a pronk portrait. The centerpiece of the composition is not a pronk goblet but a nautilus cup. Again to the right a skull is half-hidden under a book. This motif of a half-hidden skull under a book is seen in a number of vanitas paintings by Claesz, e.g. in a work of 1634 in the J. Paul Getty Museum in Malibu, California.[13] What is the meaning of a book in this context? A book can either imply wisdom (or the acquisition of wisdom) or the vanity of gathering knowledge that does not reach beyond earthly life. This symbolism was linked to the belief that the spirit can triumph over material things and thus attain immortality. In addition to the old literary sources we shall consider here several recent authors who have treated this subject.[14] Sambucus (1564) devoted an emblem to the famous Venetian printer Paulus Manutius with the motto 'In morte vita' (In death there is life). In the explanation we read that by learning we can obtain fame in both life on earth and life hereafter: 'This is shown by the skull, the horn, the hourglass, the book, the laurel wreath of fame and the globe.'[15] Rollenhagen (1611) uses in his first emblem the motto 'Vivitur ingenio; caetera mortis erunt' (Man lives by the spirit, the rest is death's portion). He adds to this that man should study the sciences but should despise transient things. His illustration shows precious objects set out on a table. Among them are gold and silver articles, and nearby Death is holding a crown and scepter. Roemer Visscher (1614) calls reading 'herbs for the wild savage,' medicine for the uneducated to remedy their spiritual emptiness.[16] In the Pers edition of Ripa we read about the printing of books: '...From it we have obtained the knowledge of good and evil, of virtue and vice, of learning and ignorance: Through it Man has become immortal....'[17] A skull crowned with laurel leaves indicates eternal spiritual achievement, and the damaged and fragmentary books represent transiency.

The overturned glass in both still lifes could refer to 'emptiness', which was often linked

GERRIT WILLEMZ. HEDA
Private Collection

MAERTEN BOELEMA DE STOMME
Charles Roelofsz Gallery, Amsterdam

with vanity. We see in many vanitas still lifes a broken glass, indicating that life is just as vulnerable as glass. The document with wax seals and the burnt-out but still-smoking oil lamp need no explanation. The pomander on a gold chain is a token of vanity.

The splendid nautilus cup depicted in Claesz's painting has been preserved and is in the Toledo Museum of Art in Ohio. It was made by the Utrecht silversmith Jan Jacobsz. van Royesteyn in 1596.[18] We shall come across a modified version of it in one of Willem Kalf's still lifes (cat. no. 55). Perhaps the silversmith made two versions, or perhaps one or both of the artists has taken liberties. The large, toothy jaws on the nautilus cup are those of the whale which disgorged Jonah upon the shore.[19] He had spent three days and three nights in the belly of the animal after he had been cast into the sea by the crew.[20] The belly of the whale has been compared to the sepulchre of Christ, and the escape from the whale is seen as a prototype of the Resurrection, a sign of the hope of redemption and the salvation of the soul out of distress. Christ himself mentioned the experience of Jonah as a 'sign'.[21]

The stem of the beaker is a figure, sitting on a foot in the form of a dolphin. This reminds us of the story of Arion, the gifted singer from Lesbos who was forced to jump from a ship into the sea to escape from murderous sailors who coveted his wealth. Picked up by a dolphin who loved his music, Arion was brought back to the shore. In emblem books this tale evokes Virtue which spurns danger and triumphs over it. Arion and Jonah are linked to each other in Meyster (1579) and Joost van den Vondel.[22]

When we look analytically at the compositions of Pieter Claesz, we notice a striking rhythm of forms, a well-thought-out, harmonious and coherent construction. Such mastery as this we see in other great still-life painters as well, each applying it in his own individual manner. Again and again we see a repetition of horizontally aligned curves and ovals (for example in the plates and bowls), vertical curves (of the cups of the glasses and beakers), and lines which run obliquely through the compositions and sometimes converge in the foreground. Sometimes these sinuous rhythms are echoed in a single detail, such as a walnut. In the Münster painting the walnut has been carefully positioned between the belt pendant[23] and the skull. The smooth surfaces of the glass, the nautilus shell and the skull are also interesting repetitions, as are the small ovals of the chain links, the prunts of the glass and the handle of the oil lamp. We see other repetitions in the shapes of the teeth and fins of the nautilus cup, the thornlike projections on the prunts of the *roemer* and the wick of the lamp.

The vanitas pronk still lifes of Claesz are distant echoes of the work of Clara Peeters — e.g. the paintings shown in cat. no. 9 and fig. 4.8, both painted in 1612 and both containing a pronk goblet with a *Miles Christianus*. In fig. 4.8 we also see shells, a golden chain and a flower on the table.

The still lifes of Pieter Claesz and Willem Claesz. Heda, the two most important painters of monochrome banquet pieces, have often been confused, and the works of Heda and his son even moreso. In order to study the development of Claesz's work and to compare it to that of Heda, I have analyzed the dated *banketjes* of both artists and charted the data in tables. In the more than 100 works of Claesz we can see clear lines of development, but I will not go deeply into this here. Neither shall I discuss all the differences between Claesz and Heda, but I would like to mention a few significant points.

We see in the case of both painters that their brushwork gradually becomes broader and more fluent. They seem to have taken to heart, as many other painters did, the words of Carel van Mander, who wrote in 1604 that a painter must begin by working very precisely and only later should he develop a freer brush stroke.

Generally speaking, Claesz's brushwork is freer than that of Heda, who gave more attention to the rendering of details. From a technical point of view the work of Claesz seems closer to that of his fellow-townsman Frans Hals. Heda achieved a more optical vision by focusing on the depth of field in which objects lie, treating the foreground a little more superficially. Claesz usually painted simple objects, such as a pewter saltcellar, or herrings and onions, while Heda chose more luxurious objects, such as a knife with auricular ornament, or a silver ewer. Claesz, who was also a vanitas painter, occasionally depicted vanitas objects in his *banketjes*.

It is probable that Claesz began to work as an independent artist at an earlier age than Heda: a dated work by Claesz is known from as early as 1621, but by Heda not before 1629. Heda's earlier works must bear false signatures or have been wrongly attributed. At the beginning of the 1630s we see that Heda was a follower of Claesz, but he soon found his own way. In Heda's works the point of view, in general, is somewhat lower, and the compositions are such that the top of the triangle formed by the objects shifts more to the middle of the picture, while in Claesz's works it is nearer to the top. Heda was always on the lookout for new objects; these were often adopted later by Claesz. Claesz was the first to paint a saltcellar mounted on three columns. We see this from 1630 onwards, but Heda was the first to introduce cylindrical, engraved silver saltcellars, and hexagonal ones, in 1635 and 1642 respectively. Claesz in turn was the first to depict a *bekerschroef*, though Heda depicted them in more varieties. Heda also showed the way in the use of beer glasses: the waffle glass, in 1634; a pass-glass (a glass with notched threads around the body used for communal drinking), in 1637; and a glass with flat prunts, in 1642. Surveying their whole oeuvre one can say that Claesz's work is especially attractive in his smaller, simpler paintings, while Heda shows his strength in the larger pronk still lifes.[24]

The most serious problem in the study of Heda's oeuvre is that his paintings have not always been correctly distinguished from those of his son Gerret and some of his pupils. In Vroom (1980) this led to the same painting's being attributed to various artists, and to a definition of the styles of Willem and Gerret which, in my opinion, needs some correction.[25] It is known that in 1642 Willem had three pupils: his son Gerret, Hendrick Heerschop from Haarlem and Maarten Boelema from Leeuwarden.[26] From Van Mander we know that the work of pupils or apprentices was the lawful property of the master and that pupils could be called upon to assist in parts of a painting.[27] It is therefore possible that some works of 1642 and the years thereafter which carry Heda's signature are joint efforts. It is quite possible that Willem Heda used certain paintings from the preceding years as examples for his pupils to copy and that they were allowed to sign these with their own names if they were in great part by their own hands, even though the compositions were copied. Perhaps Cornelis Mahu from Antwerp was also an apprentice, as we know of several replicas of Heda's work signed by him.

Apart from paintings signed HEDA (usually with a date), we know of eight signed *jonge* HEDA,

35

JAN JANSZ. DEN UYL
Charles Roelofsz Gallery, Amsterdam

Jan Jansz. Treck
National Gallery, London

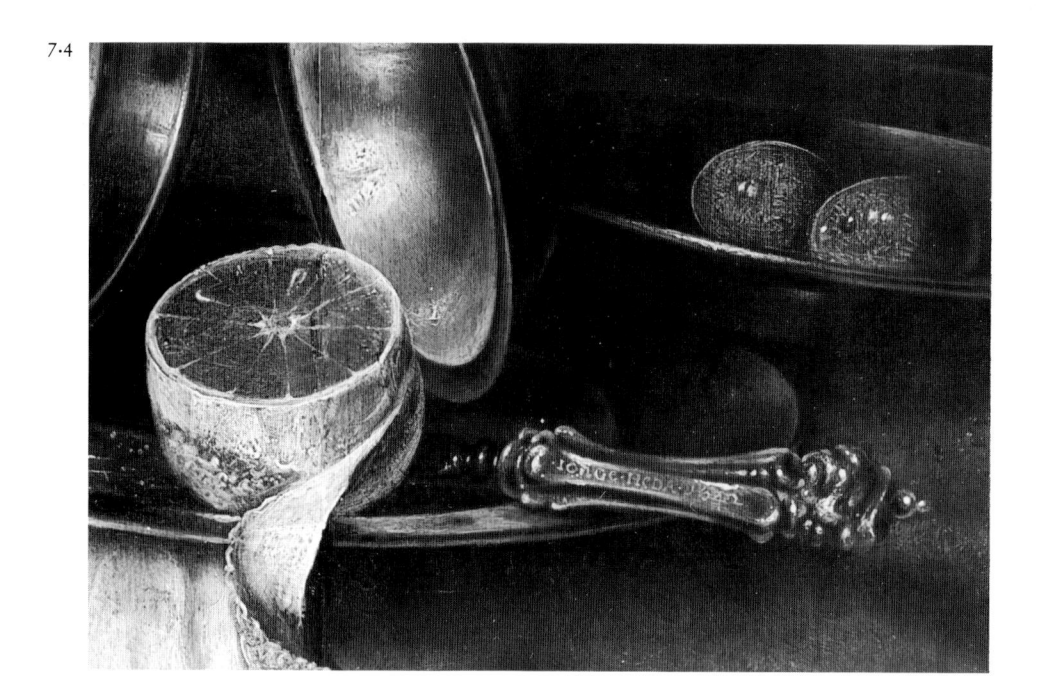

GERRET HEDA
Detail of a Painting, 1642
Rijksdienst Beeldende Kunst, The Hague

with dates between 1642 and 1644 (fig. 7.4);[28] eight paintings are signed *Gerret* HEDA (between 1644 and 1646) or GERRET HEDA *1646* (two examples), and one is signed ^G_HEDA · F · *1665*. Some of the signatures are now fragmentary. In others the words 'jonge', 'Gerret' or the initial 'G' have been rubbed out, probably in order to suggest an attribution to Willem Heda. Vroom (1980) wrote that a son of Willem died in or before 1649.[29] This is correct, but it is incorrect to state that it was his son Gerret, as Gerret was still listed as an active member of the Haarlem Guild in 1658.[30]

After examining the works of the generation of Heda followers we are better able to understand their development and to pinpoint some differences from the work of Willem Heda himself. First I must say that it is not always easy to distinguish between the works of these artists. Theoretically it is not impossible that, apart from Gerret, a second son was also a painter, a younger Willem who signed as 'jonge Heda.' In 1648 or 1649 a son died about whom we know nothing. The paintings that are signed 'jonge Heda' do indeed differ somewhat from the works signed 'Gerret Heda,' but the differences could be accounted for in the artistic development of a single painter. The paintings from 1642-1644 have stronger contours, with lighter lines around the darker colors of pewter, which makes for a somewhat harder impression. Later all the shades become softer. Personally I would prefer to follow the tradition of one son who painted, Gerret. This is also supported by the fact that in inventories paintings were listed as by 'the young Heda.'[31] From our research it seems likely that all the paintings after 1657 are by Gerret. Before 1642 he produced no works, but the father, Willem, was painting in a vertical format as early as 1638, which has confused art historians, since this format has usually been considered a specific characteristic of Gerret. One of the differences between father and son — and the one that is the most noticeable in the period directly after 1642 — is the degree of pictorial unity, which is greater in Willem's work. An objective criterion for distinguishing the works of the two is the degree of overlapping of objects, which indeed can be quantified. Another is the distribution of objects over the total surface area of the painting, which can also be expressed in objective values.[32] In Gerret's work the tall objects extend relatively higher above the others, while in Willem's the difference in height is less and the transition more gradual. With Gerret we often see objects that are tilted at a small angle to the horizontal, usually ascending toward the left, while with Willem horizontal lines dominate, or the slanting lines are more concealed or run in shifting directions. There are many more differences, for instance a more crumpled tablecloth often contributes to a certain restlessness in the works of Gerret.

In contrast to Vroom, who does not attribute a single dated work from the period 1645-1647 to Willem, I am of the opinion that both Willem and Gerret were painting at that time. Works signed HEDA were made by the father, and works signed HEDA or all the signed works with an F (for Fecit) added to the signature were painted by Gerret.[33] It must also be said that Gerret, in his later works from around 1650 onwards, surpassed his father in quality. It was only during a short period, around 1647, that some works are really difficult to distinguish on grounds of style. Gerret was at his best about 1647 and 1648.

Cat. no. 31, from the Rijksmuseum in Amsterdam, is a work by Willem Claesz. Heda of 1634. The composition is similar to that of a work of 1630 with a different tazza in the same place. The latter also has a deep pewter plate, a lemon, walnuts, hazelnuts, a *roemer* and a knife.[34] In Willem Heda's paintings the presence of a silver tankard and a knife with a golden handle are unique. The combination of walnuts and hazelnuts is only seen in his early period (a constant feature in the work of Pieter Claesz). Walnuts disappear quickly and almost completely from Heda's work. The silver beer tankard is a German product, close to one made by Elias Geyer in Leipzig about 1610.[35]

Cat. no. 32, also from 1634, is a *banketje* with rather expensive food, a Ming basin and a knife with an ivory and ebony handle. A sheet of paper from an almanac has been twisted into a cone and filled with pepper, which, together with cloves, nutmeg and mace, was an expensive foreign spice. A sheet from an almanac represents in vanitas still lifes the fleetingness of time, and together with costly pepper it links the themes of transiency and vanity. The silver spoon is known as a *torentgenslepel* (little tower spoon) because the top looks like a tower. Examples of such spoons still exist. The sort of sauce that we see in the Ming basin is a kitchen secret. We can, however, divulge that in still lifes with oysters little *façon the Venise* glass jugs are seen which are probably filled with vinegar. Cloves and mustard are most often seen in combination with ham.

A larger, more extensive *banketje*-pronk still life of 1635 is the panel in the Rijksmuseum, Amsterdam (fig. 7.5).[36] A twisted glass jug for vinegar stands behind the oysters beside the cylindrical, chased silver saltcellar. We recognize the tazza from the painting of 1634, cat. no. 31. The pronk goblet reminds us of the painting by Pieter Claesz from 1624, but the particulars of design are different. The pewter jug is an example of the influence of Jan Jansz. den Uyl, about whom we shall speak later. It seems as if Heda has wanted to give a summing-up of all his talents in his large-scale compositions.

7.5

WILLEM CLAESZ. HEDA
Pronk Still Life with Oysters, 1635
Rijksmuseum, Amsterdam

33 Cat. no. 33 is a magnificent work of 1647, but it is a painting which makes one hesitate over the attribution to Willem or to Gerret Heda. On the one hand, it could easily belong to Willem's oeuvre because of its balanced composition and its atmosphere of grandeur and relative calm. On the other hand, one sees a number of characteristics of Gerret, and the painting could well represent the culmination of his development in which he reached maturity. We must in any case conclude that if this piece is by Gerret it is in no way inferior to the works which his father Willem made in the 1640s. I support Vroom's attribution to Gerret, and the signature confirms this. Also by Gerret is the splendid, related work from the same year belonging to the Staatliches Museum in Schwerin (with oysters instead of a mackerel), while the brilliant, large canvas in the Hermitage in Leningrad, painted in 1648[37], shows Gerret's influence on his father. At this point Gerret had reached the height of his talent, as can also be seen later in a few pieces of this quality, while Willem had already passed his peak by 1642.

The rendering of texture in cat. no. 33 is perfect. In a delicate manner the differences between copper, pewter and silver have been precisely defined. There are still examples of this accolade-shaped platter in existence. An example of such a platter made by the Amsterdam silversmith Lucas Draef in 1647 is illustrated by Dirkse (1980). The tilted berkemeier affords the artist a chance to demonstrate his skill in foreshortening. The silver jug is close to one made by Evert Kettwyck in Hamburg about 1640.[38] The piled pewter plates were copied from Jan Jansz. den Uyl. The small quantity of wine in the *berkemeier* and the centrally placed *façon de Venise* flute glass are not necessarily signs of a finished meal but could also be admonitions of moderation.

Maerten Boelema, as mentioned already, was a pupil of Willem Heda in 1642. Cat. no. 34 is one of his best works and was painted in that year. We can see by comparing it to a work by Willem Heda of 1641 (fig. 7.6, from the Musée des Beaux-Arts in Strasbourg) that he was still very much under Heda's influence.[39]

Boelema's works distinguish themselves by their brownish tone. In his later compositions he showed in his choice of objects that he had become less dependent on his teacher, using silver which had been made in Friesland, his place of origin. In cat. no. 34 we see an empty nautilus cup lying on its side. The same one is seen in Heda's compositions, though sometimes with the figure of Fortuna on the top with a bulging sail in her hands. The ham is as usual accompanied by a mustard pot, but a silver one of this shape is now unknown.

Less well-known than Heda, Jan Jansz. den Uyl was, nevertheless, an artist of extraordinary gifts. Den Uyl had a short and stormy career. His earliest dated still life, painted in 1632, is in

WILLEM CLAESZ. HEDA
Still Life with a Nautilus Cup, 1641
Musée des Beaux-Arts, Strasbourg

JAN JANSZ. DEN UYL
Banquet Piece with Plovers' Egg, 1632
Národní Galerie, Prague

the Národní Galerie in Prague (fig. 7.7).⁴⁰ He was already ill by 1639 and died in 1640, a respected artist and a well-off citizen of Amsterdam. Rubens possessed three works by Den Uyl, and Rembrandt was the owner of several. One of his most beautiful pieces is a vanitas still life with books in the Rijksmuseum in Amsterdam, with the reflection of an owl in a pewter jug.⁴¹ Den Uyl usually 'signed' his works with the reflection of an owl (the Dutch word for owl was *uyl*). Reflections of owls can, in fact, be seen in several places in the still life in cat. no. 35, a late work painted probably around 1638. The reflection can be most clearly seen in the cover of the pewter jug, but there are also vague impressions of an owl or an owl's head in other places. (The same applies in a number of other still lifes by Den Uyl, although not everyone seems to be able to detect these owls.⁴²) The silver saltcellar with vertical ridges in this work is of a type not known to have survived. The lobed silver cup lying on its side is probably what was known as a *Hansje-in-de-kelder* (Little John in the cellar). When the cup is filled with wine, a small doll floats to the top through a little hole in the bottom. These bowls were used to congratulate a woman, and to wish her well, when she announced that she was in the happy expectation of a child. The painting could, in fact, be an occasional piece, commissioned at the birth of a child, since the cup is lying on its side. A similar cup is known by the Dordrecht silversmith Jan Hermansz. van Ossevoort, made in 1622.⁴³ This painting is a true exercise in the definition of the textures of various materials: pewter, gold, glass and porcelain, as well as silver in both mat and gleaming finishes. An unusual peculiarity of Den Uyl's works is that certain objects are seen through glass; another is the very subtle greenish reflection of the cloth in the pewterware.

Den Uyl worked now and again with his brother-in-law, Jan Jansz. Treck, who was ten years younger than he and also died at an early age. Among the latter's most beautiful works is cat. no. 36 from the National Gallery in London, a work painted in 1649. The atmosphere is completely different from that in Heda's work of the same period. This is partly due to the warmer, browner tonality and also to the less orderly composition. The rather rustic pewter jug, the vine leaves and the surprisingly colorful accent of the red cherries (or, in another work, of berries) contribute to this atmosphere. Although Treck copied much from Den Uyl, he clearly introduced his own ideas into his works. One of his characteristics was the use of vine branches around pewter jugs. The silver spoon and the silver knife are decorated with auricular ornaments. Such knifes also appear in paintings by the Hedas. Spoons with auricular ornaments are known to us from this period, around 1650, but similar knifes have only survived from a later date. We can compare the one in the painting to an object by Johannes Lutma of Amsterdam, made in 1648, one year before the execution of the still life.⁴⁴ In the jug can be seen the reflections of the nearby objects and the artist's studio. It is obvious that the painter enjoyed his work from the manner in which he signed it, namely in a coat of arms, as if it had been embroidered in the cloth. We can still partake in his enjoyment 330 years later.⁴⁵

CHAPTER 8

DE HEEM AND HIS CIRCLE

Jan Davidsz. de Heem was born in 1606, the son of David de Heem (Utrecht, 1570-1632), a painter by whom no works are known. Jan's earliest works are in the style of Balthasar van der Ast, with whom he had studied in Utrecht. Jan Davidsz. moved to Leiden in 1626 and there he worked in various still-life formats, more or less following the monochrome tendency. He painted still lifes with books, a type of vanitas still life, breakfast pieces influenced by Pieter Claesez (but usually with grapes or other fruit), stable pieces with kitchen utensils, and pronk still lifes in sober colors. Jan married in 1626 and moved with his family to Antwerp in 1635. There he developed the large-scale lavish still life with a landscape vista in the background, a type of work that had a widespread influence throughout Europe. It is known that he came back to the northern Netherlands quite often. Some of his works are thought to have been made there (in Utrecht, 1649), and he was a member of the Utrecht Guild of St. Luke between 1669 and 1672. He died in Antwerp in 1683 or 1684.[1]

Jan Davidsz. de Heem was an enormously successful painter, in his own time as well as later. He possessed not only the most prodigious technique but also a protean inventiveness which enabled him to introduce many innovations that were adopted by his colleagues. He was the most highly-esteemed still-life painter in the world, not just during his lifetime but ever since, except for a period during the 18th century when some critics awarded the palm to Jan van Huysum. It is therefore not surprising that his works were widely copied, even while he lived.[2]

De Heem's success was grounded in the integration of the different methods, tendencies and ideas of his contemporaries, which in turn led him to new and original concepts. He absorbed, while still young, the style of Balthasar van der Ast, as can be clearly seen in his early fruit pieces (painted up to 1628). He also absorbed the ideas of Jacques de Gheyn the Younger, as is shown in his book still lifes. He was further influenced by Pieter Claesz in his banquet pieces, and finally by some vanitas painters from Leiden. Jan Davidsz. brought a compelling sense of atmosphere to works in the monochrome style by emphasizing the shimmer of light on the surfaces of precious objects which he gave a dominate role, along with fruits and other foods depicted with unparalleled sensitivity. Gradually he violated the severity of the monochrome tonality of his contemporaries, introducing red or reddish hues to add tension. Thus the lobster which he painted in 1634 in the still life from the Staats-

JAN DAVIDSZ. DE HEEM
Staatsgemäldegalerie, Stuttgart

Jan Davidsz. de Heem
Rijksdienst Beeldende Kunst, The Hague

37 galerie in Stuttgart (cat. no. 37) achieves its stunning effect. When we compare this work to one of his first still lifes in this genre (fig. 8.1, of 1632)[3], we can appreciate De Heem's breakaway from the monochrome tradition and how quickly he distanced himself from painters like Pieter Claesz, Willem Heda and Jan den Uyl. He succeeded by tinging the reds and other hues which might have made a harsh contrast with hints of silvery gray or bronze, thus attaining a harmony of colors which contributed to the sense of atmospheric units. His light effects are also striking and seem to be produced by a light entering obliquely from the left. Not only are the colors in subtle balance, but the composition is also unspoiled by any exaggerated piling-up of objects. The lemon peel has the supple curl which a thin and already somewhat dried-out peel has by nature, and it contrasts subtly with the nautilus shell on its silver stand. The tone of the *bekerschroef* fits beautifully between the lobster, the peaches and the silver beaker. Curves and horizontal lines alternate in a well-balanced pattern, while the diagonal thrust of the beaker is continued in the lines of the wall above on the right. The berkemeier glass is empty, and the position of the beaker suggests that it is empty too. This beaker is not heavily chased but is nearly smooth. A smooth beaker is rare in still lifes. The prototype, as far as we know, comes from Culemborg, The Netherlands, and was made around 1606.[4]

De Heem's brushwork is thin and fluent in certain places, but in others the paint is applied in a thick impasto. Such variations in technique within a given painting become even more

8.1

JAN DAVIDSZ. DE HEEM
Pronk Still Life with a Nautilus Cup, 1632
Barber Institute of Arts, Birmingham

striking in his later works. It is characteristic of a great master that his technique and style cannot be forced into oversimplified ideas of chronological development, as he is often able to use them in all their varieties at various moments in his career.

In Antwerp, the city of Peter Paul Rubens, De Heem encountered a much more courtly and expansive style than he had known in his native Utrecht. He absorbed the broader brush technique, the larger sense of scale, greater dynamic range and varied palette, and especially the spatial effects of Frans Snyders and his Flemish colleagues. These characteristics he amalgamated with the more intimate and static tonal compositions of the Dutch, creating a new form of still life. In these large-sized, elaborate and opulent works, we find combinations of objects arrayed on several planes, new compositional elements like pillars and vistas of landscapes beyond a curtain, and a new color harmony which is masterfully balanced between monochrome tonality and coloristic richness.

The famous pronk still life from the Musée du Louvre (fig. 8.2), painted in 1640, was possibly the first example.[5] The curtain with tassels, the lute and the gilt goblet are among the new elements. The spatial complexity of this work is staggering in comparison to anything we have seen before. The bronze wine cooler, in the foreground at the right, and the lute, leaning against the table to the left, establish the plane of the table with the main still-life composition as a middle ground, which is further defined by the background with its curtain, the walls, the pillar and the view of palatial architecture and a landscape.

JAN DAVIDSZ. DE HEEM
Pronk Still Life with a World Map, 1640
Musée du Louvre, Paris

JAN DAVIDSZ. DE HEEM
Pronk Still Life with Shells, 1642
Sale Christie's, New York, 1988

In 1642 De Heem painted what has to be considered as his absolute magnum opus (fig. 8.3). In size it is his largest work;[6] it is also his most complicated, the peak achievement at the end of a development in which all his mastery is brought to bear. This remarkable painting[7] was probably a direct commission from the English royal family for the decoration of Windsor Castle. We know that King Charles I had a work by Jan Davidsz. de Heem in his collection; it is described in the inventory as follows: 'Baeht bij de king don by hemeson itm a pis in a blak fram auff some silffr shel and wijt wijnpot standing opan a tabel.'[8] Most descriptions in this catalogue are as short as this, often even shorter. The shells and the wide wineglass are conspicuous elements in this work.

The large table is set on a terrace, bordered by three pillars and looking over a landscape, with a river and a boat under full sail in the distance behind trees and a town. The small table with shells in the foreground and the chair with a lute (theorbe) articulate the space in front of the large table. The vine climbing over the wall and the landscape are broadly brushed to establish a background for the still life, which is filled with subtle and delicate observations.

The transparent flesh of the sliced lemon and the many delicate reflections throughout the painting are thinly and transparently painted, contrasting with the heavy impasto in such details as the citrus peels and the highlights on silver and gold ware, especially the goblet. This varied touch strengthens the composition and adds to its visual unity. The painter's workshop can be recognized in a reflection on one of the copper nails and on the knobs of the gilt goblet; in both cases we can see the artist at his easel.

The color scheme is harmonious. Brighter colors dominate the center, with yellowish shades and silvery gray along both sides of an imaginary diagonal from upper left to lower right. Red and pink tones are spread mainly along the other diagonal. The brighter parts are kept in soft contrast to the greenish, bluish and grayish hues of the background.

The shells include species from the East and West Indies.[9] The silver saltcellar is very close to somewhat later examples produced in Amsterdam in 1646. They were probably made by Anthony Grill.[10] The *bekerschroef* is related to another one attributed to Anthony Grill, dated 1642,[11] the year in which this painting was made.

For a fuller understanding of the meaning of his still lifes De Heem himself (and also his brother David and sons Cornelis and Jan Jansz.) gave us some clues in the form of legends and inscriptions on some of his works. The following texts are examples, and, in my opinion, they are applicable also to many works without such texts by De Heem and his contemporaries. A vanitas piece, with a recorder and a watch, dated 1652, in the Nostitz Gallery in Czechoslovakia,[12] bears the inscription 'SPIEGEL' (mirror), and the little note says: 'Hoe dat je pypt of hoeje fluyt/ o Mensch, Dat is/ u Erve, / t'sy ryck, arm, geleert of bott, / dat leeuen heeft, moet sterve' (No matter how you squirm or squeak, oh Man, this is your Fate: Whether rich or poor, learned or dumb, what lives, must die). One observes a skull with a fly, signifying decay, and several other objects implying transiency, for example the withering rose. The watch clearly indicates that the end is near: the hand is pointing at five to twelve.

A related vanitas painting, in the Musée Royaux des Beaux-Arts in Brussels,[13] contains several similar objects. It includes a traverse flute and a big recorder, the latter leaning against a pillar. The vista of a landscape under an evening sky, with a vine along the open window, is seen on the right. Texts on the books read: 'Rekening' and 'Navolging Christi' (Account and Imitation of Christ); this is a translation of *De Imitatione Christi* by Thomas à Kempis. A slip of paper protruding from a book reads 'BIBLIA', and a label on a flask says 'Aqua vita.'

A large sumptuous still life in the Kunstakademie in Vienna[14] bears two elaborate inscriptions on letters. One is hardly legible but it refers, as one can infer from the words that are legible, to Heaven's Blessing, Hope, Fortune, Happiness and Prosperity. The other inscription reads: 'De schoonste die mijn oogh oyt sach / die metter sonne maackt den dach / en mette nacht sluijt's hemels oogen / die doet mijn siecke herte drooghen / dat soete schepsel Aerdigh dier / dat goddelijck vonckie vier / doet stadich mijn gemoet vermijen / als d'heete son de landerijen' (The most beautiful that my eye ever met / that by the sun generates the day / and by the night closes heaven's eyes / that is the comfort of my sick heart. / That sweet and pretty earthly creature, / that divine spark of fire / does always give pleasure to my mind / like the hot sun does to the land).[15] The paintings can possibly be understood as an allusion to the second marriage of Jan Davidsz. in 1644.

8.4

JAN DAVIDSZ. DE HEEM
Niet hoe veel... (Not how much...), 1652
Private Collection, formerly Kraus Gallery, Paris

A work of 1651 (fig. 8.4)[16] bears the inscription on the large glass vessel: 'NIET hoe veel' (Not how much), and another work, of which only copies are known,[17] is inscribed 'Niet hoe veel, Maer hoe Eel' (Not how much but how noble, or, it is not the quantity that counts but the quality). Both works depict fruit, wine and crayfish. De Heem's exhortation to moderation is echoed later in Samuel van Hoogstraeten's *Inleyding tot de hooge schoole der schilderconst* (Introduction to the Superior School of Painting), in which he advises young painters to apply moderation in their arrangements and adds: '...You should not overburden your work with too many unnecessary things: as De Heem has already written, 'Niet hoe veel, maer hoe eel.' A host of objects which do not perform any function is disgusting.'[18]
Temperance and Vanity are probably the central themes of the painting of 1642, at least if we want to seek symbolism in it. Could the sailing boat be a metaphor for Man who is dependent on the winds or the forces around him but, in some ways, is able to control them, so that Fate, to a certain extent, is in his own hands?[19]
Another of these large, lavish still lifes by De Heem, probably painted before or in 1645, is

that in the Rijksdienst Beeldende Kunst in The Hague (cat. no. 38).[20] There are several characteristics that correspond to the work of 1642: the small table and the chair in right foreground, the pillar and the curtain, and the wall with vine leaves in the background. No example has been preserved of the rich repoussé silver basin in the front, decorated with strawberries, morning glory, tulips and roses. The gilt goblet is related to one from Nürnberg of the early 17th century.[21] The *bekerschroef* is known in a work by De Heem's of 1641[22] and is also included in fig. 8.3, of 1642. We see the same object in the later work of other artists. The stem is in the form of a putto sitting on a sphere with a flower in his hand. The pepper pot is a rare object in still lifes. A remarkable detail of this painting is the broken pillar at the upper right, on the base of which a snail is crawling. A pillar can be a symbol of spiritual strength and steadfastness,[23] but a broken pillar points rather to transiency. The snail is usually a symbol of 'earthly disposition'[24] and sluggishness, but can also mean cautiousness.[25] The eucharistic interpretation of the bread, wine and grapes in this type of composition has been proposed earlier in this study. The goldfinch, above right, was a well-known symbol of Christ, or a symbol of man's soul which always returns to Christ.[26] It is a bird that seeks its food among the thistles.

The Seville orange, in the right foreground on a velvet cushion, could be interpreted as the fruit of the Knowledge of Good and Evil. It also played a role in the Judgment of Paris. The three golden apples which Hercules succeeded in obtaining from the garden of the Hesperides became a symbol for the three virtues of a hero: reconciliation after anger, moderation and contempt for lust.[27]

We see in the center of the painting a partly-cut melon. This, or slices of melon, can be observed in many paintings of laid tables and pronk still lifes and might be associated with the theme of moderation. Melons were thought to produce insanity when eaten in large amounts. Dodoens (Dodonaeus) warned, in 1554, against consuming too much cucumber: '...It yeeldeth small nourishment & evil, insomuch that the immesurable use thereof, fylleth the vaynes with colde noughtie humours, the whiche (because they may not be connected into good blood) doo at the length bryngh foorth long and great agues and other diseases, as Galen writeth.' Dodoens states that melons are of the same nature. In a similar way he quotes, in his 1644 edition, Aëtius's compilation *Tetrabiblion* (Aëtius of Amida was a physician at the Byzantine court in the sixth century). Dodoens' herbal was very popular, and several reprints and translations were produced. Jacques Pons, who was the first to make a study of melons, in 1583, also warned against overindulging and illustrated his argument with examples of famous persons who died from eating too much melon. He made King Henry IV, to whom he later became personal physician, an example, since he loved melons a great deal. Vicaire, in 1607, wrote a poem entitled 'Le proces du melon' in memory of one of Henry's attacks of indigestion due to swallowing melon.[28]

Cat. no. 39, a painting from the Boymans-Van Beuningen Museum in Rotterdam, has to be dated around 1648.[29] The lobster in this case, as in many pronk still lifes, is a striking feature. Contrary to crabs and shrimps from the North Sea, lobsters are not fished off the Dutch coast, since they inhabit a rocky sea bottom. A supply of fresh lobsters was therefore not a simple matter, and the same goes for grapes, figs, peaches and citrus fruit.

39

JAN DAVIDSZ. DE HEEM
Museum Boymans-van Beuningen, Rotterdam

JAN DAVIDSZ. DE HEEM
Thomas Brod Gallery, London

The symbolism of the lobster and the crab is practically identical. It is based on the fact that they are able to crawl backwards as well as forwards and do not move in a straight line, which can lead to both negative and positive interpretations. In a woodcut of Jost Amman (Zürich, 1539-1591, Nürnberg) we see three lobsters drawing a chariot in three different directions. On the chariot is a figure of Fortuna, and above it floats Fama, fame.[30] Much earlier Giotto had painted the lobster as an attribute of the allegorical Inconstantia (Instability), who is trying to keep her balance on a rolling ball.[31] Also in Ripa the lobster is an attribute of Inconstantia.[32] Its crooked progress makes it a 'rake'.[33] Roemer Visscher uses the crab which moves in all directions with the motto 'Don't teach it to your children,' meaning that one should not set a bad example by drinking, gambling or whoring.[34] The maneuverability of the lobster was regarded by Aristotle and Pliny[35] as something useful, and La Perrière (1553) adopted this in an emblem in which it was considered sensible to adapt oneself to circumstances. The lobster can, says Taurellus (1602), move, if necessary, on the land or in the water.[36] When a lobster and a nautilus shell appear together in a painting, as in cat. no. 37 and fig. 8.3, they may refer to instability and steadfastness respectively, but we have no way of knowing whether this entered De Heem's mind.

Another striking feature in the Boymans painting is the wreath of vine leaves around the *roemer* which stands on the jewelry box. De Heem several times expressed a 'Praise of the wine' in a similar manner. Does this mean a wine that gratifies the senses and the body, or the spiritual wine, the Teaching of Christ?

This painting also lends itself well to a closer study of De Heem's methods of composition. Striking is the repetition of ovals (circles projected on a nearly horizontal plane), which, following a diagonal from lower left to upper right, increase in size in five stages: a shrimp, a crab, the piece of bread, a pewter platter with fruit, and a pewter basin with ham. The jaunty lines of the twigs and the antennae of the lobster make for a playful, nearly calligraphical impression. The blistered leaves of the peaches and the grapes, and the autumn-colored, curling leaves of the chestnut contribute to the lively effect of the painting. The ham reminds us that this follows in the tradition of the Rich Kitchens of early still lifes.

40   A magnificent work, painted in 1649, is cat. no. 40. Like the Rotterdam still life, it combines both fruit and pronk objects, but it is richer still. The painter in his studio is reflected several times in the bosses of the pronk goblet, and part of the display on the table can be seen mirrored in the gleaming surface of the silver ewer. Also subtly rendered is the reflection of the window of the studio in the *roemer*. Major parts of the precious objects are hidden behind the fruit. The stem and foot of the flute glass and the goblet are not visible, and one can only guess at the form of the *bekerschroef*. Some motifs on the ewer point to vintage time, the time of grape harvest when the swans also begin to migrate to the south. The swan that forms the spout is reined by a putto. This reminds us of the bridle of temperance (fig. 2.2). The handle is formed by Hercules who defeats the Nemean lion, the shining example of Man who by his
39   virtue and good works earns eternal life. We also see the tazza which we saw in cat. no. 39 from another side. The blue of the silk shawl perfectly complements the Chinese basin: precious lapis lazuli blue has been used to paint both. The gilt goblet is close to one made by Friedrich Hirschvogel in Nürnberg about 1638.[37]

The branch of the Seville orange, at the front left, has both fruit and blossoms as in nature.

They do not shed their leaves before winter and therefore are used as a symbol of eternity and eternal youth. The yellow citrus fruit behind them is a citron, which has a thicker and more irregular skin and also has a more bitter taste than a lemon.

Before giving our attention to De Heem's pupils, we should consider François Ryckhals, who worked in Middelburg on the island of Walcheren, between Antwerp and Holland. Together with De Heem he brought the pronk still life to the pinnacle of its development. Perhaps we can regard the still life in fig. 8.5 as a kind of derivation of the work of Rubens with the sleeping Silenus in Vienna (fig. 1.2) and the still life with the smithy by Adriaen van Utrecht, of 1636, in Brussels (fig. 1.3). Unfortunately this painting, which used to be in the former Kaiser Friedrich Museum in Berlin, was destroyed during the war.[38] It is filled with spectacular examples of the metalsmith's art. Several specimens of an octagonal pointed silver dish (a *puntschotel*) are known, the earliest examples from Antwerp, c. 1615, two from Middelburg, 1628 and 1631, and others mostly from Amsterdam before 1635. They are usually engraved, often with representations of the four seasons.[39] We shall see other examples in cat. no. 49 and figs. 8.8, 9.3 and 11.1. *Plooischotels* (silver basins with rims composed of gadroons) as we see at the lower right were probably quite unusual in such a large size, but a related specimen of a smaller size is in the Frans Hals Museum in Haarlem.[40] The silver ewer goes with the salver which has been depicted upright. Both are decorated with episodes from the story of Jonah. The pronk goblet is crowned with the figure of Fortuna. *Façon de Venise* glasses, such as those at the back to the left, we have already seen in paintings by Pieter Claesz and Willem Heda from around 1630.

FRANÇOIS RYCKHALS
Pronk Still Life, 1640
formerly Kaiser Friedrich Museum, Berlin (burnt)

41

François Ryckhals
Szépmüvészeti Múzeum, Budapest

PIETER DE RING
Indiana University Art Museum, Bloomington (Indiana)

Two panels of about the same size and from the same year are in the collections of the Szépmüvészeti Múzeum in Budapest (cat. no. 41) and the Hermitage in Leningrad.[41] The Budapest painting shows the independent character of Ryckhals. The composition is disorderly, and, just as in the Berlin painting, we encounter objects which we have not seen before. One such is the slanting silver ewer on the right, which is normally placed on the ring in the middle of the salver to the left. A comparable ewer, made in Amsterdam, is in the State Armory of the Kremlin in Moscow.[42] A related nautilus cup, made in Utrecht in 1634, is in the Victoria and Albert Museum in London.[43] The hart on top of the little cupboard is probably a reference to Christ. The *Akeleipokal* to the right, a goblet in a shape of a bunch of grapes, is related to one made by Hinrich Lamprecht in Hamburg, c. 1627;[44] the goblet to the left is related to one by Winterstein in Augsburg, c. 1605.[45] The *Miles Christianus* is different from the type with which we are familiar. Several of the Ming jugs have a cover and are mounted in precious metals. A knife with an agate handle is protruding. Ivy is wound around the flute glass that forms the middle axis of the work. As ivy stays green in the winter, it is a symbol of eternal life after death. The companion piece in Leningrad has laurel leaves around the wine glass, a symbol of eternal fame.[46]

Ryckhals was also a painter of stable interiors, such as those painted by Willem Kalf in the 1640s and by Abraham and David Teniers in Antwerp. The earliest known stable painting with kitchen utensils was painted by Jan Davidsz. de Heem in 1631 and is in the Lakenhal Museum in Leiden. The date of a stable interior by Ryckhals reads 1638, and not 1628, as has been misread by several art students.

De Heem had pupils and followers in Leiden, Utrecht and Antwerp. In Leiden, where he worked until 1635, Pieter de Ring was a follower, and Nicolaes van Gelder and Johannes Hannot took De Ring as their guide. Jan's brother David Davidsz. de Heem worked in Utrecht. He was less successful than Jan Davidsz. During the periods that Jan Davidsz. returned to Utrecht he gave lessons to Jacob Marrell and the latter's pupil Abraham Mignon, of Frankfurt. In Antwerp he taught his sons Cornelis and the much younger Jan Jansz. de Heem. Alexander Coosemans, Jan Pauwel, father and son Gillemans, Joris van Son and Christiaen Luyckx were all influenced by De Heem. Many works by these painters and other followers carry attributions to Jan Davidsz., and the number of altered or forged signatures is countless. It is not always simple to distinguish all these hands, and it will take much time and patience to sort this all out. This is only possible by a minute examination of the original works, something which has not been systematically done.

One of the most gifted followers of De Heem was Pieter de Ring. He signed not only with his own name but also with its latinized form, *P. Ab. Annulo*, or simply with a ring, usually set with a small, pyramidal diamond. In later times the latin variant of his name was no longer understood, and this explains why we sometimes read about an artist called P. Ab. Annulo.[47] In cat. no. 42 we see a work from the Museum of Indiana University in Bloomington, Indiana. A lobster is given the central position in this elaborate composition, and from the barnacles on its shell we can see that it has been depicted with truth to nature. The 'Praise of the wine' is indicated by the laurel wreath. The work is signed with a ring on the right. The gray parrot with a red tail, shown on his perch at the left nibbling at a cherry, is an element which we also encounter in early works by Frans Snyders, Adriaen van Utrecht and other Flemish painters, but less frequently in work of their Dutch colleagues.[48]

The parrot signifies in many old paintings an exhortation to praise God. The basis of this symbolic interpretation in the bird's ability to imitate the human voice. The influential author Physiologus writes: 'Man, imitate the voices of the Apostles who praise the Lord, and you should praise Him too. Imitate the Congregation of the Righteous so that you deserve to achieve their radiating place.'[49] In Valerianus, Sambucus, Ripa and others the parrot is a symbol of Eloquentia.[50] But the parrot is not always praised for its gift of the tongue, as it is also regarded as a symbol of empty imitation, for instance in Camerarius.[51] Hans Baldung Grien depicts a parrot amidst seven women who represent the seven stages in the life of woman. The painting dates from 1544 and is in the collection of the Museum der Bildenden Künste in Leipzig. Apparently Grien considered women as great talkers, from the cradle to death.

In 1660 Pieter de Ring made one of his most sumptuous pronk still lifes (cat. no. 43), which is now at Squerryes Court, south of London. It is even a little larger than the large still life by De Heem of 1642. In it we see an ensemble of pronk objects with all sorts of food, vegetables, roses, a parrot and a monkey. The top of the pronk goblet is formed by an eagle, as in other work by De Ring and in several paintings of Nicolaes van Gelder. In our painting it bends with spread wings away from the parrot. The silver-gilt and the mother-of-pearl ewer resembles an example from the first half of the 17th century which Hayward ascribes as English or Dutch.[52] If this ewer goes with the large, gilt salver placed in an upright position, then it is most probably Dutch, as the salver bears the coat of arms of the Van der Dussen family, prominent citizens of Leiden where De Ring worked. A comparable dish, made in Amsterdam in 1608 and commissioned by the Municipality of Vlissingen (Flushing), is in the Rijksmuseum in Amsterdam.[53] A bronze wine cooler like the one at the front left can be seen in Castle Twickel in the Dutch province of Overijssel. The *roemer* is again crowned with laurel leaves.

The monkey, like the parrot, is an animal which is depicted in the work of Frans Snyders, and it is also linked to the theme of imitation. In this case, however, the chained animal symbolizes the restraint of lust, as we noted in Chapter 3. In series depicting the Senses the monkey is a symbol of Taste. If one wishes, he could regard this painting as representing the Senses, in which case the theme of the whole work would be Abundance, which implies the temptation of the senses. Several elements in both works by De Ring can also be observed in another painting by him in the Rijksmuseum in Amsterdam.[54]

Nicolaes van Gelder's work is closely related to that of De Ring. Dated work by Van Gelder is known from 1660. Cat. no. 44 is a painting from the Rijksmuseum in Amsterdam, painted in 1664. The oriental carpet on the marble table is a new element. Such carpets are typical of this period, as can also be seen in the works of other painters, such as Abraham van Beyeren. The rug has been identified as a 'column prayer rug,' possibly from West Anatolia (Ydema 1988). The Chinese jug reappears later in a work in the Museum Narodowe in Warsaw.[55] Related examples of the silver dish with auricular ornaments have been preserved,[56] and a similar saltcellar, made in Leiden by Barend Gast in 1655, is in the Lakenhal Museum in Leiden.[57] Hexagonal saltcellars with three knobs on the top were made in many varieties. The silver

PIETER DE RING
Squerryes Court Collection, Westerham (Kent, Great Britain)

NICOLAES VAN GELDER
Rijksmuseum, Amsterdam

8.6

PIETER DE RING
Still Life with a Lobster
Rijksmuseum, Amsterdam

8.7

JORIS VAN SON
Detail of cat.no. 47

models were probably developed from pewter examples. The olive-shaped knobs are sometimes replaced by tulips, as in fig. 8.3, or by little monsters, as in the richly decorated saltcellar with flower motifs in the painting by Pieter de Ring in the Rijksmuseum in Amsterdam (fig. 8.6).

In a work by Johannes Hannot (cat. no. 45) a hexagonal saltcellar is given a prominent place. It is related to that in cat. no. 44 and was perhaps also made by a goldsmith from Leiden. We can wonder whether salt itself had a meaning in still lifes, or whether the saltcellar was only depicted as a pronk object. We do not know, but I suspect that salt in scenes of the Last Supper or the Supper at Emmaus had a meaning, and I shall therefore not exclude the possibility that salt also had a meaning in these still lifes. It can be linked with sacrifice according to the text 'And every oblation of thy meat offering shalt thou season with salt; neither shalt thou suffer the salt of the covenant of thy God by the lacking from thy meat offering: with all thine offerings thou shalt offer salt.'[58] Salt was regarded as a holy substance. God confirms his covenant with David as a covenant of salt.[59] At the blessing of the Jewish Sabbath meal, the bread is dipped in salt, and in the Roman Catholic christening ceremony salt is administered as a symbol of wisdom and the 'seed of the Church.'[60] Christ calls his disciples 'the salt of the earth' when he speaks about their task. If they have no salt, no spirit in themselves, their activities lead to nothing.[61] It should be noted that the Latin work *sal* means salt or sea, as well as intelligence, astuteness or good taste and humor.

The painter and theoretician Gerard de Lairesse writes that according to the philosophers everything grows by the salt of the earth, and so does the fertile teaching of the Gospel. With reference to Hesychius he compares the salt that improves the odor and taste of food to divine wisdom in things that are good: hope, belief and love.[62] Otto van Veen uses the motto 'Animae sal est amor' (Love is the salt of the soul) with the following explanation: 'The love of God is the true salt which supports all that has received life and will not let us down at death.'[63] Salt as a symbol of eternity perhaps has something to do with its function as a preservative. Salt may also refer to the 'exact measure.' It is a necessary ingredient to bring something to the correct taste and, equally, says Job,[64] words need to have an exact content. Hildegard van Bingen points to the 'exact measure:' lightly salted food strengthens people, insipid food makes people lazy, and too strongly salted dishes make them dry and arid.[65]

Until recently not many works by Johannes Hannot were known. Part of his oeuvre was falsely signed with the name of Jan Davidsz. de Heem, or the signatures were completely rubbed out. When recently a number of paintings were being cleaned in the museums of Lille and Bonn,[66] vestiges of old signatures appeared. On the basis of specific characteristics some more paintings could be credited to this painter.[67]

Among the Antwerp painters of still lifes Pieter Boel (1622-1674) was one of the most original. He did not produce pronk still lifes in the true sense of the work but rather vanitas still lifes with pronk objects, such as in fig. 2.4. They were often on a large scale.[68] He specialized in game still lifes, also often with pronk objects.

Apart from De Heem's son Cornelis the most important Antwerp painter in the style of De Heem was Joris van Son. The silver ewer (fig. 8.7) in cat. no. 46 is a beautiful example of the art of the silversmith. No similar ewer is known to exist any longer. On the lid of the spout is a little dog. The ewer is ornamented with festoons of fruit, with a devilish mask and with

JOHANNES HANNOT
Private Collection

JORIS VAN SON
Hohenbuchau Collection, Schlangenbad-Georgenborn
(Federal Republic of Germany)

cherubs, a combination that represents something of a contradiction. The painting is related to works dated 1652 which are signed in the same manner on a cartouche on the wall.[69] The rummer is bedecked on this occasion with a spray of a strawberry plant with its ternary leaves. The depiction of strawberries, medlars and gooseberries distinguishes Joris van Son from his contemporaries, especially by the way in which he incorporates these fruits into his compositions.[70]

Fig. 8.8 is a work from a series of the Four Elements, in this case the element Fire.[71] We see here coins, gold and silver objects, porcelain, stoneware and glass, though in a different context than previously. The silver platter and beaker were probably made in Antwerp.[72] It is also a destructive force, an appropriate reminder of transiency. The ivy, however, is a hopeful sign of eternal life.

An engraved platter called in Dutch a *puntschotel* is often seen in still lifes. An example can be seen in cat. no. 47, a work by Christiaen Luyckx, and is very similar to that in fig. 8.5 by Ryckhals. The spoon with a lion-and-shield finial resembles a Haarlem spoon.[73] A comparable *bekerschroef*, of 1609, made by the Amsterdam goldsmith Leendert Claesz. van Emden, is in the Historical Museum of Amsterdam.[74] A comparable tazza from the Delft silversmith Cornelis Jansz. van der Burch dates from about 1600.[75] A comparable pronk goblet was made by Hans Endres in Augsburg, about 1654.[76] The little crown in the fruit pastry is actually a little 'chimney' by which the hot air can escape during baking. The column in the background in front of the curtain occupies an important position in the composition. A column is a traditional symbol of Constantia (Steadfastness) and Fortitudo (Spiritual strength).[77] The warm colors of the curtain were overpainted before the painting's very successful recent cleaning.

8.8

JORIS VAN SON
Fire (from a Series of Elements), 1656
Van Haeften Gallery, London

CHAPTER 9

PAINTERS OF THE BROAD BRUSH: ABRAHAM VAN BEYEREN

Running parallel to the polished, virtuosic style of many Dutch still-life painters, we can detect a broader, more painterly tendency usually associated with Abraham van Beyeren. This tendency did not just emerge full-blown in the work of Van Beyeren, however; and we can see the roots of it in certain older artists who are today less well known.
Pieter Potter was working toward the end of the 1620s in Leiden, at the same time as Jan Davidsz. de Heem. Later he was to work both in Amsterdam and The Hague. It is unlikely that he made his first vanitas still life with books as early as 1620, as has been assumed in the literature,[1] but is more probable that he was inspired by De Heem's book still lifes in Leiden from around 1628-29. His earliest paintings, from possibly around 1630, are still quite detailed, but soon became vanitas still lifes. The earliest dated one that we know of, painted in a rugged manner, is from 1636 and is even broader than those of Pieter Claesz. Later a number of other vanitas painters, such as Pieter Steenwijck and Franciscus Gijsbrechts in Leiden, Jacques de Claeu in The Hague and Leiden, and Petrus Schotanus of Friesland all worked in this broad manner. The same also applies to Pieter de Putter, the Hague painter who was the earliest specialist in fish still lifes and who was in all likelihood the spiritual father of Abraham van Beyeren, the greatest painter of fish still lifes. The broad-brush technique was less appropriate for painting flowers and fruit. Nevertheless, artists such as Jacob van Es in Antwerp, Anthony Claesz in Amsterdam and Hans Bollongier in Haarlem painted in a freer way than their contemporaries - but not like De Putter and Potter. The few known flower pieces by Jacques de Claeu and Abraham van Beyeren are among the most beautiful and sensitive of their time.
A beautiful still life formerly attributed to Van Beyeren illustrates the confusion that surrounds these lesser-known artists and suggests a fruitful path for further study. Cat. no. 48 was formerly attributed to Abraham van Beyeren, partly on the basis of a false signature. Recently it was also thought to be a work by Jacques de Claeu. Its broad brushwork is indeed characteristic of both these artists, but this is the only thing it has in common with either. Neither the composition nor the color nor the rendition of detail nor the subject nor even the majority of the objects are typical of either Van Beyeren or De Claeu. The composition it too forced for van Beyeren and too orderly for De Claeu. The transitions in color are too harsh for Van Beyeren, and the color scheme is too bright for De Claeu; for both artists there

CHRISTIAEN LUYCKX
Peter Tillou Gallery, Litchfield (Connecticut)

48

Hans Bollongier
Rijksdienst Beeldende Kunst, The Hague

9.1

HANS BOLLONGIER
Flower Piece, 1638
Private Collection, formerly Knoedler Gallery, New York

are deviations from characteristic brushwork. The subject matter is also wrong for both artists: there is too much mingling of pronk and vanitas objects. In Van Beyeren's work vanitas objects are usually subordinate, while in De Claeu's pronk objects are practically non-existent. Roses are sometimes present in both their pronk and vanitas still lifes, and some other flowers appear in De Claeu's paintings as well, but never a complete bouquet with many varieties of flowers, such as we find in this still life. Van Beyeren and De Claeu both painted some flower pieces, but they differ strongly in composition from the bouquet in this still life. In some respects the style of painting resembles that of Pieter Potter, but this attribution is also problematical. I think that the small bouquet offers the best starting point for determination of a new attribution, and this leads us to Hans Bollongier of Haarlem. The composition, arrangement and colors of the bouquet are typical of this artist.[2] Fig. 9.1 is evidence of this.[3] We see here several identical flowers, such as the double columbines in the same place lower down in the vase. We know of numerous flower pieces by Bollongier, and of some fruit pieces or combinations of flowers and fruit, the majority of which are dated between 1627 and 1672. But I do not know of any signed pronk or vanitas still life by him.

The tazza in this work is identical to one used by Willem Heda and his pupils in Haarlem.[4] Among the vanitas objects it depicts are: an hourglass, writing materials, documents, a celestial globe and bag of money. There are also pronk objects: the watch and a casket of jewelry with a string of pearls and a gold chain. Amor with his arrow connects life and death through love. The flowers are both pronk and transiency symbols. The tulip at the top is the 'Viceroy', for which, in 1637, the highest price ever was paid for a single tulip bulb — 4,600 guilders. Vanity is also symbolized here: at the back to the left we see the feathers of a bird of paradise. In Australia and New Guinea there are about 40 species of these birds, some of which have long feathery tails — a yard long. The East Indiamen caught these exotic birds and prepared their skins for the curio cabinets of collectors. Since the bones, muscles and intestines were removed during the preservation process, people in Europe got the impression that the birds had no feet. The symbolism of this bird is therefore based on a misconception: that it can only fly and never touches the earth. It is mostly interpreted *in bono* as the contemplative spirit which ignores earthly things, as in Camerarius and in other emblem books.[5] A letter is sticking out of the book under the pronk goblet, and we can read a date: 'De 16 July.' This allows us to suppose that this is a commemorative piece. If it was meant to honor a wedding, then the meaning of Amor would be obvious.

As we mentioned above, the great master of the broad brush among painters of pronk still lifes was Abraham van Beyeren. He was born in The Hague in 1620 and was taught by his brother-in-law, Pieter de Putter. By 1638-39 he had been in Leiden for about a year. He married there. In 1640 he became a member of the Guild in The Hague, where, after the death of his first wife, who had borne him three daughters, he remarried in 1647. In 1657 he was inscribed as a member of the Guild in Delft, and in 1663 he returned to The Hague. From 1669 to 1674 he lived in Amsterdam. Later he went to Alkmaar and Gouda, and finally, from 1678, he went to live in Overschie, where he died in 1690.[6] He led a restless life which is reflected in his work. His oeuvre consists not only of pronk still lifes but also fruit and some flower pieces, kitchen still lifes with plucked birds, many excellent fish still lifes and seascapes. In contrast to De Heem's his work was not highly valued either during his lifetime or up to the 19th century in Holland. It is, however, possible that his work was understood and appreciated by artists like the Frenchman Chardin, in whose kitchen still lifes from around 1730 a similar atmosphere can be seen.[7]

Van Beyeren was not rich and was often in debt. One may then ask: Why did he paint these large sumptuous still lifes? De Jongh bases his answer on the fact that excess and ostentation were considered blameful and sinful in the eyes of orthodox Calvinists and Baptists. Moderation was strongly recommended from the pulpit. Church councils complained about the 'pompous and delicate treats and sumptuous meals.' The authorities in several parts of the country were put under pressure by the Church to intervene and make laws to restrict the spending of money on weddings and other festivities. Pronk still lifes, according to this view, were not simply excellent renderings of food and articles of luxury but included remonstrances against excess and ostentation.[8] In one way the pronk still lifes of Van Beyeren seem to be less rich than those of Willem Heda, Jan Davidsz. de Heem and Willem Kalf, but this can only be judged in the light of their complete oeuvre: the precious objects that Van Beyeren painted are generally of a lesser quality and value than those of his colleagues. Cer-

ABRAHAM VAN BEYEREN
Rijksdienst Beeldende Kunst, The Hague

ABRAHAM VAN BEYEREN
Ashmolean Museum, Oxford, Ward Collection

tain objects are repeated in several paintings. Some, however, such as a *bekerschroef,* a salt-cellar or a silver beaker, appear only a few times, and it is clear that they were only available to him for a short period. When they do appear in paintings, the attributions are sometimes doubtful. Specific objects in Van Beyeren's repertory include a silver brandy-wine bowl and silver *plooi-*platters (dishes with a rim composed of gadroonings). We shall not find insects in his work.

We may, perhaps, consider Van Beyeren's fish still lifes as the counterpart of his pronk still lifes. Fish was, generally, food for the poor. On a Dutch faïence colander of the early 18th century (private collection, Amsterdam), decorated in blue on white with fishes, we read: 'Gelooft mijn vriend de Rog en Bolk is int Gemeen voor 't Arme volk' (Believe me, friend, the Ray and Bolk are, usually, for poor folks). The fish still life, thus, would follow the tradition of the Poor Kitchen, the pronk still life that of the Rich Kitchen.

Van Beyeren's technique was extraordinarily delicate. He worked in a fluent manner, sometimes painting thickly, sometimes with broad passages of transparent glazing, with touches of impasto. His work has a directness and spontaneity that appeals to the modern age. Sometimes it seems as if he has attacked the canvas, almost violently. His tonality is golden-brown and velvety, rather than the silver tonality of the Haarlem painters and De Heem, and he delights such subtle optical effects as the lustre of mother-of-pearl, the sheen of silver, and the sparkle of glass. A certain softness is achieved by the use of rounded lines instead of straight lines and angles. The compositions are not always so well thought-out as De Heem's. Sometimes they look a little cramped, and from close by the coherence between the objects is not very strong. The viewer's attention is not usually directed at one single object. The paintings of this artist are, however, not meant to be looked at from nearby. Like the works of the Impressionists, they must be appreciated from a certain distance. Van Beyeren asks the viewer to participate actively and lets him fill in the details himself. Though little attention is devoted to detail, great skill has been used to evoke an atmosphere. The colors of a tablecloth or of leaves, for example, have been completely keyed to the silver or brown tones of the whole composition.

Van Beyeren painted many large works, usually in a vertical format, but sometimes square. Like De Heem he also produced small, simple compositions in which his broad brushwork is more noticeable than in larger works. In the beginning he painted fish still lifes and marines. His earliest dated pronk still life is a work of 1651 (fig. 9.2).[9] In a niche which reminds one of a church window we see a *roemer* containing wine encircled by vine foliage. This is probably a reference to Christ, the 'true vine,' and also to the eucharistic wine: the teaching of the New Testament. A garland of flowers has been draped across the niche between vertically hanging sprays of ivy, signs of eternity. The pronk attributes are lying on a marble slab which shows signs of damage, a symbol of transiency and the antithesis of the ivy. The overturned pronk goblet is 'empty', but the *Miles Christianus* stands upright on the lid. Are the nautilus shell and the lobster here intended as signs of steadfastness and instability?

The accolade-shaped silver plate and the pronk goblet also appear in a painting belonging to the Rijksdienst voor Beeldende Kunst in The Hague (cat. no. 49). This painting dates from around 1653. The same plate can also be seen in another work dated 1653.[10] Some other similarities can be observed in fig. 9.3, a work of 1654.[11] Here we see a similar Chinese bowl with

ABRAHAM VAN BEYEREN
Still Life with a Garland of Flowers, 1651
Kunstmuseum, Düsseldorf, Bentinck-Thyssen Collection

ABRAHAM VAN BEYEREN
Pronk Still Life with Roses, 1654
Brod Gallery, London

candied lemon and Seville oranges, a similar silver *plooi*-platter, similar fruit and a similar watch. The silver jug is related but not identical.[12] The gilt pronk goblet might be an Augsburg product.[13] Another related work of 1654 shows some of the elements and also a cut melon.[14] Two undated paintings show a relationship with cat. no. 49 and must have been made in the same period. Both have the same silver jug, accolade-shaped platter, knife with an agate handle, a basket, Ming basin and fruit. One of them, probably the first painted (around 1652-53), has a horizontal format with a lobster and oysters and, through an opening in the wall, a vista. These and other aspects remind us of De Heem.[15] The most closely related work has the pronk goblet, cut melon, practically identical grapes and foliage, but a wall with a closed niche.[16]

Ter Kuile has said that the paintings of Van Beyeren are difficult to date.[17] This is only partly true. Van Beyeren indeed used objects from an earlier period in his paintings dated from 1666 to 1667, but by careful examination one can see that they usually differ in certain details and in many cases are painted differently. Between 1657 and 1666, however, we know of no dated pronk still life, only some kitchen still lifes with a few pronk elements. Presumably

Abraham van Beyeren
Cleveland Museum of Art, Cleveland (Ohio)

ABRAHAM VAN BEYEREN
Los Angeles County Museum of Art, Los Angeles

9.4

ABRAHAM VAN BEYEREN
Still Life with a Silver Ewer
Toledo Museum of Art, Toledo (Ohio)

the artist made many relatively simple paintings in that period, such as the pronk still life from 1666,[18] and kitchen still lifes. Cat. nos. 50 and 51 could be dated between 1660 and 1665. Marble plinths are hardly known in paintings of the 1650s, and the plinth of 1651 is painted quite differently. The one in fig. 9.4[19] shows an obvious similarity to those in cat. nos. 50 and 51 (the same objects have been painted in a closer view) and is very much like the plinth in cat. no. 52, of 1667. Oranges (insofar as that they were not candied ones) do not appear in dated paintings before 1659. The watch in cat. no. 51 is the same as the one in cat. no. 52. Many objects from previous periods are missing. In the silver ewer we can see a reflection of the artist, a trick familiar to us from Clara Peeters and other artists. This silver ewer appears in at least eight other paintings that support this dating.[20]

Cat. no. 52 is a work from 1667 from the Los Angeles County Museum of Art. It is an extraordinary example of Van Beyeren's work. A napkin has been placed, in a familiar manner, over a warm red oriental rug. The colorist Van Beyeren knew how to link and make contrasts simultaneously. The folds of the napkin are shaded so that the white planes are not too strongly contrasted, and the silver platter has assimilated the tonality of the shading. The color transitions have been subtly rendered in this way throughout the entire composition. The accolade-shaped platter has auricular ornaments, and an example like this is known; it was made by Gerrit Vuysting in The Hague in 1656.[21] The silver *plooi*-platter on the basket is like the one in cat. no. 49, but this time it is decorated with a floral motif. In an earlier work by Van Beyeren's there is another *plooi*-platter which also has floral motifs.[22] This type of platter was made in Amsterdam and Haarlem during the 1650s.[23] The *krulbeker* has also been seen in an earlier work, but it was then decorated with a different figure.[24] The same goblet with or without various ornaments seems to support the argument that there were interchangeable parts for these goblets. An example of such a *krulbeker* was made in Augsburg about 1642.[25] The little mouse creeping along the edge of the silver platter is here a surprising element. A mouse represents in general the mundane, sinful life and in particular gluttony. In the Bible it is an unclean and abominated animal that destroys the land.[26] A number of sources link gluttony to all sorts of temptation and to inevitable punishment: the mouse is either poisoned or caught in a trap.[27]

WILLEM KALF
Charles Roelofsz Gallery, Amsterdam

WILLEM KALF
National Gallery, London

Chapter 10

The sparkling light of Willem Kalf

Willem Kalf is one of the few important Dutch still-life painters for whose pictures a critical oeuvre catalogue has been written. This work is to the credit of Grisebach,[1] who has quoted comprehensively from the archival data and source literature on the artist's life. We know that Kalf was born in Rotterdam in 1619, the son of a cloth merchant. From around 1640 to 1645/46 he was working in Paris. In 1651 he married in Hoorn (northern Holland) a clergyman's daughter, Cornelia Pluvier, who was a calligrapher, poetess and glass etcher. They both became Roman Catholic converts. From 1653 until his death in 1693 Kalf lived in Amsterdam. He had probably also lived there on his return from Paris, before his marriage, but nothing is known about that period. It is known that he, like Vermeer and other artists of his time, dealt in works of art and prints, but when and to what extent is not clear. According to Houbraken, Kalf was a friendly, entertaining and well-read man.[2] Early in his career he painted many stable interiors and farm exteriors with figures and still-life details of kitchen utensils, vegetables and fruits. The majority of these were made while he was living in Paris. In these works we often see food that was practically unknown in Dutch markets, such as pumpkins, cardoons and celery. Such pictures are usually small in size but painted with a broad brush. At the same time, however, he also painted still lifes in a more delicate technique. He often elaborated his depiction of objects with touches of wet-in-wet paint resulting in small points, lines, scratches or sweeps of paint that lend vibrancy to the surface. He applied thin layers of white over gray to define subtle planes of spreading highlights. Later he made use of glazing in specific areas. Unfortunately, many of his paintings have been damaged by inexpert cleaning, and these subtle layers of paint have been rubbed. In addition, thinly painted objects sometimes have sunk into the darkened backgrounds.
The mysterious beauty of Kalf's still lifes is due in large measure to the quality of their light, an obliquely falling light that gives gentle relief to lustrous objects in a deep but transparent darkness. Only the highlighted areas are elaborated with much detail, as the light and shade establish a clear but richly somber aerial perspective. If Van Beyeren were called the master of brilliance, then Kalf would be the master of sparkle. His colors remind us of those of Rembrandt: they are warm but with less brown and red, more blue and orange.
Kalf was highly esteemed in his lifetime, though not to the same degree as Jan Davidsz. de Heem. The quality of his attributed oeuvre is variable, because he, like De Heem, allowed

his pupils to make copies of his paintings to which he himself would add the finishing touches. Besides numerous copies by others, we also know of contemporary replicas signed by Kalf himself. In some cases these differences in quality are easily distinguishable, but not always and not clearly.

The dating of Kalf's works is not always a simple task, as relatively few of them — fewer than 20 percent of the total — have legible dates; moreover, the dates appear sporadically throughout his lifetime (not one between 1644 and 1653 and more than two-thirds of the total between 1658 and 1663). A number of his dated works also depict objects which appear in no other still life, rendering useless this sometimes-helpful guide. On the other hand there are objects which are painted repeatedly over long periods. Nevertheless, some useful points of reference can be identified. Just as in the case of Van Beyeren, there are objects which were obviously, or presumably, at Kalf's disposal for only a restricted amount of time. Furthermore, the apparent similarity of some objects can be misleading. We have already noticed in the works of De Heem, Van Beyeren, Heda and others that certain objects appear to have been made of interchangeable parts arranged in different ways by the painters, or that the painters used their imaginations in depicting these objects. This semblance of similarity is very strong in Kalf's work, but if we examine carefully, the differences between the nautilus cups and pronk goblets are greater than is apparent at first glance. The same is true for other types of objects as well. For example, among the still lifes painted in 1643 and 1644, we can count five different but related gilt ewers, a degree of variety that went unremarked by Grisebach. Some objects which we see once or only a few times appear in what we could call 'pronk portraits,' standing out from other subordinate objects in the compositions. Some kinds of things which we see less frequently in the works of other artists have a striking presence in the works of Kalf, such as certain gilt and silver objects and knives with agate handles, but no less striking is the absence of familiar objects which we see in De Heem. Abraham van Beyeren seldom painted animals, but in Kalf's work there is not one fly, butterfly, snail or mouse to be seen. In that respect his paintings are 'clean'. Neither are flowers often seen, only now and again a rose or, on a sprig of Seville oranges, some leaves and a blossom. The representation of seashells is almost entirely confined to the smaller group of specialized shell still lifes or to a nautilus or shell cup. Kalf was apparently not very interested in depicting nature's riches. Or could it be that he did not feel the need to employ what for others had been symbolic elements? Even his fruits are restricted to a small number of species: citrus fruits and peaches, now and again hazelnuts and, rarely, grapes, a melon, a pomegranate or plums. Usually they are few in number, and this also applies to the hazelnuts and olives. One of Kalf's preferred motifs was the peach stone. The Seville orange is often seen with lengthwise grooves or with protuberances.

We could ask ourselves whether we should expect to find as much symbolic content in Kalf's work as in De Heem's: several authors have their doubts about this. De Lairesse himself wrote on the subject in his book of 1707, which was partly written as a guide for young artists. He wrote that not every still-life painter approached the matter of 'private meanings' with conscious intent and that Kalf 'could give us little Reason for what he did as others before or after him: He only depicted what occurred to him, a Porcelain Pot or Dish…without any thought of doing something of Importance which might bear some particular Meaning

WILLEM KALF
Thyssen-Bornemisza Collection, Castagnola (Switzerland)

WILLEM KALF
Cleveland Museum of Art, Cleveland (Ohio)

WILLEM KALF
Still Life with a Temperantia Jug, 1639
Mrs. and Mrs. Edward William Carter Collection, Los Angeles

WILLEM KALF
Still Life with Armor
Private Collection, formerly Speelman Gallery, London

or be applicable to something.'[3] Yet we shall see that sometimes there are indications (and not only in the frequently depicted watch) that we should see more in them than mere pronk objects.

Kalf had a following in Holland, among which was Juriaen van Streeck. Most of his followers were also influenced by De Heem, and, as in the case of Willem van Aelst, they combined the style of both artists. From the time that Kalf was working in France he had followers there too, such as Meiffren Conte and Hupin. These followers, however, began to load their compositions with large numbers of baroque gilt objects, and the quiet atmosphere of the Dutch still life was lost. The German artist Georg Hinz and the Swedish Ottmar Elliger were also greatly influenced by Kalf during his Dutch period.

Until recently two dated paintings of 1643 and 1644 were considered to be the earliest dated works by Kalf.[4] A few years ago, however, I saw a work that was signed and had indistinct vestiges of a date: W KALF 163(?), probably to be read as 1639 (fig. 10.1).[5] Grisebach, who had not seen the original, illustrated and mentioned it in his book, giving only some technical information, but without mentioning the signature or the date. The low point of view is striking, drawing our attention to the edge of the tabletop. In a medallion on the gilt ewer we see the figure of Temperantia pouring wine. It is possible that this is one of the first paintings that Kalf made in Paris; he might have been there already in 1639 following his mother's death the year before (his father had died in 1625). The Wan-li bottle with prunts is the same as one seen in another painting.[6] The gilt ewer is closely related to one made by François Briot in the last quarter of the 16th century which has allegorical scenes of the seasons and the continents of the world and belongs to a salver with a Temperantia scene in the center.[7] The silver knife with a little horseshoe can also be seen in another painting of a possibly early date.[8]

Kalf introduced his own portrait into an elaborate early still life (fig. 10.2),[9] of which there is an even larger version without the self-portrait.[10] This picture was probably painted in 1643 or 1644, and Grisebach supports this plausible dating for the larger version by noting the presence of a commemorative coin dated 1643 in honor of Louis XIV and that the nautilus cup appears in a painting that is a version of one dated in 1644.[11]

Cat. no. 53 is a painting from the Paris period, one of Kalf's most mature early works and perhaps among the last he painted there. It came to light after the publication of Grisebach's book, just like fig. 10.1. It too is a replica of a known work, a painting in the Wallraf-Richartz Museum in Cologne[12] which has been mentioned and reproduced frequently in the literature as the most important example of Kalf's Paris period.[13] Various copies of this work are not by Kalf's own hand but are from a later date.[14] Goethe made the following note on this painting on August 19, 1797, when he saw it in the Städelsche Kabinett in Frankfurt: 'Gold – und silberne Gefässe von Kalff – Die Meisterschaft dieses Mannes in diesem Teil der Kunst zeigt sich hier in ihrem höchsten Lichte. Man muss dieses Bild sehen um zu begreifen, in welchem Sinne die Kunst über die Natur sei und was der Geist des Menschen den Gegenständen leiht, wenn er sie mit schöpferischem Auge betrachtet. Bei mir wenigstens ist's keine Frage, wenn ich die goldnen Gefässe oder das Bild zu wählen hätte, dass ich das Bild wählen würde.'[15] (Gold and silver vases by Kalff [sic] – they highlight the masterly skill of this man in this branch of art. One must see this painting in order to understand in what respect art is superior to nature and what the spirit of man lends to these objects when he observes them with a creative eye. For me there is no question: If I would have to choose between the golden vases or the painting, I would choose the painting). What Goethe did not know, as did many after him, was that he was looking at a copy.

When I first saw cat. no. 53, I was convinced that it was an authentic work by Kalf and that it could be a version of the Cologne painting. In order to be quite sure, however, I asked the owner if he would agree to a direct confrontation of the two works. He agreed, and the staff of the museum was also willing to cooperate. Side by side it was obvious that the newly-discovered work was much superior to the one in the museum in Cologne and that the latter must be a copy.[16] The two gilded ewers, or at least one of the two, must be seen in connection with the large salver that is leaning against the wall. The ewers differ a little from each other but resemble greatly the examples in figs. 10.1 and 10.2. Though not identical, they could have been made by the same goldsmith, and such differences as there are could be due to Kalf's artistic licence. In the middle of the salver is a coat of arms which has not yet been identified but about which Grisebach offers some sound suggestions. The same object is also depicted in a still life by Simon Renard de Saint André painted around 1650.[17] Inscribed

57

WILLEM KALF
Indianapolis Museum of Art, Indianapolis (Indiana)

WILLEM VAN AELST
Statens Museum for Kunst, Copenhagen

on a letter in that still life we can read: 'A Monsieur / Monsieur du Vaulx / officier du roy en /sa maison a Paris' (To M. / Squire of Vaulx / officer of the king at / his house in Paris). Still lifes with such letters or documents often bear the name or the signature of the artist or, in some cases, of the man who had commissioned the work. Grisebach speculated that the coat of arms on the salver in the Cologne version of Kalf's composition could be that of Simon de Vaulx, who left a large collection upon his death in 1651.[18]

A silver pilgrim's bottle occupies the central place in this painting. The same object is also depicted in a number of other works by Kalf from his Paris period.[19] The name 'pilgrim's bottle' is derived from the medieval leather bottles carried by travelers, which were often used to hold wine. Only a few examples of such bottles have been preserved, even though they were still being made at the end of the 17th century.[20] In a dated family portrait of the goldsmith Hans Rudolf Faesch, painted in 1559 by the Basle artist Hans Hug Kluber, we see a pilgrim's bottle and a ewer in a bronze wine cooler.[21] We can also recognize the candlestick from Kalf's still life in other paintings. Like the bottles, it was probably made towards the end of the 16th century.[22] The glass basin with cover and the rippled glass on the shelf at the upper right also appear in other works.[23] Thus a number of objects can be seen in three dated paintings of 1643 and 1644, but none in the painting of 1639. The paintings of the Amsterdam period are of a different character, and not a single object from the Paris years can be found in them. Kalf must have got the idea of a chair or, in the case of this painting a bench, and the drapery with cords and tassels from De Heem.

54 In cat. no. 54, which belongs to the National Gallery in London, we also see a chair in the foreground to the left. This work is one of the jewels of Dutch still-life painting.[24] Another version of it exists with a number of small differences. Neither Grisebach nor I have seen the work itself, but Grisebach believes it to be authentic. I still have considerable doubts. In this painting more of the chair and the persian rug can be seen. Like nearly all of Kalf's still lifes, it is vertical in format with plenty of space at the top.[25] One of these two paintings was auctioned in 1706 with the description: 'A capital piece by Kalf including a drinking horn, the best one known by him.'

We know of no dated works by Kalf from the years between 1644 and 1653, and we have no idea what he was doing during this time. Presumably he was sufficiently well-off to be able to live for a few years without earning money from his painting. He could also have lived from his stock in trade as a dealer in works of art. In any case there are hardly any known paintings that could possibly have been painted earlier than 1653. The still life of 1653 (fig. 10.3) in the Alte Pinakothek in Munich is a key work for the dating of his paintings made in Holland, especially since there is no other dated work prior to the large group made between 1658 and 1663.[26] The 1653 piece does not offer many clues for the dating of undated works, either because most of the objects are only seen once or because they appear throughout his oeuvre. The Chinese jug and the silver spoon with auricular ornaments are seen only once, and a pomegranate only a few times. The composition and technique, however, do offer bases for dating other works. Kalf still makes use of small dots of pigment as highlights. These give an almost tangible thorniness to the prunts of the rummer, yet they lend a slight optical blur to the decoration on the vase. These vibrant little strokes of paint are smaller and more pointed than during his Paris period and are distributed differently. In a similar way we can notice other changes in his later work.

Willem Kalf
Still Life with a Ming Jug, 1653
Alte Pinakothek, Munich

From a technical point of view the London painting is very close to fig. 10.3. We need only compare the rummers and the reflections seen in them. We can group a small number of paintings made about the same time around this London piece. Once again, however, the objects are only partially a basis for analysis. The drinking horn, the lobster, the hunting knife, the cylindrical prunt glass and the chair are objects which we see only twice (in the London picture and the other version of it), as is the marble table which is decorated underneath with a putto. A pewter plate appears only seldom, except for the Paris period. It is not impossible that the London painting and two related works[27] were made before the Munich picture and therefore around 1652. It is reasonable to assume that the group of other paintings must have been made in the period between the London/Munich pieces and the work dated 1658.

We can well imagine that on his return to Holland Willem Kalf first had to find his bearings. It is likely that he was again inspired by De Heem and by the artist Simon Luttichuys, who was working in Amsterdam. The lobster in the London painting was probably a result of De Heem's influence, and this painting is one of the few in which that artist's approach is still recognizable. The central object is the drinking horn, which belonged to the St. Sebastian

59

Willem van Aelst
Private Collection

DIRCK DE BRAY
Stichting Museum Amstelkring, Amsterdam

GABRIEL METSU
Tuning of the Lute
Staatliche Kunstsammlungen, Kassel

WILLEM KALF ATTRIBUTED
Sketch of a Drinking Horn
Fondation Custodia (Collection F. Lugt), Paris

Archers' Civic Guard of Amsterdam (the original horn is now in the Amsterdams Historisch Museum).[28] It consisted of a buffalo's horn mounted in silver with the coat of arms of Amsterdam and an inscription under the lion: 'Anno Domini 1565 factum est.' The stem was made in the shape of the tree trunk to which St. Sebastian was tied, with an archer on either side of it. The drinking horn could be drunk from in turn in a company of friends, but it could also be regarded as a horn of plenty. Kalf has not painted the horn exactly as it is, as can be seen in the detail of the little dog and the three figures. There are also differences between the horn cups in the two versions that Kalf made. The depiction of it is more accurate in a painting by Bartholomeus van der Helst, of 1653, and in two works by Gabriel Metsu in which the horn can also be seen.[29] Fig. 10.4 is from Metsu's *Lute Player* in the museum in Kassel, a playful rendering of the Senses as a harmonious attunement between two persons. Two drawings attributed to Kalf also depict this object. One, fig. 10.5,[30] is a composition with a drinking horn and a ginger jar in front of an arched niche. This could relate to two

WILLEM KALF
Still Life with a Silver Jug
Rijksmuseum, Amsterdam

paintings with a ginger jar which were made between 1653 and 1658.[31] But all these paintings, including those made up to 1659 (and some later ones) have a straight, flat plinth. A table such as the one in the sketch is seen in dated works from 1660 to 1680. The other drawing is in the same technique and of about the same size.[32] It seems in every respect to be a pendant of the first drawing. The second composition relates to paintings made around 1662. I see the drawings as composition sketches, possibly compiled from other ones and not necessarily preparatory for specific paintings.[33]

Fig. 10.6 illustrates a well-known painting by Kalf from the Rijksmuseum in Amsterdam.[34] The ewer is ornamented with lobes and resembles one made by Christiaen van Vianen of Utrecht, on loan to the Victoria and Albert Museum in London,[35] but it is not identical. The absence of a work by Kalf with a Van Vianen auricular-ornamented ewer is compensated by a painting with such an ewer by Willem van Aelst (cat. no. 58.1). It differs somewhat from Kalf's ewer and the one in London. The object is seen again in paintings by Kalf in Leningrad

THE SPARKLING LIGHT OF WILLEM KALF

and Weimar, the latter being dated 1680.³⁶ In the Amsterdam and Leningrad paintings the colorful citrus fruits are striking: a citron, a half-peeled lemon and Seville oranges. Both works were probably painted around 1656, perhaps the Amsterdam work a little later. The Rembrandtlike atmosphere supports this dating. Cat. no. 55 is another superb example by Willem Kalf, a painting of 1660 from the collection of Baron Thyssen-Bornemisza in Castagnola. It also is distinguished by a Rembrandtlike quality. The warm color, the loving light and the shadowy atmosphere, in which three glasses and a glass carafe faintly sparkle, create an effect of great subtlety and delicateness. The coloring, with lapis lazuli-blue against white, and the air of tranquility and intimacy make it comparable to works by Vermeer, whose *Woman reading a Letter* (fig. 10.7), in Dresden,³⁷ was painted about 1658 and has a similar persian rug. We can recognize this similarity to Vermeer in the earliest works by Kalf from his Amsterdam period. The Ming bowl with fruit in Vermeer's Dresden painting is comparable to the slanting bowl in the Amsterdam Kalf.³⁸ Vermeer used the pointillist technique for the first time in this work. Could he have been inspired to do this by Kalf? The fruit in Vermeer's work have a specific meaning: they are an allusion to fertility.

JOHANNES VERMEER
Woman reading a Letter, with Fruits
Gemäldegalerie Alte Meister, Dresden

We have seen the nautilus cup already in a work by Pieter Claesz, a painting made in 1636 (cat. no. 30). Here the effect is totally different, however: the personality of the painter asserts itself more strongly, even over such an opulent object. The fleeing Jonah is clearly seen; Neptune on the head of the whale is an elderly god, just as we always imagined him. In another work by Kalf, Jonah has disappeared and the nautilus cup has been placed in the opposite direction.[39] Kalf indeed made variations on his motifs, just as Vivaldi did in his concerti grossi. Things seem to be alike, and the same elements are used repeatedly, but each time with subtle differences.[40]

The Wan-li sugar bowl is ornamented with figures in high relief. They are the Eight Taoist Immortals arranged in pairs; a Fu-lion has been placed on the cover. The Fu-lion (or dog) was in China a symbol of prosperity and, particularly, of valor and energy. A few of these sugar bowls have been preserved.[41] In a number of Kalf's paintings, of which five are dated between 1660 and 1662, such a sugar bowl with cover appears.[42] A chased silver platter is an almost obligatory object in Kalf's still lifes from the Amsterdam period. Some are recognizable, but many are less important objects and are not painted with great detail. The platter in the Thyssen painting, like the one in the Oxford Van Beyeren (cat. no. 50), is similar to a platter made in Amsterdam in 1659.[43]

In 1663 Kalf painted the beautiful still life in the Cleveland Museum of Art (cat. no. 56). The same relationship to both Vermeer and Rembrandt is also noticeable in this work, and it can also be compared to fig. 10.7. A peach stone is lying on the silver plate. The same Ming Chinese bowl is seen in many of Kalf's paintings dated between 1660 and 1678. The most striking object in the painting is the glass goblet in the Thyssen still life, but that one is narrower. This slender type of goblet appears often in Kalf's paintings with a winged glass stem and not, as in this case, with a silver foot. With the help of this object we can examine the variations in Kalf's objects. The stem of the goblet has perhaps been broken, leading to its mounting on a silver foot. Once again the question arises whether this could also have been a matter of interchangeable parts or of the artist's fantasy. The same foot can be seen in a painting by Kalf in Leipzig (fig. 10.8),[44] but this time with a Turbo shell mounted on it and without the crown that envelopes the glass knob in the Cleveland painting. It can also be seen mounted under a nautilus cup in a dated work (1678) in Copenhagen (fig. 10.9).[45] The same or otherwise very similar glass goblet is seen on the same foot as the Kalf painting in Heino (cat. no. 16), and in a work of 1663 in Schwerin.[46]

The variation on the 'shell goblet' motif, based on the painting in Leipzig, makes this problem even more knotty. The same shell can be seen on four different feet.[47] I find it difficult to imagine how parts could have been exchanged in all these cases. The operation of doing this on a nautilus cup would entail much work. I believe that Willem Kalf did indeed allow himself to take liberties in the depiction of this objects for the sake of variety and composition in his work. This does not necessarily exclude the possibility of interchangeable parts: perhaps Kalf got his inspiration from them. Neither does this necessarily imply that his method was adopted by other artists. We have seen already in his Paris period that he was painting the same glasses with different feet. In the 1669 painting in the Indianapolis Museum of Art (cat. no. 57) Kalf falls back on his earlier style of composition. The fall of light through the rummer onto the ginger jar, creating an amber-colored half-light above the gray shadows cast by the gilt *bekerschroef*, is masterly. We see similarly subtle effects in the reflections of the silver plate in the glass objects on the table. The stem of the *bekerschroef*, the foot of which is half-hidden, is familiar. We recognize it from the glass goblet in the Cleveland painting (cat. no. 56), the nautilus cup from Copenhagen (fig. 10.9), the Turbo-goblet from Leipzig (fig. 10.8), and so on, although always with small variations in the depictions.[48] The silver putto is holding in his hand a gilt horn of plenty, meant as the antithesis of Measure, the watch.

The large ginger jar is a typical object of the Transitional period, i.e. the time between the end of the Ming and the beginning of the K'ang-hsi dynasties (1644-1662). Spriggs (1965) discusses a number of these which are related to the ginger jars that Kalf painted in five of his works. It seems to me that the one closest to this painting is in the Burghley House Collection.[49] Also here we see again small differences in Kalf's jars.[50]

Fig. 10.9 is one of Kalf's last works, dated 1678.[51] The *pièce de resistance* is a rock crystal bowl made around 1540 after a design of Hans Holbein. On the foot of the bowl we read 'Holbein Fe.' On the foot of the original bowl, which still exists, are other texts.[52] The history of this bowl is well documented:[53] at one time it belonged to Henry VIII, but we do not know how Kalf could have set eyes on it. Perhaps it passed through his hands in the art trade in Amsterdam. It is seen in the last dated work by Kalf, of 1680, in Weimar.[54] From the three peach stones we can infer that three peaches have already been eaten. We certainly see in this painting the aspect of pomp that so characterizes the pronk still life, but with the distinction that Measure, or restraint, is not forgotten.

WILLEM KALF
Still Life with a Shell Cup
Museum der Bildenden Künste, Leipzig

WILLEM KALF
Still Life with a Holbein Bowl
Statens Museum for Kunst, Copenhagen

CHAPTER 11

Sparkle and Smoke

Many eminent artists were working in the second half of the 17th century in Amsterdam, which had become one of the most important trading cities of the world. Haarlem was still a center for still-life painters, but as the distance between the two cities was only a few hours' walk it was quite easy for the artists to keep in contact with each other. Utrecht, Leiden, The Hague, Delft and Dordrecht were smaller centers of still life painters, and again the relatively small distances between these cities (100 kilometers) enabled the artists to keep up to date.

The majority of the good still-life painters worked in a precise and detailed style and gave a great deal of attention to the description of texture. The broader brushwork used by Van Beyeren was sometimes combined with this finer style, as, for example, in the works of Simon Luttichuys in Amsterdam, Barend van der Meer in Haarlem, and Abraham Susenier in Dordrecht. The great period of pronk still lifes in Holland and Antwerp lasted from around 1640 to 1670. Toward the end of the century pronk still lifes had had their day.

Simon Luttichuys worked in Amsterdam and painted vanitas and pronk still lifes and banquet pieces with fruit. He worked to begin with in the style of De Heem but developed an individual approach, and his technique is a little like that of Van Beyeren, especially in some paintings with small casks of oysters and breakfast pieces with fish. We know of dated works from the 1640s and 1650s which look like forerunners of Kalf's works from his Amsterdam period. An example is fig. 11.1, a painting of 1649 in the Národní Galerie in Prague.[1] It is a beautiful, well-balanced work that can compete with many paintings by the 'great masters.' Lying on a *puntschotel*, the pointed octagonal platter, are sweetmeats and candied oranges. Some of these *puntschotels* still exist.[2] The sauceboat in the Van Vianen style is unknown. The Chinese ginger jar with cover is from the Transitional period and must have been imported to Holland immediately after its manufacture. A similar jar is seen in other paintings of Luttichuys.[3] The theme of transiency is not only expressed here by the watch, of which only the silver lid and the ribbon to which the key is attached are visible, but also by the falling petal of the blown rose. These are wonderfully subtle details. Other Amsterdam still-life painters who are interesting for their pronk pieces are Paulus van den Bosch, G(illis?) van Berkborgh and Isaac van Kipshaven. Paulus van den Bosch was probably born in 1615 and died in 1664.[4] Several of his works dated between 1649 and 1655 are known. In the

11.1

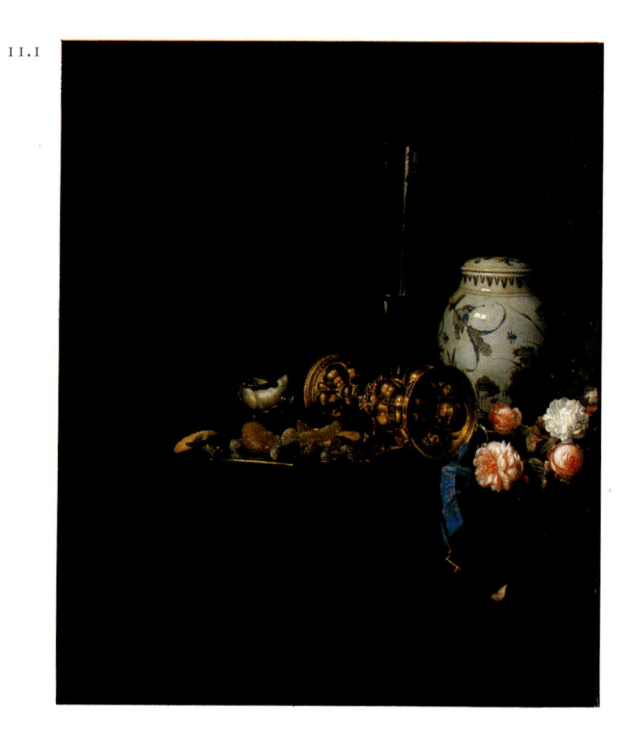

SIMON LUTTICHUYS
Still Life with a Transitional Ginger Jar, 1649
Národní Galerie, Prague

11.2

PAULUS VAN DEN BOSCH
Still Life with a Hercules Tazza, 1652
Private Collection

11.3

G. VAN BERKBORGH
Still Life with a Silver Dish and Tazza
Schlossmuseum, Weimar (German Democratic Republic)

literature and the art trade they are often confused with the works of Pieter van den Bosch, who was a painter of stable interiors. An example of Paulus's work is shown in fig. 11.2,[5] painted in 1652. The stem of the tazza is formed by Hercules holding in one hand his club and in the other a cornucopia which evolves into the bowl. It is possible that both the silversmith and the artist saw in Hercules a parallel to Christ's endeavors for fertility and abundance in the spiritual sense. Perhaps — to continue in this train of thought — the artist placed the grapes and the vine leaves in the center as a foil to the 'earthly' fruits on either side.[6] Similar interpretations could be made of other works by Paulus van den Bosch in which radishes, tobaccoware, a lobster or a Turbo shell are placed in opposition to eucharistic symbols or a *Miles Christianus*.[7] The same Hercules tazza is seen in other works of Paulus van den Bosch.[8] I include among the works attributed to him a splendid painting in Hamburg with a *façon de Venise* glass and a platter with bread in a niche.[9]

Little is known of G. van Berkborgh. Renckens (1967) was the first to pay him any attention as a painter.[10] Just as Paulus van den Bosch he seems to have been influenced by Luttichuys, and he may have been about the same age, since his dated work is from the same period. Fig. 11.3 is an example of his work which has been attributed to Willem Heda and belongs to the Schlossmuseum in Weimar.[11] We know even less about Isaac van Kipshaven. He painted still lifes and portraits. In a work of 1661, in the Mauritshuis in The Hague,[12] we can perhaps detect the influence of Luttichuys. A work attributed to Willem Gabron in the Staatsgalerie in Aschaffenburg[13] (fig. 11.4) is undoubtedly from Kipshaven's hand. Barend van der Meer painted pronk still lifes in the tradition of Luttichuys during the last quarter of the 17th century in Amsterdam.[14]

11.4

Isaac van Kipshaven
Still Life with a Silver Dish and Goblet
Staatsgalerie, Aschaffenburg (Federal Republic of Germany)

Willem van Aelst was born in 1627 in Delft. We know of works by him dated as early as 1642, when he was only fifteen years of age. On November 9, 1643, he became a master in his guild. He traveled in France and Italy from 1645 to 1656, and it is possible that he met Willem Kalf in Paris. During his travels he continued with his painting. He returned to Amsterdam in 1657, where he must have been very impressed by the work of Kalf. One of his paintings of this period (cat. no. 58), dated 1657, is in the National Museum in Copenhagen. The silver Van Vianen ewer is identical to the ewer in the signed work by Kalf in the Hermitage in Leningrad[15] and to one that is lying on its side in an unsigned work where another Van Vianen ewer is also present.[16] The *façon de Venise* glass is similar to one in other paintings by Kalf. The painting of such glassware was nothing new for Van Aelst; it occurred in earlier works.[17] A similar but more complicated glass is found in many of his paintings, such as fig. 11.5. The façon de Venise glass goblet cannot be identified in Kalf's pictures. It recurs in Van Aelst's later works.[18] Van Aelst also painted a Van Vianen ewer in this work of 1659, in the Bode Museum in Berlin (fig. 11.5), one of his most complex compositions.[19] The *bekerschroef* in this piece is strongly related to a silver saltcellar made by the Amsterdam silversmith Johannes Lutma in 1643.[20]

Van Aelst's compositions are usually quite simple, depicting only a few objects which he used repeatedly. On the other hand there are also things which we see only once or rarely. There is none of the variation in the depiction of objects that we found in Kalf's oeuvre. The details are often painted with great precision. In his fruit pieces, with their exaggerated relief in the veins of the leaves, we sometimes feel his sense of detail is too deliberate. Van Aelst painted flower and fruit pieces, bird still lifes and banquets with pronk objects. His range of color is wide, with blues and greens that can be cold and detached but which add to the distinction of the work and never lead to hardness. This distinction is increased by the silky and velvety modeling which he achieved by the subtle use of glazing. The still life in Copenhagen (cat. no. 58) is very restrained in its color scheme: silky and velvety gray and brown tints dominate. Small patches of red from the wine and of blue from the glass carafe break through in a very sensitive manner. Cooler touches, no less important, are seen in the blue-gray leaves of the shallots, of which the tips are defined in a masterly way. Such details as the way the agate-handled knife rests on the gold-threaded fringe of the velvet cloth are at once enriching and delicate in their nuances of color. Van Aelst demonstrates his mastery in the description of texture. The dry, thin, withered onion skin is almost palpably true to nature and painted with obvious affection. It is reasonable to see the bread and wine in the light of the Eucharist, and perhaps the fish too. Many, however, will consider that this is carrying interpretation too far.

Cat. no. 59 is a work of 1678, more than twenty years later. In many ways it is comparable to the Copenhagen painting, yet there are noticeable differences, especially in color and rendition of detail. The warm red of the velvet cloth is a wonderful foil for the silver and gold tints of the objects. These are painted rather broadly. In his later years Van Aelst characteristically used a freer brush stroke than in his youth. Again we see a masterpiece of silver, a saltcellar with auricular lobe ornaments in the tradition of the Van Vianens. The figure sitting against a gilded tree trunk is Orpheus playing a violin. He is placed between the gilt foot and the cup of the goblet. The same object can be seen in earlier paintings up to 1681,[21] as in fig. 11.6.[22] A

WILLEM VAN AELST
Still Life with a 'Bekerschroef' and Silver Jug
Bodemuseum, Berlin (German Democratic Republic)

WILLEM VAN AELST
Still Life with an Orpheus Salt Cellar, 1679
Private Collection, formerly Hoogsteder Gallery, The Hague

closely related stand, with Orpheus standing upright with a violin, onto which a nautilus shell has been mounted,[23] belongs to the group of objects that Van Aelst often used in his compositions. After Orpheus had had to leave his beloved Eurydice behind in the Underworld he consoled himself by playing, and his music was so sweet that he could even charm the beasts. Later he was stoned to death by the Thracian women.[24] He was, as Good Shepherd, already depicted as a Christ symbol in the Early Christian times.

Among the followers of Van Aelst were Ernst Stuven, Jacob Denys, Nicolaes Lachtropius and Hendrik de Fromantiou. Their works are often mistaken for Van Aelst's. An example of this is a painting by Lachtropius with Van Aelst's own nautilus cup in a niche, with fruit and a garland of flowers.[25] The influence of Van Aelst remains noticeable among Dutch still-life painters throughout the 18th century.

An exceptional type of still life, of which we know only a few examples, is that with religious objects. Some still lifes by Jan Davidsz. de Heem incorporated objects such as a crucifix (fig. 6.10) which were even an essential part of the composition. In another example a chalice

61

PIETER GERRITSZ. VAN ROESTRAETEN
Richard Green Gallery, London

PIETER GERRITSZ. VAN ROESTRAETEN
Museum Boymans-van Beuningen, Rotterdam

JAN ANTON VAN DER BAREN
Ecclesiastical Still Life
Kunsthistorisches Museum, Vienna

is depicted with a cartouche of fruit, ears of corn and flowers.[26] The origin of these pieces were the flower wreaths and cartouches encircling religious subjects, as painted respectively by Jan Brueghel the Elder and Daniel Seghers in Antwerp. Jan Anton van der Baren worked in the wake of Seghers. Pieter van Kessel painted, respectively, a chalice and a monstrance in a pair of cartouches of flowers.[27]

Van der Baren painted a still life with exclusively religious objects when he was in the service of Archduke Leopold Wilhelm in Vienna; this work is now in the Kunsthistorisches Museum in Vienna (fig. 11.7).[28] The objects are lying on a table in front of a background of buildings where one can see, on a small scale, a Nativity at the entrance of a temple or church. Hairs (1970) mentions this work as lost in her biography of the artist. It escaped her notice that this work was listed under no. 292 in the inventory of 1659 of the gallery of the Archduke as follows: 'Christi Geburt, seitlich ein Tisch mit einem roten Teppich, darauf die Opfer der heiligen drei Könige, Leinwand, in einer schwarzen Ramen, 4 Spann 5 Finger x 4 Spann 6 Finger, Original von dem Canonico van der Baren' (Birth of Christ, on the side of a table with a red rug, on which the gifts of the Holy Magi, canvas, in a black frame, 4 Spann and 5 Fingers x 4 Spann and 6 Fingers. Original painting by Canon Van der Baren). Since this description mentions the presents of the Magi, we know what the objects are supposed to be: gold, frankincense and myrrh. We see on the table: coins in an ornamented lacquer box, a silver incense burner[29] and a rock crystal goblet with perfumes.

A still-life tradition based on Catholicism hardly existed in the northern Netherlands, but in Antwerp in the south the followers of Seghers remained active until the beginning of the 18th century. A work like cat. no. 60 by Dirck de Bray is unique. The De Bray family were Roman Catholics living in the bishopric of Haarlem. Dirck made many woodcuts between 1656 and 1676 and a few still lifes in oil in the 1670s, which are jewels of Dutch still-life painting. De Bray's painting was made in 1672 and is now in Museum Amstelkring in Amsterdam. In front is a rosary of cut rock crystal, a rose, a sprig of rosemary and a morning glory. The rose is a symbol of godly love, the Christian, neighborly love of Mary. Rosemary is a symbol of eternity, but its name makes it also a Marian symbol. The morning glory is a tri-colored flower — white, yellow and blue — and as such a symbol of the Holy Trinity, like the pansy. It is a flower that opens in the morning and closes at the end of the afternoon so that it also represents the Day, the time of wakefulness and awareness. In some still lifes it has this meaning in contrast to a Night symbol, such as the opium poppy. The small incenser and the gilt Virgin's crown set with precious stones are the most striking objects. A reliquary decorated with saints is almost hidden by the crown. Another meditative still life by Dirck de Bray shows a crucifix, a Bible and roses with a glass in a niche.[30]

A still life which at first glance seems to be more worldly is fig. 11.8, also by Dirck de Bray.[31] A stuffed bird of paradise has been attached to a red velvet cap. Birds of paradise are sometimes seen in vanitas still lifes and represent the spiritual life, or redemption, to which man must aspire.[32] The meaning of the sword is manifold. It can refer to power and its transiency or to the fight for virtue; it is also a weapon of the *Miles Christianus*.[33] The manner in which the gold hilt of the sword has been painted by De Bray is reminiscent of Rembrandt.

Pieter Gerritsz. van Roestraeten, a fellow-townsman of Dirck de Bray, was a pupil of Frans

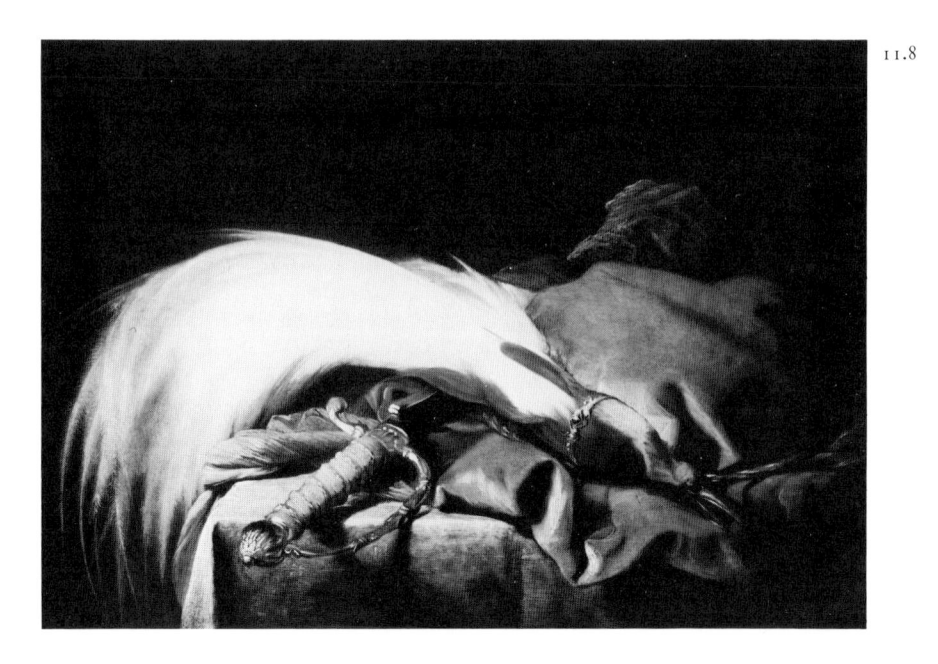

DIRCK DE BRAY
Still Life with a Bird of Paradise
Valls Gallery, London

Hals, whose daughter he married when he was twenty-four years old. He spent part of his life in England, where he died in 1698. He also painted a religious still life with a crucifix, a rosary and a watch pointing to the hour of eleven, and other vanitas objects.[34] In another work, a pronk portrait, a silver incense burner is placed between a hanging necklace of pearls and a pendant of sapphires, its profane antithesis.[35] Similar religious objects are sometimes seen in pronk still lifes with other vanitas objects.

61 Cat. no. 61 is a relatively early work in the style of De Heem, with the sparkle of Kalf and the vigor of Van Beyeren in its details. In the center is a Chinese *kendi* with a silver mount, an Amor on the top who can represent either worldly or godly love. We have already encountered a similar mount, doubtless by the same maker, in a still life, dated 1615, by Nicolaes Gillis (fig. 4.10). A *kendi* related to the one in the Roestraeten, with a similar mount, has been preserved.[36] Again we see a reference to the Eucharist in the midst of profane objects. The alabaster chalice on the back of the gilt eagle is a reference to Christ. The eagle is a divine symbol since Antiquity, when it was the bird of Zeus, the uppergod of the Greeks. It became a symbol of Christ since Melito of Sardes, based on certain texts from the Old Testament, for instance the eagle's way leading to heaven (Proverbs 30, 19). The eagle is also an attribute of St. John the Evangelist. According to Aristotle, the eagle is able to withstand the sun's glare when staring at its light. Several emblems link the mythological eagle with Christianity, for example by the representation of Ganimede, Zeus' beloved boy, as a flying eagle with motto's like 'In Deo laetandum', One should delight in God, or 'Non est Mortale quod opto', What I long for is not transient.[37]

In England, Van Roestraeten developed a new kind of still life which included foreign, mostly Chinese but also English, utensils for tea drinking: English silverware for tea, smoking tobacco and ivory tankards. There are in his oeuvre some exclusive tea still lifes but also still lifes with pots and cups for the drinking of coffee and chocolate. Such still lifes became popular, especially among French artists in the 18th century, like Liotard. In cat. no. 62, a paint-

62 ing from the Boymans-van Beuningen Museum in Rotterdam, we see at the left a Yi-shing teapot.[38] Dried tea leaves, an expensive commodity, are lying on a sheet of paper with a wax seal. The two Chinese bowls, one on its side, are reflected in the lacquered tabletop. At the back is a tea caddy with a goldcolored floral decoration. The silver spoon is a rat-tailed one.[39] Tea came to Holland with the East Indiamen from China and Japan at the beginning of the 17th century. Originally it was used as a remedy for all sorts of complaints, but in the writings of Bontekoe and Blankaart tea drinking was encouraged as a pleasure.[40] Just as in England, however, it remained for a long time only for the rich.

Let us at the end of this chapter pause for a moment over the central object in this composition, the silver candlestick. A female figure is carrying a cornucopia which becomes the drip tray for the candle. This is almost identical (only the rim of the drip tray is not octagonal but lobed) to a pair made by Anthony Nelme in 1693, which is in the collection of the Bank of England.[41] The candlestick appears in a number of Van Roestraeten's paintings, nearly all of them vanitas still lifes, one of which is dated 1696.[42] It is always seen from the same angle.[43] In the candlestick above the woman's head there is only the stump of a candle. The woman is in the flower of her life, yet from the glowing wick of the candle rises a thin plume of smoke, the last, fleeting instant of a life of fire and light.

Notes

1 INTRODUCTION

1 Since Antiquity many editions and translations of the fables have appeared. The story of the magpie with the peacock feathers can be found, among others, in the version of Edewaerd de Dene, *De Waerachtige Fabulen der Dieren...*, published in 1567 in Bruges with etchings of Marcus Gheeraerts, and in Joost van den Vondel's adaptation *Vorstelycke Warande der Dieren* of 1617 with partly the same illustration: embl. 48.

2 With monogram and dated, panel, oval, 66 x 48.5 cm; formerly Gallery P. de Boer, Amsterdam (1983), Bergström 1983, ill.; Frederiks 1961, vol 4, no. 12, pls. 11-13; J.R. ter Molen in cat. Amsterdam, Toledo and Boston 1979-80, no. 11, ill.

3 Cf. Fitzwilliam Museum, Cambridge (England), inv. no. PD 299, with monogram and dated 1630, panel, 25 x 32.7 cm; mus. cat. 1960, p. 19, pl. 10; Vroom 1980, cat. no. 92 (Pieter Claesz) and 241 (Franchoys Elout), as dated 1640 and with wrong measurements.

4 E.g., signed, panel, 44 x 40.5 cm, Vroom 1980, cat. no. 329.

5 Attention has been drawn to the still lifelike elements in Aertsen and Beuckelaer, for instance by Baldass 1923-25, p. 36; Vorenkamp 1933, p. 20; and Luttervelt 1947, pp. 4-5, but many of these works are not considered to be still lifes *sensu stricto*.

6 Herodotus 1, 29-33; Plutarch 5, 27.

7 E.g.: Härting 1983, cat. nos. A 235-238b, Kunsthistorisches Museum, Vienna, inv. no. 1049, signed, panel, 86.5 x 120 cm; mus. cat. 1973, p. 70, pl. 102; Härting no. A 235, fig. 85.

8 Livius 26, 50; Polybius 10, 17, 19; Valerius Maximus 4,3; Petrarca, *Africa* 4, 375-388.

9 Härting 1983, cat. nos. A 240-244.

10 Examples of both scenes in Pigler 1974, vol. 2, pp. 329, 424-429; vol. 3, pls. 281, 322.

11 1 Kings 10:1-13; about Solomon's wealth *ibidem* 14-29.

12 Pigler 1974, pp. 167-171.

13 Inv. no. 756; canvas, 158 x 217 cm; mus. cat. 1927, p. 344, pl. 75. A large etching after this work was made by Franciscus van den Wyngaerde.

14 Euripides, *Cyclops*, 5ff.

15 Inv. no. 4731, signed and dated, canvas, 117 x 159 cm; mus. cat. 1984, p. 399, ill.

16 Sambucus 1564, p. 185. The Dutch translation was published in 1566 in Antwerp. It was the first emblem book that appeared in Dutch and it shows a number of emblems with transiency as their theme.

17 Genesis 14:18-20.

18 Psalms 110:4.

19 Hebrews 6:20,7.

20 Inv. no. 1974.1, signed and dated, panel, 82.5 x 54 cm; mus. cat. 1980, vol. 1, pp. 70-71, vol. 3, ill. p. 395; Van Regteren Altena 1983, cat. no. P 11, fig. 3.

21 Rijksmuseum, Amsterdam, inv. no. A 2813, panel, nearly circular, 52 x 50.5 cm; mus. cat. 1976, p. 543, ill. See this cat., fig. 2.3.

22 Yale University Art Gallery, New Haven, inv. no. 1937.36, signed and dated, panel, 117.5 x 165.5 cm; Van Regteren Altena 1983, cat. no. P. 12, fig. 23.

23 The development of these still lifes and the influence of Albrecht Dürer and engravings of Hendrick Hondius have been treated in my article *Die Entstehung der Stilleben-Tradition in Hinblick auf Dürer*, in press.

24 Examples: Jan Vermeulen and Willem van Odekerken; in Italy Evaristo Baschenis among others.

25 Bergström (1947) 1956; Segal 1982a; Segal 1983a.

26 Examples in Segal 1983a, pp. 23-25.

27 Robert Lehmann Collection, signed and dated, inv. no. 1975.1.110, panel, 99 x 85 cm; mus. cat. 1980, vol. 1, p. 27, vol. 3, ill. p. 332; Friedländer 1967, vol. 1, fig. 75.

28 For the two tall ewers on the shelf, cf. a similar ewer from the Treasury of the Basel Cathedral from the first quarter of the 15th century, now in the Victoria and Albert Museum, London; Fritz 1982, fig. 648.

29 Inv. no. 1444/MR 821, signed and dated, panel, 71 x 68 cm; mus. cat. 53, pl. 51; De Bosque 1975, pp. 190-193, ill.

30 For the facet-cut rock-crystal cup, cf. the 'Burgundian Court Cup' in the Kunsthistorisches Museum, Vienna; Hahnloser & Brugger-Koch 1985, p. 179, no. 335, pl. 20.

31 Sulzberger 1965.

32 The genre paintings of Marinus van Roemerswael, who had many followers in this type of painting, were strongly influenced by Quinten Matsys.

33 Kröller-Müller Museum, Otterlo, Netherlands, inv. no. 1222-51, dated, panel, 44 x 44 cm; mus. cat. 1970, no. 27, fig. 7.

34 Oesterreichische Nationalbibliothek, inv. no. Cod. 1857, fol. 43 verso, ca. 22 x 18 cm. Depiction of Nicolaes Spierinc, c. 1477.

35 Idem, fol. 14 verso; Segal 1982, pp. 3-4, fig. 1.

36 Universitätsbibliothek, Erlangen, Ms. 2361: Christine le Pisan, *Epitre d'Orthea, Déesse de la prudence à Hector, chef des Troyens;* Wolf 1987, p. 24-25, fig. 2.

37 John 6:41.

38 Ed. Amsterdam 1634, pp. 1-28; cited: ed. Thompson 1965, p. 55.

39 Pre-stages of the meal still life include also some other scenes from the New Testament like Christ in the house of Martha and Mary (Luke 10:38-92), the Supper at Emmaus (Luke 29:30-31), the parable of the prodigal son (Luke 15:13), and the wedding in Cana (John 2: 1-11). And less common: Christ in the house of Simon (Luke 7:36-50), the parable of the royal wedding (Matthew 22:1-14), and the Meal of Herodes (Matthew 14:6). Other paintings represent profane meals with a group of guests and allegorical meals. Mythological meals are usually of a later date.

40 Inv. no. 1924-24, transferred to canvas.

41 Sources, citations and translations in cat. Ghent 1986-87, pp. 14-17.

42 Ortelius, *Album amicorum,* fo. 12 verso.

43 Regarding Aertsen's belief, Moxey's opinion is also based on premises which have no foundation whatever: Briels 1987, p. 440 n. 4.

44 Genaille 1959, pp. 275-276.

45 Segal 1982a, p. 9.

46 Anne W. Lowenthal, *Moral dilemmas in sixteenth century art,* Colloqium 'Art in the Northern Netherlands 1525-1580,' Rijksmuseum, Amsterdam 1986. Cf. Segal 1986c where the 'choice' has been elaborated upon.

47 Old inventory no. 699.

2 ON MEANING AND INTERPRETATION:
THE ABUNDANCE OF LIFE AND MODERATION IN ALL THINGS

1 E.g. De Jongh 1967; 1976.

2 E.g. De Jongh 1986.

3 Falkenberg 1985; Bruyn 1986.

4 Bergström 1947/1956.

5 De Jongh 1982; Segal div. publ.

6 Saunders 1955.

7 Aristotle's concept of the golden mean is a motto in many emblem books, for instance in Otto van Veen's *Emblemata Horatiana*, Antwerp 1607.

8 In some paintings, such as in those of Pieter Aertsen, Jacques de Gheyn and Balthasar van der Ast, the 'underdrawing' in black chalk has become visible in the course of time to the naked eye in places where the paint has become somewhat transparent. In many other painters who applied thicker layers of paint we can sometimes detect some fragments, and with the help of infra-redreflectography it is possible to make the sketch visible. Cf. fig. 3.2, and Segal 1983, pp. 53-54, fig. 19.

9 Cats 1618, p. 13; comp. De Jongh 1976, p. 25, n. 26. The comparison has been derived from Thomas Aquinas, without mention of the source, see Gombrich 1972, pp. 13-14, 199 n. 16.

10 *Prima Pars Dictionari* Nürnberg 1499 (3 vol.), and later editions or earlier manuscripts.

11 For example, Thomas Aquinas: *sensus litteralis* and *sensus spiritualis.* Cf. Cats: Minne- en Zinnebeelden, the latter with moralizing admonition.

12 For example according to neo-platonic principles, in Marsilio Ficino and in Alciatus, among others.

13 *De Doctrina Christiana* 1.2: the *sensus literalis, sensus moralis, sensus allegoricus* and *sensus anagogicus.*

14 Zohar Hadash, ed. Jerusalem 1953, col. 83a; cited in Gershom Sholem, *On the Kabbalah and its Symbolism,* New York (1965) 1986, p. 54.

15 For example, the translator, Wolfgang Hunger, of the German edition of Alciatus's *Emblematum libellus,* Paris 1542, and many emblems, among others, in Poirters. For an elaboration of the theme of *choice* in still lifes, see: Segal 1986; also, in connection with Pieter Aertsen, fig. 1.8.

16 La Perrière 1548, see Porteman 1977, pp. 31-32; Antonius a Burgundia, *Des wereldts proef-steen....,* Antwerp 1643 (*Mundi Lapis Lydius...,* Antwerp 1639).

17 The Master of the Dresdener Gebetbuch, Sachsische Landesbibliothek, Dresden, Ms. A 311; the Master of Anton of Burgundy, University Library, Wroclaw; University Library, Leipzig, see Winkler 1925, pls. 43, 45, 52; Wolf 1978, figs. 14-15.

18 Mâle (1898) 1958, p. 202-205 connects the series, among others, with *Psychomachia*.

19 Royal Library, Copenhagen, inv. no. 1605. 4; Wolf 1985, figs. 7, 8, 10, 11, 14, 15.

20 Inv. no. 2822, signed, panel, 120 x 150 cm; mus. cat. 1972, pp 66-67.

21 Museum Boymans-van Beuningen, Rotterdam, inv. no. P.B. d. O.1, signed and dated 1560, pen and brown ink, 221 x 294 mm. The anonymous burin engraving is attributed to Filips Galle, cat. Brussels 1980, p. 117, no. 57, ill.

22 A rein is also a central attribute in a still life of Torrentius of 1614 with a Temperantia-text on the sheet of music (fig. 2.2): Rijksmuseum, inv. no. A 2813, panel, nearly circular, 52 x 50.5 cm.

23 Hollstein no. 410; Van Regteren Altena 1983, vol. 1, pp. 48-49, fig. 38.

24 De Jongh 1976, p. 275, 277 n. 1 (literature), fig. 72a.

25 Franken 1881, no. 1506, no. 1 from a series of *Rampspoeden* (Catastrophies).

26 Lucas van Leyden: dated 1539; Bartsch 1808, no. 133; Lavalleye 1966, no. 181, ill. Jacques de Gheyn the Younger: Hollstein, vol. 7, p. 18, no. 46, ill; Van Thiel 1968, p. 92, fig. 2. Crispyn de Passe the Elder: in several series of the Virtues, e.g. Franken 1881, nos. 1012, 1017, and 1029, after Johannes Stradanus: dated 1600; De Jongh 1976, p. 292, fig. 72a. Hieronymus Wierix: in three series of the Virtues, Mauquoy-Hendickx 1979, vol. 2, nos. 1352, 1371, after Johannes Stradanus, 1386, ill. pp. 179, 180, 182. Rollenhagen 1614, vol. 2, embl. 84. Visscher 1614, see De Jongh 1967, pp. 57-59, ill.

27 The series *VII Virtutum theologicarum et cardinalium icones artificiosissima a Io. Strad...*, and the series *VII Peccatorum Capitalium imagines elegantissime...*, Franken 1881, nos. 1364-1371 and 1372-1379, ill. pp. 180 and 181.

28 Franken 1881, no. 1029; ill. De Jongh 1986, p. 294, fig. 72b.

29 Molsdorf (1926) 1968, no. 1062; Timmers 1947, no. 1189; Timmers 1978, no. 387.

30 Ed. 1646, p. 686.

31 Formerly Johnny Van Haeften Gallery, London (1984), with monogram and dated 1640, panel, oval, 56 x 41 cm; Bergström 1983, fig. 1.

32 *Adagia*, chil. 1, cent. 6, no. 96; ed. 1612, col. 256.

33 See n. 26 for other examples of the motto in emblem books; see also Henkel and Schöne (1967) 1978, col. 321, 1647, 1835.

34 Visscher 1614, vol. 1, embl. 21; Cats, *Liefdes Kortsprake* as proverb, ed. 1726, p. 560a.

35 In a text underneath an engraving after Jacob Savery being too generous to children is regarded as immoderation for which the reward is ingratitude; see Van Thiel 1987, p. 109, fig. 7, pp. 112-113 n. 68, cf. p. 116 n. 75, p. 127 no. II, 4.

36 Plokker 1984, cat. no. 13, with references to the literature; see also Segal 1983a, p. 31.

37 In fact a later addition: *Hadriani Iunii Adagiorum*, cent. 1, Erasmus-ed. 1612, col. 1170-1171; ed. 1646, p. 686.

38 See n. 22.

39 See n. 25; De Jongh 1967, pp. 56-60, ill. Cf. De Jongh 1982, pp. 80-82.

40 For example Alciatus 1551, p. A2b; Cats 1618, 1627, embl. 43; Zincgref 1633, embl. 97.

41 Visscher 1614, vol. 1, embl. 21.

42 Ed. Pers 1643, p. 341. About playing music and musical instruments in paintings as a sign of harmony, see also De Jongh 1976, p. 74 and Miedema 1977, p. 215 n. 47.

43 Herzog Anton Ulrich-Museum, Braunschweig, inv. no. 109; signed, canvas, 190 x 194 cm; cat. Braunschweig 1978, no. 41, ill.

44 Stechow 1938, with classical sources; De Jongh 1976, p. 45-47; and numerous other publications.

45 Musées Royaux des Beaux-arts, Brussels, inv. no. 569, canvas, 141 x 199 cm; mus. cat. 1984, p. 25, ill.

46 Musée de l'Oeuvre Notre Dame, Strasbourg, inv. no. 1249, signed and dated, canvas, 125 x 165 cm.

3 THE YOUNG HIERONYMUS AND FRANS FRANCKEN

1 Segal 1982, p. 5, cat. no. 2, ill.

2 Segal 1983, pp. 49-50, 105, cat. no. 6, ill., with literature.

3 Inv. no. 934, panel, 26.2 x 36.3 cm, mus. cat. 1959, p. 96, as Hieronymus Francken the Elder. The 4 of the date looks like a 7 because of a horizontal retouching. The painting is signed on the border of the plate: *Anno 1604 Jeronimus Francken*. Cf. Segal 1986, p. 58, 60 n. 16.

4 Enklaar 1940, p. 23, fig. 3.

5 Formerly collection Baron André Descamp, Brussels; sale Palais des Beaux-Arts, Brussels, 24/27 March 1981, no. 688, panel, 34 x 44 cm.

6 Examination on 19 December 1977 in cooperation with Dr. J.R.J. van Asperen de Boer, the photos made by Mr. Jaap Engelsman, Amsterdam.

7 Popham 1932, cat. no. 8, p. 210, pl. 88, bodycolor, 210 x 320 mm.

8 Panel, 34.2 x 44.0 cm; Segal 1986, pp. 58-60, fig. 3. I have only seen two versions in originals.

9 For a similar cup, cf. a prizes print of 1592, 'Loterije voor die arme Cranchsinnighe Menschen binnen der Stede Aemstelredamme' (Lottery in aid of the destitute lunatics within the City of Amsterdam); Municipal Record Office, Amsterdam; cf. Frederiks 1952, vol. 1, no. 17, ill.

10 Cat. Amsterdam 1970, p. 46 no. 33, ill. This version differs in the lower right corner in that it has a black and white checkered knife, a biscuit and a pretzel. These are probably very early additions and remind us of Georg Flegel and Clara Peeters.

11 Ed. 1611, pp. 101, 441-442, 510; ed. 1644, pp. 159, 622, 503.

12 Physiologus, cap. 7, ed. Curley 1979, pp. 10-12.

13 The owl can have many symbolic meanings, both positive and negative. Comp. Schwarz and Plagemann, 'Die Eule' in *Reallexikon zur deutschen Kunstgeschichte*, vol. 6, pp. 267-322.

14 Schön, Nürnberg 1540; cf. Segal 1986c, p. 60 n. 20, with text.

15 Hollstein, vol. 2, p. 96, no. 8.

16 De Brune 1636, p. 209.

17 Gillis 1566, p. 110.

18 Other meanings of the windmill which are perhaps of importance for religious scenes are related to the idea that the sails move according to God's will. This idea has later been expressed in Zincgref and Vondel. Cf. the title page of Julius Wilhelm Zincgref, *Emblematum Ethico-Politicorum Centuria*, Francfort 1619 (and later editions and books based on it) with a

vignette of a mill with the motto *Adspirante Deo* (On the breath of God) engraved by Matthias Merian. Cf. also Joost van den Vondel, *Den Gulden Winckel...*, Amsterdam 1613, pp. 14-15 with a mill as object of an emblem: 'Ziet hoe de wrake Gods (opdat wij niet en dolen)/Hier vergeleken werd bij eenen stillen Molen...' and 'De stille molen dan ons allen zij een bake, / Dat wij de goedheyd Gods erkennen voor zijn wrake....' ('See how God's wrath - so that we do not go astray - is compared here to a mill at standstill' and 'The mill at standstill is then a beacon for us all, so that we acknowledge God's goodness for his wrath...'); (ed; 1937, p. 28, without ill.; a part of the 17th- and 18th-century editions have appeared under the title *Toonneel des Mensschelijken Levens*, e.g. ed. 1699, pp. 14-15).

19 Cf. Falkenburg 1985, p. 109. Also, for example, Jeroen Bosch's *Prodigal Son* or *The Hawker*.

20 Isaiah 3:10: 'Say ye to the righteous, that it shall be well with him: for they shall eat the fruit of their doings.' Cf. Psalms 58:12.

21 Monballieu 1979.

22 *The Meat Stall*, University of Uppsala, dated 1551, panel, 124 x 169 cm, in which we see several other connections with the work of Hieronymus Francken.

23 A similar ten-lobed cup is in the Church of St. Thomas in Leipzig; cf. Fritz 1982, fig. 853. To the left an elongated version of the popular *Setzbecher* or *Häufebecher*, see cf. a set of eight, made at Speyer in 1519 and now in the Kassel State Museum, Hernmarck 1977, fig. 48.

24 Czobor 1963, p. 66, fig. 51.

25 Bergström 1956, pp. 25-26.

26 Samuel H. Kress Collection, inv. no. 1952.5.33, panel, 93 x 30.8 cm; mus. cat. 1985, p. 55, ill.: c. 1485/1490.

27 Gibson 1973, pp. 46-47, figs. 31, 32, 34.

28 Inv. no. 3825, panel, 58 x 70.5 cm; mus. cat. 1984, p. 335, ill.; attributed by Greindl 1983, p. 165, fig. 43, to Cornelis de Brier. Works attributed to Hans van Essen, such as a 'little breakfast' with a wooden plate and herrings in Bergström 1947/1956, fig. 98, deserve further study to ascertain a connection with Hieronymus Francken. In the reproduction in Bergström, a part of the inset, with some figures at a table, has been overpainted, as can be seen from the reproduction of the sale Charpentier, Paris, June 7, 1955, no. 95 (as Floris van Schooten). In a photograph of 1933 a monogram might possibly be seen on the plinth on the left.

29 English private collection; sale Sotheby's, London, 19 April 1967, no. 112, signed and dated, panel, 88.9 x 109.8 cm; Härting, cat. no. A 376, fig. 108; Müller Hofstede 1984, fig. p. 256 (no. 10, erroneously numbered 11); Ertz 1979, cat. no. 265, fig. 546. Only known to me from reproductions. Härting doubts a collaboration with Jan Brueghel, as suggested by Ertz.

30 In a stricter sense measuring a globe with compasses stands for Geometry. See for the interpretation of the scene Veldman 1985.

31 Inv. no. B 621; panel, 49 x 64 cm; cat. 1957, p. 222, ill.; Speth-Holterhoff 1957, pp. 75-77, fig. 16; Härting 1983, cat. no. A 362, a related painting in a private collection. The original is not known to me: panel, 67 x 78 cm, Speth-Holterhoff, p. 75, fig. 15; Härting, cat. no. A 364.

32 Interpreted by Luther in cat. Münster & Baden-Baden 1979-80, p. 126 and 569 ns. 82-84, as a glass sphere and connected with fortune telling or alchemy.

33 Speth-Holterhoff 1975, p. 77, fig. 17. The idea has been adopted by Härting 1983, p. 153, cat. no. A 378. The comparison is based on Ruben's famous *Four Philosophers* in the Palazzo Pitti in Florence. See also the following note.

34 The whereabouts of both paintings is unknown. 1. Coll. Widener, Philadelphia, cat. 1900, ill., panel, 63.3 x 71.8 cm; Härting 1983, cat. no. A 379. Ortelius on the grounds of resemblance to the portrait by Adriaen T. Key in the Getty Museum, Malibu, inv. no. A 54-P-2, and the engraving by Philip Galle from 1579. 2. A work which was before 1946 in Knoedler Gallery, New York, panel, 53 x 74 cm, cf. Härting 1983, p. 154 n. 364.

35 Inv. no. 1048, signed FF, panel, 74 x 78 cm; Härting 1983, cat. no. A. 361, figs. 106 and 40. Here also are some puzzles to be solved.

36 Inv. no. 96, on loan from the Government of Belgium since 1951, signed and dated 1618, panel, 56 x 85 cm; cat. 1959, p. 94; Härting 1983, cat. no. A 360.

37 There are two sagas which are examples of the stupidity of the rich Phrygian king Midas: first he obtained from Dionysos the power of turning whatever he touched into gold, and secondly, when called upon to decide a musical contest between Pan and Apollo, he decided in favor of the insignificant Pan, whereupon Apollo changed Midas's ears into those of a donkey (Ovid, *Metamorph.* 11, 85-193). The first story gives us a certain view of prosperity: if everything were turned into gold we could neither eat nor live.

38 In some cases paintings from both series of these scenes have the same size, e.g. Härting A 370 or 371 and A 378. Scholars and iconoclasts together in two small works, A 372 and 372a. Briels (1980, p. 160) sees Ignorantia as the opposite of 'recta ratio', common sense. Müller Hofstede disagrees with this contradistinction.

39 Inv. no. 31.2010, panel, 94.2 x 123.4 cm, with Archduke Albert and his wife Isabella; Härting 1983, cat. no. B 380; Ertz 1979, cat. no. 353, fig. 545, as Frans Francken the Younger and Jan Brueghel the Elder. A related but simpler painting in the Museo del Prado, Madrid, inv. no. 1405; cat. 1975, vol. I, pp. 380-381, vol. II, p. 251, as Adriaen van Stalbemt.

40 Janson 1952, pp. 145-162, with many examples.

41 Typotius (1601) 1652, pp. 22-23.

42 Inv. nos. 1394 through 1398, panel, ca. 65 x 108 cm: *Sight*, signed and dated 1617; *Taste*, signed and dated 1618; *Smell*, signed; *Touch* and *Hearing*, unsigned; cat. 1975, vol. I, pp. 40-46, vol. II, pls. 28-30; Ertz 1979, cat. nos. 327 through 331, ill.

43 Lib. 33, cap. 19; ed. 1610, p. 336. Valerianus states that he has based this on Sextus Pompeius, Lucianus and Varro.

44 John 9:1-7; Mark 8:22-25.

45 Cf. Mark 10:52; John 9:38.

46 Ertz adopted the older view that the allegorical nymph which represents Sight appears in the form of Venus who is reprimanding her small son Amor. This does not change the conclusions of this chapter.

4 LAID TABLES: FOOD FOR THOUGHT

1 Cf. Bergström 1978, pp. 136-137, fig. 93, and Segal 1984c, pp. 75-75, fig. 3, for *Spring* and *Winter*. The *Summer* was recently acquired by Johnny Van Haeften Gallery, London.

2 Ed. 1604, pp. 264, 285, 298-299; new data in the posthumhous edition of 1618, pp. 211ff. The most exhaustive publication on Badens and his work is Faggin 1969. See also Van Regteren Altena 1983, vol. 1, p. 70, and for a copy by Jacques de Gheyn the Younger after Frans Badens, vol 1, pl. 466, and vol. 3, no. 1050.

3 Inv. no. 519-187; canvas, 91.5 x 81 cm, Faggin 1969, pp. 136, 191, fig. 158.

4 *St. Jerome in His Cell*, in the Landesmuseum für Kunst und Kulturgeschichte in Oldenburg, Germany, slate, 11.5 x 20.5 cm; mus. cat. 1966, pp. 54-55, ill.; cf. Faggin 1969, p. 144. The whereabouts of a painting of a young man with a guitar, panel, 84 x 62 cm, is unknown (photo Witt Library, London).

5 Inv. no. NM 4470, signed with monogram PB and date 1620, canvas, 54 x 85 cm.

6 The painting, panel, 27 x 22.5 cm, is known to me only by a photograph made in 1939. It is probably signed. Around a burning candle in a candlestick are arranged a Ming plate with a sliced fish, a knife, half an orange, a mouse, a glass of wine, a Ming basin with olives and pieces of bread and cheese. Also this work seems to anticipate later works by Flegel. The drawing of a lobster is signed *Den 18 April/Anno 1608/FB* and belongs to a private collection in America, attributed there to F. Brendel. Dr. Heinrich Geissler of the Staatsgalerie, Stuttgart, has shown me a photograph of it. The measurements are unknown.

7 Private collection, copper, 51 x 73 cm, Bott 1961, no. 29, ill., a version of a monogrammed work, dated 1618, in Castle Schwarzenberg, Krumauz (Czechoslovakia), panel, 53 x 74 cm, Bott 1961, no. 16, ill.; Greindl 1983, p. 338, cat. nos. 19 and 5.

8 The glass holder is reminiscent of Jamnitzer's style, particularly his celebrated ewers, produced c. 1600, in the Kunsthistorisches Museum, Vienna, Kris 1932, pp. 55-57, no. 88, pl. 61; and in the Grünes Gewölbe, Dresden, cat. Nürnberg 1985, pp. 264-265, no. 89. ill.

9 Inv. no. B 1792, canvas, 120 x 146 cm.

10 Canvas, 115 x 85 cm, sale Sotheby's, Monaco, 20 June 1987, no. 351; Greindl 1983, p. 83 (as circle of Frans Snyders with monogram AS), and p. 268, fig. 161, p. 370, cat. no. 1. Cat. no. 2, which is mentioned by her, is unknown to me; no. 3 is certainly not by the same painter as no. 1. Another unsigned version or copy of the kitchen piece was recently auctioned in Paris at Ader, Picard, & Tajan, 21 November 1987, no. 24.

11 Sale Sotheby's, Monaco, 6 December 1987, no. 49, canvas 42.5 x 56 cm. The painting has, unfortunately, been greatly rubbed. There also exist connections with much later signatures on portraits from the 1640s: I.A.W. FE. A°. MDCXLII and I.A.V.W. F. A° 1644. These works are in the museums of Darmstadt and Frankfurt, respectively.

12 Resp. inv. no. 856; canvas, 83 x 57.5 cm; mus. cat. Donation d'Antoine Brasseur, 1981, pp. 138-139, ill., as after Osias Beert; fig. 4.2: private collection, canvas, 85 x 61 cm.

13 Segal 1984c. In this article the attribution to Flegel was deliberately left undecided.

14 Among others a still life in an American private collection, canvas, 29.5 x 39.5 cm, as Georg Flegel, with a pewter plate with two smoked herrings, a knife, a little basket with red currents, a silver tazza with apples, a silver beer tankard and a roll of bread.

15 I hope to report in the near future on a number of newly-found works by Flegel.

16 Canvas, 91.5 x 120.5 cm; sale Ader, Picard & Tajan, 22 November 1987, no. 10, ill.

17 Segal 1984c compared and listed the flowers in all known Flegel bouquets.

18 The attribution of cat. no. 4 to Flegel in Segal 1984c, pp. 78, 86 n. 36. The many similarities to details in signed or documented works by Georg Flegel have been stated in a report. Here we mention only that similarities regarding the knife have been noted in five other paintings, the carnation in six, the pomegranate in four, the coins in four, the orange to the left in four, the *roemer* in two, the birds, the bread with fly and the half walnut in one work. One sees again some of the objects in works by Binoit: the carnation in one work of 1615 and a related jug in works of 1616 and 1627, birds with cloves in a work of 1618, but this is perhaps a copy. Fig. 4.5: inv. no. 5026, panel, 22 x 28 cm; mus. cat. 1983, p. 201, ill.

19 Inv. no. MNR 709, panel, 50 x 77 cm; mus. cat. 1981, p. 22, ill. (Peter Binoit); Greindl 1983, pp. 60, 193, fig. 36, cat. no. 135 (Peter Binoit).

20 The painting and its similarities to and differences from works by Osias Beert have been extensively discussed in Segal 1986b.

21 Sale 16 April 1738, no. 168; cf. Hoet 1752, p. 517.

22 Luke 16:19-21; Pigler 1974, vol. 1, pp. 375-376, mentions 58 works with this theme, mostly Dutch and Italian. There are many more, for instance by Frans Francken the Younger. See Härting 1983, cat. nos. A 122, A 122a and A 123.

23 Hollstein, vol. 5, p. 47, nos. 71-74.

24 Hollstein, 1964, vol. 15, pp. 141-142, nos. 118-121; Franken 1881, pp. 196-197, nos. 1066-1069.

25 Hollstein 1974, vol. 16, p. 90, nos. 3-6; Franken 1881, pp. 195-196, nos. 1062-1065.

26 Inv. no. 2/60, copper, 50 x 65.5 cm, cat. 1975, pp. 44-45; Greindl 1983, p. 29, fig. 7, cat. no. 28.

27 With monogram, copper 51 x 44 cm, private collection. The stem has been treated asymmetrically.

28 For example, a conical glass with glassdrops on a *bekerschroef* in a painting in the Národní Galerie in Prague, inv. no. O 2730 (formerly attributed to Alexander Adriaenssen), panel, 43.5 x 36 cm, and in a painting in a private collection in Germany, panel, 53 x 79 cm, Segal 1986a, fig. 7, Greindl 1983, fig. 18, cat. no. 29; and in a work in another collection in Germany, panel, 56 x 78 cm, cat. *A Fruitful Past*, no. 25, ill., Greindl 1983, cat. no. 1, ill., also with an identical trick-glass as in our painting.

29 Segal 1982a, p. 31.

30 Segal 1983a, p. 64.

31 Only known to me from photos: panel, 46 x 65 cm, probably cut at the top, exhibited Amsterdam 1933, no. 138 (David de Heem), and in the sale Hans Lange, Berlin, 3 December 1940, no. 23, pl. 20.

32 The same applies to other misunderstandings, such as the many incorrect attributions to Elout, whose brushwork and compositions differ noticeably from Pieter Claesz, and to whom only a very few works can be attributed with certainty.

33 Segal 1987, pp. 96-97.

34 Vondel, ed. Verwey 1937, p. 881.

35 Inv. no. 2222, panel, 59.5 x 49 cm, cat. 1966, p. 236, ill., vol. p. 397; Lauts 1969, pp. 14-18, ill. (2nd ed. 1983, pp. 13-17).

36 For various interpretations of the fruit and the artichoke, see the catalogue *A Fruitful Past*. The cut pomegranate is most often interpreted as religious and *in bono*, as a symbol of Ecclesia, the Church. The artichoke was interpreted *in malo* as an aphrodisiac, e.g. by Cats, and *in bono* as a remedy for many diseases and as a symbol of Majesty (of God or rulers).

37 Poltawa, inv. no. 124; cat. Dresden 1983, no. 124, fig. 9; Segal in Bergström and Segal 1984, p. 77.

38 Signed, panel, 46 x 34 cm, sale Lepke 2059, Berlin, estate of Dr. James Simon, 29 November 1932, no. 33, pl. 9.

39 I know of eleven works in sizes between 32-35 x 45-50 cm, with compositions in oblong format. It can be assumed that in a number of these the margins have been made smaller or have disappeared in the course of time.

40 Inv. nos. 1619, 1620 and 1621, all signed and dated 1611, panel, 52 x 72 cm.

41 According to the Dutch edition by Pers, 1644, p. 433; ed. 1611, p. 204.

42 A goblet with the warrior motive in a form related to the goblet of cat. no. 9, and produced in Emden c. 1630 by Jurgen van Ham, its height 37.5 cm, was recently at gallery Neuse, Bremen; cf. *Weltkunst*, 57, no. 6 (1987), ill. p. 812. More warrior motifs can be found on preserved coconut cups.

43 Ephes. 6:10-18, especially 13-17.

44 Wisdom 5:18-21. There might be also a relation with the lance of the Passion of Christ; cf. Hrabanus Maurus, *De Universo*, lib. 22, cap. 7, Migne P.L, vol. 111, col. 539. For more literature about the lance as a weapon for the *Miles*, see Wang 1975, pp. 100-102.

45 Thes. 5:4-9.

46 Segal 1983a, pp. 76, 80 n. 20,22; Valerianus, lib. 61, cap. 3, 'Mars Ultor,' ed. 1610, p. 444, with reference to Aristophanes' *Pax*; Ripa, ed. pers, 1644, pp. 81-83. For the relationship between the pronk goblet and work by Albrecht Dürer, see Segal 1988, in press.

47 Cf. Frey 1595, fo. 119. Via Physiologus the idea was developed from Psalms 42:1 (or Vulgata 41:2): 'As the heart pantenth after the water brooks, so panteth my soul after thee, o God.' The longing of the hart, or his thirst, becomes stronger when he is chased by the dogs, comp. Koning 1723, vol. 3, p. 27. In deer hunts in the *Legenda Aurea* Christ appears as a hart (among others to St. Hubert and St. Eustache).

48 Private collection, Germany, twice signed and dated 1601, panel, 45 x 56 cm; Segal 1984a, cat. no. 6, ill.

49 Schama 1987, p. 167.

50 For more extensive discussion of the apple, citrus fruit and other fruit as fruits of the Tree of Knowledge, see: Segal 1984a, pp. 14, 36-38.

51 Formerly Gallery Schnackenburg, Munich, panel, 87 x 58 cm; Friedländer 1971, vol. 7, p. 80, cat. no. 163, pl. 111.

52 Inv. no. 79, panel, 49.5 x 77.5 cm; mus. cat. 1969, p. 59.

53 De Jongh 1982, pp. 65-66.

54 Lammers in cat. Münster & Baden-Baden 1979-80, pp. 406-408.

55 For example, the English Batman edition of Bartholomeus Anglicus's *De Proprietatibus Rerum*, London 1582, where, in lib. 19, cap. 74-76, cheese is discussed with references to many authors.

56 Editio princeps: Carolus Stephanus, *Praeludium Rusticum...*, Paris 1554; Charles Estienne and Jean Liébaut, *L'Agriculture et Maison Rustique...*, Paris 1564; Karel Stevens and Jean Liébaut, *De Veltbouw ofte Lantwinninghe...*, Amsterdam 1688. Other editions: Antwerp 1565 (French) and 1566 (Dutch), London 1600 (English), Amsterdam 1622, and several in Germany (German) and Paris until the 18th century. The London edition: *Maison Rustique, or The Countrie Farme...*, on the making of cheese and its goodness, pp. 91-92.

57 Erasmus, *Adagia...*, ed. 1544, f. 267.

58 Job 10:9-10.

59 Private collection, Switzerland, signed and dated 1615, panel, 85.5 x 111.5 cm. We shall see and discuss a similar Wan-li *kendi* mounted in gold in a much later work by Pieter van Roestraeten, cat. no. 62.

60 For example Sullivan 1984, p. 85 n. 22.

61 Fig. 4.12: Wallraf-Richartz-Museum, Cologne, inv. no. 1350, signed, panel, 99 x 156 cm; mus. cat. *Stilleben* 1980, p. 20, pl. III, fig. 56. Fig. 4.13: private collection U.S.A., signed and dated 1616, panel 56 x 80.5 cm; Greindl 1983, cat. no. 44. A study attributed to Snyders' brother-in-law Paul de Vos (possibly a design of Snyders himself?) in the Printroom in Antwerp, inv. no. XXVI, 2, comp. Greindl 1956, fig. 50. Fig. 4.14: private collection, Germany, signed, panel, 42 x 63 cm; Segal 1984a, cat. no. 30, ill.

62 Title page of Julius Wilhelm Zincgref, *Emblematum Ethico-Politicarum Centuria*, Frankfurt 1619 (and in later and derived editions).

63 Formerly Julius Böhler Gallery, Munich (1952), signed and dated 1613, canvas, 125 x 204.5 cm; Robels 1969, pp. 47-48, fig. 30.

64 Inv. no. 1191, signed, canvas, 154 x 237 cm; Segal 1984a, fig. 6.

5 Shell Still Lifes

1 For examples of extreme prices, see Cameron 1961 (1972), p. 26.

2 Vol. 1, embl. 4.

3 Ed. 1614, pp. 42-43 (ed. 1937, pp. 54-55, lines 1492-1503).

4 Coll. Mrs. Lessing J. Rosenwald, cf. Segal 1982, p. 331. E.g. vol. *Aqua - Animalia Aquatilia et Conchiliata*, no. L (= 50), the latin text from Psalms 103:22: 'Bless the Lord, all his works in all places of his dominions,'

the accompanying text with shells and other water animals.

5 Ed. 1614, pp. 42-43 (ed. 1937, p.54, line 1463).

6 Ibidem, p. 8 (p. 20, lines 202-204).

7 *Granida* 1,3. Compare Kettering 1977, p. 232. Kettering, p. 22 n. 1 opposes erroneously the opinion of Gudlaugsson 1948 that the shell in P.C. Hooft is an attribute of the wandering princess Granida.

8 Panel, diamond-shaped, 68.5 x 67.3 cm, sale Christie's, London, 24 April 1981, no. 141, ill.; Reznicek 1960, pp. 42-43, fig. 7, with incorrect measurements.

9 Boymans-van Beuningen Museum, Rotterdam, — coll. Foundation P. and N. de Boer, inv. no. Br. P. 1, with monogram and dated 1603, canvas, 107.5 x 82.7 cm; mus. cat. 1962, p. 56.

10 Wallraf-Richartz Museum, Cologne, inv. no. 1792, with monogram, canvas, 104 x 136 cm; Van Regteren Altena 1983, vol. 1, pp. 109-110, vol. 2, pl. 5, vol. 3, pp. 13-14; cat. no. P 5.

11 Härting 1983, cat. nos. A 206-A 218, with more versions of various paintings, most of them signed and some dated 1607 and 1631. Not all versions with shells.

12 Härting 1983, cat. no. A 355 and A 356. A 355, panel, 64.7 x 86.9 cm, without ill., was shown in the exhibition *World of Wonder*, Walters Art Gallery, Baltimore 1971-1972, no. 17, as Frans Francken the Elder. I know the painting that is illustrated here only from reproductions. A 356 shows many identical shells in a similar position. A literal repetition of its shells, totally different in its execution and a shell still life by its close-up composition, in a work attributed to the Neapolitan still life painter Paolo Porpora (1617-1673), canvas, 50 x 60 cm, in the Silvano Lodi collection in Campione, cat. Munich 1984-85, no. 49, ill.

13 Musée du Louvre, Paris, inv. no. R.F. 1982-51, canvas, 180 x 150 cm; mus. cat. 1983 (Nouvelles Acquisitions...), pp. 35-37, ill.; Lowenthal 1986, cat. no. A-59, pls. 82-82, XVII.

14 Coll. The Duke of Northumberland, panel, 49.5 x 80.5 cm, cat. Antwerp 1982, no. 12, ill.

15 Camerarius 1604, vol. IV, embl. 49. The depiction can also be found in Italian impresas.

16 Reusner, vol. I, embl. 26.

17 Aristotle, *Hist. Anim.* 525a, 622b; Pliny, *Nat. Hist.* IX, 88, 94; Oppianus, *Hal.* I, 338ff; Aelianus, *De Anim.* IX, 34; et alii.

18 Compare Reznicek 1960, p. 42 and Kuechen 1979, pp. 513-514, n. 206.

19 Cit. Praz 1964, p. 102: emblem 102, after Ovid, *Ars Amatoria*, vol. 2, line 519.

20 Saavedra (1640) 1659, embl. 23: 'Pretium Virtutis.' Attributes of Saints in general, according to the *Legenda Aurea*.

21 Mussel: for instance, according to the description of a painting, see Hoet 1752, p. 165; sale 10 May 1713, in The Hague, no. 65: 'A painter who cannot earn his living, and that's why he and his wife and children have to eat mussels..., by Brakenburgh.' In Brueghel's print *The Poor Kitchen*. Oysters: Van Borsselen (1611) 1614, p. 44, (ed. 1937, line 1550).

22 E.g. Huygens: '...what is the nature of the oyster: it is excellent for the pearls, but it is never healthy...,' according to De Vries c.s. 1893, vol. 10, cols. 53-54, and Johan van Beverwijck (1636) 1651, p. 141.

23 Since Pliny and Galenos in various authors, for instance Paulus Jovius, *De romanis piscibus*, Basle 1561, p. 177 (cit. in Eis 1951, p. 1719); and in Johan van Beverwijck (1636) 1651, p. 141. See also De Jongh in cat. Amsterdam 1976, pp. 204, 238 and Koning 1713, vol. 4, pp. 1-3. In Brueghel's print *Luxuria* (Voluptuousness).

24 Valerianus, liber 28, cap. 52, ed. 1610, p. 268. Johan de Brune 1624, fo. *verso, applies the metaphor of the independence of the oyster and shell differently, in connection with the relation between the picture and the texts of his Emblemata.

25 Physiologus, ed. Curley (1942) 1979, cap. XXIV, p. 35.

26 Inv. no. 1716, signed and dated 1666, canvas, 127.5 x 101 cm; cat. 1973, no. 29, ill. on back cover; Seifertová in cat. Dresden 1983, no. 77, ill.; Bastian 1984, cat. no. 55a, ill.

27 These portraits are missing in the four replicas of the painting, which are all undated. Three of them are signed: Kunstgewerbemuseum Schloss Köpenick, Berlin, inv. no. 98.474; Schloss Sanssouci, Potsdam, inv. no. GK I 30002; Museum Brukenthal, Sibiu, inv. no. 541; and one unsigned: Royal Collection of Great Britain, inv. no. DO 1137, cf. Bastian nos. 55, 55b,c,d.

28 The other shells, as far as they can be recognized, are: middle right, *Conus textile* (Indo-Pacific); below right, *Conus spec., Vascum spec.;* middle below, *Strombus pugilis* (Caribbean), *Cypraea pantherina* (Indo-Pacific, twice), *Nerita cf. polita, Strombus spec., Stomatella papyracea* (Indo-Pacific), *Turbo spec.* and *Cypraea tigris* (Indo-Pacific).

29 The Foundation Custodia owns 71 sheets, 25 of which contain shells. The highest folio number is 483. The number has disappeared from several sheets in other collections that have been cut up.

30 Galleria Doria Pamphilj in Rome, inv. no. 280/273, copper, 25.6 x 33.7 cm; cat. 1982, p. 109, fig. 170; Ertz 1979, cat. no. 3, fig. 91. It seems that Ertz has not noticed the signature and date, although he states in his book that he has seen the original. It is the earliest known dated work of Jan Brueghel the Elder. Apart from St. John's vision no further mention at all of the very interesting paradise landscapes in the same collection, inv. no. 278/274, signed and dated 1594, copper, 26.5 x 35 cm, with many small and large animals. This work is i.a. interesting in connection with scenes of Jacob and Roelandt Savery.

31 Inv. no. 27-99, panel, 47 x 64 cm. I know, apart from the three works already mentioned, another three paintings by Linard.

32 Gallery Fischer, Lucerne, 23 x 31 cm; cat. 1988, no. 4, ill.

33 Signed, panel, 52 x 73 cm, acquired in 1982; *Gazette des Beaux-Arts*, 124 (March 1982), p. 5. fig. 22. The famous *Five Senses* in the Musée des Beaux-Arts, Strasbourg, inv. no. 1690, should be dated 1638 according to numerous publications, but no date is visible, except the date 1632 on a coin, a date post quem.

34 Several identifications differ from the list in the cat. Dresden 1983, no. 6.

35 Inv. no. 13150, signed, panel, 36.2 x 51.8 cm; mus. cat. 1973, p. 12, fig. 34; 1983, p. 49, ill.

36 Segal in cat. Amsterdam 1983, no. 13; Bol 1960, cat. no. 87, fig. 45a.

37 Inv. no. 2173, signed, panel, 30 x 47 cm; cat. 1972, p. 204, ill. p. 93; Bol 1960, cat. no. 78, ill.

38 Alciatus 1550, p. 57; ed. 1621, embl. 49: 'In fraudulentos.'

39 In the Vulgate, Jeremiah 23:5; other translations as a Branch, cf. the King James version: 'a righteous Branch,' cf. also Jeremiah 33:15.

40 Physiologus, ed. Curley (1942) 1979, cap. LI, p. 67.

41 Cf. Zachariah 3:8 and 6:12; Luke 1:78: the dayspring; Malachi 4:2: Sun of Righteousness.

42 Aristotle, *Hist. Anim.* 8.17; Aelian, *Hist. Anim.* 5.47. The small crack in the wall probably has the same meaning as the 'narrow crack' through which the snake in Physiologus sneaks out, echoing the language of Matthew 7:14: 'The gate is narrow and there is tribulation on the way which leads toward life, and few are those who enter through it.' The story of the snake shows many similarities, cf. Curley (1942), 1979, p. XXIV.

43 Theobaldi 'Physiologus', cap. VII, ed. Eden 1972, pp. 52-55.

44 Private collection, signed, panel, 24 x 35.5 cm, in Segal, cat. Amsterdam 1984, p. 59, fig. 16; text has been interchanged with that of fig. 14 (p. 53).

45 The stem and foot are related to the style of Andries Grill, a German-Dutch silversmith; cf. Fredericks 1961, vol. 4, pl. 99.

46 Ruzicka Stiftung, inv. no. R 52, signed, canvas, 59 x 44 cm; coll. cat. 1968, pl. 76; Grisebach 1974, cat. no. 142, fig. 156. Of the 13 species which have been identified we mention the Indo-Pacific *Conus aucilus*, *Conus ammiralis*, a polished *Trochus nilotus*, *Mitra papalis*, *Murex tribulus*, and *Turbo potholatus*; and the Caribbean *Strombus gallus* and *Venus dione*. For the latter, high amounts were paid in the 17th century.

47 Inv. no. 4642, panel, 76 x 51 cm; mus. cat. 1972, pp. 485-500, fig. 207. The painting is part of a series of prophets and sibyls, a number of which are in the collection of the Westfälisches Landesmuseum in Münster, Germany.

48 Kuechen 1979, pp. 490, 508 nos. 138-142, fig. 8. The *Haliotis* is related to the Abalone, a well-known food in Japan.

49 Van Borsselen (1611) 1614, p. 41, the complete description pp. 41-43, (ed. 1937, pp. 53-55, lines 1448-1453-1503). Compare n. 3.

50 The large shell on the left is probably a *Cassis* and the small one in the front on the right a *Nerita*.

6 Flower and Fruit Still Lifes

1 These catalogues are out of stock but will be reprinted.

2 On the back of a panel with a portrait, 29 x 22.5 cm, cat. 1969, no. 214, ill.; Segal in catalogue Amsterdam 1982, pp. 8-9, fig. 3.

3 Examples of vases, for instance, in Jacob Floris, *Veelderhande Cierlycke Compertmenten*, Antwerp 1564, and in a series of eight copper engravings by Aegidius Sadeler after Polidoro da Caravaggio, dated 1605. In several paintings of Flegel, mostly executed in collaboration with the Valckenborchs. The baroque forms were continued in later garden vases, for example those of the Frenchman Le Pautre, and in the precious mounts in metal on Ming porcelain vases, e.g. in drawings by Jan Baptist Fornenburgh of around 1630.

4 See Briels 1987, pp. 210, 237-238; Montias 1982, pp. 55-56. He worked presumably in watercolor or bodycolor.

5 Briels 1987, p. 238.

6 Both birds are probably inspired by engravings after Adriaen Collaert. Compare also compositions by Jacob Savery and Roelandt Savery. See Segal in cat. Cologne & Utrecht 1985, pp. 55-56, 131.

7 Bergström (1947) 1956; De Jongh c.s. 1982; Segal 1982.

8 Private collection, The Netherlands, signed and dated 1605; Segal 1982b.

9 Galerie J. Herbrand, Paris, signed and dated 1612, panel, 47 x 35.5 cm. *The Burlington Magazine* 1/290 (1927), ill., p. xv; Warner 1928, cat. no. 17c, ill.; Ertz, cat. no. 268.

10 Panel, 48 x 38 cm; cat. Madrid 1978, Addenda, ill. The painting contains 33 flower species and varieties, two butterflies and three other insects. Ten versions are known to me, partly copies or adaptations by other painters, some cut from larger compositions. A preparatory drawing is in The British Museum in London, cat. 1923 (Hind), fig. XLVII-10; Ertz 1979, p. 288, fig. 358. A tazza with flowers is painted in several other flower pieces where it is combined with a flower basket.

11 Inv. no. 5013, signed and dated 1618, canvas, 47.5 x 52.5 cm; cat. 1984, pp. 40-41, ill.; Ertz 1979, cat. no. 337, fig. 374. An extremely rare example of the Renaissance gold and enamel hairpin, made in Antwerp about 1580, will figure in the exhibition *Silver of Antwerp's Golden Age*, Museum Rockoxhuis, Antwerp, 1988. For the Renaissance jewel for a pendant of c. 1610 by Arnold Lulls in the Victoria and Albert Museum, London, see Evans 1953, pl. 102.

12 In the Bible in many places; in Exodus as one of the ten plagues of the Egyptians, a scourge of God. Cf. Ripa, ed. 1611, pp. 178-179: 'Flagello di Dio,' ed. 1641, p. 440; and Valerianus (1556) 1610, lib. 28, cap. 46: 'Fames' (famine). In Alciatus, ed. 1550, p. 139: 'Nil reliqui' (nothing remains); ed. 1621, embl. 128 pp. 548-553, where a devilish locust has been depicted as a reminder of the famine in Lombardy in 1542.

13 Valerianus (1556) 1610, lib. 28, cap. 55, pp. 286-287.

14 There are many versions of Aesop's fable about the cricket and the ant in the emblemata literature, e.g. Roemer Visscher 1614, vol. 2, embl. 33, illustrated by a picture of a grasshopper.

15 Camerarius 1596, vol. 3. embl. 96, 'Expecto donec veniat' (I look forward to his coming); here a cricket is meant, but a grasshopper has been depicted. Curiously, Albrecht Dürer's engraving *The Holy Family with the Butterfly* depicts an insect sitting on the ground which has the wings and head of a butterfly but the body and legs of a grasshopper.

16 Bergström 1982, pp. 175-176, ill.; Segal in cat. Amsterdam 1984, no. 2, ill.

17 With monogram, copper, 68 x 50 cm, coll. cat. 1969, no. 37, pl. 118; Bol 1960, cat. no. 9, pl. 6.

18 Inv. no. 547, panel 50.2 x 35.3 cm; mus. cat. 1972, p. 16, pl. 26; mus. cat. 1973, p. 27, pl. 75; Bol 1960, cat. no. 10, pl. 7.

19 Both in Hessisches Landesmuseum, Darmstadt, Germany: inv. no. GK 311, with monogram and dated 1611, copper, 48 x 32 cm, and inv. no. GK 312, signed and dated *P. Binoit Francfort 1620*, panel, 110 x 87 cm; mus. cat. 1914, pp. 165-166; Bott 1962, cat. nos. 1 and 19, both ill.

20 The oldest reference to and picture of *Tropaeolum minus* in Europe is in Lobelius, *Plantarum seu stirpium historia*, Antwerp 1576, p. 338. The oldest mention of *Tropaeolum majus* dates from 1684.

21 John G. Johnson Collection, inv. no. 2481, signed and dated, copper, 37.8 x 29.2 cm; coll. cat. 1972, no. 648, fig. p. 243.

22 The similarity was first established by Merry Abbitt Outlaw in a letter of May 5, 1977, to the board of the museum in Pennsylvania, whereupon information was exchanged with the Rijksmuseum.

23 The parrot in this painting is a nearly literal repetition of one in a painting of Jeronimus Sweerts of 1626: comp. Bol 1960, fig. 58c; Bol 1982, p. 260; Segal in cat. Amsterdam 1984, no. 32, ill.

24 The auction of J.B. van den Branden in Brussels, April 13, 1801, no. 117, mentions a flower pot and shells by D. Vandelen. This might apply to our cat. no. 23.

25 Both in the exhibition *Masters of Middelburg*, Amsterdam 1984, nos. 35 and 36. A third flower piece, formerly attributed by Bol to Goedaert and included at his request as no. 37 in that exhibition was not seen by me beforehand. Upon examination, however, it appeared to me to have a forged signature. Apparently I was able to convince Bol, since he retracted the attribution in *Tableau 7*, no. 4. 1985, p. 53.

26 For example Barthel Bruyn the Elder on the reverse of a portrait in the Kröller-Müller Museum in Otterlo, The Netherlands, inv. no. 49-17, dated 1524, panel, 61 x 51 cm; mus. cat. 1970, no. 40, pp. 34-35. As *Memento Mori* on the head of the living: The Master of Frankfort, selfportrait of the artist and his wife, in the Koninklijk Museum voor Schone Kunsten, Antwerp, inv. no. 5096, dated 1496, panel, 36 x 27 cm, curved at the top, mus. cat. 1985, pp. 105-109, fig. 44; cf. Bergström 1956, p. 10, fig. 6, and Segal 1983, pp. 8-9, fig. 5.

27 For the relation between the Syrian Lord of the Flies, Baal-Zebub (from which Belzebub, the henchman of the devil, was derived), see Valerianus (1556) 1610, p. 269, and Pigler 1964. For the fly which lives on dirt and man with 'swine's mentality,' e.g. Claude Paradin 1557, p. 215; ed. 1615, pp. 340-341. As a symbol of sin in Hieronymus, cf. Picinelli (1653) 1687, lib. 8, cap. 16, p. 530.

28 For example Pliny, *Naturalis Historia*, 16.62.152: even cut pieces of ivy live and last.

29 Examples: Virgil, *Eclogae* 7.25, and Horace, *Odes* 1.1.29-30, as a crown for poets; and in Martial, *Epigrams*, lib. 8, 82.7. See also d'Ancona 1977, pp. 189-193, which refers, inter alia, to ivy as a symbol of Christ or the Virgin Mary.

30 Paradin 1557, p. 258; ed. 1615, pp. 395-396. For corn as a symbol of Resurrection: in extenso in R. Wittkower 1949. For many emblematical representations with text in Joris Hoefnagel, see: Wilberg Vignau-Schuurman 1969, vol. 1, pp. 221-224. Many other emblem books also adopted the image of ears of grain as a resurrection symbol.

31 Inv. no. 568, painted in collaboration with Nicolaes van Veerendael and signed by both artists, canvas, 103 x 85 cm; mus. cat. 1983, pp. 240-241, ill.; Segal 1982, pp. 46-74, ill. In timepieces in vanitas paintings the hour hand often stands at eleven or near twelve o'clock.

32 Signed and dated 1653, canvas, 85.5 x 65 cm; mus. cat. 1986, no. 11, pp. 59-60, fig. 68. The Dresden, Munich and Dublin paintings are also described by De Mirimonde 1970, pp. 268-271, figs. 23-25, but I follow only partly his and Bergström's interpretations. De Mirimonde mistook the roll of bread for a shell.

33 For the symbolism of these fruits see Segal in cat. *A Fruitful Past*, 1983.

34 For example: Valerianus (1556) 1610, lib. 58, cap. 17, p. 610; Junius 1565, embl. 36.

35 Typotius 1601, pp. 126-127; for emblematical images and texts and further references: Wilberg Vignau-Schuurman 1969, vol. 1, p. 153, vol. 2, p. 60.

36 As an attribute of *Goede uitkomst* (good result or *Evento Buono*) caused by a refreshing sleep in Ripa, ed. 1611, p. 153-154, ed. 1644, p. 184.

37 Inv. no. 86, PB. 538, signed, panel, 42 x 49.5 cm.

7 SUMPTUOUSNESS IN SOBER TONES

1 The development of around thirty characteristics of fruit pieces of the 17th century have been enumerated in *A Fruitful Past*.

2 Private collection, Italy, with monogram and dated, canvas, 80 x 112 cm; Vroom 1980, vol. 1, p. 15, fig. 2, vol. 2, p. 112, cat. no. 562 (with partly wrong dates).

3 A number of works in Vroom 1980 have been incorrectly attributed to Floris van Schooten, Cat. no. 588 is identical with 573.

4 E.g., a signed painting with roses, red currants, cherries and strawberries, of around 1620, at Hoogsteder Gallery, The Hague, panel, 36 x 49 cm.

5 E.g., a work of 1621 in a private collection, Switzerland, with monogram and dated, panel, 45.5 x 63.5 cm; Vroom 1980, p. 16, cat. no. 39, ill.

6 The Hague, Hoogsteder Gallery, panel, 43.3 x 66.5 cm. A work dated 1624 is probably also by Gillis, with false signature w.c. HEDA, panel, 33.5 x 55.5 cm; cf. cat. Lohr & Dortmund 1984, no. 16, ill. (Willem Claesz Heda). Also with a *bekerschroef* with a berkemeier glass.

7 Other works possibly by Nicolaes Gillis: The Art Institute of Chicago, inv. no. 1935.300, panel, 48 x 77 cm (attributed to Pieter Claesz), Vroom 1980, vol. 1, p. 92, fig. 119, vol. 2, p. 102, cat. no. 511 (Clara Peeters); and Gammelbo 1960, vol. 2, p. 15, cat. no. 37, ill.; panel, 39.5 x 78.5 cm (Floris van Schooten), Vroom 1980, vol. 2, p. 114, no. 575, ill. (Floris van Schooten or Franchoys Elout). These works are known to me only from photos.

8 p. 58; not in the original Italian editions.

9 About this and other general trends, see Segal 1984a.

10 The smallest size in Vroom 1980, vol. 2, p. 22, cat. no. 72, on canvas (!), 14 x 17 cm, forming a pair with no. 71, which is slightly larger. These paintings are unknown to me; the attribution seems implausible. A tour de force is a dated work of 1653 in the Walraff-Richartz Museum in Cologne, inv. no. 1505, canvas, 150 x 200 cm; mus. cat. *Stillleben* 1980, no. 12, ill.

11 Hollstein, vol. 11, p. 232, no. 320.

12 Hermitage, Leningrad; Hernmarck 1977, fig. 106; Ter Molen 1984, vol. 2, no. 406.

13 J. Paul Getty Museum, inv. no. 70.PB.37, monogrammed and dated 163 · (?), panel 54 x 71.5 cm, with a pronk goblet, shells, a glass sphere and other objects; Vroom 1980, vol. 1, p. 100, fig. 131, vol. 2, p. 21, cat. no. 66, ill. (Pieter Claesz) and p. 104, cat. no. 520 (Clara Peeters).

14 Miedema 1975; Becker in cat. Münster and Baden-Baden 1979-80; Bialostocki 1982; Eikemeier 1984; Schwarz 1987.

15 Sambucus 1564, p. 116.

16 Vol. 1, embl. 30: 'kruijt voor de wilde woeste.'

17 p. 66; not in the original Italian editions.

18 Roodenburg 1959, pp. 14-16, ill.; Frederiks 1961, vol. 4, p. 20, no. 35, ill. Roodenburg, p. 23, n. 46, uses the well-chosen word 'portrait' for this painting.

19 Jonah 2:10.

20 Jonah 1:12-15.

21 Matthew 12:40; comp. 16:4, and Luke 11:30.

22 The story of Arion is told by a number of classical authors, for instance Herodotus I. 23-24. Emblems, among others in Alciatus 1531, p. (A6); Meyster 1579, no. 64; Rollenhagen 1611, vol. 1, no. 10; and Van den Vondel 1613, nr. 64 (ed. 1699, pp. 124-125). Vondel is a revised edition of Meyster with the same plates. (Meyster has been listed in Henkel & Schöne erroneously as Laurentius Haechtanus — Laurens van Haecht — to whom the book was dedicated). The bearded figure on the nautilus cup bears some resemblance to the figures in Meyster and Rollenhagen. For the young figure on the whale with the trident of Neptune, I have no explanation, unless it might be an adaptation of the *Miles Christianus*.

23 Such belt pendants (and pomanders) are known in two examples from Vienna, datable 1590-1600; in the Metropolitan Museum, New York; and the National Gallery of Art, Washington, D.C. See: Hackenbrock 1979, p. 188, nos. 510 and 511 respectively. Cf. De Jongh 1986, p. 117, fig. 17 for a portrait.

24 In Vroom's work there are, in my opinion, many attributions which are incorrect. In the oeuvre catalogue we find under Pieter Claesz, apart from many dubious attributions to Clara Peeters and Franchoys Elout, works by Cornelis Kruys (no. 158), Pieter de Putter (no. 167) and Willem Claesz. Heda (no. 172).

25 A number of works which had been attributed to Gerret are in reality by Willem Claesz., and vice versa, while others are by neither.

26 Wurzbach, vol. 1, pp. 654-655 with references to older sources. Miedema 1980, p. 532, according to data from the municipal archives of Haarlem, fol. 75verso, no. 3. In 1637 a certain Arnoldus Beerensteyn was a pupil of Willem Heda.

27 Miedema 1981, pp. 134-135.

28 Detail of a painting from the collection of the Rijksdienst Beeldende Kunst, The Hague, inv. no. B 2213, panel, 83 x 60 cm; Vroom 1980, vol. 1, fig. 225, vol. 2, p. 58, cat. no. 285.

29 Vroom 1980, vol. 1, pp. 66, 76, 166, 169. Information about the death of a son, from Dr. P. Biesboer, conservator of the Frans Halsmuseum, Haarlem.

30 Miedema 1980, p. 1035.

31 Cf. Bredius 1915, vol. 1, p. 107, estate of the art dealer Cornelis Doeck, Amsterdam, 1664, no. (101): 'A banket by the young Heda.'

32 By measurement of the surface area of the objects separately, their sum and the ratio to the area above the table and to the total surface area of the painting.

33 One work by Willem is signed differently: *Heda. fecit · /1643*.

34 Private collection, Germany, signed and dated, panel, 45 x 60 cm; Vroom 1980, p. 66, cat. no. 328, ill.; cat. The Hague 1982, no. 42.

35 Cat. Nürnberg 1987, no. 40, ill. p. 154: Germanisches Nationalmuseum, on loan, height 14.2 cm.

36 Signed and dated, panel, 87 x 113 cm; purchased 1984, Vroom 1980, vol. 1, fig. 76, vol. 2, p. 70, cat. no. 351a.

37 Schwerin: inv. no. G 151, signed and dated, panel, 103.5 x 82 cm; Vroom 1980, vol. 1, fig. 229, vol. 2, p. 65, no. 321 (Gerret Willemsz. Heda); Leningrad: inv. no. 5606, signed and dated, canvas, 118 x 118 cm: Vroom 1980, vol. 2, p. 77, cat. no. 372 (Willem Claesz. Heda).

38 Schliemann 1985, vol. 1, fig. 128: dated between 1631 and 1643.

39 Inv. no. 1745, signed and dated, panel, 60 x 77 cm; Vroom 1980, vol. 2, p. 75, no. 366a, ill.

40 Inv. no. O 2780, dated, panel, 80 x 67 cm, with an owl clearly visible on the cloth at the lower right and with various owl reflections in the pewter jug.

41 Inv. no. A 4090, panel, 91 x 120 cm; mus. cat. 1976, p. 473, ill., as 'milieu of Rembrandt;' Vroom 1980, vol. 2, p. 129, no. 667, ill.

42 In some still lifes by Pieter Claesz one can sometimes discern owllike reflections, but they are rare and there is never more than one such reflection per painting. In cat. no. 35, however, one sees on the pronk goblet's bosses alone three owls in positions which correspond with the various angles from which an owl sitting in the place of the artist would be reflected on the bosses.

43 Cat. Dordrecht 1975, no. 14, ill.

44 The handel of a trowel for laying the first stone of the Amsterdam Town Hall (now the Royal Palace); cat. Amsterdam 1984, no. 38a, ill.

45 A painting in Prague was thus signed by Jan Jansz. den Uyl with an owl on the cloth (fig. 7.7). Also in a painting that was sold on January 14, 1988, at Sotheby's, New York, cat. no. 41, panel, 90 x 72 cm, from the Linda and Gerald Guterman collection.

8 DE HEEM AND HIS CIRCLE

1 Jan Davidsz. de Heem's biography was written in 1888 by Toman, who quotes the sources. There is

often confusion between works by Jan Davidsz., his brother David Davidsz., and his sons Cornelis Jansz. and Jan Jansz. I hope to publish in the future a survey of the work of De Heem and his followers.

2 Mention of copies in 1649 in Obreen, vol. 1, 1880, pp. 76-77, 83, 85, 86, 91.

3 The Barber Institute of Fine Arts, University of Birmingham, signed and dated, panel, 77.5 x 64.7 cm; coll. cat. 1952, p. 60, ill.; Greindl 1983, cat. no. 27 (as dated 1652). Regarding both paintings: Bergström 1956, pp. 178-183, figs. 7, 8.

4 Cat. Arnhem 1955, no. 192, pl. IV. For the beaker in the painting, cf. cat. Amsterdam 1984, no. 19, ill., by Abraham van der Plaetsen, Amsterdam 1613.

5 Inv. no. 1321, signed and dated, canvas, 149 x 203 cm; mus. cat. 1979, p. 68, ill. An interesting 'version' of this painting was made by Henri Matisse around 1916. It is even bigger in size.

6 Larger in size is a signed work, canvas, 144 x 239 cm, in the Abbaye de Châalis in France, inv. no. 350, but it is not by De Heem. Possibly by his son Johannes Jansz., the painting hangs high of the wall of a staircase so that an accurate examination was impossible.

7 At Christie's, New York, 15 January 1988, no. 107. It fetched the highest price ever paid for a Dutch old master, $ 6,600,000.

8 Manuscript Ash. 1514, fo. 180 verso, published in Millar 1960, p. 196; cf. Talley 1983.

9 They are: *Nautilus pompilius* (Indo-Pacific, left), *Lioconcha castrensil* (Indo-Pacific, front left), *Melolonga corona* (Indian Ocean, on top of the nautilus), *Conus spectrum* (Indo-Pacific, center), *Strombus gigas* (Caribbean, front center), *Tonna perdrix*? (Indian Ocean, at the back), *Cimatium pileare* (Indo-Pacific, at the front to the right).

10 Ter Molen, in cat. Rotterdam 1976, no. 24; cat. The Hague, Amsterdam, Toledo & Boston 1984-85, no. 36.

11 With a young Bacchus on a barrel in the Gemeentemuseum, The Hague; Frederiks 1961, vol. 4, no. 99.

12 Inv. no. DO 5040, signed and dated, panel, 56 x 40 cm; mus. cat. 1905, no. 87; exh. cat. Prague 1984-85, no. 37, fig. 27.

13 Inv. no. 2661, signed, canvas, 88 x 116 cm; mus. cat. 1984, p. 135, ill.

14 Inv. no. 612, signed, canvas, 116 x 169 cm; mus. cat. 1927, p. 186, fig. 104; Cat. *Meisterwerke der Tier- und Stilllebenmalerei*, Akademie, Vienna, 1952, no. 10; Greindl 1983, p. 362, cat. no. 140.

15 The transcription and, accordingly, the translation differ in detail from that given by Lincoln 1985, p. 52.

16 Private collection, Germany, signed and dated 1651, panel, 87.5 x 61.5 cm; Segal 1984, pp. 31-32, fig. 15.

17 A copy, signed: 'Jacob Marrellus ab Heem' private collection, Germany, canvas, 76.5 x 61.5 cm, cf. Segal 1984, cat. no. 21, ill.; a falsely signed and illegibly dated (1661?) copy is in the Quimper Museum of Fine Arts, inv. no. 673-1-183, canvas, 65.5 x 56 cm, incorrectly given to Cornelis de Heem: mus. cat. (Paris) 1987, p. 85, ill.

18 Book 5, Chapter 4, p. 186.

19 A number of other texts on works by De Heem have become known in the meantime, some of them short vanitas texts. An extensive text about Neptune, who drives a four-in-hand and restrains and subdues the horses, can be found on a work of Cornelis de Heem of 1658: Greindl 1983, pp. 123, 251, fig. 132, p. 362, cat. no. 142 (Jan Davidsz. de Heem). The text 'MODICUM ET BONUM' appears on a work by Guilliam van Deynum in the Musée de Picardie in Amiens as attributed to Jan Davidsz. de Heem. Another work with the same text appears in Bergström 1947, p. 196, fig. 163, ed. 1956, p. 190, fig. 165 (Jan Davidz. de Heem). Works by Van Deynum are ususally easily recognizable, but the signatures have often been changed, e.g. in a work in the Museo del Prado, Madrid, inv. no. 2072 (Coosemans) and Greindl 1983, cat. no. 108, fig. 126 (Jan Davidsz. de Heem).

20 Ter Kuile (1985) dates the painting around 1670. His arguments that it shows similarities to paintings by Abraham Mignon have little meaning, since objects in De Heem's paintings can be recognized in those of all his pupils. The style of the later works is also completely different, and thus the painting shows many connections with dated works of the 1640s and early 1650s.

21 According to Ter Kuile 1985, p. 206 n. 13: by Hanns Wasmundus, early 17th century, height 39 cm, in the Bayerisches Nationalmuseum, Munich, inv. no. R 7821; information from Dr. M. Koch.

22 Leonard Koetser Gallery, London, cat. Autumn 1969 no. 23, ill., signed and dated, panel, 45.3 x 53.2 cm. A related *bekerschroef* with a putto on a dolphin and a flower in his hand can be seen in several works by Joris van Son.

23 Tervarent 1958, cols. 106-108, with sources. The column is also seen in Pieter Brueghel's engraving *Fortitudo*.

24 In Van Mander 1604, *Uytbeeldinge der figuren...*, fo. 132; comp. Valerianus, lib. 28, cap. 59, ed. 1610, p. 287; Cats 1627, *Emblemata Moralia*, embl. 23, pp. 46-47, based on Cantimpré.

25 In the work of the German Jacobus à Bruck (1615) is an emblem in which a snail is climbing up a tall complete column, with the motto 'Tandem sero licet,' (At last, even though too late); Henkel & Schöne 1978, col. 620. It is not likely that this emblem was known by De Heem. For the snail as a symbol of cautiousness, see, among others, Rollenhagen 1611, vol. 1, embl. 11: 'Lente sed attente' (Slowly but carefully). See also Kuechen 1979.

26 Comp. Friedmann 1946.

27 Ripa ed. 1611, p. 538: 'Virtu Heroica;' ed. Pers 1644, p. 85. As a sign of 'Opulenza,' Wealth, ed. 1610, p. 394; ed. 1699, p. 439.

28 Dodoens 1554, pp. 626-626, 630; ed. 1644, pp. 1036-1037; French ed. 1557, p. 408; cited the English ed. of 1578, p. 587. Pons (1583) 1680, pp. 24-30. Vicaire 1607, cols. 711-712; cf. Ketcham-Wheaton (1983) 1988, p. 56.

29 Some points of reference for the date are: a work of 1646 in the Toledo Museum of Art, inv. no. 55.33, canvas, 59.3 x 92.6 cm, with a similar crab, melon, shrimps, table and cloth; and cat. no. 40, of 1649, with a similar rummer and tazza, as well as other similarities. The same tazza appears in a work dated 1651 in a New York private collection, canvas, 41.5 x 58 cm and in another signed from the Toledo Museum of Art, inv. no. 52.25, canvas, 63.5 x 84.5 cm.

30 In *Kunst- und Lehrbüchlein für die anfahenden Jungen. Daraus reissen und Malen zu lernen.* Durch Jos Aman von Zürijch. Im 1578 Jar. I.A. (2nd ed.). *The Illustrated Bartsch*, 1985, vol. 20, pt. 2, p. 434, no. 447, ill. (original ed. Bartsch vol. 9, no. 368, pl. 3); Hollstein (German engravings...), vol. 2, p. 51.

31 Capelle degli Scrovegni, Padua, one of the frescoes in a series of virtues and vices; Vigorelli & Baccheschi 1966, p. 109, no. 105, ill. p. 107.

32 Ed. 1611, pp. 244-245; Pers ed. 1644, pp. 367-368.

33 Cf. Ripa ed. Pers 1644, p. 459, under the motto 'Simonia', Sale of spiritual yarn.

34 Visscher 1614, vol. 2, embl. 40. Cf. Poirters, ed. 1935, pp. 71-73: lobster in connection with the example of the parents.

35 Aristotle, *Hist. Anim.* 487b, 590b; Pliny *Nat. Hist.* 9, 98.

36 La Perrière 1533, embl. 61; Taurellus 1602, embl. A; cf. Camerarius, vol. 4, 1604, embl. 55.

37 Germanisches Nationalmuseum, inv. no. HG 8598, height 62.1 cm; cat. Nürnberg 1987, no. 35, ill.

38 Cat. nr. 905 A, panel, 64 x 98 cm; photo from the Staatliches Museum in Berlin (German Democratic Republic).

39 Citroen 1963.

40 Citroen 1988, fig. 24.

41 Inv. no. 3775, signed and dated, panel, 70 x 118 cm, Kuznetsov & Linnik 1982, no. 252, ill.

42 Cat. 1958, fig. 349.

43 Frederiks 1961, vol. 4, pl. 37.

44 Schliemann 1985, vol. 1, no. 227, ill., datable 1625-28.

45 Seling 1980, no. 116, ill., datable 1600-10.

46 It is not certain whether the two paintings were painted as pendants. The compositions do, however, suggest this. In the Budapest painting the diagonal descends from upper left to lower right, in the Leningrad work it ascends from lower left to upper right. The latter painting includes lobsters and crabs, as well as silver ewers and a Ming pot with cover.

47 For instance in the inventory list of paintings published by Talley 1983, p. 185. The artist was described as obscure.

48 E.g. in the work of the Hague artist Jan Baptist van Fornenburgh. Sometimes in that of Jan Davidsz. and Cornelis de Heem. A cockatoo is quite often seen in the work of Jacob Marrell.

49 Physiologus ed. Seel (1960) 1987, p. 81. Probably meant in this sense in Dürer's famous engraving of Adam and Eve; in Niccolo dell' Abbate's *Man with a Parrot* in the Kunsthistorisches Museum in Vienna; in Joachim Patinir's *Landscape with the Penitent St. Jerome* in the Louvre in Paris (cf. Falkenberg 1905, p. 119: symbol of redemption or sin); and in Anthony van Dyck's portrait of William Fielding in the National Gallery in London. Comp. also Joris Hoefnagel's illuminations in the *Missale Romanum*, Austrian Nationalbibliothek, Vienna, Cod. 1784 fo. 328 recto and 403 verso, with texts (Wilberg 1969, p. 211, no. 409), and other Hoefnagel drawings. The parrot can also be a symbol of Mary, and Dürer might have linked it with the reversal of EVA and AVE, a greeting from the bird. Eve is seen as a prototype of Mary: comp. Molsdorf 1926, p. 145, no. 880, and p. 148, no. 917, after the Dominican Franz von Retz. The parrot is, among other things, a symbol of Touch in series of the Senses.

50 Valerianus. lib. 23, cap. 15, ed. 1610, pp. 231-232; Sambucus 1569, p. 54; Ripa ed. 1611, p. 139; Pers ed. 1644, pp. 595, 597.

51 Camerarius 1596, vol. 3, embl. 45: 'Alienae vocis aemula,' Imitation of another's voice. In Holzwart 1581, embl. 19, the parrot has a negative sound: 'Qualis rex, talis grex' (like master, like man, as he imitates without discernment).

52 Hayward 1976, fig. 690.

53 Mus. cat. 1952, cat. no. 73, fig. 20; cat. Amsterdam 1984, no. 16, ill. A somewhat similar example by Adam van Vianen, Utrecht 1614, is also in the Rijksmuseum in Amsterdam, mus. cat. 1952, cat. no. 81, fig. 21.

54 Inv. no. A 335, signed with a ring, canvas, 100 x 85 cm; mus. cat. 1976, p. 476, ill.

55 Inv. no. 128047, signed, panel, 57.5 cm x 43 cm; mus. cat. 1967, cat. no. 405, ill. A different ewer, related in shape and decoration, is seen in a work by Nicolaes van Gelder, with a parrot, dated 1667: Richard Green Gallery, London, catalogue 10th Biennale in Paris, 1980, no. 12, canvas, 110 x 87 cm.

56 E.g. Frederiks 1952, vol. 1, no. 149: a dish by Johannes Grill, made in Amsterdam in 1650, preserved in the Rijksmuseum, Amsterdam.

57 With the arms of Leyden, one of a pair, cat. Amsterdam, Toledo & Boston 1979-80, no. 59, ill.

58 Leviticus 2:13; cf. Mark 9:49.

59 2 Chronicles 13, 5.

60 See J.R. ter Molen in cat. Rotterdam 1976, p. 20, with sources.

61 Matthew 5:13; Luke 14:34; Mark 9:50.

62 De Lairesse 1740, vol. 2, p. 286.

63 Vaenius 1615, pp. 104-105.

64 Job 6:6-7.

65 Ed. Riethe 1980, p. 51, 'De Sale.'

66 Musée des Beaux-Arts, Lille, inv. no. 914, canvas, 75 x 92 cm, mus. cat. 1981, pp. 75-76, ill; Rheinischer Landesmuseum, Bonn, inv. no. 35.256, signed and dated (16)54, canvas, 47.5 x 64 cm, cat. *A Fruitful Past*, no. 44, ill. Both with an added false signature.

67 E.g. Glasgow Art Gallery and Museum, inv. no. 11, falsely signed, canvas, 36.5 x 52.7 cm, mus. cat. 1961, p. 65, ill. p. 51. Also one listed as a painting by Pieter de Ring in the Museum De Lakenhal in Leiden is by Hannot: inv. no. 373, vestiges of a signature and dated (16)56, canvas, 97.5 x 77 cm, mus. cat. 1983, p. 274, ill.

68 Akademie der Bildenden Künste, Vienna, inv. no. 757, signed with initials, canvas, 129 x 168 cm; Musée des Beaux-Arts, Lille, inv. no. 78, signed and dated 1633, canvas, 207 x 261 cm; Greindl 1983, cat. nos. 28 and 15, fig. 42 (Lille).

69 Private collection, Spain, canvas, 89 x 119 cm; cat. Madrid 1977/78, no. 141, ill.; Greindl 1983, cat. no. 4, fig. 218 (with wrong measurements). Signatures in a cartouche are also seen later, at least up to 1660.

70 Segal 1983b, pp. 76-81.

71 A series of four paintings in the Johnny Van Haeften Gallery, London, of which *Earth* (with fruit) and *Water* (with fish) are signed and dated 1656. *Air* (with live and dead birds) is monogrammed CL by Christaen Luyckx, not Cornelis Leliebergh; all four have a landscape in the background; canvas, 40.5 x 57.5 cm.

72 The silver tazza with a swan in the center is remarkably close to a Dutch one made in 1727 and given to the Evangelist Lutheran Church in Zaandam; cf. Frederiks 1952, vol 1, no. 246, ill. A swan was a symbol of the Lutherans.

73 Citroen 1988, pl. 19b.

74 Cat. Amsterdam, Toledo & Boston 1979-80, no. 14, ill.; cat. Amsterdam 1984, no. 17, ill.

75 Frederiks 1952, vol. 1, no. 18, ill.

76 Seling 1980, no. 423, ill., dated 1653-55.

77 See n. 23. Also De Jongh 1982, pp. 155-158, with examples in portraits and sources.

9 Painters of the Broad Brush; Abraham van Beyeren

1 Bergström 1947, p. 172 / ed. 1956, p. 166; an opinion adopted by other authors.

2 The specific characteristics of Bollongier's flower pieces have been described in Segal 1983c.

3 Knoedler Gallery, New York (before 1948), signed in monogram and dated 1638, panel, 27 x 21 cm.

4 This type of Dutch tazza must have been fairly common; we see a great quantity in a prizes print for an Amsterdam lottery of 1592; Frederiks 1952, vol. 1, no. 17, ill, see chapter 3, n. 9.

5 Camerarius 1596, vol. 3, embl. 43, 'Negligit ima' (He ignores what is below). Cf. Boria 1581, embl. 49 and De Soto 1599, p. 58, both quoted in Henkel & Schöne 1978, col. 799; see also col. 798 for Sambucus's meaning: 'Vita irrequieta' (A restless life).

6 For his biography see Van Gelder (1942), pp. 21-25.

7 Comp. Conisbee, pp. 90-91, figs. 82-84. Géricault copied Van Beyeren: Van Gelder (1942), p. 39.

8 De Jongh in cat. Auckland 1982, pp. 80, 82, with sources.

9 Collection Bentinck-Thyssen, on loan to the Kunstmuseum in Dusseldorf, inv. no. D 37/1974, panel, 115.5 x 87.5 cm.

10 Alte Pinakothek, Munich, inv. no. 1620, signed in monogram and dated, canvas, 125.7 x 105.3 cm; mus. cat. 1983, pp. 71-72, ill. Also a similar lobster, fruit, watch and napkin. The glass goblet is similar except for the lid, which could be the same one if the top had been broken and the lid reground.

11 Thomas Brod Gallery, London, signed in monogram and dated, canvas 101 x 100 cm. The interesting gilt *krulbeker* with a silver dolphin and Fortuna figure appears in another work of 1654, (see n. 24) and without a figure in a dated work of 1655, in the Worcester Art Museum (Mass.), 1953.1, signed and dated, panel, 133.7 x 85.1 cm; mus. cat. 1974, pp. 80-82, ill. vol. p. 552. The same *krulbeker* with another figure on the top is seen in cat. no. 52, from 1667.

12 Cf. a jug by Evert Kettwyck of Hamburg, 1631-43; Schliemann 1985, vol. 1, pl. 128.

13 Cf. one by Melchior I Gelb, c. 1641; Seling 1980, no. 420, ill.

14 Boymans-van Beuningen Museum, Rotterdam, inv. no. St.90, signed in monogram and dated, canvas, 126 x 106 cm; cat. 1972, p. 204. ill. vol. p. 99. See also n. 11.

15 Galerie Hohenbuchau, Schlangenbad-Georgenborn (West-Germany), signed in monogram, canvas, 118.2 x 167.6 cm.

16 City Art Gallery, York, inv. no. 761, canvas, signed in monogram, 109.2 x 88.9 cm; mus. cat. 1961, vol. 1, pp. 47-48. pl. 61.

17 Ter Kuile 1985, pp. 72, 73 n. 12, 74.

18 Kunsthistorisches Museum, Vienna, inv. no. 562, signed in monogram and dated, panel, 74 x 57.9 cm; mus. cat. 1972, p. 10, pl. 38: mus. cat. 1973, p. 23, pl. 120.

19 Toledo Museum of Art, inv. no. 52.24, signed in monogram, canvas, 79.3 x 63.5 cm; mus. cat. 1976, no. 126, ill.

20 Among others in the Bode-Museum, Berlin (German Democratic Republic), the Mauritshuis in The Hague and the Boymans-van Beuningen Museum in Rotterdam.

21 Frederiks 1952, vol. 1, pp. 258-259, no. 167, ill.

22 For example in a painting in Worcester, (see n. 11) and in two paintings which were made around 1654-55: Musée Royaux des Beaux-Arts, Brussels, inv. no. 2987, signed in monogram, canvas, 99 x 89 cm, mus. cat. 1984, p. 22, ill., and Rijksdienst Beeldende Kunst, The Hague, inv. no. NK 1600, signed in monogram, canvas, 98.5 x 120 cm; cat. Ter Kuile 1985, pp. 74-75, ill.

23 Comp. a shallow platter with floral motifs made by Lucas Draef, Amsterdam 1657, in cat. Amsterdam, Toledo & Boston 1979-80, no. 66, ill.

24 See n. 11.

25 By Hans Otto: Seling 1980, vol. 1, fig. 406, height 26.9 cm, in the Schweizerisches Landesmuseum, Zurich.

26 Leviticus 11:29; Isaiah 66:17; 1 Samuel 6:45. See also Wilberg Vignau-Schuurman 1969, vol. 1, pp. 173-174, no. 330, with a reference to Corrozet (1590): symbol of sin, which, like the owl, cannot bear the daylight; also in a poem by Vondel about the Night (next to one about the Day) of 1644, ed. 1937, p. 940. Other meanings are cautiousness, thoughtlessness, might of the small, fertility, theft and hearing.

27 For instance in the emblem books of Alciatus 1531, p. (E3b): 'Captivus ob gulam', (A prisoner of gluttony); Camerarius 1606, vol. 4, embl. 60; Vischer 1614, vol. 2, embl. 31; Cats 1627, pp. 68-73, embl. 12. Comp. also Picinelli (1653) 1687, pp. 225, 229, 230, 231. In Horapollo (1505) 1551, p. 73, the mouse is a symbol of destruction but also has the power of discernment.

10 THE SPARKLING LIGHT OF WILLEM KALF

1 Grisebach 1974. Since the publication of that book some new material has come to light. I do not always share Grisebach's views, though we differ mostly on matters of little importance.

2 Houbraken (1718) 1753, vol. 2, pp. 218-220.

3 From the English translation: *The Art of Painting, in All its branches,* London 1738, p. 555, cited from Talley 1983, p. 141.

4 Musée de Tessé, Le Mans, inv. no. 10-89, signed and dated 1643, canvas, 74 x 58 cm, mus. cat. 1932, no. 385 Gemäldegalerie, Berlin-Dahlem, inv. no. 2137, signed and dated 1643, canvas, 66.3 x 53 cm, mus. cat. 1957, p. 212, ill.; Lord Brooke of Warwick, Warwick Castle, signed and dated 1644, canvas, 100 x 79 cm; Grisebach 1974, cat. nos. 61, 63, 70, figs. 65, 68, 71, respectively. See also ns. 10-12.

5 Collection Mr. and Mrs. Edward William Carter, Los Angeles, canvas, 55.3 x 44 cm; Grisebach 1974, cat. no. 65, fig. 69.

6 Private collection, canvas, 76 x 62.2 cm; Grisebach 1974, cat. no. 67, fig. 77.

7 After designs by Briot pewter models were made in Nürnberg: Haedeke 1968, cat. nos. 226-227, ill., with literature. For a related gilt ewer by Bartel Jamnitzer, see Nürnberg 1985, no. 58, ill.; this ewer resembles closely that in the painting in the Getty Museum in Malibu, inv. no. 54. PA. 1; mus. cat. 1972, p. 83, no. 107; Fredericksen 1980, no. 32, ill.; Grisebach 1974, cat. no. 62, fig. 67.

8 Private collection, Germany, signed, canvas, 77 x 60 cm; Grisebach 1974, cat. no. 59, fig. 66. Arguments for an early dating include: the loose composition, the simply hanging linen cloth and the bowl of a tazza without a foot, as in some monochrome banquet pieces.

9 Private collection, formerly Edward Speelman, Ltd., London (1979), canvas, 153 x 166 cm; not in Grisebach.

10 Musée de Tessé, Le Mans, canvas, 200 x 170 cm; mus. cat. 1932, no. 384; Grisebach 1974, no. 66, fig. 72; dated wrongly as 1643 by Bergström 1947, p. 270, fig. 221; ed. 1956, p. 266, fig. 221.

11 Grisebach 1974, pp. 108-109, 238. Incorrect that the gilt ewer is identical to that in the painting in Cologne, n. 12, whose inscribed date is, moreover, not authentic.

12 Inv. no. 3233, canvas, 114.5 x 85.5 cm; mus. cat. 1967, pp. 62-63, fig. 81; mus. cat. *Stillleben* 1980, p. 32, pl. IX; Grisebach 1974, pp. 236-237 cat. no. 64, figs. 63 (and 84, pp. 90 n. 186, 92, 93, 94 n. 193, 96 n. 196, 98, 100, 101, 102, 103 n. 212, 105-108, 109, 110, 208, 234 no. 60, 235 no. 61, 236 no. 63, 241 nos. 70-70A) always as signed and dated 1643.

13 For example illustrated in Bode (1917), ed. 1965, fig. 83; Bergström 1947/1956, fig. 218; Von der Osten 1966, fig. 232; Bergström c.s. 1977/1979, fig. 54; Haak 1984, fig. 1096. Mentioned without an illustration in many other books since the beginning of the 19th century.

14 Grisebach 1974, p. 237, mentions three copies; there are more.

15 Goethe (1797), ed. 1954, p. 121.

16 Taking part in this examination were Dr. E. Mai, the curator of the museum; the restorer of the museum; and a Dutch restorer, who all agreed with the results. Afterwards the linen was examined and compared with that of other works from the Paris period, and the result was in the affirmative.

17 Staatsgalerie Aschaffenburg, inv. no. 6436, canvas, 65.5 x 81 cm; mus. cat. 1975, pp. 92-93 (French, 2nd half 17th century); Faré 1974, ill. p. 175.

18 In the inventory of Vaulx's estate, however, there were no paintings listed which seemed connected to Kalf or Renard de Saint André.

19 Grisebach, cat. nos. 61, 63, 67, 68, 69, 70, figs. resp. 65, 68, 77, 70, 78, 71. No. 76 is another example, with a coat of arms.

20 A gilt example in the Musée du Louvre in Paris, with the arms of King Henri III, is attributed to Noël Delacroix, 1581-82, on the basis of Nocq c.s. vol. 1, pl. IV. A gilt example by Adam Loofs, The Hague, 1688, in cat. Washington 1986, no. 116, ill.

21 Kunstmuseum, Basle; illustrated in cat. Nürnberg 1985, p. 14. fig. 10.

22 Grisebach 1974, cat. nos. 67, 70, figs. resp. 77, 71. Nocq c.s., vol. 1, pl. VIIIB. See also Bergström 1947, p. 320 n. 23, ed. 1956, p. 315 n. 25.

23 The glass box: Grisebach 1974, cat. nos. 60, 61, 67, figs. resp. 64, 65, 77; the rippled glass cat. nos. 61, 62, figs. resp. 65, 67 and with another foot, cat. no. 65, fig. 69, and again another foot, cat. no. 67, fig. 77.

24 The painting's importance and surpassing quality are recognized despite the fact that it has probably been cut down. This applies, however, to many great works, such as Rembrandt's *Night Watch*.

25 Whereabouts unknown, canvas, 128 x 106 cm; Grisebach 1974, cat. no. 78, fig. 86. The painting has two olives which are missing in the London painting. If this picture is authentic this could be an argument for a relatively early dating, because olives are otherwise seen only in the still lifes from the Paris period. An argument against the possibility is the technique, which seems atypical. This could, however, be the result of overpainting. The drinking horns in both versions differ slightly.

26 Alte Pinakothek, Munich, inv. no. 10763, signed and dated, panel, 44.9 x 35.7 cm; mus. cat. 1967, p. 39, fig. 55; mus. cat. 1983, p. 268, ill. A painting in Budapest is generally recognized as being from 1656, but it is probably from 1658; Grisebach 1974, cat. no. 85, fig. 92.

27 The glass goblet appears in Grisebach 1974, cat. no. 73, fig. 80, a painting related to cat. no. 74, fig. 81.

28 Height 46 cm; Frederiks 1961, vol. 4, no. 2, ill.; mus. cat. 1952, no. 40.

29 B. van der Helst, *The Four Governors of the Archers' Civic Guard (the St. Sebastian Guard)*: Rijksmuseum, Amsterdam, inv. no. C3, signed and dated 1653, canvas, 183 x 268 cm, mus. cat. 1976, p. 268, ill.; G. Metsu, *The Oyster Eaters*: Hermitage, Leningrad, inv. no. 920, signed, panel, 55.5 x 42 cm; Robinson 1974, figs. 137, 200, Kuznetsov & Linnik 1982, pp. 105, 108-109 with a large detail photograph of the drinking horn; G. Metsu, *Girl Playing the Lute*: Kassel, Museum Wilhelmshöhe, inv. no. 301, signed, panel, 36 x 30 cm, Robinson 1974, p. 85, fig. 141. Also in a drawing after a lost painting by Dirck Barentsz, 1586, in the British Museum.

30 Fondation Custodia (Collection F. Lugt), Paris,

inv. no. J100, pen and ink in brown, 182 x 145 mm; Grisebach 1974, cat. no. 147, fig. 155.

31 Grisebach 1974, cat. nos. 92, 93, figs. 100, 101.

32 Kupferstichkabinett, Berlin-Dahlem, 180 x 143 mm; mus. cat. 1931, no. 2851, pl. 116; Grisebach 1974, cat. no. 146, fig. 154.

33 Grisebach 1974, pp. 163-165, is not definite about the authenticity.

34 Inv. no. A199, canvas, 71.5 x 62 cm, enlarged all around; mus. cat. 1976, p. 310, ill.

35 Frederiks 1952, vol. 1, p. 265, no. 1706, ill., with matching salver, p. 264, no. 170a, ill.; Ter Molen 1984, vol. 2, p. 110, cat. no. 609. This object dates back to a model from 1619 by Adam van Vianen: Ter Molen 1984, vol. 2, p. 8283, cat. Utrecht 1985, resp. no. 87 and 65, both ill. Van Gelder (1941), p. 55 n. 2 refers to a ewer in the collection of the Marquis de Sligo.

36 Hermitage, Leningrad, inv. no. 2822, signed, canvas, 105.5 x 87.5 cm, mus. cat. 1981, p. 134, Grisebach 1974, cat. no. 79, fig. 88, Kuznetsov & Linnik 1982, pp. 263-264, ill.; Schlossmuseum, Weimar, inv. no. G169, Grisebach 1974, cat. no. 141, fig. 152.

37 Gemäldegalerie, Dresden, inv. no. 1336, vestiges of a signature, canvas, 83 x 64.5 cm; mus. cat. 1982, p. 332, ill.

38 Or to a work in Leningrad, n. 36. Also other works by Vermeer and Kalf are comparable.

39 Collection E.G. Bührle, Zurich, 66.5 x 56 cm; Grisebach 1974, cat. no. 118, fig. 136. I have not seen the original.

40 Two nautilus shells and two mounts are seen in five variations in Kalf's work. See Grisebach 1974: (a) cat. no. 111, fig. 117; (b) cat. no. 112, fig. 118; (c) cat. nos. 109, 121, figs. 120, 110 (shell as 111, mounted as 118); (d) cat. no. 119, fig. 122 (like 109, with a figure of Fortuna); cat. no. 120, fig. 123 (like 112, with a figure of Neptune). Possibly the same shell as in another (third) mount: cat. no. 138, fig. 146.

41 Spriggs 1967, p. 78, fig. 66c; Lunsingh Scheurleer 1966, p. 45, fig. 24; Grisebach 1074, p. 123 n. 271.

42 The same sugar bowl in Grisebach 1974, cat. nos. 114, 115, 116, 139, 140, figs. resp. 126, 124, 125, 150, 151. The nos. 139 and 140 are painted differently and are obviously from a later date. Another sugar bowl with the Eight Taoistic Immortals, only partly colored and not in pairs, with a Buddha on the cover, in cat. nos. 106, 107, 108, figs. resp. 114, 110, 111.

43 Amsterdam 1984, no. 50, ill.

44 Museum der bildenden Künste, Leipzig, inv. no. 1034, signed, canvas, 52.5 x 43 cm; mus. cat. 1979, p. 103, ill. p. 303; Grisebach 1974, cat. no. 136, fig. 135.

45 Statens Museum for Kunst, Copenhagen, inv. no. 1531, signed and dated, canvas, 68 x 56 cm; mus. cat. 1951, p. 151, ill.; (this cat. fig. 10.9) Grisebach 1974, cat. no. 138, fig. 146. See also n. 40.

46 Staatliches Museum, Schwerin, inv. no. 71, signed and dated, canvas, 61 x 48 cm; mus. cat. 1982, p. 105, no. 174; Grisebach 1974, cat. no. 125, fig. 133. But with a knob of rock-crystal on the head of the masculine figure.

47 Besides the paintings in Leipzig and Heino, in Grisebach 1974, cat. no. 139, fig. 150 on a foot with a knob of rock crystal on the head of the putto, and in cat. no. 140, fig. 151 on another foot. The figure of the stem is related to works of the Amsterdam silversmith Lutma, but not so the ornaments.

48 *Bekerschroeven* are seen in Kalf's work in three other shapes.

49 Cat. Washington 1985, no. 134, p. 208, ill. The style reminds us of works by Andries Grill of the Hague.

50 The ginger jar in this painting by Kalf can be seen in a still life in the Musée du Louvre, inv. no. R.F. 796, canvas, 58 x 71 cm, mus. cat. 1979, p. 80, ill., Grisebach 1974, no. 137, fig. 149, with a clearly different upper rim and cover. In a private collection there is an even lovelier version of this painting: private collection, Germany, canvas, 55 x 65.5 cm, not in Grisebach. A somewhat divergent jar can be seen in a painting attributed to Kalf in the Musée des Beaux-Arts in Valenciennies, canvas, 67 x 55 cm, inv. no. 46.1.98, mus. cat. 1931, no. 144 (not in Grisebach) which has been in the museum since the French Revolution. This painting which has a Holbein bowl, as in two works by Kalf dated 1678 and 1680, and also a pilgrim's bottle as in the Paris period, I do not think is authentic.

51 See n. 45.

52 Schatzkammer der Residenz, Munich, cat. 1964, no. 40.

53 Hayward 1965.

54 See n. 36.

11 SPARKLE AND SMOKE

1 Národní Galerie, Prague, inv. no. DO 4208, signed in monogram and dated 1649, canvas, 102 x 83 cm; mus. cat. Still Life 1967, no. 20, ill.

2 Citroen 1963; cf. chapter 8.

3 Private collection, Germany, signed in monogram, panel, 30.8 x 22.8 cm, cat. *A Fruitful Past*, no. 20, ill.; in the Rijksbureau voor Kunsthistorische Documentatie, The Hague, is a photograph of a work in a Swedish collection, signed in monogram, without measurements, representing the ginger jar, a tazza and a rose. For a related pot see Spiggs 1965, p. 84, pl. 75b.

4 According to material collected by Bredius in the archive of the Rijksbureau voor Kunsthistorische Documentatie in The Hague, the marriage banns were read on March 27, 1651 when he was 'about 34 years old.' He was mentioned already as a painter in 1644. He was buried on October 17, 1664. See further Vroom 1980, vol. 1, pp. 130.132, vol. 2, pp. 14-15, cat. nos. 31-37, with some wrong attributions (fig. 175 reserved).

5 Private collection, Germany, signed and dated, canvas, 66 x 52 cm.

6 For the meaning of the peach, orange and quince as earthly symbols see cat. *A Fruitful Past*. The foot of the tazza is related to a work by the silversmith Adam van Vianen of 1627, cf. cat. Utrecht 1984-85, nos. 78 and 79, both ill., but not so the figure.

7 Examples in Vroom, see n. 4, cat. nos. 31, 33 (1655 not 1645), 34 and 35.

8 Richard Green Gallery, cat. 1974, no. 20, signed and dated 1652, canvas, 70 x 61 cm, Gammelbo 1960, no. 115 (Pieter van den Bosch); present whereabouts unknown, signed and dated 1652, measurements

unknown, photograph from the Rijksbureau voor Kunsthistorische Documentatie, The Hague, with grapes, a peach and a quince in a niche; P. de Boer Gallery, Amsterdam (1983), canvas, 76.5 x 58 cm.

9 Hamburger Kunsthalle, inv. no. 73, panel 53.5 x 40.5 cm, mus. cat. 1966, p. 90, ill. (manner of Willem Kalf), cf. Bergström, c.s. 1977/1979, p. 236, ill., pl. XXVI (Barend van der Meer).

10 See also Vroom 1980, vol. 1, pp. 124-126, vol. 2, pp. 10-11, cat. nos. 7-14 (as Gerret van Berkborch, with some wrong attributions); Bergström 1984.

11 Inv. no. G 1171, panel, 71 x 55.6 cm.

12 Inv. no. 814, signed and dated, canvas, 84 x 73 cm; mus. cat. 1977, p. 134, ill.

13 Inv. no. 6496, canvas, 73.8 x 60.5 cm; mus. cat. 1975, pp. 96-97.

14 For example: Alte Pinakothek, Munich, inv. no. 6598, signed, canvas, 150.8 x 117.6 cm; mus. cat. 1983, p. 313, ill.

15 Inv. no. 2822, canvas, 101.5 x 87.5 cm; mus. cat. 1981, p. 134; Grisebach 1974, cat. no. 79, fig. 88; Kuznetsov & Linnik 1982, pp. 263-264, ill.; see also chapter 10, n. 36.

16 Formerly in the Kaiser Friedrich-Museum, Berlin, inv. no. 948 J, burned in 1945, canvas, 67.5 x 82.5 cm; Grisebach 1974, cat. no. 71, fig. 79.

17 For example: a related but simpler *façon de Venise* rippled glass in a work in Museum Narodowe, Poznan, inv. no. Mo 200, signed and dated 1650, canvas, 52.5 x 40 cm, mus. cat. 1958, no. 1, fig. 1; a *façon de Venise* glass carafe in a work in the Palazzo Pitti, Florence, inv. no. 509, signed and dated 1652, canvas 71.5 x 50.5 cm.

18 For example: Pushkin Museum, Moscow, inv. no. 1842, signed and dated 1659, canvas, 67 x 52 cm, mus. cat. 1961, p. 8, Kuznetsov & Linnik 1982, p. 267, ill., pp. 269-270; Musée du Louvre, Paris, inv. no. RF 666, canvas, 74.5 x 58 cm; mus. cat. 1979, p. 19, ill.

19 Cat. no. 975, signed and dated, canvas, 86.3 x 72 cm; mus. cat. 1976, p. 10, ill. p. 113.

20 Frederiks 1952, vol. 1, p. 221, ill.

21 Hermitage, Leningrad, inv. no. 9677, signed and dated 1681, canvas, 58 x 47 cm; Fechner 1981, p. 170, ill., figs. 70-71.

22 Hoogsteder Gallery, The Hague (1983), signed and dated 167(8?), canvas, 57 x 47 cm.

23 Staatsmuseum, Schwerin, inv. no. 52, signed and dated 1672, canvas, 63.5 x 52.5 cm, mus. cat. 1962, no. 3, ill.; 1982, p. 94, no. 3; Richard Green Gallery, London (1977), signed and dated 1678, canvas, 66 x 53.5 cm. In the second painting the shell has been painted as damaged and in the first painting there is no handle.

24 Ovid, *Metamorphoses* 10, 1-77 and 11, 1-43.

25 Private collection, Switzerland, signature changed, panel, 71.5 x 58 cm. The nautilus goblet as the second example of n. 23.

26 Kunsthistorisches Museum, Vienna, inv. no. 571, signed and dated 1648, canvas, 138 x 125.5 cm; mus. cat. 1972, p. 40, fig. 39; 1973, p. 83, pl. 97. Jan Davidsz. de Heem also painted some fruit and flower cartouches in which a glass of wine makes a eucharistic reference.

27 Staatsgalerie Bamberg (Bayerische Staatsgemäldesammlungen), inv. no. 5963, signed and dated 1658, canvas, 110 x 89 cm; inv. no. 6108, same measurements.

28 Inv. no. 8608, canvas, 71 x 74 cm; cat. Münster & Baden 1979-80, no. 228, fig. p. 436.

29 A simular, slightly simpler silver censer, from the Basle Cathedral treasury, is now in the Metropolitan Museum, New York, Fritz 1982, p. 230, fig. 306.

30 On loan to the Overijssels Museum, Zwolle (Holland), inv. no. 961, signed and dated 1678, panel, 49 x 37 cm.

31 Rafael Valls Gallery, London, signed and dated 1672, panel, 37.5 x 52 cm.

32 For example: a signed and dated 1627 painting of Jacques Linard in the National Museum of Algiers, canvas 104 x 154 cm, illustrated in Faré 1974, p. 17; and in a work by Broderus Matthisen, signed and indistinctly dated in the Gemäldegalerie of Dresden, inv. no. 1966A, canvas 138 x 119 cm, exh. cat. Dresden 1983, no. 109, fig. 25.

33 In the symbolic sense one can find in heraldry, in the emblem literature and the iconological literature (Ripa) many meanings on themes such as power, strength, virtue (especially justice), vice (especially wrath).

34 P. de Boer Gallery, Amsterdam, signed, canvas, 45.5 x 42 cm.

35 Alfred Brod Gallery, London, cat. Spring 1957, no. 25, signed, canvas 38 x 28 cm.

36 Collection Nicolaus F. Landau, Paris; Lunsingh Scheurleer 1980, fig. 32.

37 Melito of Sardes, cap. VIII, 7, in Pitra, vol. 21, p. 480-484; Aristotle, *Historia Animalium*, 618 b; Alciatus 1531; p. (B) 65; Rollenhagen 1613, vol. 2, embl. 22; and many more sources.

38 Cf. Spriggs 1965, p. 86.

39 Cf. Wttewaall 1987, p. 137.

40 Schama 1987, pp. 171-172, with sources and prices.

41 Hayward 1963, p. 19, fig. 4; Oman 1967, no. 94, pl. 24.

42 Rijksmuseum Twenthe, Enschede (Holland), signed and dated 1696, canvas, 71.5 x 57.5 cm, mus. cat. 1976, pp. 94-95, fig. 198; Ter Kuile 1969, ill.; Lodi Gallery, Munich (1968), canvas, 76 x 62.5 cm, illustrated Ter Kuile 1969, fig. 5; Museo de Arte de Ponce, Puerto Rico, inv. no. 67.0621, signed and dated 1678, canvas, 257.5 x 205 cm, mus. cat. 1984, p. 256, ill. In the last-mentioned large still life we see many objects which also appear in other still lifes, among which is a Yi-shing teapot. It is also seen in a vanitas still life by Jacob van Walscapelle of 1685, cf. Bol 1969, p. 317, fig. 290. We can see the candlestick in some of the innumerable 18th-century paintings by Van Roestraeten's followers.

43 Van Roestraeten painted other types of silver candle sticks too.

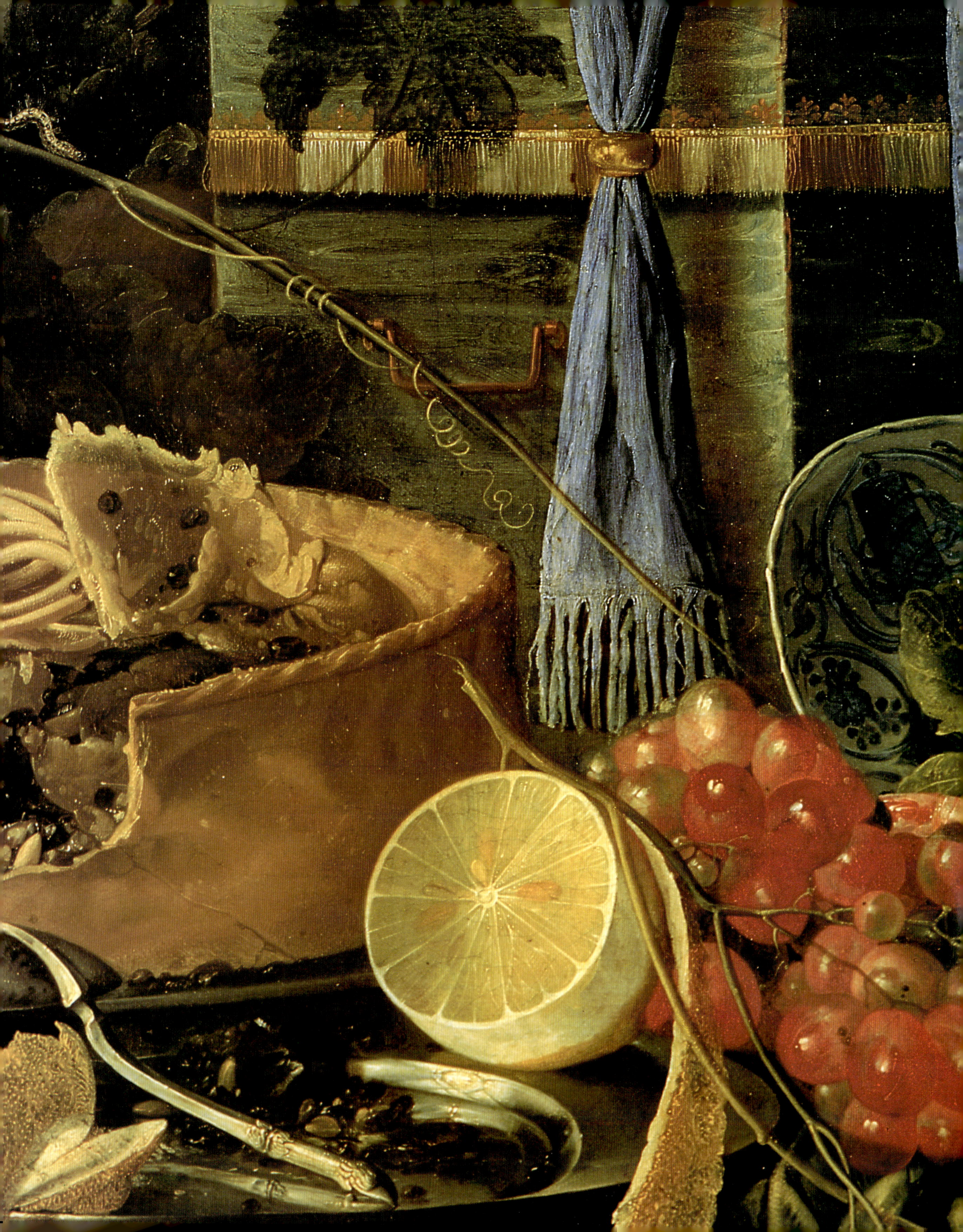

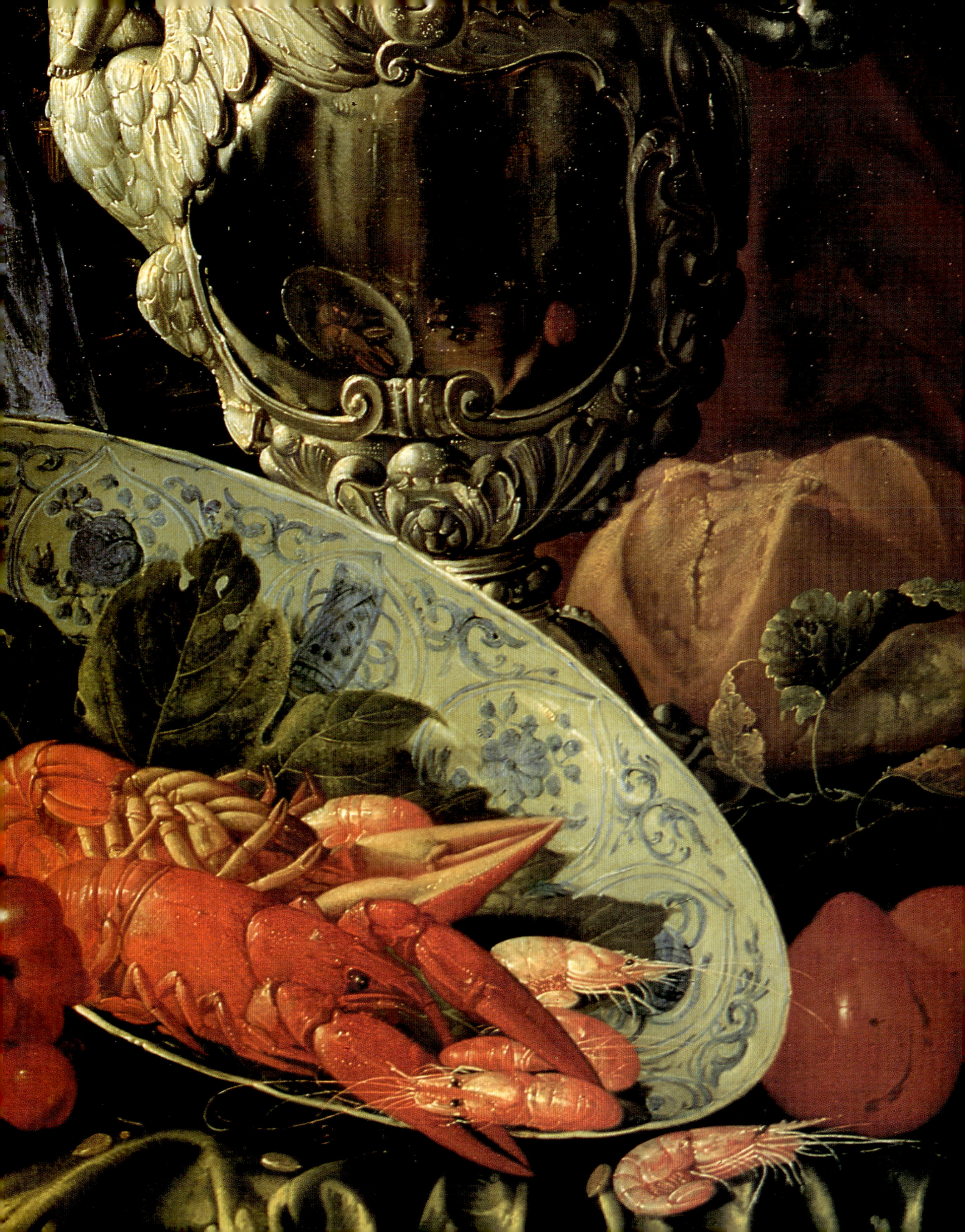

1 Text, p. 39

HIERONYMUS FRANCKEN THE YOUNGER
1578-Antwerpen-1623

Monogrammed and dated on the blade of the knife, in gray, a hand, and underneath: 'H F / 1599'? (H F linked).
Panel, 36 x 46 cm.
Private collection, Germany.
Provenance: Coll. Manteau, Brussel (until 1934); Gallery P. de Boer, Amsterdam; Coll. Dr. R.T. Mees, 's Gravenhage; Gallery P. de Boer, Amsterdam.
Literature: Bergström 1947, p. 30-31, 296 n. 50; ed. 1956, p. 24, 297 n. 64; Greindl 1956, p. 14; ed. 1983, p. 8-9; Luttervelt in cat. Liège & Luxembourg 1957, p. 32; Segal 1986b, p. 24, 29 n. 13; Segal 1986c, p. 58-59, fig. 4.
Remarks: Formerly attributed to a follower of Pieter Aertsen. Several versions are known, all about the same size, a.o., in the Koninklijk Museum voor Schone Kunsten, Antwerpen, inv. no. 846; the Musées Royaux des Beaux-Arts, Brussel, inv. no. 3357; and the Museum Boymans-Van Beuningen, Rotterdam, inv. no. 2288 (on loan from the Rijksdienst Beeldende Kunst, 's Gravenhage).
They have, formerly, been attributed to Pieter Brueghel the Elder, Pieter Aertsen, and Joachim Beuckelaer. They all bear remains of a signature or a monogram and date, probably 1599, 1600 or 1601. They form pairs with versions of fig. 3.4.

2 Text, p. 56

FRANS BADENS
Antwerpen 1571-1618 Amsterdam

Monogrammed left on the plinth in green-brown: 'F B'.
Copper, 10.8 x 14.0 cm.
Private Collection, Germany.
Provenance: Sale Sotheby's, London, 14 December 1977, no. 101, ill. (as Gotthardt de Wedig); Gallery P. de Boer, Amsterdam (1978) (as Wolfgang Heimbach).

CATALOGUE

3   Text, p. 57

JEREMIAS VAN WINGHEN
Brussel 1578-1645 Frankfurt am Main

Monogrammed and dated on the right of the plinth in black: 'I v W. 1607'.
Copper, 45.5 x 39 cm.
Rijksdienst Beeldende Kunst, 's Gravenhage, inv. no. NK 1493 (as Jacob van Walscapelle, and dated 1667).
Provenance: Gallery J. Goudstikker, Amsterdam; *Reichskanzlei*, Berlin; recuperated Stichting Nederlands Kunstbezit, Amsterdam (cat. 1946, no. 1225.)
Literature: Wright 1980, p. 488.
Remark: Hitherto as by Jacob van Walscapelle.

4   Text, p. 64

GEORG FLEGEL
Olmütz 1563-1639 Frankfurt am Main

Panel, 50.5 x 85 cm.
Private collection, The Netherlands.
Provenance: Coll. R.G. de Boer, Laren (1961); Gallery P. de Boer, Amsterdam (1983-84); Gallery Hoogsteder, 's Gravenhage (1985).
Exhibited: Laren 1963, no. 11, fig. 13 (as Peter Binoit); Amsterdam & Braunschweig 1983, no. 26, ill. (as Peter Binoit).
Literature: Greindl 1956, p. 46, 150, fig. 23 (as Peter Binoit); ed. 1983, p. 60, 191, fig. 33, p. 338, cat. no. 16 (as Peter Binoit); Bott 1961-62, p. 83, cat. no. 23, ill; Veca 1983, p. 212-213, fig. 155 (as Peter Binoit); *Tableau* 6, no. 2 (1983), ill. p. 41 (as Peter Binoit); Segal 1984c, p. 78, 86 n. 36; *Weltkunst* 54, no. 5 (1984), fig. p. 515 (as Peter Binoit).
Remark: Two replicas are known, one of them in the Musée du Louvre, Paris, inv. no. MNR 709 (as Peter Binoit).

5   Text, p. 65

JACQUES DE GHEYN II
Antwerpen 1565-1629 's Gravenhage

Monogrammed on the knife in gray: 'IDG' and a hand.
Panel, 52 x 79.8 cm.
Private collection, U.S.A.
Provenance: Gallery Konrad O. Bernheimer, München (1981); Private collection, Germany; Gallery P. Tillou, Litchfield, Connecticut.
Exhibited: Lohr & Dortmundt 1984, no. 4, 2 ill. (as Gottfried de Wedig, ca. 1615-1620).
Literature: Segal 1986a, p. 28-29; Segal 1986b, 5 ills.; Briels 1987, p. 226-227, fig. 288.

6   Text, p. 65

OSIAS BEERT I
1580-Antwerpen-1624

Panel, 49.5 x 71.5 cm.
Private Collection, England.
Provenance: Coll. Elisabeth Fichter, Baden-Baden; Gallery Abels, Köln (1953-56); Coll. Dr. Hans A. Wetzlar, Amsterdam (1956); Gallery A. Brod, London (1958); Coll. Ph. Linstedt, Göteborg; Sale Sotheby's, London, 11 July 1973, no. 27, ill. (as Hieronymus Francken); Gallery A. Stein, Paris; Sale Christie's, London, 12 December 1980, no. 45, ill.; Gallery Hoogsteder, 's Gravenhage (1981).
Exhibited: Köln 1956, no. 10, fig. p. 5 (as Osias Beert 1622-1678); London 1958, no. 4, ill.; 's Gravenhage 1982, no. 6, ill.
Literature: Greindl 1956, p. 149; ed. 1983, p. 336, cat. no. 59; *The Burlington Magazine* 98, no. 644 (1956), ill. p. 420; *Weltkunst* 26, no. 22 (1956), ill. p. 10; Lammers 1979-80b, p. 408-409, ill.; Härting 1983, p. 146; Haak 1984, p. 123, fig. 232.
Remark: Another version without vista is known, on panel, 46 x 65 cm, falsely signed 'D. de Heem' (Gallery P. de Boer, Amsterdam, before 1965).

7   Text, p. 67

CLARA PEETERS
?1583-Antwerpen-?1657

Signed and dated at the left on the plinth in dark gray: 'CLARA. P 1607'.
Panel, 23.7 x 36.7 cm.
Private collection, England.
Provenance: Private collection, Switzerland; Gallery Hoogsteder, 's Gravenhage.

8   Text, p. 69

CLARA PEETERS
?1583-Antwerpen-?1657

Signed and dated at the left on the plinth in gray-black: 'CLARA P. A° 1612'.
Panel, 45.5 x 33.5 cm.
Private collection, U.S.A.
Provenance: Gallery Speelman, London (1977).
Remark: Forms a pair with the following painting.

CATALOGUE

9   Text, p. 69

CLARA PEETERS
?1583-Antwerpen-?1657

Signed at the left on the plinth in gray-black: 'CLARA PEETERS'.
Panel, 45.5 x 33.5 cm.
Private collection, U.S.A.
Provenance: Gallery Speelman, London (1977).
Remark: Forms a pair with the foregoing painting.

10   Text, p. 70

NICOLAES GILLIS
? ca.1580-after 1632 Haarlem

Signed and dated upper left in gray, partly in brown glaze: 'Nicolaes Gillis fecit/ A° 1612'.
Panel, 59 x 79 cm.
Private collection, The Netherlands.
Provenance: Gallery L. Spik, Berlin; Sale Mak van Waay, Amsterdam (before 1962); Coll. Mr. Willem M.J. Russell, Amsterdam.
Exhibited: 's Hertogenbosch 1959, no. 59 I; Dordrecht 1962, no. 54, fig. 12; Amsterdam 1970, no. 37, ill.; London 1976b, no. 44, ill.; Münster & Baden-Baden 1979-1980, no. 213, ill.; Rutgers 1983, no. 42, fig. 23; Madrid 1985-86, no. 2, p. 26-29, col. ill.
Literature: Bergström 1963, p. 451, fig. 6; Lunsingh Scheurleer 1966, p. 46, fig. 13; Bol 1969, p. 15, fig. 11; Forbes n.d., fig. 25; Lammers 1979-1980b, p. 410, fig. p. 407; *Weltkunst* 50, no. 4 (1980), ill. p. 396; Veca 1983, p. 187-188, fig. 138; Haak 1984, p. 181, fig. 370; Segal 1984a, p. 50, 57 n. 5; Schama 1987, p. 161; Briels 1987, p. 227-229, fig. 290.
Remark: Before 1983 (exhibition Rutgers) the date has been read as 1611.

11   Text, p. 73

FLORIS VAN DIJCK
1575-Haarlem-1651

Monogrammed and dated upper right in gray: 'FVD Fecit./ A° 1610' (FVD interlaced).
Panel, 49 x 77.7 cm.
Private collection, Europe
Provenance: Private collection, 's-Gravenhage (1983).
Literature: Segal 1984d, ill. p. 33; Jordan 1985, p. 6-7, fig. 8.

12

JACQUES LINARD
Paris? 1600-1645 Paris

Signed and dated on the box to the right in cream: 'J Linard/à Paris/1624'(or 1621).
Panel, 38 x 51.7 cm.
Private collection, U.S.A.
Provenance: Gallery Wildenauer, Berlin; Gallery Speelman, London.

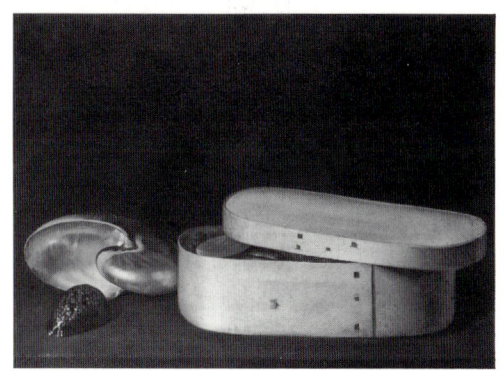

13

SEBASTIAN STOSKOPFF
Strasbourg 1597-1657 Idstein

Canvas, 47 x 59.5 cm.
Private collection, Germany.
Provenance: Gallery Joseph Hahn, Paris (1985).
Literature: Apollo 115, no. 242 (1982), p. 287, fig. 11; Apollo 120, no. 271 (1984), p. 208, fig. 2; L'Estampille 173 (1984), fig. p. 52.

14

BALTHASAR VAN DER AST
Middelburg 1593/94-1657 Delft

Signed lower right in brown: '.B. van der Ast.'.
Panel, 29 x 37.5 cm.
Gemäldegalerie Alte Meister der Staatlichen Kunstsammlungen Dresden, inv. no. 1722/28, A654; cat. 1930, no. 1257; mentioned in the inventory of 1722 by Wackerbarth.
Exhibited: Dresden 1955-56, p. 124, no. 1257; Dresden 1983, no. 6, fig. 10.
Literature: Von Wurzbach 1906-1911, vol. 1, p. 33; Bergström 1947, p. 298 n. 65; ed. 1956, p. 301 n. 66; Bol 1955, p. 154; Bol 1960, p. 81, cat. no. 85; Bénézit 1966, vol. 1, p. 270; Bol 1980, p. 81, cat. no. 85; Segal 1984a, p. 60, 62 n. 48.

15   Text, p. 89

BALTHASAR VAN DER AST
Middelburg 1593/94-1657 Delft

Signed on the plinth left from the centre in brown: ' · B. vander. Ast.'
Panel, 27 x 36 cm.
Private collection, England.
Provenance: Sale Knight, Frank & Rutley, Nethercourt, Bournemouth, 25 October 1960, no. 267, ill. pl. IV; Gallery Leonard Koetser, London (1960); Gallery David Koetser, Zürich; Private Collection, England.

16   Text, p. 92

WILLEM KALF
Rotterdam 1619-1693 Amsterdam

Signed on the right of the plinth in gray: 'w. KALF'.
Canvas, 52 x 43 cm.
Stichting Hannema-de Stuers Fundatie, Kasteel Het Nijenhuis, near Heino, The Netherlands; cat. 1967, no. 150, fig. 19.
Provenance*:* Probably Sale Lepke, Berlin, 20 March 1900, no. 11; Private collection, Berlin (1901); Gallery E. Bolton, London (1924); Sale London, 18 June 1924, no. 66; Sale Frederik Muller, Amsterdam, 25 November 1924, no. 50, ill.; Coll. A.W. Mensing, Amsterdam (1926); Sale Frederik Muller, Amsterdam, 10-11 December 1935, no. 22; Sale Frederik Muller, Amsterdam, 29 November 1939, no. 919; Gallery D.A. Hoogendijk, Amsterdam (1939-1941); Coll. Dr. D. Hannema, Castle Weldam, Goor.
Exhibited: 's Gravenhage 1926, no. 65; Almelo 1953, no. 24, fig. 50; Dordrecht 1954, no. 61; Rotterdam 1955, no. 81, fig. 124; Luxembourg & Liège 1957, no. 40, fig. 127; Eindhoven 1957, no. 40; Tokio & Kyoto 1968-1969, no. 31, ill.; Madrid 1985-86, no. 23, p. 102-105, ill.
Literature: Bergström 1947, p. 285-286, fig. 232; ed. 1956, p. 283, fig. 232; Hannema 1952, p. 30, fig. 14; *Connaissance des Arts* 110, no. 4 (1961), ill. cover.; Grisebach 1974, p. 117, 159, 160, 177, 178, 278, 279, 280-281, cat. no. 143, fig. 157; Bergström 1977/1979, ill. p. 196; Wright 1980, p. 196.

* According to Hannema (cat. 1967) too: Coll. Mulliner, London and Coll. F. von Hochberg, both ca. 1924.

17 — Text, p. 92

ADRIAEN COORTE
active in Middelburg 1683-1707

Signed and dated left on the plinth in dark brown: 'A, Coorte, *1697*'.
Paper on panel, 17.2 x 22.2 cm.
Dutch Renaissance Art Collection, Amsterdam.
Provenance: Sale Sotheby's, London, 26 March 1969, no. 35, ill., Coll. T.A. Samuel; Private collection, Germany; Gallery J. Kraus, Paris (1977); Gallery Charles Roelofsz, Amsterdam; French & Company, Inc., New York.
Literature: Bol 1977, p. 21 n. 57, p. 42, cat. no. 31, fig. 19; *Kunstbeeld* 9, no. 1 (1985), p. 44, ill. p. 45.
Remark: Formed a pair in the T.A. Samuel collection with another shell piece, signed and dated 1698 (Bol 1977, cat. no. 32).

18 — Text, p. 101

JAN BRUEGHEL THE ELDER
1568-Antwerpen-1625

Signed lower right on the plinth in brown: 'Brveghel'.
Copper, 44.6 x 31.7 cm.
Private collection, Germany.
Provenance: Coll. Graham Baron Ash, Wingfield Castle, Diss, Norfolk (1949); Coll. Rev. John Arthur Rushton Reed, Blackburn, Lancashire; Sale Christie's, London, 4 October 1967, no. 155, ill., to G. Winner; Private collection, France (until 1979); Gallery Silvano Lodi, Campione (1980); Gallery Speelman, London.
Exhibited: London 1949, no. 2; Norwich 1955, no. 6; Gent 1960, no. 31, fig. 54; Brussel 1980, no. 128, ill.
Literature: Hairs 1955, p. 38, 201; ed. 1965, p. 42, 60, 359; ed. 1985, vol. 1, p. 46, 48, fig. 8, p. 82, 427 n. 204, vol. 2, p. 11; Hawcroft 1960, ill. p. 8; Spriggs 1967, p. 78, fig. 69b; *Apollo* 86, no. 70 (1967), p. 521, fig. 3; *Connaisseur* 166, no. 670 (1967), p. 250, fig. 3; Ertz 1979, p. 283, 285, fig. 355, ill. p. 326, p. 530-531 n. 364, 592-593, cat. no. 208a; Strachwitz 1980, p. 2875, 2876, fig. 5; Ertz 1981, p. 120-121, cat. no. 35, ill.; Jordan 1985, p. 9, fig. 16.

19 — Text, p. 104

PETER BINOIT
Köln? ca. 1590-1632 Hanau

Monogrammed lower right in gray-black: 'PB'.
Panel, 41.2 x 28.2 cm.
Private collection, Germany.
Provenance: Hermitage, Leningrad, inv. no. 3131; Coll. H.L. Straat, Leeuwarden; Gallery S. Nystad, 's Gravenhage (1959); Private collection, The Netherlands.
Exhibited: Amsterdam 1934, no. 241, ill.; Amsterdam 1935, no. 15, ill.; Rotterdam 1951, no. 6; Laren 1963, no. 13.
Literature: King 1954, p. 43; Hairs 1955, p. 252; ed. 1965, p. 250, 349; ed. 1985, vol. 1, p. 368, vol. 2, p. 5; *Weltkunst* 29, no. 17 (1959), ill. p. 5; Bott 1961-62, p. 49, 76, cat. no. 2, ill.; Lunsingh Scheurleer 1980, p. 29; Veca 1982, p. 148-149, fig. 171.

20

BALTHASAR VAN DER AST
Middelburg 1593/94-1657 Delft

Signed lower left in gray-brown: 'B. vandeR. Ast...'
Panel, 36.3 x 27.7 cm.
Private Collection, U.S.A.
Provenance: Coll. Victor D.Spark, New York (before 1956); Coll. Sidney J.van den Bergh, Wassenaar (cat. 1968, p.14, 15, ill.); Gallery Hans Cramer, 's Gravenhage (1972); Coll. Eugene Slatter, London.
Exhibited: Laren 1959, no. 21, fig. 14; Gent 1960, no. 7, fig. 72; Delft 1962, no. 9; Leiden 1965, no.2.
Literature: Bol 1955, p. 139, fig. 1, p. 141 n. 18; Bol 1960, p. 37, 38, 70, cat. no. 6, pl. 33; Pavière 1962, p. 9; De Vries 1964, p. 353-354, fig. 3; Spriggs 1967, p. 76, fig. 62c; Lewis 1973, p. 9.
Remark: There is a replica in the Suermondt-Museum, Aachen, cat. 1932, no. 19.

21   Text, p. 108

BALTHASAR VAN DER AST
Middelburg 1593/94-1657 Delft

Signed at the lower right in brown: '· B. vander. Ast. fe..'
Panel, 67.5 x 37.5 cm.
Staatliche Galerie Dessau, Schloß Georgium; cat. 1929, no.63.
Provenance: Sale Frankfurt 1784, no. 365; Amalienstiftung, no.322.
Literature: Zeitschrift für bildende Kunst 1879, p. 344; Parthey 1863-1864, vol. 1, p. 45; Von Wurzbach 1906, vol. 1, p. 33; Thieme & Becker 1907-1950, vol. 2, p. 203; Gerson 1950, p. 52-53, fig. 140; Bol 1960, p. 38, 39, 40, 86, cat. no. 120, pl. 47a; Lunsingh Scheurleer 1980, p. 30-31; Segal 1984a, p. 54, 61 n. 22; Haak 1984, p. 205, fig. 424.

22   Text, p. 108

JAN BAPTIST VAN FORNENBURGH
ca. 1585-1649? 's Gravenhage

Monogrammed and dated lower right of the centre in gray: 'IB.F: 1629' (IB connected).
Panel, 24.5 x 31 cm.
Private collection, Germany.
Provenance: Gallery P. de Boer, Amsterdam; Coll. W.Reineke, Amersfoort (1962).
Exhibited: Dordrecht 1962, no. 51, fig. 5; Laren 1963, no. 70, fig. 11; Amsterdam & 's Hertogenbosch 1982, p. 94, no.47, ill.
Literature: Van Gelder 1931, p. 242; Bergström 1963, p. 448, 450, fig. 2; Gammelbo 1965, p. 9, cat. no. XIII; Bol 1982a, p. 260, fig. 3; Bol 1982b, p. 87-88, fig. 3.

23

DIRCK VAN DELEN
Heusden 1604/05-1671 Arnemuiden

Signed and dated lower right in gray-brown: 'DVDELEN/1637' (DVD in monogram).
Panel, 38.3 x 29 cm.
Museum Boymans-van Beuningen, Rotterdam, inv. no. 2887.
Provenance: Coll. Marquis du Blaisel, Paris; Probably sale J.B. van den Branden, Brussel, 13 April 1801, no. 117; Sale Christie's, London, 17 May 1872, no. 117; Coll. Ad. Schloß, Paris, before 1940; Stolen during World War II; Coll. Dr. Vitale Bloch, 's Gravenhage, bequeathed to the Museum Boymans-van Beuningen in 1979.
Exhibited: Rotterdam 1978, no. 14, ill.; Paris 1979, no. 14, ill.; Amsterdam & 's Hertogenbosch 1982, p. 39, 91, no. 40, ill.; Kobe 1982, no. 243, ill. p. 79; København 1983-84, no. 3, fig. p. 15, cover; Amsterdam 1984, p. 79, 184-185, no. 34, ill.
Literature: Jantzen 1910, p. 68; Thieme & Becker 1907-1950, vol. 9, p. 11; Vorenkamp 1933, p. 119-120; Bol 1960, p. 55-56, 99, fig. 62; Pavière 1962, vol. 1, fig. 29a; Bloch 1966, p. 24, fig. 17; Bol 1969, p. 56, fig. 47; Lewis 1973, p. 26; Bergström 1977/79, ill. p. 185; Hoetink 1978, p. 104-110, fig. 5; 'The Vitale Bloch Bequest', in *Apollo* 107, no. 194 (1978), p. 323, ill.; Wright 1980, p. 96; Bol 1981, p. 582, ill.; Bol 1982b, p. 55-56, fig. 8; Veca 1982, p. 182-184, fig. 210; Blade 1983, p. 109-111, no. 57, fig. 54; Haak 1984, p. 118, fig. 217; Krafft 1986, ill. cover; Segal 1987, p. 92, fig. 32.

24

JOHANNES GOEDAERT
1617-Middelburg-1668

Signed lower right in gray: 'Joh: Goedaert'.
Panel, 28 x 22 cm.
Private collection, Germany.
Provenance: Coll. Ir. J.Th. Berkemeier, Rotterdam.
Exhibited: Amsterdam 1935, no. 55, ill.; Dordrecht 1955, no. 50; Amsterdam 1984, no. 35, ill.
Literature: Bol 1959, p. 13-14, fig. 7; Bol 1969, p. 57-60, fig. 40; Bergström c.s.1977/1979, ill. p. 191; Bol 1980, p. 369, fig. 4; Bol 1982b, p. 31-32, fig. 4; Segal 1984a, p. 77, fig. 27c, p. 79-80, 186-187, no. 35, ill.; Bol 1985, p. 53, fig. 24.

25   Text, p. 112

JAN DAVIDSZ. DE HEEM
Utrecht 1606-1683/84 Antwerpen

Signed on the letter in brown, in calligrafic writing: 'J D De Heem'.
Canvas, 87.5 x 65 cm.
Gemäldegalerie Alte Meister der Staatlichen Kunstsammlungen Dresden, inv. no. 1722/28, A 187, gallery no. 1265; cat. 1982, p. 203, ill. Mentioned in the inventory of 1722 by Wackerbarth.
Exhibited: Zürich 1971, no. 24; Tokyo & Kyoto 1974-1975, no. 53, ill.; Mexico City 1980-1981, no. 22, ill.; Dresden 1983, no. 75, col. fig. 12; New Delhi 1984, no. 19.
Literature: Von Wurzbach 1906, vol. 1, p. 657; Bergström 1947, p. 216-219, fig. 179; ed. 1956, p. 212-214, fig. 179; Bergström 1955, p. 343-345, fig. 15; Hairs 1955, p. 140, 220; ed. 1965, p. 271, 384; ed. 1985, vol. 1, p. 397, vol. 2, p. 29; Greindl 1956, p. 122, 172; ed. 1983, p. 146, 3-60, cat. no. 45; Mitchell 1973, p. 134-137; Kuechen 1979, p. 512 n. 196; Veca 1981, p. 119, fig. 139; Ter Kuile 1985, p. 40-41, fig. 20.

26   Text, p. 117

JAN DAVIDSZ. DE HEEM (former attribution) *Utrecht 1606-1683/84 Antwerpen*

Inscribed upper left in dark-brown: 'J De Heem F.'. Panel, 43 x 59.6 cm.
Szépművészeti Múzeum, Budapest, inv. no. 3538 (590a); cat. 1967, p. 304, fig. 322. Acquired 1907.
Provenance: Sale Ch. Sedelmeyer, Paris 1907.
Literature: Takács 1908, p. 666; Takács 1911, p. 874; Greindl 1956, p. 172; ed. 1983, p. 360, cat. no. 38 (measures 40.5 x 55.5 cm); Bénézit 1966, vol. 4, p. 631.
Remark: The painting is by a follower of Jan de Heem from whom we know other works, e.g., a festoon of fruits in the Centraal Museum, Utrecht, mus. cat. 1952, no. 136, panel, 39.5 x 49,5 cm. A copy of cat. no. 26 in sale Sotheby's, London, 27 March 1974, no. 116, ill., panel, 48.5 x 63.5 cm (as by Joris van Son).

27   Text, p. 121

PIETER CLAESZ
Burgsteinfurt 1597/98-1661 Haarlem

Monogrammed on the knife blade, recumbent, in grey: 'P C'.
Panel, 50 x 74 cm.
Private collection, The Netherlands.
Provenance: Gallery A. Brod, London (Winter 1957-1958); Coll. Dr. Hans A. Wetzlar, Amsterdam.
Exhibited: Laren 1959, no. 38; Dordrecht 1962, no. 36, fig. 17; Laren 1963, no. 63; Amsterdam & Braunschweig 1983, p. 51-52, 107, no. 9, 2 ill.
Literature: Weltkunst 27, no. 24 (1957), ill. p. 11.

28

PIETER CLAESZ
Burgsteinfurt 1597/98-1660 Haarlem

Monogrammed and dated lower right in brown: 'PC'/.A 1647'.
Panel, 64 x 82 cm.
Rijksmuseum, Amsterdam, inv. no. A1857; cat. 1976, p. 168, ill.; Acquired 1900.
Provenance: Coll. H. Bols, Groningen (1900).
Exhibited: Rotterdam 1976, no. 118, ill. detail.
Literature: Bye 1921, p. 82, fig. p. 84; Martin 1935, p. 407-408, fig. 245; Vroom 1945, p. 191, fig. 178, p. 201, cat. no. 64 (with wrong measurements); ed. 1980, vol. 1, p. 242-243, fig. 327, vol. 2, p. 33, cat. no. 136; Van Schendel & Haak 1966, no. 40, ill.; Crébas 1972, p. 3, 4, 7, fig. 10; Wright 1978, p. 75, ill.; ed. 1980, p. 75, ill.; Wright 1980, p. 76; Wright 1981, p. 12; Walsh & Schneider 1981-82, p. 34-35, fig. 2.

29

PIETER CLAESZ
Burgsteinfurt 1597/98-1660 Haarlem

Monogrammed and dated left on the plinth in brown: 'PC A° 1624'.
Panel, 65 x 55.5 cm.
Gemäldegalerie Alte Meister der Staatlichen Kunstsammlungen Dresden, gal. no. 1370; cat. 1982, p. 133, ill. Acquired 1875 from trade.
Exhibited: Dresden 1983, no. 31, fig. 44.
Literature: Von Wurzbach 1906, vol. 1, p. 285; Zarnowska 1929, p. VIII, XII; Vorenkamp 1933, p. 31, 98; Vroom 1945, p. 21, 23, fig. 8, p. 198, cat. no. 22; ed. 1980, vol. 1, p. 92, 94, fig. 122, vol. 2, cat. no. 506 (as Clara Peeters); Menz 1962, ill. p. 295; Wright 1981, p. 12; Bergström & Segal 1984, p. 74, 77-78, fig. 2.

30 Text, p. 129

PIETER CLAESZ
Burgsteinfurt 1597/98-1660 Haarlem

Monogrammed and dated left on the plinth in gray: 'PC 1636'.
Panel 47 x 61 cm.
Westfälisches Landesmuseum für Kunst und Kulturgeschichte, Münster, inv. no. 1369 LM (74-36); cat. 1975, p. 20, fig. 28.
Provenance: Coll. Fritz Marcus, New York (1966); Gallery Agnew, London (1969); Gallery C.P.A. & G.R. Castendijk, Rotterdam (1973).
Exhibited: San Francisco, Toledo & Boston 1966-67, no. 100; Münster & Baden-Baden 1979-80, no. 115, ill.; Lohr & Dortmundt 1984 (only in Dortmundt, not in catalogue).
Literature: Jones 1930, p. 225, fig. 111, p. 222; Olbrich & Möbius 1951, p. 320f., fig. 5; Roodenburg 1959, p. 23 n. 46; Frederiks 1961, vol. 4, no. 35, fig. 44; *Apollo* 85, no. 60 (1967), p. 141, fig. 4; *Antiek* 8, no. 2 (1973), p. 146, ill.; Klemm 1979-80, p. 202-203, 206, no. 115, ill.; Vroom 1980, vol. 1, p. 99, 105, fig. 138, vol. 2, p. 20, cat. no. 64, p. 104, cat. no. 521 (Clara Peeters); Veca 1981, p. 92-93, fig. 108; Dittrich 1981, ill. p. 10; Uhlig 1986, p. 11-13, fig. 10.
Remark: The date has hitherto been read as 1634.

31 Text, p. 137

WILLEM CLAESZ. HEDA
1594-Haarlem-1670

Signed and dated at the right on the plinth, in gray: '.HEDA./1634'.
Panel, 44.5 x 62 cm.
Rijksmuseum, Amsterdam, inv. no. A137; cat. 1976, p. 262, ill. Purchased 1809.
Provenance: Cabinet van Heteren Gevers, 's-Gravenhage-Rotterdam.
Literature: Moes & Van Biema 1909, p. 146, 159; Vroom 1945, p. 58-59, fig. 47, p. 72 (wrong data), 211, cat. no. 188; ed. 1980, vol. 1, p. 54, fig. 67, p. 69, vol. 2, p. 68, cat. no. 341.
Remark: Apocryphally signed also: 'Johannes de Heem .f.'.

32 Text, p. 137

WILLEM CLAESZ. HEDA
1594-Haarlem-1670

Signed and dated on the plinth in dark gray: 'HEDA 163.' (probably 1634).
Panel, 36.5 x 49 cm.
Private collection, England, Courtesy of John Mitchell & Son.
Provenance: Coll. Hoog, Haarlem; Sale Van Marle, Sille & Baan, Rotterdam, 28 February 1951, no. 130 (as dated 1631, measures 40 x 57 cm); Gallery Nystad, Lochem & 's-Gravenhage (1957); Coll. W. Mak, Blaricum (1962); Sale Lempertz 472, Köln, 14 March 1963, no. 46; Gallery John Mitchell & Sons, London (1980).
Exhibited: Leiden 1950, no. 27; Luxembourg & Liège 1957, no. 28, fig. 16 (as dated 1634); Eindhoven 1957, no. 27 (as dated 1634); Dordrecht 1962, no. 59, fig. 51 (as dated 1639); London 1976a, p. 32-33, ill.
Literature: Vroom 1980, vol. 1, p. 58, fig. 73, p. 155, 158, fig. 211, vol. 2, p. 50, cat. no. 238 (as Franchois Elout), p. 68, cat. no. 344.

33 Text, p. 138

GERRET WILLEMSZ. HEDA
c. 1622-Haarlem-1702?

Signed and dated along the border of the linen cloth, in green-gray: '.HEDA. 1647..'
Panel, 89.5 x 76.5 cm.
Private collection.
Provenance: Collection Baron van der Borgh, sale Castle Vorden, 7 October 1936, no. 322, ill.; Gallery D. Katz, Dieren (1936); Gallery Frederik Muller, Amsterdam; Gallery P. de Boer, Amsterdam; Coll. Mr. H. Haga, 's-Gravenhage (1955); Coll. Mrs. W.J. van der Meer-Solkes, 's-Gravenhage.
Exhibited: Rotterdam 1955, no. 72, ill.
Literature: Van Gelder [1941], p. 16-17, ill. (as W.C. Heda); Vroom 1945, p. 132, fig. 114, p. 134-135, 209, cat. no. 167; ed. 1980, vol. 1, p. 175, vol. 2, p. 64, cat. no. 320.

34 Text, p. 139

MAERTEN BOELEMA
active 1642-1664

Signed and dated on the knifeblade in gray: 'M.BOELEMA. DE STOMME. 1642'.
Panel, 59.8 x 79.4 cm.
Gallery Charles Roelofsz, Amsterdam; cat. 1988, no. 3, ill..
Provenance: Private collection, Switzerland.

35 Text, p. 140

JAN JANSZ. DEN UYL THE ELDER
1595/96-Amsterdam-1640

Signed with reflections of owls
Canvas, 74.5 x 86.5 cm.
Gallery Charles Roelofsz, Amsterdam; cat. 1988, no. 2, ill.
Provenance: Coll. Baron Kuffner; Los Angeles County Museum of Art, Gift of Jacob M. Heimann 1950, inv. no. A. 5608.50-9 (cat. 1965, p. 70); Sale Sotheby's, New York, 17 January 1986, no. 22.
Exhibited: La Jolla 1964, no. 13; Rutgers 1983, no. 69, p. 97 (as W.C. Heda or G. Heda).
Literature: Bulletin Los Angeles County Museum 4 (1951), p. 11 (as W.C. Heda); Wescher 1954, vol. 2, p. 38, cat. no. 38, ill. (as Heda); Sutton 1986, p. 132.

36

JAN JANSZ. TRECK
ca. 1606-Amsterdam-1652

Signed and dated lower left in the coat-of-arms on the napkin in brown: 'JJ Treck/1649' (JJ connected).
Canvas, 76.5 x 63.8 cm.
The Trustees of the National Gallery, London, inv. no. 4562; cat. 1986, p. 626, ill.; cat. N. MacLaren, *The Dutch School*, 1960, p. 409-410; Illustrated in cat. *Continental Schools*, 1937, p. 365; *Dutch School-Plates*, 1958, p. 334. Acquired 1931.
Provenance: Gallery Robson & Sons, Newcastle-upon-Tyne (1930); Sale Christie's, London, 21 November 1930, no. 87 (as Heda); Gallery Ascher & Welcker; Gallery A. Tooth & Sons, London (cat. 1931, no. 15).
Exhibited: London 1945, no. 38.

Literature: Vorenkamp 1933, p. 26, 41-42, 44; De Boer 1940, p. 11-12, fig. 8; Vroom 1945, p. 161, 162, 217, cat. no. 265, fig. 142; ed. 1980, vol. 1, p. 209, 211, fig. 284, vol. 2, p. 126, cat. no. 647 (as dated ca. 1649); Bergström 1947, p. 156, 159, fig. 132; ed. 1956, p. 151-152, fig. 133; Gwynne Jones 1954, p. 52, pl. 41; Pavière 1962, p. 59; Bénézit 1966, vol. 8, p. 371; Bol 1969, p. 75-76, fig. 63; Lewis 1973, p. 72; Von Graevenitz 1973, p. 303 n. 718; Wright 1976, p. 203; Bergström c.s. 1977/1979, p. 236, ill., pl. 23; Haak 1984, p. 310, fig. 663; Ember in cat. Köln & Utrecht 1987, p. 122.

37

JAN DAVIDSZ. DE HEEM
Utrecht 1606-1683/84 Antwerpen

Signed and dated upper right in green-brown: 'JDHeem F A 1634:' (JDH connected).
Canvas, 61.5 x 55 cm.
Staatsgalerie Stuttgart, inv. no. 3323; Acquired 1978.
Provenance: Coll. Dr. Philip Lindstedt, Göteborg (1956); Sale Sotheby's, London, 11 July 1973, no. 30, ill.; Gallery Herner Wengraf, London (1975); Gallery Julius Böhler, München (cat. 1978, no. 7).
Exhibited: Münster & Baden-Baden 1979-1980, no. 232, ill.; Lohr & Dortmundt 1984, no. 20, ill.
Literature: Bergström 1956, p. 194-195, pl. V; Bergström 1956a, p. 180-183, fig. 8; Grisebach 1974, p. 168, fig. 197; cat. New York 1974-1975, no. 7, ill.; *Gazette des Beaux Arts* 121, no. 4 (1979), p. 18, fig. 94; Veca 1981, p. 98, fig. 120; Greindl 1983, p. 362, cat. no. 125.

38

JAN DAVIDSZ. DE HEEM
Utrecht 1606-1683/84 Antwerpen

Signed at the centre below on the music sheet in brown: 'J.D De Heem'.
Canvas, 140 x 115.5 cm.
Rijksdienst Beeldende Kunst, 's-Gravenhage, inv. no. NK 2711; since 1948 on loan to the Centraal Museum, Utrecht; cat. Centraal Museum 1952, p. 56-57, no. 137.
Provenance: Coll. Dr. James Simon, Berlin (1906); Sale Frederik Muller, Amsterdam, 16 December 1919, no. 29, ill.; Gallery P. Cassirer, Berlin (ca. 1925); Coll. S.P.D. May and Mrs. May-Fuld, De Breul, Zeist; Private collection, The Netherlands; Sale Frederik Muller, Amsterdam, 14-17 October 1941, no. 311, ill.; Taken to Germany by the German occupation during World War II; recuperated, Stichting Nederlands Kunstbezit, Amsterdam, inv. no. 1010 (cat. 1946, p. 19).
Exhibited: Berlin 1906, no. 57; Utrecht 1969; Leiden & Groningen 1985, no. VI-27 (see Ter Kuile).
Literature: Van Luttervelt 1947, p. 46, 50, fig. 23; Greindl 1956, p. 103, 105, 174; ed. 1983, p. 124, 249, fig. 130, p. 362, cat. no. 131 (as no. 416); Foucart 1965, ill.; Houtzager c.s. 1967, p. 238-239; De Mirimonde 1970, p. 282; Grisebach 1974, p. 125 n. 285; Wright 1980, p. 165; Ter Kuile 1985, p. 50-51, fig. 33, p. 116-117, cat. no. VI-27, ill., p. 206; J.A.L. de Meyere in cat. Köln & Utrecht 1987, p. 41, fig. 8.
Remark: A copy, signed 'David de Heem', probably false: Coll. Rudolf Tewes, Bremen; exh. *Historische Gemälde aus Bremischen Privatbesitz*, Kunsthalle, Bremen 1904, no. 197; purchase Kunsthalle, Bremen 1912; C. Stoermer in *Der Cicerone* 5 (1913), p. 789-790, fig. 5; Sale Lempertz, Köln, 27 november 1935, no. 147, ill.

39

JAN DAVIDSZ. DE HEEM
Utrecht 1606-1683/84 Antwerpen

Signed at the left on the plinth in gray-black: 'J. De heem f'.
Canvas, 75 x 105 cm.
Museum Boymans-van Beuningen, Rotterdam, inv. no. 1289; cat. 1972, p. 211, fig. p. 108. Purchased in 1856.
Provenance: Sale Roos & Engelberts, Amsterdam, 4 November 1856, no. 17, Coll. H. Eijmer Az.
Exhibited: Rotterdam 1909, no. 37; Kobe 1982, no. 245, ill.
Literature: Burger 1860, vol. II, p. 319; Lafenestre & Richtenberger 1898, no. 99; Von Wurzbach 1906, vol. 1, p. 658; Warner 1928, no. 45d, ill.; ed. 1975, idem, add. p. 246; Martin 1936, p. 415, 428, fig. 217; Martin 1950, p. 44, 113, fig. 313; Greindl 1956, p. 103, 104, 105, 172; ed. 1983, p. 124, 127, 362, cat. no. 114; Pavière 1962, p. 34; Foucart 1965, p. 33, ill.; Bénézit 1966, vol. 4, p. 631; Lewis 1973, p. 36; Brandt Corstius 1973, fig. p. 138; Wright 1980, p. 165.
Remark: A copy, signed 'J.P.C. Leemans', 80 x 115 cm, was in 1954 in the New York trade, together with a pendant.

40

JAN DAVIDSZ. DE HEEM
(Utrecht 1606-1683/84 Antwerpen

Signed and dated on the plinth on the lower left in brown: 'J.De heem f. A° 1649'.
Canvas, 75 x 111.5 cm.
Gallery Thomas Brod, London.
Provenance: Coll. E.H. Davenport, Davenport House, Bridgnorth, Shropshire (1881); Inherited by his daughter, Mrs. Leicester-Warren (1931); Sale Christie's, London, 12 June 1931, no. 74, ill., coll. Leicester-Warren, purchased by Collings; Coll. Alexander Jergens, Cincinnati, Ohio (1931); Gallery French & Co. Inc., New York; Coll. Linda and Gerald Guterman, New York; Sale Sotheby's, New York, 14 January 1988, no. 19, ill., coll.Guterman.
Exhibited: St. Jude's, London-Whitechapel 1886, no. 138; Museum of Art, Cincinnati, extended loan of Mr. Jergens.

41

FRANÇOIS RYCKHALS
c. 1600-Middelburg-1647

Signed and dated lower left in a booklet in gray: 'FRHALS 1640' (FRHALS connected).
Panel, 70 x 117 cm.
Szépművészeti Múzeum, Budapest, inv. no. 265; cat. 1967, vol. 1, p. 609-610, vol. 2, fig. 317.
Provenance: Coll. Esterházy (inv. 1820, no. 978, as Willem Kalf).

Literature: Mündler 1869, p. X, 6 (as W. Kalf); Frimmel 1892, vol. 1, p. 191 (as Frans Hals the Younger); Von Wurzbach 1906, vol. 1, p. 641 (as Frans Hals the Younger); Moes 1909, p. 81 (as Frans Hals the Younger); Posse 1911, p. 257 (as Frans Hals the Younger); Bredius 1917, p. 3, 6; Térey 1926, p. 51; Vorenkamp 1933, p. 105; Thieme & Becker 1907-1950, vol. 29, p. 253; Bergström 1947, p. 182, 266, fig. 216, p. 276, 277; ed. 1956, p. 176, 262, fig. 216, p. 274; Spriggs 1967, p. 82, 83; Bol 1969, p. 101, fig. 86; Bergström c.s. 1977/1979, ill. p. 212; Bol 1980, p. 310-311, fig. 19; Bol 1982b, p. 28-29, fig. 19; Haak 1984, p. 408, fig. 880.

42   Text, p. 156

PIETER DE RING
1615-Leiden-1660

Signed with a ring.
Canvas, 86 x 114.5 cm.
Indiana University Art Museum, Bloomington, inv. no. 73.22. Acquired 1973.
Provenance: Coll. Sir Francis Cook, Doughty House, Richmond, Surrey; thence by inheritance to his eldest son, Sir Frederick Cook, 2nd Baronet; thence inherited by Sir Herbert Cook, 3rd Bart.; inherited in 1939 by Sir Francis Cook, 4th Bart.; Gallery Herbert Shickman, New York.
Exhibited: Lincoln 1946, no. 37; London 1948, no. 45; London 1952-1953, no. 466.
Literature: Kronig 1914, p. 81, no. 324, ill.; Brockwell 1932, p. 86, no. 324; Kinder 1979, p. 26-43, 2 ills. & cover; Wright 1980, p. 386; Sutton 1986, p. 14, fig. 17.

43   Text, p. 157

PIETER DE RING
1615-Leiden-1660

Signed and dated on the plinth of the pillar-base in brown with beige and gray-white: 'P: Ab. Annulo. fe 1660'.
Canvas, 160.5 x 205 cm.
Collection Mr. John Warde of Squerryes Court, Westerham, Kent, England.
Provenance: Probably sale at Cock's, London, 29 May 1746, no. 131 ('A large piece of Fruit, and still life P. Ab. Annulo'), coll. Mrs. Mary Edwards; and/or Sale Cock's, London, 8 May 1747, no. 138 ('Still life, large P. Annulo'), coll. Henry Bridges, 2nd Duke of Chandos; bought by John Warde of Squerryes Court, in 1759 for 12, 1s, 6d; thence by inheritance.
Literature: Richard Houldich, *Sale catalogues of the Principal Collections of Picture (One Hundred & Seventy one in number) sold by Auction in England within the years 1711-1759, the greater part of them with the Prices and Names of Purchasers* (mnscr. cited by Talley 1983, p. 157-158); Talley 1983, p. 185; J. Warde n.d., *Squerryes Court*, p. 11, ill.

44

NICOLAES VAN GELDER
Leiden ca. 1636-1677 Amsterdam

Signed and dated lower right in grayish ochre: 'N.v. Gelder f.Anno 1664'.
Canvas, 110.5 x 88 cm.
Rijksmuseum, Amsterdam, inv. no. A1536; cat. 1976, p. 239, ill.; Acquired 1890.
Provenance: Purchased from M. Cohen Stuart, Alkmaar.
Literature: Von Wurzbach 1906-1911, vol. 1, p. 574; Warner 1928, no. 34d, ill.; Vorenkamp 1933, p. 68; Bernt 1948, vol. 1, no. 305, ill.; ed. 1962, idem; ed. 1969, no. 415, ill.; ed. 1980, no. 444, ill.; Pavière 1962, p. 28; Bénézit 1966, vol. 4, p. 196; Bol 1969, p. 303; Lewis 1973, p. 31; Wright 1980, p. 136; Ydema 1988, p. 24-25, ill.

Text, p. 157

45

JOHANNES HANNOT
1633-Leiden-1685

Signed lower left in gray-black: 'J hannot. fe'.
Canvas, 83.8 x 72 cm.
Private collection, U.S.A.
Provenance: Gallery J & S. Goldschmidt, Amsterdam (1923); Private collection.
Exhibited: Worcester 1979, p. 34-37, no. 9, ill. & cover-ill.; Columbus 1985.

Text, p. 161

46

JORIS VAN SON
1623-Antwerpen-1667

Signed upper left on the shield in brown: 'J/ VAN.SON/F' (VAN connected).
Canvas, 80 x 116.8 cm.
Hohenbuchau collection, Schlangenbad-Georgenborn.
Provenance: Sale Christie's, London, 10 July 1981, no. 63, ill.
Literature: Greindl 1983, p. 381, cat. no. 45.

Text, p. 161

47   Text, p. 164

CHRISTIAEN LUYCKX
1623-Antwerpen-after 1670

Signed at the left on the underplinth in dark brown: '.Carstian Luckx. fecit,'.
Panel, 45.5 x 71 cm.
Gallery Peter Tillou, Litchfield (Connecticut).
Provenance: Sale Mak van Waay 169, Amsterdam, 24 May 1966, no. 319, ill.; Gallery Leonard Koetser, London, (cat. autumn 1966, no. 11, ill.; Sale Sotheby's, London, 2 July 1986, no. 169, ill.

48   Text, p. 165

HANS BOLLONGIER
c. 1600-Haarlem-1670?

Signed falsely at the right on a book: 'A beyren'.
Panel, 83.5 x 102 cm.
Rijksdienst Beeldende Kunst, 's-Gravenhage, inv. no. NK 1724 (as Jacques de Claeuw).
Provenance: Gallery P. de Boer, Amsterdam (1936); Coll. Dr. Hugo Oelze; Coll. Mühlmann, 's-Gravenhage; taken to Germany by the German occupation during World War II; recuperated, Stichting Nederlands Kunstbezit, Amsterdam, no. 925.
Exhibited: 's-Hertogenbosch 1965; Leiden & Groningen 1985, cat. no. VI-19, ill. (see Ter Kuile, as Jacques de Claeuw).
Literature: Bergström 1947, p. 182-183, 248, fig. 151 (as Abraham van Beyeren); ed. 1956, p. 176-177, 246, fig. 151 (as Abraham van Beyeren); Ter Kuile 1985, p. 36, fig. 15, p. 100, cat. no. VI-19, ill. (as Jacques de Claeuw).

49

ABRAHAM VAN BEYEREN
's-Gravenhage 1620-1690 Overschie)

Monogrammed at the right on the plinth in brown: 'A V B f.' (A V B connected).
Canvas, 99 x 119 cm.
Rijksdienst Beeldende Kunst, 's-Gravenhage, inv. no. N K 1685; Acquired 1948.
Provenance: Coll. J.J.M. Chabot, Rotterdam, on loan to the Rijksmuseum, Amsterdam, 1923-1943 (cat. 1934, no. 506a); Sold to Hitler in 1942 (acc. to R K D); recuperated Stichting Nederlands Kunstbezit, Amsterdam (cat. 1946, no. 815).
Exhibited: Oude Kunst, Kasteel-Raadhuis, Helmond 1961-62 (no catalogue); *Kan een kan kunst zijn?,* Provinciaal Museum voor Drenthe, Assen 1979 (no catalogue); Leiden & Groningen 1985, no. VI-5 (see Ter Kuile 1985).
Literature: Bergström 1947, p. 244-245, fig. 200; ed. 1956, p. 240-242, fig. 200; Wright 1980, p. 34; Ter Kuile 1985, p. 48-49, fig. 31, p. 72-73, cat. no. V I-5, ill., p. 204 (facs. signature).

50

ABRAHAM VAN BEYEREN
's Gravenhage 1620-1690 Overschie

Canvas, 100 x 84 cm.
Ashmolean Museum, Oxford; cat. Ward Collection, 1950 (by Van Gelder), no. 10, ill.; cat. 1980, no. A. 534, p. 17. Acquired 1940.
Provenance: Coll. I. van Eyck (1818); Sale Christie's, London, 12 March 1892, no. 6; Coll. Earl of Clancarty, London; Gallery Charles Sedelmayer, Paris (cat. 1898, no. 2); Coll. Rudolf Kann, Paris (1907); Gallery G. von Hollitscher, Berlin (cat. 1912, no. 31); Sale Fievez, Brussel, 10 December 1928, no. 3, ill., Coll. C. Bayard; Gallery Benedict & Co., Berlin; Coll. Mandelbaum, Berlin; Gallery Duits, London (1929); Gallery Van Diemen, Berlin (1930); Gallery J. & S. Goldschmidt, Berlin (1935); Coll. T.W.H. Ward & Daisy Linda Ward; bequethed to the museum.
Literature: Martin 1936, p. 421, pl. 220; Wright 1976, p. 17; Broos in cat. Parijs 1986, p. 148-151, fig. 3; Broos 1987, p. 65-67, fig. 3.

51   Text, p. 176

ABRAHAM VAN BEYEREN
's Gravenhage 1620-1690 Overschie

Monogrammed below the plinth left, in brown: 'A V B f.'.
Canvas, 99.7 x 82.6 cm.
Cleveland Museum of Art, Inv. no. 60.80; Purchased by the Mr. and Mrs. William H. Marlatt Fund, 1960; cat. 1982, p. 220-221, no. 93, ill.
Provenance: Coll. Huldschinsky, Berlin (before 1928); Coll. Bornheim, München; Gallery Lempertz, Köln, cat. 1956, no. 2a, fig. 31; Gallery Drey, New York.
Exhibited: Cleveland 1960, no. 55; Cleveland 1979, no. 1, ill.
Literature: Francis 1960, p. 212-214; Sullivan 1974, p. 271-282; Moore 1979, p. 26, 83, ill. p. 85; Alpers 1983, p. 19-21, fig. 9-10; Sutton 1986, p. 67; Broos in cat. Paris 1986, p. 148-151, fig. 2; Broos 1987, p. 65-67, fig. 2.
Remark: A copy after this painting, with a monogram on the plinth, canvas 108 x 85 cm, can be traced in several sales since 1921, lately sale Christie's, London, 20 July 1984, no. 212, ill. (follower of Abraham van Beyeren).

52   Text, p. 176

ABRAHAM VAN BEYEREN
's Gravenhage 1620-1690 Overschie

Monogrammed and dated on the wall above the centre in gray : '.A V B f./1667.'.
Canvas, 141.5 x 122 cm.
Los Angeles County Museum of Art, inv. no. M86.96; Gift of the Ahmanson Foundation 1986.
Provenance: Coll. Pietro Camuccini, Roma (until 1833); his nephew Giovanni Battista Camuccini, Roma (until 1856); Coll. 4th Duke of Northumberland, Alnwick Castle, Algernon Percy, since 1865 by descent; Gallery Agnew, London, cat. 1978, no. 24, ill.; Gallery Rob Noortman, Hulsberg; Gallery Herbert Shickman, New York.
Exhibited: London 1859, no. 22 (Jan Davidsz. de Heem); Newcastle-upon-Tyne 1929, no. 895 (Jan Davidsz. de Heem)
Literature: Platner 1842, vol. 3, p. 269-273.

53   Text, p. 185

WILLEM KALF
Rotterdam 1619-1693 Amsterdam

Signed above the table on the right in dark brown: 'W. Kalf...' (difficult to read).
Canvas, 144 x 101 cm.
Gallery Charles Roelofsz, Amsterdam; cat. 1988, no. 4, ill.
Provenance: Private collection, Germany; Gallery A. van der Meer, Amsterdam; Private collection, Paris.
Literature: Weltkunst 44 no. 6 (1974), p. 407;
Remark: The version in the Wallraf-Richartz Museum in Köln, inv. no. 2598, is mentioned and reproduced in numerous handbooks and publications, through a copy.

54

WILLEM KALF
Rotterdam 1619-1693 Amsterdam

Text, p. 188

Signed below the plinth left in gray, in calligrafic writing: 'W kalf'.
Canvas, 86.4 x 102.2 cm.
The Trustees of the National Gallery, London, inv. no. 6444; cat. 1986, p. 300, ill.; bequeathed by Mr. R.S. Newall, 1978.
Provenance: Probably coll. Arnout Stevens, Amsterdam (died 1706); Probably sale Amsterdam, 31 March 1706, no. 1; Coll. William Newall, London (ca. 1860); hence by inheritance, before 1978 on loan to the National Gallery.
Exhibited: London 1938, no. 191; London 1976b, no. 64, ill.
Literature: Hoet 1752, vol. I, p. 85-87; Bredius 1925, p. 267-268; *The Studio* 115 (1938), p. 61, ill.; *The Connaisseur* 101 (1938), p. 63, 65, ill.; Van Luttervelt 1947, p. 57; Van Gelder [1941], p. 56-57, fig. 53; L. Thyssen in cat. Leiden 1966, p. 133; Grisebach 1974, p. 119, 120, 122 n. 266, 133, 154, 155, 156, 157, 167 n. 375, 244 (no. 74, 75), 244-245, cat. no. 77, p. 245 (no. 78, 79), 278 (no. 138), 279 (no. 141), fig. 85; *The National Gallery. Year in review* 1978-79, p. 21, ill.; *Gazette des Beaux Arts* 121, no. 4 (1979), p. 57, fig. 294; Haak 1984, p. 494-495, fig. 1098; Schama 1987, p. 160, fig. 83.

55

WILLEM KALF
Rotterdam 1619-1693 Amsterdam

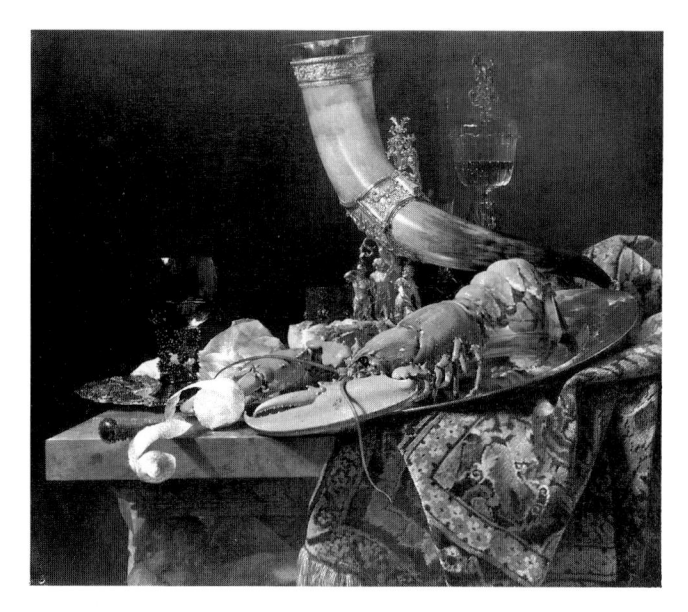

Text, p. 194

Signed upper left in gray: 'W. KALF FECIT', and dated upper right in grey: 'A° 1660'.
Canvas, 79.4 x 67.3 cm.
Thyssen-Bornemisza Foundation, Lugano-Castagnola; cat. 1986, no. 150, p. 162, col. ill. Acquired in 1962.
Provenance: Possibly Sale Amsterdam, 16 March 1778, no. 43, Coll. Pieter van den Bogaerde; Coll. Count Alexis Orloff-Davidoff, St. Petersburg (Leningrad); Coll. Michel van Gelder, Uccle near Brussel; Inherited by his wife; Gallery D. Katz, Dieren, cat. Eindhoven 1936-37, no. 31, ill., cat. Dieren 1937, no. 41; Coll. H.E. ten Cate, De Lutte near Almelo (1938).
Exhibited: Amsterdam 1911, no. 7; London 1929, no. 299, ill.; Amsterdam 1933, no. 172, fig. 41; Rotterdam 1933, no. 46, fig. 7; Brussel 1935, no. 739; Amsterdam 1936, no. 84, ill.; Rotterdam 1938, no. 92, fig. 125; Providence 1938, no. 24, fig. 24; New York 1939a, no. 7; New York 1939b, no. 206; Detroit 1939, no. 26; San Francisco 1939-1940, no. L-68, ill.; Detroit 1941, no. 34; New York 1942, no. 32, ill.; Montreal 1944, no. 67, fig. 78; Paris 1952, no. 45; Almelo 1953, no. 25, fig. 49; New York, Toledo & Toronto 1954-1955, no. 47, ill.; Brussel 1971, no. 58, ill.; Washington etc. 1979-1981, no. 39, p. 132-133, ill. p. 61; Moskou & Leningrad 1983-84, no. 11, p. 34-35, col. ill.; Atlanta 1985, no. 38, ill.; Basel 1987, no. 50, p. 152-153, ill.

Literature: Schneider & Constable 1930, p. 67, fig. 32; Benedict 1938, p. 314, fig. 316; Vorenkamp 1938, p. 12, ill. p. 10; Frankfurter 1939, p. 21, ill. p. 7; Van Gelder [1941], p. 54, ill. p. 51; Ottema 1946, fig. 209; Gerson 1952, p. 60, fig. 179; Sterling 1952, p. 51, pl. 33; ed. 1959, p. 51, pl. 33; ed. 1981, p. 71, 76, pl. 33; English ed. 1959, p. 54, pl. 33; English ed. 1985, p. 49, 51, pl. 33; *Illustrated London News*, 12 February 1955, p. 266, ill.; Hannema 1955, no. 8, fig. 15; Hering 1955, p. 80; Roodenburg 1959, p. 21; Argan 1964, ill. p. 211; Lunsingh Scheurleer 1966, p. 44, 48, 194, fig. 25; Rosenberg & Slive 1966, p. 200, fig. 167; ed. 1972, p. 341, fig. 268; ed. 1977, p. 340-341, fig. 268; Ter Kuile 1970, p. 141, 143, fig. 222; Grisebach 1974, p. 117, 122 n. 267, 268, p. 126, 151, 162 n. 361, p. 173, 260 (no. 106), 261 (no. 107, 108), 262 (no. 110), 263 (no. 111, 112), 265 (no. 114), 266 (no. 115), 266-267, cat. no. 117 (as dated 1662), p. 268 (no. 118), 269 (no. 119, 120), 276 (no. 135), fig. 128; De Gaigneron 1977, p. 37, fig. 12; Bergström c.s. 1977/1979, ill. p. 196; Wohlgemuth 1978, p. 23-25, ill.; 'The Baron Thyssen-Bornemisza Collection', in *Museum*, March-April 1980, p. 45, ill.; De Grace 1980, p. 8, cover ill.; Alpers 1983, p. 115, fig. 59; Kingzett 1986, p. 21.

56   Text, p. 195

WILLEM KALF
Rotterdam 1619-1693 Amsterdam

Signed and dated below the plinth left in gray: 'W.KALF 1663'.

Canvas, 60.3 x 50.2 cm.

The Cleveland Museum of Art, Cleveland, Leonard C. Hanna Jr. Bequest (1962), inv. no. 62.292; cat. 1982, p. 250-251, no. 109, ill.

Provenance: Private collection, Basel; Gallery M. Schulthes, Basel (1959); Coll. G. Vegting, Amsterdam; Gallery Duits, London; Gallery Frederick Mont, New York.

Exhibited: Oslo 1959, no. 36, ill.; Cleveland 1963, no. 90; Cleveland 1973, *Dutch art and life in the 17th century* (no catalogue); Cleveland 1982, *The Porcelain Connection: East and West* (no catalogue); Chicago 1985, no. 51, ill.

Literature: Jörgensen 1959, no. 36, ill. p. 217 (detail); *The Art Quarterly* 26 (1963), p. 354, ill. p. 358; *Bulletin of the Cleveland Museum of Art* 50 (1963), p. 114, ill. p. 109; *Gazette des Beaux-Arts* 106, no. 63 (1964), p. 58, fig. 196; *The Connaisseur* 184 (1973), p. 136, fig. 13; Nash 1973, p. 27, fig. 73; Grisebach 1974, p. 122 n. 267, 147, 148, 149, 160, 161, 165, 272 (no. 125), cat. no. 126, p. 273 (no. 127), 277 (no. 136), 278 (no. 139), 279 (no. 240), fig. 134; Fabri 1974, p. 11; Kahr 1978, p. 202-203, fig. 154; Preisner 1980, p. [1X]; Sutton 1986, p. 67, fig. 93.

57   Text, p. 195

WILLEM KALF
Rotterdam 1619-1693 Amsterdam

Signed and dated lower left in gray: 'W KALF 1669'.

Canvas, 77 x 65.5 cm.

Indianapolis Museum of Art, Gift of Mrs. James W. Fesler in memory of Daniel W. and Elisabeth C. Marmon (1945), inv. no. 45.9; cat. 1951, fig. 23.

Provenance: Sale Hôtel Drouot, Paris, 4 April 1864, no. 50, Coll. Dr. Van Cleef, Utrecht; Gallery Drey, München; Gallery Julius Böhler, München (1934); Gallery Dr. Herman Burg, Haarlem (1936); Coll. Mrs. E. Reiffenberg, Köln; Coll. Rye, New York; Gallery M. Knoedler & Co., New York, cat. 1945, no. 6, ill.

Exhibited: Amsterdam 1936, no. 85 (ill. only in the preliminary «voorlopige catalogus»).

Literature: Bulletin of the Art Association of Indianapolis, Indiana, John Herron Art Institute 22 (1945), p. 28-29, ill.; cat. Marmon Memorial College of Painting, 1948, p. 22-24, ill.; Spriggs 1965, p. 95, 100, fig. 10; Grisebach 1974, p. 118, 128, 144, 145, 146, 150, 158, 159, 160, 164, 276, cat. no. 135, p. 277 (no. 136, 137), fig. 145; Sutton 1986, p. 118, fig. 169.

58 Text, p. 200

WILLEM VAN AELST
Delft 1626/27-after 1683 Amsterdam

Signed and dated lower right in ochre-orange: 'W.V. aelst 1657'.
Canvas, 58 x 46 cm.
Den kgl. Maleri- of Skulptursamling, Statens Museum for Kunst, København, inv. no. 379; cat. 1951, no. 1, p. 1, ill., facsimile signature p. 397 (as dated 1651); From Castle Fredensborg 1840.
Provenance: Sale 's-Gravenhage, 4 July 1763, no. 2, Coll. Willem Lormier ; Royal Danish Collection, since 1764.
Exhibited: Utrecht 1984-1985, no. 115, ill.
Literature: Terwesten 1770, p. 313, no. 2; Von Wurzbach 1906, vol. 1, p. 5; Thieme & Becker 1907, vol. 1, p. 98; Bergström 1947, p. 286-287, fig. 233; ed. 1956, p. 285-286, fig. 233; Gammelbo 1960, no. 104, ill.; Bénézit 1966, vol. 1, p. 41; Grisebach 1974, p. 125; De Jongh 1982a, p. 75-76.

59 Text, p. 200

WILLEM VAN AELST
Delft 1626/27-after 1683 Amsterdam

Signed and dated lower left in gray: 'Guill^{mo} van/Aelst.1678'.
Canvas, 51.5 x 45 cm.
Private Collection, France.
Provenance: Gallery Heim, Paris (1960); Sale Angers, 1975.

60 Text, p. 205

DIRCK DE BRAY
active in Haarlem ca. 1650-1680

Signed and dated in dark gray inside a double curl: '1672 D d bray f'.
Panel, 37 x 30.5 cm.
Stichting Museum Amstelkring, Amsterdam, inv. no. AK 365. Acquired 1954.
Provenance: Coll. Mrs. Tarleton, Harefield, Middlesex; Gallery Knoedler, London (1954).
Literature: Pavière 1962, p. 17; De Wolf 1967, p. 9; Van Haaren 1968, p. 7, ill. p. 5; Lewis 1973, p. 17; Wright 1980, p. 57; Walsh & Schneider 1981-1982, p. 27 n. 6; De Jongh 1982a, p. 32, fig. V; Kuretsky 1987, p. 86-87, fig. 6.

61   Text, p. 206
PIETER GERRITSZ. VAN ROESTRAETEN
Haarlem 1629/30-1698 London

Signed at the centre below in brown-rose: 'P Roestraten'.
Canvas, 61 x 76 cm.
Richard Green Galleries, London.
Provenance: Gallery Dowdeswell (ca. 1900); Coll. A. Schloss, Paris; Stolen during World War II; Sale Sotheby's, London, 2 July 1986, no. 165, ill.
Literature: Moes 1909, ill. opposite p. 92; Lunsingh Scheurleer 1980, fig. 31.

62   Text, p. 206
PIETER GERRITSZ. VAN ROESTRAETEN
Haarlem 1629/30-1698 London

Signed lower right in ochre: 'P:Roestraeten'.
Canvas, 72 x 59.5 cm.
Museum Boymans-van Beuningen, Rotterdam, inv. no. St. 131; cat. 1972, p. 219, fig. p. 109. Acquired 1966.
Provenance: Private coll. in Broome Park, Kent; Coll. Lord Kitcher (1912); Coll. Oxenden, London (1914); Gallery Herbert N. Bier, London; Sale Sotheby's, London, 8 July 1964, no. 171, Coll. A. Gattetly, sold to Dr. Scharf; Gallery Marianne Feilchenfeldt, Zürich (1966).
Exhibited: Berlin 1985, no. 4/38, ill.
Literature: Manners 1915, p. 207, fig. p. 208; H. Gerson in Thieme & Becker 1907-1950, vol. 28, p. 505; Lunsingh Scheurleer 1966, p. 48, 195, fig. 32 (as W. Kalf); Ter Kuile 1969, p. 201; Ter Molen in cat. Utrecht 1979, fig. 57; Wright 1980, p. 391; De Jongh 1982a, p. 219, fig. 43a; Haak 1984, p. 392, fig. 840.

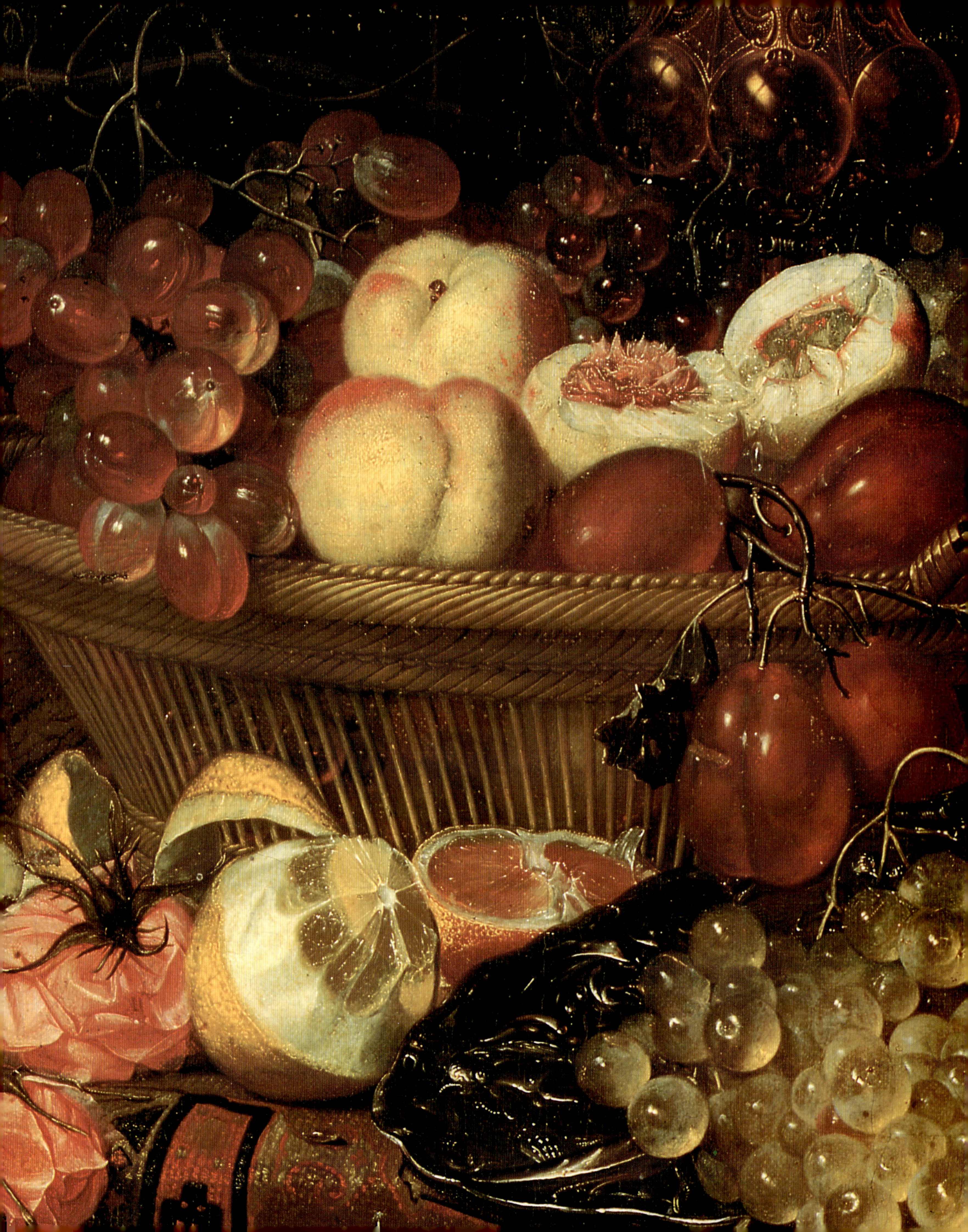

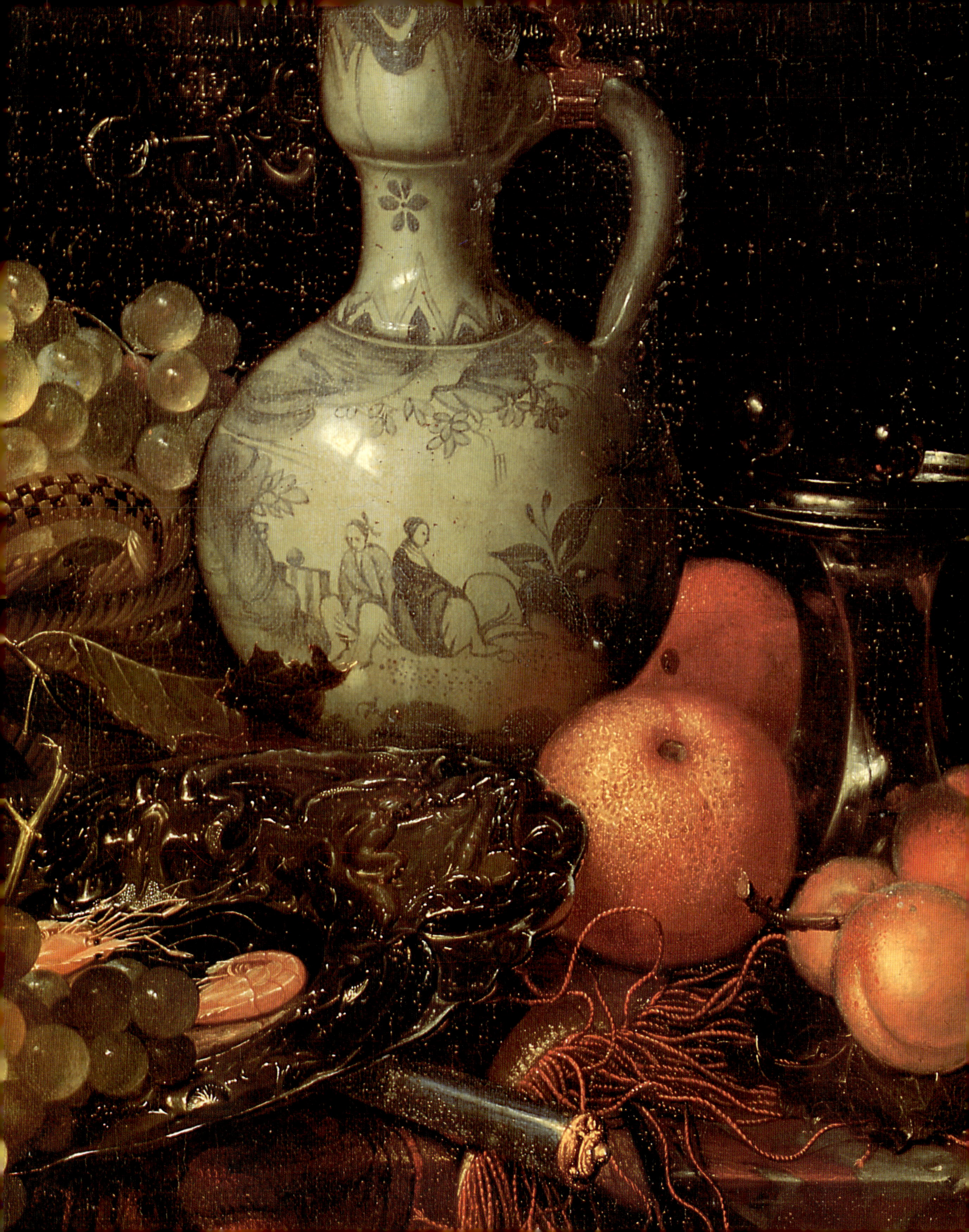

Sam Segal

Addendum to the Exhibition *A Prosperous Past*

PIETER CLAESZ
Private collection

Masters of the Monochrome Banquet Piece

The great painters of the monochrome banquet piece, Pieter Claesz and his fellow-townsman Willem Claesz. Heda of Haarlem, produced both small-sized, simple compositions and large-sized, intricate pictures. The larger paintings are mostly later works. Willem's son Gerret Heda only occasionally did smaller pictures. Fig. 1 shows the distribution of sizes of dated banquet pieces by Pieter Claesz between 1621 and 1658.[1] We can observe a slight overall tendency to an increase of size, with greater variations after 1640. The year 1627 is an exception to this trend, however.
In 1627 Pieter Claesz produced some very small panels as well as a large one. The smallest measures 19.5 x 24.5 cm.[2] Its composition is very simple and it depicts, on a stone ledge: a *berkemeier* glass of wine, a small bunch of grapes, a whole and a half-peeled lemon, and a knife with an inlaid, checkered handle of ebony and mother-of-pearl. The large-sized work, now in the Rijksmuseum in Amsterdam, is a panel of 75 x 132 cm.[3] This is an anomalous work in several ways: its large size, its atypical composition, its color scheme and the objects themselves. The pewter dishes and other objects shown at the left of the table are displayed so that they do not overlap, while a relatively small nautilus cup at the right is overwhelmed by a large turkey pie behind it, in which are stuck various parts of the bird: head and neck, wings and tail. The fruits and vine leaves, as well as the decoration of the stand of the nautilus cup, remind us of the earlier works of Floris van Schooten.

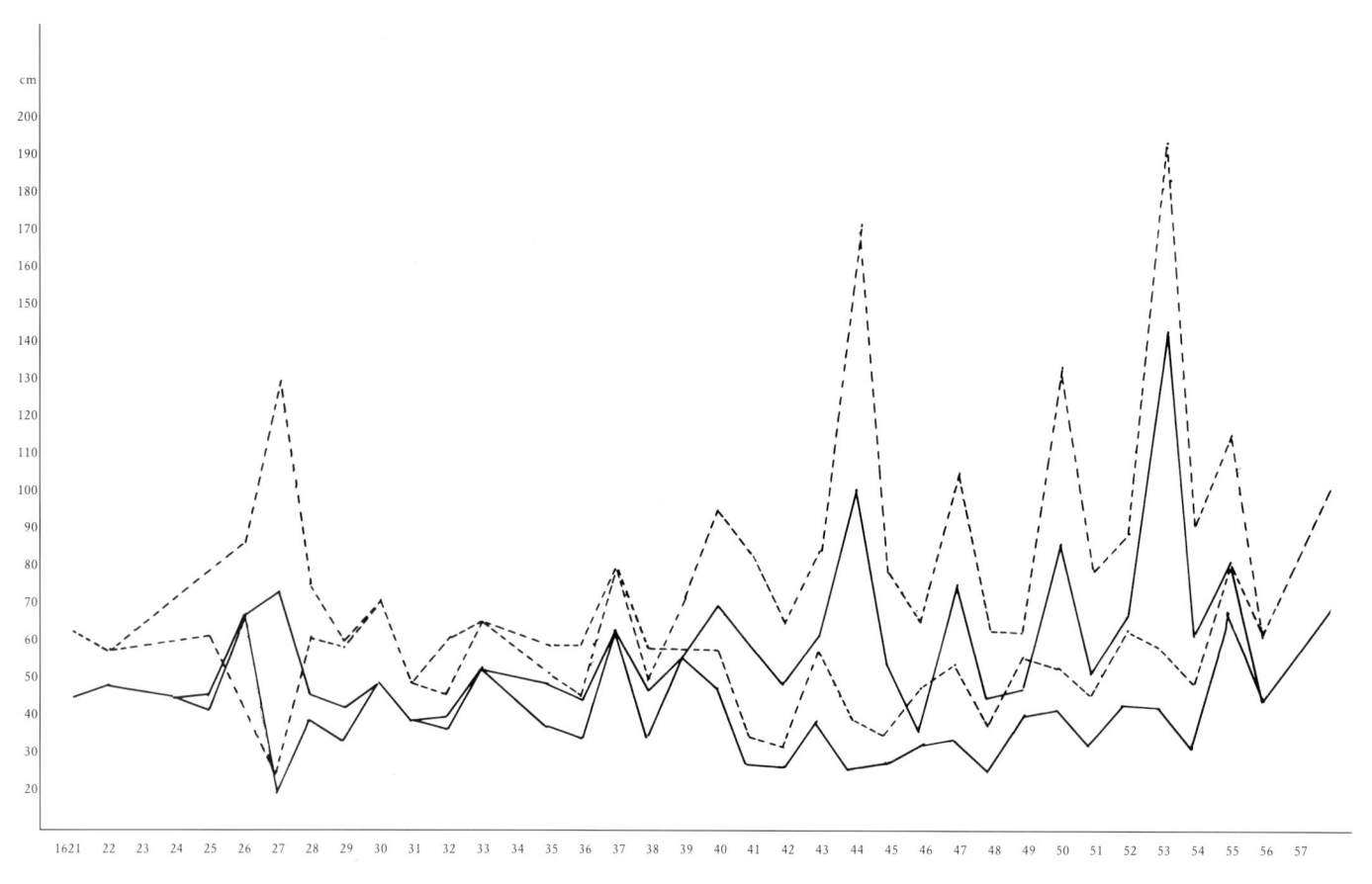

1 *Annual distribution of the sizes of 118 dated banquet pieces by Pieter Claesz between 1621 and 1658*
– smaller dimension (usually height), -- larger dimension (usually width)

Apart from the pie and the nautilus cup, other things which are unusual are the silver knife with auricular ornament, the wine jug with a long, narrow spout and the oriental rug, objects which we usually see in works of a later date. The works of smaller size in the same period have, in fact, a more harmonious structure. Pieter Claesz might have concluded as much for himself, since it took many years before he ventured onto a large scale again.

In the catalogue *A Prosperous Past* I have mentioned, as the largest work by Pieter Claesz, a painting in the Wallraf-Richartz Museum in Cologne, a canvas measuring 150 x 200 cm.[4] It is dated 1653 and represents, as it were, a kind of summary of different aspects of Claesz's work. One might, at first glance, perceive the influence of Jan Davidsz. de Heem. Such influence is probable, but we should not forget that Claesz had painted many of the same objects, including musical instruments, even earlier than De Heem in a composition of 1623 in the Musée du Louvre in Paris.[5]

Recently I saw another large canvas in a private collection, measuring 136 x 206 cm, signed with a monogram but undated (fig. 4). It is another compendium of Claesz's usual components. There is a turkey pie, for example, like the one in the 1627 painting in the Rijksmuseum, which also occurs in another, undated work.[6] The painting represented in fig. 4 lacks the tail: a small wooden pin has been kept. Other elements relate to a large composition of 1650.[7] The fruits and vine leaves of both works remind us of Roelof Koets, with whom Pieter Claesz collaborated more than once. We also find a similar jug and pronk goblet in earlier still lifes by Claesz.[8]

Willem Heda and his son Gerret painted objects similar to those of Claesz. We often see identical jugs and similar pies in the still lifes of Gerret Heda of the 1650s and 1660s. When the pie is decorated, he also used a peacock design instead of a turkey.[9] We have already observed that Willem Heda sometimes borrowed from Claesz[10], which he also did, by the way, from the Amsterdam painter Jan Jansz. den Uyl. Willem Heda's paintings are distinctive: they are refined, intimate and atmospheric. But Pieter Claesz shows more directness and, sometimes, more originality. The difference between their dispositions is also reflected in their brush strokes. Claesz has a strong, taut and spontaneous brush stroke, like Frans Hals but on a smaller scale. Willem Heda's style is more nervous and searching. His stroke is short and thin, sometimes itching, or moving in small flowing coils. He must have worked more slowly than Claesz. Indeed, Heda's production was considerably smaller: more paintings are known by Pieter Claesz than by Willem and Gerret Heda combined.

A SIMPLE WORK BY PIETER CLAESZ

The general observations above are intended as a prelude to consideration of a picture added to the exhibition *A Prosperous Past* in the Fogg Art Museum and the Kimbell Art Museum, a painting by Pieter Claesz (fig. 2), signed with a monogram, painted on panel and measuring 38.5 x 55.3 cm. It is lent from an American private collection.[11] The painting is a monochrome banquet piece in which the objects share the tonal gray, green and brown hues of the background and the stone ledge. Depicted are glasses, pewter dishes, a silver knife, oysters and a knife case with a ribbon. A yellow lemon and touches of white, standing out locally, enliven the composition. This is a perfect example of the intimate, simple type of composition that shows Claesz at his best: an optimal result by minimal means. If we compare this painting with an attractive work by Willem Heda in an English collection (*A Prosperous Past* cat. no. 32), the differences in the two artists' brushwork become apparent at once, especially by comparing details of the oyster shell, the lemon peel, the pewter, and the highlights on the glass.

Unusual in Claes'z paintings are the silver, partly gilt knife and the *façon de Venise* glass. But the same glass was used in a related work of 1629.[12] Our painting must have been executed in the same year or, perhaps in 1630. We find and equally simple compositional scheme, with similar objects, in other works by Claesz, especially from the period 1627-1632. In these, the placement of the objects forms a scalene or nearly right triangle, the vertical axis of which is established by a glass. Several features of the artist's usual way of composing are clearly visible, especially the repetition of ornamental patterns and rhythmic motifs. We can observe this in the ornamental curls of the knife handle, in the lemon peel and the ribbon, or in the irregularly gnarled edges of the lemon peel and one of the oyster shells. The crumbs of ground pepper on the pewter dish behind establish an awareness of texture that is heightened by the scales on the rough surface of the other oyster shell. The sectioned planes of the lemon with their regular radials assert a pattern of formal reiteration. The bulges of the Venetian glass are, as it were, repeated in those of the prunts and the foot of the rummer. The four-fold reflection of the studio window in the glasses is the final touch. (We find the repetition of horizontal ovals in most banquet pieces.)

Pieter Claesz's compositions are carefully constructed, with deliberate forethought given to the system of intersecting diagonals. In the paintings of Gillis and Van Schooten, and in the early ones of Pieter Claesz, some objects are arranged in rows parallel to the picture plane, while others are in parallel rows receding obliquely. The two usually meet at angles of 30° to 45° or more. But Claesz, in addition to lowering the point of view, begins in 1627 to reduce these angles of intersection and eliminates the need for multiple lines of recession to run parallel to each other (fig. 3). This allows some objects to overlap others and gives his compositions a more natural look. This is not Claesz's only compositional scheme, for he also produced horizontal compositions, but it is one of his principal contributions. In 1627 the sober tonality also becomes a common feature of his work.

2 PIETER CLAESZ
Still life with a façon de Venise glass
Private collection, USA

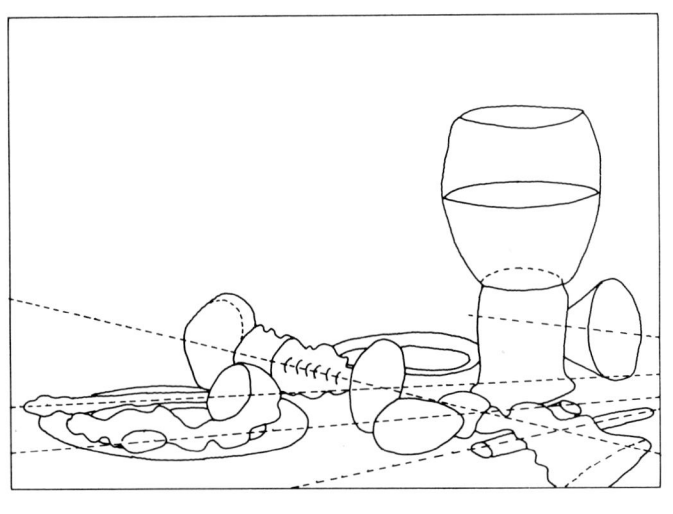

3 *Compositional scheme of the still life in fig. 2*

A related composition by Willem Heda of 1630, quite soon after Claesz's 1629 painting, shows another *façon de Venise* glass.[13] Heda followed the scheme of oblique lines, but his lines are mainly formed by rows of circular or voluminous objects rather than, as with Claesz, slender ones like a knife, a spoon, a stalk, a pipe, a bundle of matches, a ribbon, a squill, a herring, or a folded almanac leaflet.

The idea of an overturned glass might have been borrowed from Nicolaes Gillis. In his painting of 1625 (*A Prosperous Past* fig. 7.2) we also find some other elements which can be traced in Pieter Claesz's pictures, for example the half-peeled lemon with its peel running over the edge of the dish. The *façon de Venise* glass seems to be a deliberate replacement of Gillis's *bekerschroef* and *berkemeier* together. The overturned *berkemeier* is seen again in several works by Claesz of the 1630s. The same rummer appears in many paintings between 1628 and 1644.

One of the smaller still lifes by Pieter Claesz, produced when his skill and inventive powers were at their peak, this painting is a poetic work, full of elegance and restraint. The secrets of its mystery lie partly in the fleeting quality of light and the spatial void surrounding the fragile objects.

4 PIETER CLAESZ
Laid table with a pronk goblet and a turkey pie
Private collection, Germany

NOTES

1 The vanitas and tobacco pieces are not considered.
2 David Koetser Gallery, Geneva (1979); Warner 1928 (1975), no. 22a, ill.; Vroom 1980, vol. 1, pp. 154-155, fig. 206, vol. 2, p. 49 no. 225, as by Franchoys Elout.
3 Inv. no. A 4646, mus. cat. 1976, p. 168, ill.; Vroom 1980, vol. 1, p. 19 fig. 10, vol. 2, p. 18 no. 50, p. 49 no. 227, as by Pieter Claesz or Franchoys Elout.
4 Cat. *A Prosperous Past*, p. 216 no. 10; not in Vroom 1980. The painting needs a careful cleaning and restoration.
5 Inv. no. RF 1939-11, signed with a monogram and dated.
6 Private collection, USA, signed with a monogram, panel, 36.5 x 77 cm; cat. Lohr & Dortmund 1984, no. 9, ill.
7 The Sarah Campbell Blaffer Foundation, signed with a monogram and dated, panel 93.4 x 139.7 cm, collection cat. *A Golden Age of Painting* (by Ch. Wright), San Antonio, Texas, 1981, pp. 124-125, ill. There is also a strong similarity in coloring.
8 The jug in the 1627 painting in the Rijksmuseum is related in its design, but works of the 1640s and 1650s depict similar or identical specimens. A related goblet can be seen in a still life of 1624 in Dresden, cat. *A Prosperous Past*, no. 29, ill.
9 Some examples of Gerret Heda: cat. *A Prosperous Past*, no. 33, dated 1647: jug; Frans Halsmuseum, Haarlem, signed with a monogram and dated 1650, canvas, 103 x 123 cm, Vroom 1980, vol. 1, p. 77 fig. 94, vol. 2, pp. 77-78 no. 377, as by Willem Claesz. Heda: jug, pie, knife in case; Rijksdienst Beeldende Kunst, The Hague, inv. no. NK 2585 (on loan to the Frans Halsmuseum, Haarlem), signed and dated 1658, canvas, 89 x 109,5 cm, as by Willem Claesz. Heda, not in Vroom: jug, pie; sale Christie's, Amsterdam, 29 May 1986, no. 163, signed and dated 1665, canvas, 94 x 73.5 cm, Vroom 1980, vol. 2, p. 80 no. 391, ill., as by Willem Claesz. Heda (and panel): jug, peacock pie.
10 Cat. *A Prosperous Past*, p. 133.
11 The monogram in greyish ochre on the knife blade. Provenance: Private collection, The Netherlands; Noortman Gallery, Maastricht & London (1988).
12 Private collection, Switzerland, signed with a monogram and dated, panel, 44.5 x 61 cm; Vroom 1980, vol. 1, p. 26 fig. 20, p. 156 fig. 209, vol. 2, p. 19 no. 57, p. 50 no. 232, as by Pieter Claesz or Franchoys Elout.
13 Formerly Speelman Gallery, London, signed and dated, panel, 41.5 x 57.5 cm; Vroom 1980, vol. 1, p. 153 fig. 205, vol. 2, p. 50 no. 235, as by Franchoys Elout (with wrong measures). Another related *façon de Venise* glass was used by Pieter Claesz in a work of 1635: sale Wertheim, Berlin, coll. Josef Cremer, Dortmund, 29 May 1929, no. 39, ill., signed with a monogram and dated, panel 40 x 55 cm; not in Vroom 1980.

Literature

ALCIATUS 1531
Viri clarissimi, D. Andreae Alciati ..., Augsburg 1531 (facsimile reprint Hildesheim & New York 1977).

ALPERS 1983
S. Alpers, *The art of describing - Dutch art in the seventeenth century*, Chicago 1983.

ARGAN 1964
G.C. Argan, *L'Europe des Capitales 1600-1700*, Paris 1964.

BALDASS 1923
L. Baldass, 'Sittenbild und Stilleben des Niederländischen Romanismus', IN *Jahrbuch der Kunsthistorischen Sammlungen in Wien* 36 (1923), pp. 15-46.

BARTSCH 1803-1821
A. Bartsch, *Le peintre graveur*, 21 vols., Wien 1803-1821.

BARTSCH 1985
The illustrated Bartsch, vol. 20, *German masters of the sixteenth century - Jost Amman: Woodcuts*, ed. J.S. Peters, New York 1985.

BASTIAN 1984
K. Bastian, *Georg Hinz und sein Stillebenwerk*, Hamburg 1984 (diss. 1982).

BECKER 1979-1980
J. Becker, 'Das Buch im Stilleben — Das Stilleben im Buch', in cat. Münster & Baden-Baden 1979-80, pp. 448-478.

BENEDICT 1938
C. Benedict, 'Un peintre oublié des nature mortes — Osias Beert', in *L'Amour de l'Art* 19 (1938), pp. 307-314.

BÉNÉZIT 1966
E. Bénézit, *Dictionnaire critique et documentaire des peintres, sculpteurs, dessinateurs et graveurs de tous les temps et de tous les pays par un groupe d'écrivains spécialistes français et étrangers*, 8 vols., Paris 1966 (other editions not considered).

BENGTSSON & OMBERG 1951
Å. Bengtsson & H. Omberg, 'Changes in Dutch seventeenth century landscape, still life, genre and architecture painting', in *Figura*; Studies edited by the Institute of Art History, University of Uppsala, I (1951), pp. 13-56.

BERGNER 1905
P. Bergner, *Verzeichnis der Gräflich Nostitzschen Gemäldegalerie zu Prag*, Praha 1905.

BERGSTRÖM 1947/1956
I. Bergström, *Studier i Holländskt Stillebenmåleri under 1600-talet*, Göteborg 1947; English rev.ed. *Dutch still-life painting in the seventeenth century*, London & New York 1956.

BERGSTRÖM 1949
I. Bergström, 'Twee onbekende stillevens van François Rijckhals', in *Oud Holland* 64 (1949), pp. 18-24.

BERGSTRÖM 1955
I. Bergström, 'Disguised symbolism in 'Madonna' pictures and still life', in *Burlington Magazine* 97 (1955), pp. 303-308, 340-349.

BERGSTRÖM 1956a
I. Bergström, 'De Heem's paintings of his first Dutch period', in *Oud Holland* 71 (1956), pp. 173-183.

BERGSTRÖM 1963
I. Bergström, 'Dordrecht impressions', in *Apollo* 77 (1963), pp. 448-453.

BERGSTRÖM 1970
I. Bergström, 'Notes on the boundaries of Vanitas significance', in cat. Leiden 1970, pp. (6-14).

BERGSTRÖM a.o. 1977/1979
I. Bergström c.s., *Natura in Posa - La grande stagione della natura morta Europea*, Milano 1977/ *Stilleben - Die große Zeit des europäischen Stillebens*, Stuttgart & Zürich 1979.

BERGSTRÖM 1983
I. Bergström, " 'Portraits' of gilt cups bij Pieter Claesz", in *Tableau* 5 no. 6 (1983), pp. 440-445.

BERGSTRÖM 1984
I. Bergström, 'A quartet of rare still-life masters — Jacob Flegel, Thomas de Paep, G. van Berkborch and Georg Held', in *Tableau* 7 no. 1 (1984), pp. 40-54.

BERGSTRÖM & SEGAL 1984
I. Bergström & S. Segal, 'A feast for the eye and mind — The Dresden still-life exhibition', in *Tableau* 6 no. 6 (1984), pp. 73-78.

BERNT 1948
W. Bernt, *Die Niederländischen Maler des 17. Jahrhunderts*, 3 vols., München 1948 (2nd ed. with Ergänzungsband, vol. 4, 1962 ; 3rd ed. 1969 ; 4th ed. 1979-80).

BIALOSTOCKI 1982
J. Bialostocki, 'Books of wisdom and books of vanity', in *In Memoriam J.G. van Gelder 1903-1980*, Utrecht 1982, pp. 37-67.

BILLE 1961
C. Bille, *De Tempel der Kunst of het Kabinet van den Heer Braamcamp*, 2 vols., Amsterdam 1961.

BLADE 1983
T.T. Blade, *The paintings of Dirck van Delen*, Ann Arbor 1983 (xerox diss. University of Minnesota 1976).

LE BLANC 1854-1889
Ch. le Blanc, *Manuel de l'amateur d'estampes*, 4 vols.,Paris 1854-1889.

BLOCH 1966
V. Bloch, 'Over het stilleven', in *Bulletin Museum Boymans-van Beuningen* 17 (1966), pp. 23-31.

BOCHARTUS 1712
Samuele Bocharto, *Hierozoicon, sive Bipartitum opus de Animalibus S. Scripturae, [...]*, Leyden & Utrecht 1712 (ed. princeps 1663).

VON BODE 1965
W. von Bode, *Die Meister des holländischen und flämischen Malerschulen*, rev. ed. by E. Plietsch, Leipzig 1965 (ed. princeps Leipzig 1917).

DE BOER 1940
P. de Boer, 'Jan Jansz den Uyl', in *Oud Holland* 57 (1940), pp. 49-64.

BOGLEY & OUTLAW 1980
B.A. Bogley & M. Abbitt Outlaw, 'In the Archaeologist's Laboratory', in *Notes on Virginia* 21 (1980), pp. 27-37.

BOL 1952-1953
L.J. Bol, 'Adriaen S. Coorte, stilleven-schilder', in *Nederlandsch Kunsthistorisch Jaarboek* 4 (1952-1953), pp. 193-232.

BOL 1955
L.J. Bol, 'Een Middelburgse Brueghelgroep, III, In Bosschaerts spoor - 1. Balthasar van der Ast', in *Oud Holland* 70 (1955), pp. 138-154.

BOL 1956
L.J. Bol, 'Een Middelburgse Brueghelgroep, V, Christoffel van den Berghe: Bloemen en landschap - recuperatie voor een schilder die zijn oeuvre verloor', in *Oud Holland* 71 (1956), pp. 183-195 (summary pp. 203).

BOL 1959
L.J. Bol, 'Een Middelburgse Brueghelgroep, IX, Johannes Goedaert, schilder-entomoloog', in *Oud Holland* 74 (1959), pp. 1-19.

BOL 1960
L.J. Bol, *The Bosschaert Dynasty. Painters of flowers and fruit*, Leigh-on-Sea 1960.

BOL 1969
L.J. Bol, *Holländische Maler des 17.Jahrhunderts nahe den großen Meistern - Landschaften und Stilleben*, Braunschweig 1969.

BOL 1977
L.J. Bol, *Adriaen Coorte - A unique late seventeenth century Dutch still-life painter*, Assen & Amsterdam 1977.

BOL 1979
L.J. Bol, 'Goede onbekenden - Hedendaagse herkenning en waardering van verscholen, voorbijgezien en onderschat talent I.', in *Tableau* 2, no. 3 (1979), pp. 132-137 (reprinted in Bol 1982b).

BOL 1980
L.J. Bol, 'Goede onbekenden [...] IV: Schilders van het vroege Nederlandse bloemstuk met klein gedierte als bijwerk', in *Tableau* 3 no. 1 (1980), pp. 368-373 (reprinted in Bol 1982b).

BOL 1981
L.J. Bol, 'Goede onbekenden [...] VII: Schilders van het vroege Nederlandse bloemstuk met klein gedierte als bijwerk (vervolg). - Balthasar van der Ast (1593/941657)', in *Tableau* 3 no. 4 (1981), pp. 578-586 (reprinted in Bol 1982b).

BOL 1982a
L.J. Bol, 'Goede onbekenden [...] XII: Invloed van Jacques de Gheyn II als schilder van bloemstukken', in *Tableau* 4 no. 3 (1982), pp. 260-268 (reprinted in Bol 1982b).

BOL 1982b
L.J. Bol, *Goede onbekenden - Hedendaagse herkenning en waardering van verscholen, voorbijgezien en onderschat talent*, Utrecht 1982 (reprints of various articles in *Tableau*).

BOL 1985
L.J. Bol, 'Johannes Goedaert, schilder-entomoloog' III, in *Tableau* 7 no. 4 (1985), pp. 48-54.

VAN BORSSELEN 1611
Philibert van Borsselen, *Strande, oft Ghedichte van de schelpen, Kinckhornen [...] tot lof vanden Schepper aller Dinghen*, Haarlem 1611 (facsimile ed. of Amsterdam 1614 in P.E. Muller, *De dichtwerken van Philibert van Borsselen*, Groningen & Batavia 1937, pp. 13-67).

BOTT 1961-1962
G. Bott, 'Stillebenmaler des 17. Jahrhunderts, Isaak Soreau - Peter Binoit', in *Kunst in Hessen und am Mittelrhein* 1-2 (1961-1962), pp. 27-93.

BRANDT CORSTIUS 1973
L. Brandt Corstius, 'Jeroen Bosch en het fantastische in de schilderkunst', in *Openbaar Kunstbezit* 17 (1973), pp. 137-140.

BREDIUS 1915-1922
A. Bredius, *Künstler-Inventare - Urkunden zur Geschichte der Holländischen Kunst des XVIten, XVIIten und XVIIIten Jahrhunderts*, 6 vols., Nachträge & Register, 's Gravenhage 1915-1922.

BREDIUS 1917
A. Bredius, 'De schilder François Rijckhals', in *Oud Holland* 35 (1917), pp. 1-11.

BREDIUS 1925
A. Bredius, 'Rembrandtiana', in *Oud Holland* 42 (1925), pp. 263-276.

BRIELS 1980
J. Briels, 'Amator Pictoriae Artis - De Antwerpse kunstverzamelaar Peeter Steevens (1590-1668) en zijn Constkamer', in *Jaarboek Koninklijk Museum voor Schone Kunsten Antwerpen* 1980, pp. 137-226.

BRIELS 1987
J. Briels, *Vlaamse schilders in de Noordelijke Nederlanden in het begin van de Gouden Eeuw*, Antwerpen 1987.

BROCKWELL 1932
M.W. Brockwell, *Abridged catalogue of the pictures at Doughty House, Richmond, Surrey, in the Collection of Sir Herbert Cook, Bart.*, London 1932.

BROOS 1987
B. Broos, *Meesterwerken in het Mauritshuis*, 's Gravenhage 1987.

DE BRUNE 1624
Johannes de Brune, *Emblemata of Zinne-werck: voorghestelt in Beelden, ghedichten en breeder uijtlegginghen tot uijt-druckinghe, en verbeteringhe van verscheijden feijlen onser eeuwe*, Amsterdam 1624.

DE BRUNE 1636
Johannes de Brune, *Nieuwe wijn in oude leerzacken*, Middelburg 1636.

BURGER 1860
W. Burger, *Musées de la Hollande*, vol. 2, Paris 1860.

BYE 1921
A.E. Bye, *Pots and pans. - Studies in still-life painting*, Princeton, London & Oxford 1921.

CAMERARIUS 1590-1604
Joachim Camerarius, *Symbolorum & Emblematum [...]*, 4 vols., Nürnberg 1590-1604.

CATS 1618/1627
Jacob Cats, *Sinne- en Minne-Beelden.../Silenus Alcibiadis, sive Proteus...*, Amsterdam 1618. *Proteus ofte Minnebeelden Veranderd in Sinne-beelden*, Rotterdam 1627. (Ca. 20 editions between 1618 and 1630, and many afterwards.)

CITROEN 1963
K.A. Citroen, 'Een zilveren puntschotel uit 1633', in *Bulletin Museum Boymans-van Beuningen* 14 no. 3 (1963), pp. 86-95.

CITROEN 1988
K.A. Citroen, *Haarlemse zilversmeden*, Haarlem 1988, in print.

DE COO 1958
J. de Coo, 'Addenda bij 'Een Middelburgse-Brueghelgroep': Christoffel van den Berghe en Mattheus Molanus', in *Oud Holland* 73 (1958), pp. 229-231.

CRÉBAS 1972-1973
A. Crébas, 'Stil leven in stillevens', in *Kunstrip* 3, no. 24 (1972), pp. 1-7.

CZOBOR 1963
A. Czobor, 'Recherches faites dans le fonds Hollandais et Flamand de la Galerie des Maitres Anciens', in *Bulletin du Musée Hongrois des Beaux-Arts* 23 (1963), pp. 53-77.

VAN DANTZIG 1934
M. van Dantzig, 'Eenige opmerkingen over verftechnieken', in *Maandblad voor Beeldende Kunsten* 2 (1934), pp. 134-137.

DE DENE 1567
Edewaerd de Dene, *De vvarachtige Fabvlen der dieren [...]*, Brugge 1567 (rev. ed. see Vondel 1617).

DIRKSE 1980
P.P.W.M. Dirkse, " 'God gheeft die wasdom'. Rondom een Utrechtse puntschotel uit 1624", in *Nederlands Kunsthistorisch Jaarboek* 31 (1980), pp. 122-136.

DITTRICH 1981
S. Dittrich, 'Perlboote', in *Der Zoofreund. Zeitschrift der Zoofreunde Hannover* 40 (1981), pp. 8-12.

DODOENS 1554/1644/1557/1578
Rembert Dodoens (Dodonaeus), *Cruijdeboeck [...]*, Antwerpen 1554 (facs. eds. Nieuwendijk 1971; Amsterdam 1978); rev. ed.Antwerpen 1644; French ed. *Histoire des Plantes [...]*, Antwerpen 1557 (facs. ed. Bruxelles 1978); English ed. *A Niewe Herball [...]*, London 1578.

DUPARC 1985
See cat. Atlanta 1985.

DUYVENÉ DE WIT-KLINKHAMER & GANS 1958
Th.M. Duyvené de Wit-Klinkhamer & M.H. Gans, *Geschiedenis van het Nederlandse zilver*, Amsterdam 1958 (English ed. *Dutch silver*, London 1961).

EIKEMEIER 1984
P. Eikemeier, 'Bücher in Bildern', in *De Arte et Libris*, (Erasmus) Amsterdam 1984, pp. 61-67.

EIS 1951
G. Eis, 'Austerschalen', in *Studien zur altdeutschen Fachprosa*, Heidelberg 1951, pp. 11-29 (reissued in G. Baarder & G. Keil, *Medizin im Mittelalterlichen Abendland*, Darmstadt 1982, pp. 125-150).

EMBER 1987
See cat. Köln & Utrecht 1987.

EMMENS 1973
J.A. Emmens, 'Eins aber ist nötig. - Zu Inhalt und Bedeutung von Markt- und Küchenstücken des 16. Jahrhunderts', in *Album Amicorum J.G. van Gelder*, 's Gravenhage 1973, pp. 93-101.

ENKLAAR 1940
D.T. Enklaar, *Uit Uilenspiegel's kring*, Assen 1940.

ERASMUS 1544
Desiderius Erasmus, *Adagiorum [...]*, ed. Lyon 1544; (ed. Genève 1612; ed. Frankfurt 1646; ed. princeps *Adagia [...]*, Paris 1500)

ERASMUS 1634
Desiderius Erasmus, *Colloquia Familiaria, of Gemeensame t'samen-spraken, [...]*, Haarlem 1634 (ed.princeps in latin, Basel 1516; Translated edition in English by C.R. Thompson,*The Colloquies of Erasmus*, Chicago & London 1965).

ERTZ 1979
K. Ertz, *Jan Brueghel der Ältere (1568-1625) - Die Gemälde mit kritischem Oeuvrekatalog*, Köln 1979.

ERTZ 1981
K. Ertz, *Jan Brueghel der Ältere (1568-1625)*, Köln 1981.

EVANS 1953
J. Evans, *A history of jewellry 1100-1870*, London 1953.

FABRI 1974
R. Fabri, 'What we can learn from the old masters', in *The Ohio Art Graphic* 22 (1974).

FALKENBURG 1985
R.L. Falkenburg, *Joachim Patinir: Het landschap als beeld van de levenspelgrimage*, Nijmegen 1985.

FARÉ 1974
M. Faré, *Le Grand Siècle de la nature morte en France le XVIIe siècle*, Friburg & Paris 1974.

FECHNER 1981
E.U. Fechner, *Hollandskii naturmort XVII weka*, Moskwa 1981.

FORBES n.d.
W.A. Forbes, *De oud Hollandse keuken*, Bussum n.d.

FOUCART 1965
J. Foucart, *Musées de Hollande, la peinture néerlandaise*, Paris 1965.

FRANCIS 1960
H.S. Francis, 'Abraham van Beyeren: Still life with a silver wine jar and reflected portrait of the artist', in *Cleveland Museum of Art Bulletin* 47 (1960), pp. 212-214.

FRANCKEN 1881
D. Francken Dz., *L'Oeuvre gravé des Van de Passe*, Paris 1881 (facs. ed. Amsterdam 1975).

FRANKFURTER 1939
A.M. Frankfurter, '17 pictures of the XVIIth century', in *The Art News*, February 4, 1939.

FREDERIKS 1952-1961
J.W. Frederiks, *Dutch silver*, 4 vols.,'s Gravenhage 1952-1961.

FREY 1595
Hermannum Heinrychum Frey, *Therobiblia - Biblisch Thierbuch [...]*, Leipzig 1595 (facs. ed. Graz 1978).

FRIEDMANN 1946
H. Friedmann, *The symbolic goldfinch [...]*, New York 1946.

FRIMMEL 1892
Th. Frimmel, *Kleine Galeriestudien*, vol. 1, Bamberg 1892.

FRITZ 1982
J.M. Fritz, *Goldschmiedekunst der Gotik in Mitteleuropa*, München 1982.

DE GAIGNERON 1977
A. de Gaigneron, 'Nouveau regard sur la collection Thyssen', in *Connaissance des Arts* 306 (1977), pp. 52-63.

GAMMELBO 1960
P. Gammelbo, *Dutch still-life painting from the 16th to the 18th centuries in Danish collections*, Amsterdam 1960.

GAMMELBO 1965
P. Gammelbo, 'Some flower still-lifes by Jan Baptist Fornenburgh', in *Artes, Periodical of the Fine Arts*, København, 1 (1965), pp. 5-16, pl. 1-xx.

VAN GELDER 1931
H.E. van Gelder, 'Jan Baptist van Fornenburgh de Oude', in *Mededelingen van de Dienst voor Kunsten en Wetenschappen 's Gravenhage*, 2 (1931), pp. 242-243.

VAN GELDER 1935
H.E. van Gelder, 'De schilderkunst in de tweede helft der zeventiende eeuw', in H.E. van Gelder c.s., *Kunstgeschiedenis der Nederlanden van de Middeleeuwen tot onze tijd*, vol. 2, Utrecht 1935 (2nd ed. 1946; 3rd revised ed. 1955, pp. 185-226).

VAN GELDER [1941]
H.E. van Gelder, *W.C. Heda - A. van Beyeren - W. Kalf*, Amsterdam n.d. [1941].

VAN GELDER 1950
J.G. van Gelder, *Catalogue of the collection of Dutch and Flemish still-life pictures bequeathed by Daisy Linda Ward*, Ashmolean Museum, Oxford 1950.

GENAILLE 1954
R. Genaille, 'L'Oeuvre de Pieter Aertsen', in *Gazette des Beaux-Arts* 44 (1954), pp. 267-288.

GERSON 1950
H. Gerson, *De Nederlandse schilderkunst*, vol. 1: *Van Geertgen tot Frans Hals*, Amsterdam 1950.

GERSON 1952
H. Gerson, *De Nederlandse schilderkunst*, vol. 2: *Het tijdperk van Rembrandt en Vermeer*, Amsterdam 1952 (2nd ed. 1962).

GIBSON 1973
W. Gibson, *Hieronymus Bosch*, London 1973 (Am. ed. New York 1972; Dutch ed. Amsterdam 1974).

GLÜCK 1917
G. Glück, *Niederländische Gemälde aus der Sammlung des Herrn Dr. Leon Lilienfeld in Wien*, Wien 1917.

VON GOETHE 1797
J.W. von Goethe, *Zur Erinnerung des Städelsches Kabinetts* (1797), in *Gedenkausgabe der Werke, Briefe und Gespräche*, vol. 13, Zürich 1954.

GOMBRICH 1972
E.H. Gombrich, *Symbolic images - Studies in the art of the Renaissance*, London & New York 1972.

DE GRACE 1980
M. de Grace, 'Still life with nautilus cup (1662) by Willem Kalf: In special Exhibition Old Master paintings from the collection of Baron Thyssen-Bornemisza', in *D.A.C. News*, March 1980.

VON GRAEVENITZ 1973
A-M. von Graevenitz, *Das niederländische Ohrmuschel-Ornament-Phänomen und Entwicklung dargestellt an den Werken und Entwürfen der Goldschmiedefamilien van Vianen und Lutma*, Bamberg 1973 (diss. München 1971).

GREINDL 1956/1983
E. Greindl, *Les peintres flamands de nature morte au XVIIe siècle*, Brussel 1956 (2nd rev. ed. 1983).

GRISEBACH 1974
L. Grisebach, *Willem Kalf 1619-1693*, Berlin 1974.

GROSJEAN 1974
A. Grosjean, 'Toward an interpretation of Pieter Aertsen's profane iconography', in *Konsthistorisk Tidskrift* 43 (1974), pp. 121-143.

GUDLAUGSSON 1948
S.J. Gudlaugsson, 'Representations of Granida in Dutch seventeenth-century painting, I', in *The Burlington Magazine* 90 (1948), pp. 226-230.

GWYNNE-JONES 1954
A. Gwynne-Jones, *Introduction to still-life*, London & New York 1954.

HAAK 1984
B. Haak, *Hollandse schilders in de Gouden Eeuw*, Amsterdam 1984 (English ed. *The Golden Age - Dutch painters of the seventeenth century*, New York 1984).

VAN HAAREN 1968
H. van Haaren, 'Ons' Lieve Heer op Solder', in *Openbaar Kunstbezit* 12, no. 8 (1968), pp. 1-8.

HACKENBROCH 1979
Y. Hackenbroch, *Renaissance jewellry*, München 1979.

HAEDEKE 1968
H.U. Haedeke, *Zinn*, Cat. Kunstgewerbemuseum, Köln 1968.

HÄRTING 1983
U.A. Härting, *Studien zur Kabinettbildmalerei des Frans Francken II, 1581-1642 - Ein repräsentativer Werkkatalog*, Hildesheim, Zürich & New York 1983.

HAHNLOSER & BRUGGER-KOCH 1985
H.R. Hahnloser & S. Brugger-Koch, *Corpus der Hartsteinschliffe des 12.-15.Jahrhunderts*, Berlin 1985.

HAIRS 1955/1965/1985
M.L. Hairs, *Les peintres flamands de fleurs au XVIIe siècle*, Paris & Brussel 1955, 2nd ed. 1965, 3rd ed. 1985, 2 vols.

HANNEMA 1938
See cat. Rotterdam 1938.

HANNEMA 1952
D. Hannema, *Kunst in oude sfeer*, Rotterdam 1952.

HANNEMA 1955
D. Hannema, *Catalogue of the H.E. ten Cate collection*, 2 vols., Rotterdam 1955.

HAVERKAMP BEGEMANN 1978
E. Haverkamp Begemann, *Wadsworth Atheneum Paintings - Catalogue I: The Netherlands and the German-speaking countries, fifteenth-nineteenth centuries*, Hartford 1978.

HAWCROFT 1960
F.W. Hawcroft, 'Wingfield Castle, Suffolk', in *Connaisseur Yearbook* 1960.

HAYWARD 1963
J.F. Hayward, 'Candlesticks with figure stems', in *The Connoisseur* 36 (1963), pp. 16-21.

HAYWARD 1965
J.F. Hayward, 'The Mannerist goldsmiths: 4 — England. Part 1 — The Holbein designs', in *The Connoisseur* 159 (1965), pp. 80-84.

HAYWARD 1976
J.F. Hayward, *Virtuoso goldsmiths and the triumph of mannerism 1540-1620*, London 1976.

HENKEL & SCHÖNE 1978
A. Henkel & A. Schöne, *Emblemata - Handbuch zur Sinnbildkunst des XVI. und XVII. Jahrhunderts*, Stuttgart 1978 (1st ed. 1967).

HERING 1955
K.H. Hering, *Silberschmiedegefäße auf Niederländischen Stilleben des siebzehnten Jahrhunderts* (diss. Freie Universität Berlin, typescript 1955).

HERNMARCK 1977
C. Hernmarck, *The art of the European silversmiths 1430-1830*, 2 vols., Amsterdam, London & New York 1977.

HILDEGARD VON BINGEN 1980
Hildegard von Bingen, *Physica*. Ed. P.Rietke, *Naturkunde. Das Buch von dem inneren Wesen der verschiedenen Naturen in der Schöpfung*, 3rd ed., Salzburg 1980 (1st ed. 1959).

HOET 1752
Gerard Hoet, *Catalogus of Naamlyst van schilderyen*, 3 vols., 's Gravenhage 1752, vol. 3 by E. Terwesten, 's Gravenhage 1770 (facs. ed. Soest 1976).

HOETINK 1978
H.R. Hoetink, 'Beschouwingen naar aanleiding van een schilderij', in *Boymans Bijdragen* (1978), pp. 104-110.

HOFRICHTER 1983
F. Fox Hofrichter, *Haarlem in the seventeenth Century*, Jane Voorhees Zimmerli Art Museum, Rutgers (New Jersey) 1983.

HOLLSTEIN 1949-
F.W.H. Hollstein, *Dutch and Flemish etchings, engravings and woodcuts*, vol. 1 - , in progress, Amsterdam 1949- .

HOLLSTEIN 1954
F.W.H. Hollstein, *German engravings, etchings and woodcuts 1400-1700*, vol. 1 - , in progress, Amsterdam 1954 -.

VAN HOOGSTRATEN 1678
Samuel van Hoogstraten, *Inleyding tot de hooge schoole der Schilderconst [...]*, Rotterdam 1678.

HOUBRAKEN 1753
Arnold Houbraken, *De Groote Schouburgh der Nederlantsche Konstschilders en Schilderessen [...]*, 3 vols., 's Gravenhage 1753 (ed. princeps Amsterdam 1718; reprint ed. P.T.A. Swillens, Maastricht 1943).

HOUTART 1935
See cat. Brussel 1935.

HOUTZAGER a.o. 1967
M.E. Houtzager c.s., *Röntgenonderzoek van de oude schilderijen in het Centraal Museum te Utrecht*, Utrecht 1967.

HUIZINGA 1961
J. Huizinga, *Holländische Kultur im 17.Jahrhunderts. - Ihre sozialen Grundlagen und nationale Eigenart*, Basel 1961 (Jena 1933); Dutch ed. *Nederland's beschaving in de zeventiende eeuw*, Haarlem 1941; English ed. *Dutch civilization in the 17th century*, London & New York 1968.

IRMSCHER 1986
G. Irmscher, 'Ministrae voluptatum: stoicizing ethics in the market and kitchen scenes of Pieter Aertsen and Joachim Beuckelaer', in *Simiolus* 16 no. 4 (1986), pp. 219-232.

JANSON 1952
H.W. Janson, *Apes and ape lore in the Middle Ages and the Renaissance*, London 1952.

JANTZEN 1910
H. Jantzen, *Das Niederländische Architekturbild*, Leipzig 1910.

JÖRGENSEN 1959
R. Jörgensen, 'Hollandsk kunstnerliv i det 17. Århundre', in *Kunst og Kultur* 42 no. 4 (1959), pp. 197-233.

JONES 1930
E.A. Jones, 'Some old foreign silver in the collection of Mr. William Randolph Hearst', in *The Connoisseur* 86 (1930), pp. 220-225.

DE JONGH 1967
E. de Jongh, *Zinne- en minnebeelden in de schilderkunst van de zeventiende eeuw*, Amsterdam & Antwerpen 1967.

DE JONGH 1976
See cat. Amsterdam 1976.

DE JONGH 1982a
See cat. Auckland etc. 1982.

DE JONGH 1982b
E. de Jongh, 'Bol vincit amorem', in *Simiolus* 12 no. 2/3 (1982), pp. 147-161.

DE JONGH 1986
See cat. Haarlem 1986.

JORDAN 1985
See cat. Fort Worth 1985.

JUNIUS 1565
Hadrianus Junius, *Emblemata [...]*, Antwerpen 1565.

KAHR 1978
M. Millner Kahr, *Dutch painting in the seventeenth century*, New York, Hagertown, San Francisco & London 1978.

KETCHAM - WHEATON 1988
De smaak van het verleden - De Franse keuken van 1300 tot 1789, Amsterdam 1988 (transl. from *Savouring the past*, University of Pennsylvania 1983).

KINDER 1979
T. Tucker Kinder, 'Pieter de Ring: A still-life painter in seventeenth-century Holland', in *Indiana University Art Museum Bulletin* 2 no. 1 (1979), pp. 26-43.

KING 1954
E.S. King, 'Notes on a still life by Jan Soreau', in *The Journal of the Walters Art Gallery* 17, Baltimore 1954, pp. 35-43.

KINGZETT 1986
R.N. Kingzett, 'Dutch treat for Atlanta', in *Apollo* 123, no. 287 (1986), pp. 19-23.

KLEMM 1979-1980
Ch. Klemm, 'Weltdeutung - Allegorien und Symbole in Stilleben', in cat. Münster & Baden-Baden 1979-1980, pp. 140218.

KNUTTEL 1926
G. Knuttel Wzn., 'Het Nederlandse stilleven', in *Mededeelingen van den Dienst voor Kunsten en Wetenschappen der gemeente 's Gravenhage*, vol. 2 nr. 1 (1926), pp. 1-37.

KONING 1722-1727
Martinus Koning, *Lexicon Hieroglyphicum sacro-profanum of Woordboek van Gewyde en Ongewyde Voor- en Zinnebeelden; [...]*, 6 vols., Dordrecht & Amsterdam 1722-1727.

KRAFFT 1986
B. Krafft, 'Börsenkrach in Hollands Tulpenbeet', in *PAN-Zeitschrift für Kunst und Kultur* 4/1986, pp. 42-47.

KRONIG 1914
J.O. Kronig, *A Catalogue of the paintings at Doughty House Richmond & elsewhere in the collection of Sir Frederick Cook Bart.*, Vol. 2: Dutch and Flemish Schools, London 1914.

KUECHEN 1979
U.-B. Kuechen, 'Wechselbeziehungen zwischen allegorischer Naturdeutung und der naturkundlichen Kenntnis von Muschel, Schnecke und Nautilus - Ein Beitrag aus literarischer naturwissenschaftlicher und kunsthistorischer Sicht', in Walter Haug (ed.), *Formen und Funktionen der Allegorie*, Symposion Wolfenbüttel 1978, (ed. Stuttgart 1979).

TER KUILE 1969
O. ter Kuile, 'Een Hollands stilleven door Pieter van Roestraeten in 1696 te Londen geschilderd', in *Antiek* 4 no. 4 (1969), pp. 196-203.

TER KUILE 1970
O. ter Kuile, *500 jaar Nederlandse schilderkunst*, Amsterdam 1970.

TER KUILE 1985
O. ter Kuile, *Seventeenth-century North Netherlandish still lifes* (Rijksdienst Beeldende Kunst), Amsterdam & 's Gravenhage 1985.

KURETSKY 1987
S. Donahue Kuretsky, 'Het schilderen van bloemen in de 17e eeuw', in *Kunstschrift Openbaar Kunstbezit* 1987 no. 3, pp. 84-87.

KUZNETSOV & LINNIK 1982
Y. Kuznetsov & I. Linnik, *Dutch paintings in Soviet museums*, Amsterdam & Leningrad 1982.

LAFENESTRE & RICHTENBERGER 1898
G. Lafenestre & E. Richtenberger, *La peinture en Europe - La Hollande*, Paris 1898.

DE LAIRESSE 1740
Gerard de Lairesse, *Groot schilderboek [...]*, Haarlem 1740 (facs. ed. Utrecht 1969; ed. princeps 1707).

LAMMERS 1979-80a
See cat. Münster & Baden-Baden 1979-80.

LAMMERS 1979-80b
J. Lammers, 'Fasten und Genuß - Die angerichtete Tafel als Thema des Stillebens', in cat. Münster & Baden-Baden 1979-80, pp. 402-429.

LAMMERS 1979-80c
J. Lammers, 'Innovation und Virtuosität', in cat. Münster & Baden-Baden 1979-80, pp. 480-512.

LAUTS 1969
J. Lauts, *Stilleben alter Meister, I. Niederländer und Deutsche* (Staatliche Kunsthalle), Karlsruhe 1969 (2nd ed. 1983).

LAVALLEYE 1966
J. Lavalleye, *Lucas van Leyden - Peter Brueghel l'Ancien - Gravures - Oeuvre complet*, Paris 1966.

LEVI D'ANCONA 1977
M. Levi d'Ancona, *The garden of the Renaissance: botanical symbolism in Italian painting*, Firenze 1977.

LEWIS 1973
F. Lewis, *A dictionary of Dutch & Flemish flower, fruit and still life painters 15th to 19th century*, Leigh-onSea 1973 (most repetitions from Pavière 1962).

LINCOLN 1985
See cat. Minneapolis, Houston & San Diego 1985.

LORENZELLI & VECA 1986
P. Lorenzelli & A. Veca, *Orbis pictus – Natura morta in Germania, Olanda e Fiandra, XVI-XVIII secolo* (cat. Galleria Lorenzelli), Bergamo 1986.

LOWENTHAL 1986
A.W. Lowenthal, *Joachim Wtewael and Dutch mannerism*, Doornspijk 1986.

LUNSINGH SCHEURLEER 1966
D.F. Lunsingh Scheurleer, *Chine de commande*, Hilversum 1966.

LUNSINGH SCHEURLEER 1980
D.F. Lunsingh Scheurleer, *Chinesisches und Japanisches Porzellan in europäischen Fassungen*, Braunschweig 1980.

LUTHER 1979-80
G. Luther, 'Stilleben als Bilder der Sammelleidenschaft. - Die Entstehung der Kunstkammer', in cat. Münster & Baden-Baden 1979-80.

VAN LUTTERVELT 1947
R. van Luttervelt, *Schilders van het stilleven*, Naarden 1947.

MADSEN 1925
K. Madsen, *Catalogue de la collection de M. & Mme. Karl Bergsten – Art Ancien, I, Peinture*, Stockholm 1925.

MALE 1958
E. Mâle, *L'Art réligieux du XIIIe siècle en France*, 2 vols. Paris (1898) 1958.

MANNERS 1915
V. Manners, 'The Oxenden collection, part III', in *The Connoisseur* 43, no. 172 (1915), pp. 200-208.

MARTIN 1935
W. Martin, *De Hollandsche schilderkunst in de 17e eeuw*, vol. 1, *Frans Hals en zijn tijd – Onze 17e eeuwsche schilderkunst in het algemeen, in hare opkomst en rondom Frans Hals*, Amsterdam 1935.

MARTIN 1936
W. Martin, *De Hollandsche schilderkunst in de 17e eeuw*, vol. 2, *Rembrandt en zijn tijd – Onze 17e eeuwsche schilderkunst in haren bloeitijd en nabloei*, Amsterdam 1936; 2nd ed. Amsterdam 1942.

MARTIN 1950
W. Martin, *De schilderkunst in de tweede helft van de zeventiende eeuw*, Amsterdam 1950.

MAUQUOY-HENDRICKX 1978-83
M. Mauquoy-Hendrickx, *Les estampes des Wierix conservées au Cabinet des Estampes de la Bibliothèque Royale Albert Ier – Catalogue raisonné [....]*, 4 vols., Brussel 1978-83.

MELITO OF SARDES (1865)
Melito Sardinensis, *Clavis cum variorum commentariis*, in J.B. Pitra, *Spicilegium solesmense completens Sanctorum Patrum...*, 4 vols, Paris 1865.

MENZ 1962
H. Menz, *Les chefs-d'oeuvres de la Galerie de Dresde*, Paris 1962.

MEYSTER 1579
Everhard Meyster, *Mikrokosmos – Parvvs Mundus*, Antwerpen 1579 (several reprints, and translations into French and Dutch; cf. Vondel 1613)

MIEDEMA 1975
H. Miedema, 'Over het realisme in de Nederlandse schilderkunst van de zeventiende eeuw', in *Oud Holland* 89 (1975), pp. 2-18.

MIEDEMA 1977
H. Miedema, 'Realism and comic mode: the peasant', in *Simiolus* 9 nr. 4 (1977), pp. 205-219.

MIEDEMA 1980
H. Miedema, *De archiefbescheiden van het St. Lukasgilde te Haarlem, 1497-1798*, 2 vols., Alphen aan de Rijn 1980.

MIEDEMA 1981
H. Miedema, *Kunst, kunstenaar en kunstwerk bij Karel van Mander - Een analyse van zijn levensbeschrijvingen*, Alphen aan de Rijn 1981.

MIGNE 1844-65
J.P. Migne, *Patrologiae cursus completus, [...] Series Latina [...]*, 221 vols., Paris 1844-65 (facs. ed. Turnhout in progress).

MILLAR 1960
O. Millar, 'Abraham van der Doort's Catalogue of the Collections of Charles I', in *Walpole Society* 37 (1960), pp. 1-243.

DE MIRIMONDE 1970
A.P. de Mirimonde, 'Musique et symbolisme chez Jan Davidszoon de Heem, Cornelis Janszoon en Jan II Janszoon de Heem', in *Jaarboek van het Koninklijk Museum voor Schone Kunsten*, Antwerpen 1970, pp. 241-296.

MITCHELL 1973
P. Mitchell, *European flower painting*, London 1973 (2nd ed. Schiedam 1981).

MITCHELL 1976
See cat. London 1976a.

MOES 1909
E.W. Moes, *Frans Hals, sa vie et son oeuvre*, Brussel 1909.

MOES & VAN BIEMA 1909
E.W. Moes & E. van Biema, *De Nationale Konstgallerij en het Koninklijk Museum: bijdrage tot de geschiedenis van het Rijksmuseum*, Amsterdam 1909.

TER MOLEN 1984
J.R. ter Molen, *Van Vianen – Een Utrechtse familie van zilversmeden met een internationale faam*, 2 vols., diss. Leiden 1984.

MONBALLIEU 1979
A. Monballieu, 'De «Hand als teken op het kleed» bij Brueghel en Baltens', in *Jaarboek van het Koninklijk Museum voor Schone Kunsten*, Antwerpen 1979, pp. 197-209.

MOORE 1979
J.G. Moore, *The Eastern Gate*, Cleveland & New York 1979.

MOXEY 1976
K.P.F. Moxey, 'The «Humanist» Market scenes of Joachim Beuckelaer: Moralizing exempla or «Slices of life»?', in *Jaarboek van het Koninklijk Museum voor Schone Kunsten*, Antwerpen 1976, pp. 109-187.

MOXEY 1977
K.P.F. Moxey, *Pieter Aertsen, Joachim Beuckelaer and the rise of secular painting in the context of the Reformation*, New York & London 1977.

MÜLLER 1956
W.J. Müller, *Der Maler Georg Flegel und die Anfänge des Stillebens*, Frankfurt am Main 1956.

MÜLLER HOFSTEDE 1984
J. Müller Hofstede, '«Non Saturatur Oculus Visu» — Zur «Allegorie des Gesichts» von Peter Paul Rubens und Jan Brueghel d. Ä.', in H. Vekeman & J. Müller Hofstede, *Wort und Bild in der niederländische Kunst und Literatur des 16. und 17.Jahrhunderts*, Erftstadt 1984.

MÜNDLER 1909
O. Mündler, 'Schätzungsliste von Otto Mündler über die Bestände der Esterházy-Galerie', [1869], in *Az Országos Magyar Szépmüvészeti Múzeum állagai* 1 (1909), pp. 3-40.

NASH 1973
J.M. Nash, *The Age of Rembrandt and Vermeer — Dutch painting in the seventeenth century*, London 1973.

NOCQ, ALFASSA & GUÉRIN n.d.
H. Nocq, P. Alfassa & J. Guérin, *Orfèvrerie civil français du XVI au début du XIXe siècle*, Paris n.d.

NOVOTNY 1942
V. Novotny, *Hollandské zátisí*, Prameny & Praha 1942.

OBREEN 1877-1890
D.O. Obreen, *Archief voor Nederlandsche Kunstgeschiedenis [...]*, 7 vols., Rotterdam 1877-1890 (facs. ed. Soest 1976).

OLBRICH & MÖBIUS 1951
H. Olbrich & H. Möbius, 'Wahrheit und Wirklichkeit zum Realismus holländischer Kunst', in *Bildende Kunst* 7 (1951), pp. 320f.

OMAN 1967
Ch. Oman, *A catalogue of plate belonging to the Bank of England*, London 1967.

VAN OMMEREN 1909
See cat. Rotterdam 1909.

ORTELIUS 1969
Album Amicorum Abrahami Ortelij, facs. ed.Amsterdam 1969.

OTTEMA 1970
N. Ottema, *Chinese ceramiek - Handboek geschreven naar aanleiding van de verzamelingen in het Gemeentelijk Museum Het Princessehof te Leeuwarden*, 3rd ed., Lochem 1970, revised by J. Romijn (1st ed. 1943, 2nd ed. 1946).

PARADIN 1557
Claude Paradin, *Devises Heroïques*, Lyon 1557 (ed. princeps 1551); Dutch ed. *Princeliicke Deuiisen*, Leyden 1615.

PARTHEY 1863-1864
G.F.C. Parthey, *Deutscher Bildersaal: Verzeichnis der in Deutschland vorhandenen Oelbilder verstorben Maler aller Schulen*, 2 vols., Berlin 1863-1864.

PAVIERE 1962
S.H. Pavière, *A dictionary of flower, fruit, and still life painters*, Amsterdam & Leigh-on-Sea 1962.

DE LA PERRIERE 1553
Guillaume de la Perrière, *La Morosophie [...]*, Lyon 1553.

PHYSIOLOGUS (1972)
Theobaldi 'Physiologus', ed. P.T. Eden (Mitellateinische Studien und Texte, vol. 6), Leiden & Köln 1972.

PHYSIOLOGUS (1979)
Physiologus, ed. M.J. Curley, Austin & London 1979.

PHYSIOLOGUS (1987)
Der Physiologus - Tiere und ihre Symbolik, ed. O. Seel, Zürich & München 1987, 5th ed. (1st ed. 1960).

PICINELLI 1687
Ph. Picinelli, *Mondo simbolico*, Köln 1687 (facs. ed. Hildesheim & New York 1979; ed.princeps Milano 1653).

PIGLER 1964
A. Pigler, 'La mouche peinte: un talisman', in *Bulletin du Musée Hongrois de Beaux-Arts* 24 (1964), pp. 47-64.

PIGLER 1974
A. Pigler, *Barockthemen — Eine Auswahl von Verzeichnissen zur Ikonographie des 17. und 18. Jahrhunderts*, 2nd rev. ed., 3 vols., Budapest 1974 (1st ed. 1956).

PLATNER a.o. 1842
E. Platner c.s., *Beschreibung der Stadt Rom*, vol. 3, Stuttgart 1842.

PLINIUS (1635)
Cajus Plinius Secundus, *Historiae Naturalis, [...]*, 1635; English ed. by H. Rackham, W.H.S. Jones & D.E. Eichholz, *Natural history*, 10 vols., Cambridge (Mass.) & London 1938-62.

PLOKKER 1984
A. Plokker, *Adriaen Pietersz van de Venne (1589-1662) - De grisailles met spreukbanden*, Amersfoort 1984.

POIRTERS (1646) 1935
Adrianus Poirters, *Het Masker vande Wereldt afgetrocken*, Oisterwijk 1935 (ed. princeps Antwerpen, 1646, many reprints, rev. ed. of *Ydelheyt des Werelts*, Antwerpen 1645, adapted from A. Tellier et al., *Typus Mundi [...]*, Antwerpen 1627).

PONS (1583) 1680
Jacques Pons, *Traité des melons ou il est parlé de leur nature, de leur culture, de leurs vertus et de leur usage [...]*, Lyon 1680 (ed. princeps: *Sommaire traité des melons et l'usage d'iceux, avec les commodités et incommodités qui en reviennent*, Lyon 1583).

POPHAM 1932
A.E. Popham, *Catalogue of drawings by Dutch and Flemish artists preserved in the Department of Prints and Drawings in the British Museum. Vol. 5: Dutch and Flemish drawings of the XV and XVI centuries*, London 1932.

PORTEMAN 1977
K. Porteman, *Inleiding tot de Nederlandse emblemataliteratuur*, Groningen 1977.

POSSE 1911
H. Posse, *Die Gemäldegalerie des Kaiser FriedrichMuseums*, vol. 2, *Die germanischen Länder*, Berlin 1911.

VAN DE PIJL-KETEL 1981
C. van der Pijl-Ketel, 'Zijn de wijnkopjes van Wan-Li porselein uit de Oostindiëvaarder de «Witte Leeuw» soms «pimpelkens»?, in *Antiek* 15 (1981), pp. 510-512.

VAN DER PIJL-KETEL 1982
C. van der Pijl-Ketel, *The ceramic load of the «Witte Leeuw» (1613)*, Amsterdam (Rijksmuseum) 1982.

RENCKENS 1967
B.J.A. Renckens, 'G. van Berkborch', in *Oud Holland* 82 (1967), pp. 236-239.

REUSNER 1581
Nicolas Reusner, *Emblemata Nicolai Reusneri lc. Partim Ethica, et Physica [...]*, Francfort 1581.

REZNICEK 1960
E.J. Reznicek, 'Het begin van Goltzius' loopbaan als schilder', in *Oud Holland* 75 (1960), pp. 30-49.

RIPA 1611/1644
Cesare Ripa, *Iconologia, overo descrittione d'imagini delle virtu, [...]*, Padua 1611 (facs. ed. New York & London 1976); Dutch ed. *Iconologia of Uijtbeeldinghe des Verstants [...]*, D. Pz. Pers, Amsterdam 1644 (ed. princeps Roma 1593).

ROBELS 1969
H. Robels, 'Frans Snijders' Entwicklung als Stillebenmaler', in *Wallraf-Richartz Jahrbuch* 31 (1969), pp. 43-94.

ROBINSON 1974
F.W. Robinson, *Gabriel Metsu (1629-1667) — A study of his place in Dutch genre painting of the Golden Age*, New York 1974.

ROLLENHAGEN 1611, 1613
Gabriel Rollenhagen, *Les Emblèmes*, Arnhem 1611; *Selectorum Emblematum Centuria Secunda*, Arnhem 1613.

ROODENBURG 1959
M-C. Roodenburg, *Een hollands pronkstilleven*, Rotterdam 1959 (private ed. Bank voor Handel en Scheepvaart N.V.).

ROSENBERG & SLIVE 1966
J. Rosenberg & S. Slive, 'Painting: 1600-1675', in J. Rosenberg, S. Slive & E.H. ter Kuile, *Dutch art and architecture: 1600 to 1800*, Middlesex etc. (Penguin books) 1966; 2nd rev. ed. 1972; 3rd rev. ed. 1977.

RUDOLPH 1938
H. Rudolph, '«Vanitas». Die Bedeutung mittelalterlicher un humanistischer Malerei des 17. Jahrhunderts', in *Festschrift Wilhelm Pinder zum sechzichsten Geburtstage*, Leipzig 1938, pp. 405-433.

SAAVEDRA 1659
Diego de Saavedra Fajardo, *Idea de un Principe Politico Christiano [...]*, Amsterdam 1659 (ed. princeps München 1640).

SAUNDERS 1955
J. Saunders, *Justus Lipsius, the philosopher of Renaissance Stoicism*, New York 1955.

SCHAMA 1987
S. Schama, *The embarrasment of riches — An interpretation of Dutch culture in the Golden Age*, New York 1987.

SCHENCKEVELD-VAN DER DUSSEN 1984
M.A. Schenckeveld-van der Dussen, Book review on A. McNeil Kettering, The Dutch Arcadia, in *Simiolus* 14 no. 3/4 (1984), pp. 231-233.

VAN SCHENDEL & HAAK 1966
A.F.E. van Schendel & B. Haak, *Kunstschatten uit het Rijksmuseum*, Amsterdam 1966.

SCHLIEMANN 1985
E. Schliemann (ed.), *Die Goldschmiede Hamburgs*, 3 vols., Hamburg 1985.

SCHNEIDER & CONSTABLE 1930
See cat. London 1929.

SCHÖN 1540
Erhard Schön, *Unterweissung der Proportion rund Possen*, Nürnberg 1540 (facs. ed. of 1542, Frankfurt 1920).

SCHWARZ 1987
S. Schwarz, *Das Bücherstilleben in der Malerei des 17. Jahrhunderts*, Wiesbaden 1987.

SEGAL 1982a
See cat. Amsterdam & 's Hertogenbosch 1982.

SEGAL 1982b
S. Segal, 'Een vroeg bloemstuk van Jan Brueghel de Oude/ An early flower piece by Jan Brueghel the Elder', in *Tableau* 4 no. 5 (1982), pp. 490-499.

SEGAL 1982c
S. Segal, 'The flower pieces of Roelandt Savery' in *Leids Kunsthistorisch Jaarboek* 1982, pp. 309-337.

SEGAL 1983a
See cat. Amsterdam & Braunschweig 1983.

SEGAL 1983b
S. Segal, 'Joris van Son', in cat. *A selection of Dutch and Flemish seventeenth-century paintings*, Gallery Hoogsteder-Naumann, Ltd., New York 1983, pp. 76-81.

SEGAL 1983c
S. Segal, 'Un bouquet de fleurs par Hans Bollongier', in *La Revue du Louvre et des Musées de France* 33 (1983) no. 5/6, pp. 370-372.

SEGAL 1984a
S. Segal, 'Still-lifes by Middelburg painters', in cat. Amsterdam 1984, pp. 25-95.

SEGAL 1984b
S. Segal, 'Die Pflanzen im Genter Altar', in *«De Arti et Libri»*, (Erasmus) Amsterdam 1984, pp. 403-420.

SEGAL 1984c
S. Segal, 'Georg Flegel as flower painter', in *Tableau* 7 no. 3 (1984), pp. 73-86.

SEGAL 1984d
S. Segal, 'De beleving van het stilleven', in *Beeld - Tijdschrift voor kunst, kunsttheorie en kunstgeschiedenis* 4 (1984), pp. 30-34.

SEGAL 1985
S. Segal, 'Symbol and meaning in still-life painting', in H.R. Hoetink (ed.), *The Royal Picture Gallery Mauritshuis*, Amsterdam & New York 1985, pp. 92-101.

SEGAL 1986a
S. Segal, 'Jacques de Gheyn's plants', in cat. *Jacques de Gheyn II drawings*, Museum Boymans-van Beuningen, Rotterdam & The National Gallery of Art, Washington 1985-1986, pp. 24-30 (Dutch ed. *Jacques de Gheyn II als tekenaar*).

SEGAL 1986b
S. Segal, 'Früchte, Brot, Wein und tiefere Bedeutung - Ein Früchtestilleben von Jacques de Gheyn und seine Symbolik', in *Kunst und Antiquitäten* 11 (1986), pp. 22-32.

SEGAL 1986c
S. Segal, 'De keus in de kunst — Over de betekenis van zeventiende eeuwse stillevens', in *Tableau* 8 no. 5 (1986), pp. 56-60 (summary pp. 70).

SEGAL 1987
S. Segal, 'Exotische bollen als statussymbolen', in *Kunstschrift Openbaar Kunstbezit* 1987 no. 3, pp. 88-97.

SEGAL 1988
S. Segal, *Die Entstehung der Stilleben-Tradition im Hinblick auf Dürer*, Symposium Wien 1985 (in print).

SEIFERTOVA 1981
H. Seifertová, 'Georg Hinz a jeho projetí opichéno klamle', in *Umení* 29 (1981), pp. 530-537 (with summary in German: 'Georg Hinz und seine Auffassung der optischen Täuschung', pp. 537-539).

SELING 1980
H. Seling, *Die Kunst der Augsburger Goldschmiede 1529-1868*, 2 vols., München 1980.

SIP 1976
J. Síp, *Hollandské malírství 17. Svoletí v Prazské Národní Galerii*, Praha 1976.

SPRIGGS 1965
A. Spriggs, 'Transitional porcelain ginger jars', in *Oriental Art*, new series 11 no.2 (1965), pp. 95-100.

SPRIGGS 1967
A. Spriggs, 'Oriental porcelain in Western paintings 1450-1750', in *Transactions of the Oriental Ceramic Society* 36, 1964-1966 (1967), pp. 73-87, pl. 57-78.

STECHOW 1938a
See cat. Providence 1938.

STECHOW 1938b
W. Stechow, 'Homo Bulla', in *The Art Bulletin* 20 (1938), pp. 227-228.

STERLING 1952
See cat. Paris 1952

STERLING 1952/1959/1985
Ch. Sterling, *La nature morte de l'antiquité à nos jours*, Paris 1952; 2nd rev. ed. Paris 1959; 3rd rev. ed. *La nature morte de l'antiquité au XXe siècle*, Paris 1981; English ed.: *Still-life painting from Antiquity to the present time*, Paris 1959; 2nd rev. ed. *Still-life painting from Antiquity to the twentieth century*, New York & Toronto 1985.

STRACHWITZ 1980
A. Graf Strachwitz, 'Vier Generationen einer Malerdynastie', in *Weltkunst* 50 no. 20 (1980), pp. 2874-2876.

SULLIVAN 1974
S.A. Sullivan, 'A banquet-piece with vanitas implications', in *Cleveland Museum of Art Bulletin* 56 (1974), pp. 271-282.

SULLIVAN 1981
S.A. Sullivan, 'Frans Snijders: Still life with fruit, vegetables and dead game', in *Bulletin of the Detroit Institute of Art* 59 no. 1 (1981), pp. 30-37.

SULLIVAN 1984
S.A. Sullivan, *The Dutch gamepiece*, Towota & Montclair 1984.

SUTTON 1986
P.C. Sutton, *A guide to Dutch art in America*, Grand Rapids & Kampen 1986.

TAKACS 1908
Z. von Takács, in *Monatsheft für Kunstwissenschaft* 1 (1908), pp. 665-666.

TAKACS 1911
Z. von Takács, 'Neuerwerbungen des Museums für bildende Kunst', in *Cicerone* 3 (1911), pp. 857-882.

TALLEY 1983
M. Kirby Talley, '«Small, usual an vulgar things»: Still-life painting in England 1635-1670', in *Walpole Society* 49 (1983), pp. 133-223.

TAURELLUS 1602
Nicolaus Taurellus, *Emblemata Physico-Ethica [...]*, Nürnberg 1602.

TÉREY 1908
G. von Térey, 'A Szépmüvészeti Muzeum gyarapodásai. Nemes Marcell ajándékai', in *Vasárnapi Ujság* 1908, pp. 503, 505,970.

TÉREY 1926
G. von Térey, 'Unbekannte Werke seltener niederländischer Maler des 17. Jahrhunderts', in *Cicerone* 18 (1926), pp. 47-53.

TERWESTEN 1770
P. Terwesten, *Catalogus of Naamlyst van Schilderyen, met derzelver prysen zedert den 22. Augusti 1752 tot den 21. November 1768*, 's Gravenhage 1770 (suppl. to Hoet 1752; facs. ed. Soest 1976).

VAN THIEL 1967-1968
P.J.J. van Thiel, 'Marriage Symbols in a musical party by Jan Miense Molenaer', in *Simiolus* 2 no. 2 (1967-68), pp. 91-100.

THIEME & BECKER 1907-1950
U. Thieme & F. Becker (eds.), *Allgemeines Lexicon der bildenden Künstler von der Antike bis zur Gegenwart*, 37 vols., Leipzig 1907-1950.

TOMAN 1888
H. Toman, 'Ueber die Malerfamilie De Heem', in *Repertorium für Kunstwissenschaft* 11 (1888), pp. 123-146.

TYPOTIUS 1601
Jac. Typotius, *Symbola Divina et Humana Pontificum Imperatorum Regum. Accessit breuis & facilis Isagoge*, Praha 1601 (ed. Frankfurt 1652).

UHLIG 1986
W. Uhlig, *Stilleben - Theorie und Entwicklung der europäischen Stillebenmalerei*, Stuttgart 1986.

VAENIUS 1615
O. Vaenius (Otho van Veen), *Amoris Divini Emblemata*, Antwerpen 1615 (2nd ed. 1660).

VALENTINER 1913
W.R. Valentiner, *John G. Johnson Collection*, vol. 2: *Catalogue of Flemish and Dutch paintings*, Philadelphia 1913 (rev. ed. Philadelphia 1972).

VALERIANUS (1556) 1610
G.P. Valerianus, *Hieroglyphica [...]*, Lyon 1610 (ed. princeps 1556).

VECA 1981
A. Veca, *Vanitas - Il simbolismo del tempo*, cat. Galleria Lorenzelli, Bergamo 1981.

VECA 1982
A. Veca, *Parádeisos - Dall' universo del fiore*, cat. Galleria Lorenzelli, Bergamo 1982.

VECA 1983
A. Veca, *Simposio - Cerimonie e Apparti*, cat. Galleria Lorenzelli, Bergamo 1983.

VELDMAN 1985
I.M. Veldman, *De maat van kennis en wetenschap*, Amsterdam 1985.

VAN VIANEN 1650
Christiaen van Vianen, *Constighe Modellen van verscheyden silvere Vasen [...] gevonden ende geteeckend door E. Adam van Vianen. Uytgegeven door synen Soon Christiaen van Vianen tot Uytrecht in acht deelen*, 3 vols., Utrecht 1650.

VICAIRE 1890
G. Vicaire, *Bibliographie gastronomique*, Paris 1890.

VIGORELLI & BACCHESCHI 1966
G. Vigorelli & E. Baccheschi, *L'Opera complete di Giotto*, Milano 1966 (and later editions).

ROEMER VISSCHER 1614
Roemer Visscher, *Sinnepoppen*, Amsterdam 1614 (reprint ed. L.Brummel, 's Gravenhage 1949).

VONDEL 1613
Joost van den Vondel, *Den Gulden Winckel [...]*, Amsterdam 1613 (many reprints; revised from Everhard Meyster).

VONDEL 1617
Joost van den Vondel, *Vorsteliicke Warande der dieren [...]*, Amsterdam 1617 (many reprints; revised from Edewaerd de Dene).

VONDEL 1937
Joost van den Vondel, *Volledige dichtwerken en oorspronkelijk proza*, ed. Albert Verwey, Amsterdam 1937 (orig. ed. 1886).

VORENKAMP 1933
A.P.A. Vorenkamp, *Bijdrage tot de geschiedenis van het Hollandsch stilleven in de zeventiende eeuw*, diss. Leiden 1933.

VORENKAMP 1938
A.P.A. Vorenkamp, 'Masterpieces of Dutch painting, an important exhibition at the Providence Museum', in *The Art News*, December 10, 1938.

DE VRIES a.o. 1893
M. de Vries, E. Verwijs & A. Kluyver, *Woordenboek der Nederlandsche Taal*, vol. 10, 's Gravenhage 1893.

DE VRIES 1964
A.B. de Vries, 'Old Masters in the collection of Mr. and Mrs. Sidney van den Bergh', in *Apollo* 80 no. 33 (1964), pp. 352-359.

VROOM 1945/1980
N.R.A. Vroom, *De schilders van het monochrome banketje*, Amsterdam 1945; English rev. ed. *A modest message as intimated by the painters of the «monochrome banketje»*, 2 vols., Schiedam 1980.

WALSH & SCHNEIDER 1981-1982
See cat. Los Angeles, Boston & New York 1981-1982.

WANG 1975
A. Wang, *Der «Miles Christianus» im 16. und 17. Jahrhunderts und seine mittelalterliche Tradition - Ein Beitrag zum Verhältnis von sprachlicher und graphischer Bildlichkeit*, Bern & Frankfurt am Main 1975.

WARNER 1928
R. Warner, *Dutch and Flemish flower and fruit painters of the 17th and 18th centuries*, London 1928 (reprint ed. S. Segal, with add., Amsterdam 1975).

WESCHER 1954
P. Wescher, *Illustrated Handbook of the Los Angeles County Museum of Art*, vol. 2, Los Angeles 1954.

WIERSUM 1931
E. Wiersum, 'Het ontstaan van de verzameling schilderijen van Gerrit van den Pot van Groeneveld te Rotterdam', in *Oud Holland* 48 (1931), pp. 201-214.

WILBERG 1969
Th. A.G. Wilberg Vignau-Schuurman, *Die emblematischen Elemente im Werke Joris Hoefnagels*, 2 vols., Leiden 1969.

WILENSKI 1960
R.H. Wilenski, *Flemish painters 1430-1830*, 2 vols., London 1960.

WINKLER 1925
F. Winkler, *Die Flämische Buchmalerei des XV. und XVI. Jahrhunderts - Künstler und Werke von den Brüdern Van Eyck bis zu Simon Bening*, Leipzig 1925 (reprint ed. G. Dogaer, with add., Amsterdam 1978).

WINNER 1957
M. Winner, *Die Quellen des Pictura - Allegorien in gemalten Bildergalerien des 17. Jahrhunderts zu Antwerpen*, diss. Köln 1957 (manuscript).

WITTKOWER 1949
R. Wittkower, 'Death and resurrection in a picture by Marten de Vos', in *Miscellanea Leo van Puyvelde*, Brussel 1949, pp. 117-123.

WOHLGEMUTH 1978
M. Wohlgemuth, 'Willem Kalfs Stilleben der Amsterdamer periode: Zwei Bilder der Sammlungen Bührle und Thyssen', in *Der Landbote*, Winterthur, 8 July 1978, pp. 23-25.

WOLDBYE & VON MEYENBURG 1983-1984
See cat. København 1983-1984.

DE WOLF 1967
H.C. de Wolf, 'Kunst uit de schuilkerkentijd', in *Antiek* 1 no. 9 (1967), pp. 2-9.

WOLF 1978
H. Wolf, *Niederländisch-flämische Buchmalerei des Spät-mittelalters*, Berlin (DDR) 1978.

WOLF 1985
H. Wolf, *Kostbarkeiten flämischer Buchmalerei*, Berlin (DDR) 1985.

WRIGHT 1976
Chr. Wright, *Old master paintings in Britain – An index of continental old master paintings executed before c. 1800 in public collections in the United Kingdom*, London & Towota 1976.

WRIGHT 1978
Chr. Wright, *The Dutch painters*, London 1978 (Dutch ed. *Nederlandse schilders van de zeventiende eeuw*, De Bilt 1980.

WRIGHT 1980
Chr. Wright, *Paintings in Dutch museums - An index of oil paintings in public collections in the Netherlands by artists born before 1870*, London, Towota & Amsterdam 1980.

WRIGHT 1981
Chr. Wright, *Dutch and flemish paintings of the 17th century*, Frome & London 1981.

WTTEWAALL 1987
B.W.G. Wttewaall, *Nederlands klein zilver 1650-1880*, Amsterdam 1987.

VON WURZBACH 1906-1911
A. von Wurzbach, *Niederländisches Künstler-Lexicon*, 3 vols., Wien & Leipzig 1906-1911 (facs. ed. Amsterdam 1974).

YDEMA 1988
O. Ydema, 'Carpets in 17th Century Dutch and Flemish painting', in cat. *The European Fine Art Fair*, Maastricht 1988, pp. 15-28.

ZARNOWSKA 1929
E. Zarnowska, *La nature-morte Hollandaise - Les principaux représentants, ses origines, son influence*, Brussel & Maastricht 1929.

Exhibition Catalogues

ALMELO 1953
Oude kunst uit Twents particulier bezit - Catalogus van schilderijen en beeldhouwwerken, Kunstkring De Waag, Almelo 1953 (cat. by D. Hannema).

AMSTERDAM 1911
Importants tableaux anciens de l'école hollandaise, Gallery Frederik Muller & Co., Amsterdam 1911.

AMSTERDAM 1933
Het stilleven, Gallery J. Goudstikker, Amsterdam 1933.

AMSTERDAM 1934
Helsche en Fluweelen Brueghel, Gallery P. de Boer, Amsterdam 1934.

AMSTERDAM 1935
Bloemstukken van oude meesters, Gallery P. de Boer, Amsterdam 1935.

AMSTERDAM 1936
Oude kunst uit het bezit van den internationalen handel, Rijksmuseum, Amsterdam 1936.

AMSTERDAM 1970
17e-eeuwse schilderijen uit de verzameling Willem Russell, Amsterdams Historisch Museum, Amsterdam 1970 (cat. by B. Haak).

AMSTERDAM 1976
Tot lering en vermaak, Rijksmuseum, Amsterdam 1976 (cat. by E. de Jongh a.o.).

AMSTERDAM, TOLEDO & BOSTON 1979-1980
Nederlands zilver/Dutch silver 1580-1830, Rijksmuseum, Amsterdam, Toledo Museum of Art & Museum of Fine Arts, Boston, (ed. 's Gravenhage 1979, A. L. den Blaauwen).

AMSTERDAM & 'S HERTOGENBOSCH 1982
Een bloemrijk verleden - Overzicht van de Noord- en Zuid-Nederlandse bloemschilderkunst, 1600-heden / A flowery past - A survey of Dutch and Flemish flower painting from 1600 until the present, Gallery P. de Boer, Amsterdam & Noordbrabants Museum, 's Hertogenbosch 1982 (cat. by S. Segal).

AMSTERDAM & BRAUNSCHWEIG 1983
A fruitful past - A survey of the fruit still lifes of the Northern and Southern Netherlands from Brueghel till Van Gogh / Niederländische Stilleben von Brueghel bis Van Gogh, Gallery P. de Boer, Amsterdam & Herzog Anton Ulrich-Museum, Braunschweig 1983 (cat. by S. Segal).

AMSTERDAM 1984
Masters of Middelburg, Gallery K & V. Waterman, Amsterdam 1984 (cat. by N. Bakker, G. Jansen & S. Segal).

AMSTERDAM 1984-1985
Meesterwerken in zilver - Amsterdams zilver 1520-1820, Museum Willet-Holthuysen, Amsterdam 1984-1985, Lochem 1984 (cat. by K.A. Citroen, F. van Erpers Royaards & J. Verbeek).

ANTWERPEN 1982
Het Aards paradijs - Dierenvoorstellingen in de Nederlanden van de 16e en 17e eeuw, Zoo Antwerpen 1982.

ARNHEM 1955
Gelders zilver, Gemeentemuseum, Arnhem 1955.

ATLANTA 1985
Masterpieces of the Dutch Golden Age, High Museum of Art, Atlanta 1985 (cat. by F.J. Duparc).

AUCKLAND etc. 1982
Still life in the Age of Rembrandt, Auckland City Art Gallery, Auckland and other places 1982 (cat. by E. de Jongh a.o.).

BASEL 1987
Im Lichte Hollands - Holländische Malerei des 17. Jahrhunderts aus den Sammlungen des Fürsten von Liechtenstein und aus Schweizer Besitz, Kunstmuseum, Basel 1987 (cat. by Petra ten Doesschate Chu).

BERGEN OP ZOOM 1954
Schilders uit de zeventiende eeuw, Thalia, Bergen op Zoom 1954.

BERLIN 1906
Ausstellung von Werken alter Kunst aus dem Privatbesitz der Mitglieder des Kaiser Friedrich-Museum-Vereins, Gräflich Redernsches Palais, Berlin 1906.

BERLIN 1985
Europa und die Kaiser von China, 1240-1816, Berliner Festspiele GmbH, Martin-Gropius-Bau, Berlin 1985 (ed. Frankfurt a/M. 1985).

BRUSSEL 1935
Cinq siècles d'art, Exposition Universelle et Internationale, Brussel 1935 (cat. by Baronne A. Houtart).

BRUSSEL 1971
Rembrandt en zijn tijd/Rembrandt et son temps, Palais des Beaux-Arts, Brussel 1971.

BRUSSEL 1980
Bruegel-Une dynastie de peintres/Bruegel-Een dynastie van schilders, Palais des Beaux-Arts, Brussel 1980.

CHICAGO 1985
Blue and white, Chinese porcelain and its impact on the western world, The David & Alfred Smart Gallery, University of Chicago 1985 (cat. by J. Carswell).

CLEVELAND 1960
Year in review, Cleveland Museum of Art, Cleveland 1960.

CLEVELAND 1963
Year in review, Cleveland Museum of Art, Cleveland 1963.

CLEVELAND 1979
Chardin and the still-life tradition in France, Cleveland Museum of Art, Cleveland 1979 (cat. by G. P. Weisberg & W.S. Talbot).

COLUMBUS 1985
More than meets the eye: The art of trompe-l'oeil, Columbus Museum of Art, Columbus 1985.

DELFT 1962
Meesterwerken uit Delft, Stedelijk Museum Het Prinsenhof, Delft 1962.

DELFT 1981
De stad Delft, Cultuur en maatschappij van 1572-1667, Stedelijk Museum Het Prinsenhof, Delft 1981.

DETROIT 1939
Masterpieces of Art from foreign collections, Institute of Arts, Detroit 1939.

DETROIT 1941
Masterpieces of Art from European and American collections, Institute of Arts, Detroit 1941.

DIEREN 1937
16e en 17e eeuwse Hollandse schilderijen, Gallery D. Katz, Dieren 1937.

DORDRECHT 1954
Nederlandse stillevens uit vier eeuwen, Dordrechts Museum, Dordrecht 1954.

DORDRECHT 1955
Boom, bloem en plant - Nederlandse meesters uit vijf eeuwen, Dordrechts Museum, Dordrecht 1955.

DORDRECHT 1962
Nederlandse stillevens uit de zeventiende eeuw, Dordrechts Museum, Dordrecht 1962 (cat. by L.J. Bol).

DORDRECHT 1975
Dordrechts goud en zilver, Museum Mr. Simon van Gijn, Dordrecht 1975.

DRESDEN 1955-1956
Gemälde der Dresdner Galerie - Übergeben von der Regierung der U.d.S.S.R. an die Deutsche Demokratische Republik, National-Galerie, Dresden 1955-1956.

DRESDEN 1983
Das Stilleben und sein Gegenstand, Eine Gemeinschafts-ausstellung von Museen aus der UDSSR der CSSR und der DDR, Albertinum, Dresden 1983.

EINDHOVEN 1957
Het Hollandse stilleven 1550-1950, Van Abbemuseum, Eindhoven 1957.

FORT WORTH 1985
Spanish still life in the Golden Age 1600-1650, Kimbell Art. Museum, Fort Worth 1985 (cat. by W.B. Jordan).

GENT 1960
Fleurs et jardins dans l'art flamand / Bloem en tuin in de Vlaamse kunst, Museum voor Schone Kunsten, Gent 1960.

GENT 1985
Masterworks of silver of private collections, Oudheidkundig Museum van de Bijloke, Gent 1985.

GENT 1986-1987
Joachim Beuckelaer - Het markt- en keukenstuk in de Nederlanden 1550-1650, Museum voor Schone Kunsten, Gent 1986-1987.

'S GRAVENHAGE 1926
Nederlandsche stillevens uit vijf eeuwen, Haags Gemeentemuseum, 's Gravenhage 1926.

'S GRAVENHAGE 1982
Terugzien in bewondering, Mauritshuis, 's Gravenhage 1982.

HAARLEM 1953
Bloemenwereld van oude en moderne Nederlandse kunst, Teyler's Museum, Haarlem 1953.

HAARLEM 1986
Portretten van echt en trouw - Huwelijk en gezin in de Nederlandse kunst van de zeventiende eeuw, Frans Hals-museum, Haarlem 1986 (cat. by E. de Jongh).

'S HERTOGENBOSCH 1959
Damast, Centraal Noordbrabants Museum, 's Hertogenbosch 1959.

'S HERTOGENBOSCH 1965
Brabants zilver, Centraal Noordbrabants Museum, 's Hertogenbosch 1965.

KOBE 1982
The silk road on the sea, The Kobe City Museum, Kobe 1982.

KØBENHAVN 1983-1984
Konkylien og Mennesket, Kunstindustrimuseet, København 1983-1984.

KÖLN 1956
Blumen- und Stilleben-Gemälde von Brueghel bis Vlaminck, Gallery Abels, Köln 1956.

KÖLN & UTRECHT 1987
Niederländische Malerei des 17. Jahrhunderts aus Budapest, Wallraf-Richartz-Museum, Köln & Centraal Museum, Utrecht 1987 (cat. by I. Ember a.o.).

LA JOLLA 1964
California Annual Painting and sculpture exhibition, La Jolla Art Center, La Jolla 1964.

LAREN 1959
Kunstschatten - Twee Nederlandse collecties schilderijen vijftiende tot en met zeventiende eeuw (...), Singer Museum, Laren 1959 (cat. by R.G. de Boer).

LAREN 1963
Modernen van toen 1570-1630 - Vlaamse schilderkunst en haar invloed, Singer Museum, Laren 1963 (cat. by R.G. de Boer).

LEIDEN 1950
Kunstbezit van oud-alumni der Leidse Universiteit, Stedelijk Museum de Lakenhal, Leiden 1950.

LEIDEN 1965
17e eeuwse meesters uit Nederlands particulier bezit - Oude meesters uit de collectie van de Heer en Mevrouw Sidney J. van den Bergh-Bendix, Stedelijk Museum de Lakenhal, Leiden 1965.

LEIDEN 1970
IJdelheid der ijdelheden - Hollandse Vanitas-voorstellingen uit de zeventiende eeuw, Stedelijk Museum de Lakenhal, Leiden 1970 (cat. by M.L. Wurfbain).

LEIDEN 1977
Leids zilver, Stedelijk Museum De Lakenhal, Leiden 1977.

LEIDEN 1985
See Ter Kuile 1985.

LINCOLN 1946
Dutch and Flemish paintings of the seventeenth century from the Cook Collection, Usher Art Gallery, Lincoln 1946.

LOHR & DORTMUND 1984
Glück und Glass - Zur Kulturgeschichte des Spessart glases, Spessartmuseum, Lohr am Main & Museum für Kunst und Kulturgeschichte, Dortmund 1984 (cat. by C. Grimm).

LONDON 1859
Exhibition of the works of Ancient Masters and deceased British Artists, British Institution, London 1859.

LONDON 1929
Dutch Art 1450-1900, Royal Academy of Arts, Burlington House, London 1929 / *Commemorative catalogue of the exhibition of Dutch Art (...) London 1929* (cat. by H. Schneider & W. Constable), Londen 1930.

LONDON 1938
Seventeenth Century Art in Europe, Royal Academy of Arts, London 1938.

LONDON 1945
Dutch Paintings of the seventeenth century, Arts Council, London 1945.

LONDON 1948
Five centuries of European painting, Whitechapel Art Gallery, London 1948.

LONDON 1949
Masterpieces of Dutch and Flemish paintings — Loan exhibition in memory of Ralph Warner, Gallery E. Slatter, London 1949.

LONDON 1952-1953
Dutch pictures 1450-1750, Royal Academy of Arts, London 1952-1953.

LONDON 1958
Annual Spring Exhibition of Old Masters, Gallery Alfred Brod Ltd., London 1958.

LONDON 1976a
The inspiration of nature — Paintings of still-life, flowers, birds and insects by Dutch and Flemish artists of the 17th century, Gallery John Mitchell & Sons, London 1976 (cat. by P. Mitchell).

LONDON 1976b
Art in seventeenth century Holland, The National Gallery, London 1976 (cat. by Chr. Brown).

LOS ANGELES, BOSTON & NEW YORK 1981-1982
A mirror of Nature — Dutch paintings from the Collection of Mr. and Mrs. Edward William Carter, Los Angeles County Museum of Art, Museum of Fine Arts, Boston & The Metropolitan Museum of Art, New York 1981-1982 (cat. by J. Walsh Jr. & C.P. Schneider).

LUXEMBOURG & LIEGE 1957
Natures mortes Hollandaises, Musée Pescatore, Luxembourg & Musée des Beaux-Arts, Liège 1957.

MADRID 1985
El siglo de Rembrandt, Museo del Prado, Madrid 1985-1986.

MANCHESTER 1949
Early Dutch flower paintings, Manchester City Art Gallery, Manchester 1949.

MEXICO CITY 1980-1981
50 obras maestras de pintura de los Museos de Dresden y Berlin de la Republica Democratica Alemana, Museo de San Carlos, Mexico City 1980-1981.

MINNEAPOLIS, HOUSTON & SAN DIEGO 1985
Dutch and Flemish Masters. Paintings from the Vienna Academy of Fine Arts, The Minneapolis Institute of Art, Minneapolis, The Museum of Fine Arts, Houston & The San Diego Museum of Art, San Diego 1985.

MONTREAL 1944
Five centuries of Dutch art, Art Association, Montral 1944.

MOSKOU & LENINGRAD 1983-84
Sedevrji iz sobranija Barona Tissen-Bornemisa. Zapadnoevropejskaja zivopisj XIV-XVII vv, Moskou, Pusjkin Museum & Hermitage, Leningrad 1983-1984 (cat. by G. Borgero).

MÜNCHEN 1984-85
Natura morta Italiana - Italian still life painting from three centuries. The Silvano Lodi collection, Alte Pinakotkek, München 1984-85 (cat. by L. Salerno).

MÜNSTER & BADEN-BADEN 1979-1980
Stilleben in Europa, Westfälisches Landesmuseum für Kunst und Kulturgeschichte, Münster & Staatliche Kunsthalle, Baden-Baden 1979-1980.

NEWCASTLE-UPON-TYNE 1929
North East Coast exhibition, Palace of Art, Newcastle-upon-Tyne 1929.

NEW DELHI 1984
Art treasures from Dresden, National Museum, New Delhi 1984.

NEW YORK 1939a
Seventeen masterpieces of the seventeenth century, Schaeffer Galleries, New York 1939.

NEW YORK 1939b
Masterpieces of Art – European painting and sculpture from 1300-1800, World's Fair, New York 1939.

NEW YORK 1942
Paintings by the great Dutch Masters of the seventeenth century, Duveen Galleries, New York 1942.

NEW YORK 1954
Magic of flowers in Painting, Gallery Wildenstein, New York 1954.

NEW YORK, TOLEDO & TORONTO 1954-1955
Dutch painting – The Golden Age. An exhibition of Dutch pictures of the seventeenth century, The Metropolitan Museum of Art, New York, Toledo Museum of Art, Toledo & The Art Gallery, Toronto 1954-1955.

NEW YORK 1974-1975
The Grand Gallery at the Metropolitan Museum of Art, 6th International Exhibition CINOA, New York 1974-1975.

NORWICH 1955
Still life, bird and flower paintings, Castle Museum, Norwich 1955.

NÜRNBERG 1985
Wenzel Jamnitzer und die Nürnberger Goldschmiedekunst 1500-1700 [...], Germanisches Nationalmuseum, Nürnberg (ed. München) 1985.

NÜRNBERG 1987
Deutsche Goldschmiedekunst vom 15. bis zum 20. Jahrhundert aus dem Germanischen Nationalmuseum, Berlin 1987.

OSLO 1959
Fra Rembrandt til Vermeer, Nasjonalgalleriet, Oslo 1959.

PARIS 1921
Exposition hollandaise - tableaux, aquarelles et dessins anciens et modernes, Galerie du Jeu de Paume, Paris 1921.

PARIS 1952
La nature morte de l'Antiquité à nos jours, Orangerie des Tuileries, Paris 1952 (cat. by Ch. Sterling).

PARIS 1960
La nature morte et son inspiration, Gallery André Weil, Paris 1960.

PARIS 1970-1971
Le siècle de Rembrandt - Tableaux hollandais des collections publiques françaises, Musée du Petit Palais, Paris 1970-1971.

PARIS 1979
Le choix d'un amateur clairé, Institut Néerlandais, Paris 1979.

PARIS 1986
De Rembrandt à Vermeer - Les peintres hollandais au Mauritshuis de la Haye, Grand Palais, Paris 1986 (cat. by B. Broos c.s.).

PHILADELPHIA 1963
A world of flowers, Philadelphia Museum of Art, Philadelphia 1963.

PITTSBURGH 1986
Gardens of earthly delight - Sixteenth and seventeenth century Netherlandish gardens, The Frick Art Museum, Pittsburgh, Pennsylvania (cat. by K. J. Hellerstedt).

PRAHA 1967
Flamská a Hollandská zátisí 17. Stol, Národní Galerie, Praha 1967 (cat. by J. Síp).

PRAHA 1984-1985
Musica picta, Národní Galerie, Praha 1984-1985.

PROVIDENCE 1938
Dutch painting in the seventeenth century, Museum of Art, Rhode Island School of Design, Providence 1938 (cat. by W. Stechow).

ROTTERDAM 1909
Het Hollandsche stilleven in de loop der tijden, Rotterdamsche Kunstkring, Rotterdam 1909.

ROTTERDAM 1933
Tentoonstelling van 115 «stillevens» 1480-1930, Museum Boymans, Rotterdam.

ROTTERDAM 1938
Meesterwerken uit vier eeuwen 1400-1800, Museum Boymans, Rotterdam 1938 (cat. by D. Hannema).

ROTTERDAM 1951
Tentoonstelling van oude schilderijen, Rotterdamsche Kunstkring, Rotterdam 1951.

ROTTERDAM 1955
Kunstschatten uit Nederlandse verzamelingen, Museum Boymans, Rotterdam 1955.

ROTTERDAM 1976
Zout op tafel - De geschiedenis van het zoutvat, Museum Boymans-van Beuningen, Rotterdam 1976 (cat. by J.R. ter Molen).

ROTTERDAM 1978
Legaat Vitale Bloch, Museum Boymans-van Beuningen, Rotterdam.

RUTGERS 1983
Haarlem: The seventeenth century, The Jane Voorhees Zimmerli Art Museum, Rutgers 1983 (cat. by F. Fox Hofrichter).

SAN FRANCISCO 1939-1940
Seven centuries of painting, California Palace of the Legion of Honor, San Francisco 1939-1940.

SAN FRANCISCO, TOLEDO & BOSTON 1966-1967
The Age of Rembrandt, California Palace of the Legion of Honor, San Francisco, The Toledo Museum of Fine Arts, Toledo & Museum of Fine Arts, Boston 1966-1967.

STOCKHOLM 1967
Holländska mästare i Svensk ägo, Nationalmuseum, Stockholm 1967.

STRASBOURG & DIJON 1949
La Hollande en Fleurs, Château de Rohan, Strasbourg & Dijon 1949 (cat. by R. van Luttervelt).

TIEL 1960
Oud Holland in de schilderkunst, Politiebureau, Tiel 1960.

TOKIO & KYOTO 1968-1969
The Age of Rembrandt - Dutch paintings and drawings of the 17th century (in Japanese), The National Museum of Western Art, Tokio & Municipal Museum, Kyoto 1968-1969.

TOKYO & KYOTO 1974-1975
Masterworks of European painting from the Gemäldegalerie Alte Meister, Dresden (in Japanese), The National Museum of Western Art, Tokio & Municipal Museum, Kyoto 1974-1975.

UNIVERSITY PARK 1980
Chinese export porcelains from the collection of Dr. and Mrs. Harold L. Tonkin, University Park, Penna 1980 (cat. by O.K. Preisner).

UTRECHT 1969
Musement, Jaarbeurs, Utrecht 1969.

UTRECHT 1979
Het goede leven - Thee, Centraal Museum, Utrecht 1979 (cat. by J.R. ter Molen).

UTRECHT 1984-1985
Zeldzaam zilver uit de Gouden Eeuw – De Utrechtse edelsmeden Van Vianen, Centraal Museum, Utrecht 1984-1985 (cat. by I. van der Zijl, based on J.R. ter Molen).

WASHINGTON ETC. 1979-1981
Old Master paintings from the Collection of Baron Thyssen-Bornemisza, Washington and eight other museums in the U.S.A. 1979-1981.

WASHINGTON 1986
The treasure houses of Britain - Five hundred years of private patronage and art collecting, National Gallery of Art, Washington 1986.

WORCESTER 1979
17th Century Dutch painting - Raising the curtain on New England private collections, Worcester Art Museum, Worcester 1979 (cat. by J.A. Welu).

WORCESTER 1983-1984
The Collector's Cabinet - Flemish paintings from New England private collections (cat. by J.A. Welu).

ZÜRICH 1956
Unbekannte schönheit, Kunsthaus, Zürich 1956.

ZÜRICH 1971
Kunstschätze aus Dresden, Kunsthaus, Zürich 1971.

Photo credits

Stichting Museum Amstelkring, Amsterdam: cat. no. 60.
Charles Roelofsz Gallery, Amsterdam: cat. nos. 28, 31, 44 / figs. 2.2, 5.8, 7.7, 8.6, 10.6.
Documentation author, Amsterdam: cat. nos. 1, 2, 5, 6, 10, 13, 19, 22, 24, 27 / figs. 3.2, 4.4, 4.9, 5.1, 6.6, 6.7, 6.8, 6.9, 7.1, 7.4, 8.1, 9.1, 9.2, 11.2.
K. & V. Waterman Gallery, Amsterdam: fig. 4.2.
Staatliche Museen, Berlin (German Democratic Republic): figs. 8.5, 11.5.
Indiana University Art Museum, Bloomington: cat. no. 42.
Herzog Anton Ulrich-Museum, Braunschweig: fig. 2.3.
Institut Royal du Patrimoine Artistique (ACL), Bruxelles: figs. 1.3, 2.4, 3.1, 3.6, 3.8, 6.3.
Szépművészeti Múzeum, Budapest: cat. no. 55 / fig. 6.4.
Cleveland Museum of Art, Cleveland: cat. nos. 51, 56.
Schlossmuseum Georgium, Dessau: cat. no. 21.
Staatliche Museen, Galerie Alte Meister, Dresden: cat. nos. 14, 25, 29.
National Gallery of Ireland, Dublin: fig. 6.10.
Historisches Museum, Frankfurt am Main: fig. 3.7.
Hoogsteder Gallery, 's-Gravenhage: cat. nos. 7-48-49 / figs. 7.2, 10.1, 11.6.
Rijksdienst Beeldende Kunst, 's-Gravenhage: cat. nos. 3, 4, 38.
Frans Halsmuseum, Haarlem: fig. 4.11.
Wadsworth Atheneum, Hartford: fig. 3.5.
Stichting Hannema-de Stuers Fundatie, Kasteel het Nijenhuis, Heino: cat. no. 16.
Indianapolis Museum of Art, Indianapolis: cat. no. 57.
Staatliche Kunsthalle, Karlsruhe: cat. no. 48.

Statens Museum for Kunst, København: cat. no. 58 / fig. 10.9.
Wallraf Richartz-Museum, Köln: figs. 4.12, 5.3.
Museum der Bildenden Künste, Leipzig: fig. 10.8.
Peter Tillou Gallery, Litchfield: cat. no. 47.
Trustees of the British Museum, London: fig. 3.3.
Thomas Brod Gallery, London: cat. no. 40 / fig. 9.3.
Richard Green Gallery, London: cat. no. 61.
John Mitchel & Sons Gallery, London: cat. no. 32.
Trustees of the National Gallery, London: cat. nos. 36, 54.
Edward & Anthony Speelman Gallery; London: cat. nos. 8, 9, 12, 15 / fig. 4.13, 10.2.
Rafael Valls Gallery, London: fig. 11.8.
Johnny Van Haeften Gallery, London: figs. 1.1, 8.8.
Los Angeles County Museum of Art, Los Angeles: cat. no. 52.
Fischer Gallery, Luzern: fig. 5.7.
Museo del Prado, Madrid: fig. 3.9.
J. Paul Getty Museum, Malibu: fig. 6.11.
Bayerische Staatsgemäldesammlungen, München: figs. 4.5, 10.3, 11.4.
Westfälisches Landesmuseum für Kunst und Kulturgeschichte, Münster: cat. no. 30.
Christie, Manson & Woods International Inc., New York: fig. 8.3.
French & Co. Gallery, New York: cat. no. 17.
Metropolitan Museum of Art, New York: fig. 1.4.
Rijksmuseum Kröller-Müller, Otterlo: fig. 1.6.
Ashmolean Museum, Oxford: cat. no. 50.
Ader, Picard & Tajan, Commissaires-priseurs associés, Paris: fig. 4.3.
Fondation Custodia (Collection F. Lugt), Paris: figs. 5.6, 10.5.
Julia Kraus Gallery, Paris: fig. 8.4.
Musée du Louvre, Paris: figs. 1.5, 8.2, 10.4.
Sotheby's Monaco S.A.M., Paris: fig. 4.1.

Philadelphia Museum of Art, John G. Johnson Collection, Philadelphia: cat. no. 6.5.
Národní Galerie, Praha: figs. 5.5, 7.7, 10.2.
Museum Boymans-van Beuningen, Rotterdam: cat. nos. 23, 39, 62 / figs. 2.1, 4.6, 5.2, 7.3.
Sammlung Hohenbuchau, Schlangenbad-Georgenborn: cat. no. 46 / fig. 8.7.
Müllenmeister Gallery, Solingen: fig. 4.14.
Conservation des Musées, Ville de Strasbourg: figs. 2.5, 7.6.
Staatsgemäldegalerie, Stuttgart: cat. no. 37.
Toledo Museum of Art, Toledo: fig. 9.4.
Schlossmuseum, Weimar: fig. 11.3.
Squerryes Court Collection, Westerham: cat. no. 43.
Akademie der Bildenden Künste, Wien: fig. 1.2.
Albertina, Wien: fig. 6.1.
Kunsthistorisches Museum, Wien: figs. 1.8, 11.7.
Österreichische Nationalbibliothek, Wien: fig. 1.7.
Div. private collections: cat. nos. 11, 18, 20, 33, 45, 59 / fig. 3.4, 4.7, 4.10, 6.2.